Art, Faith & Modernity

Edited by Sacha Llewellyn & Paul Liss

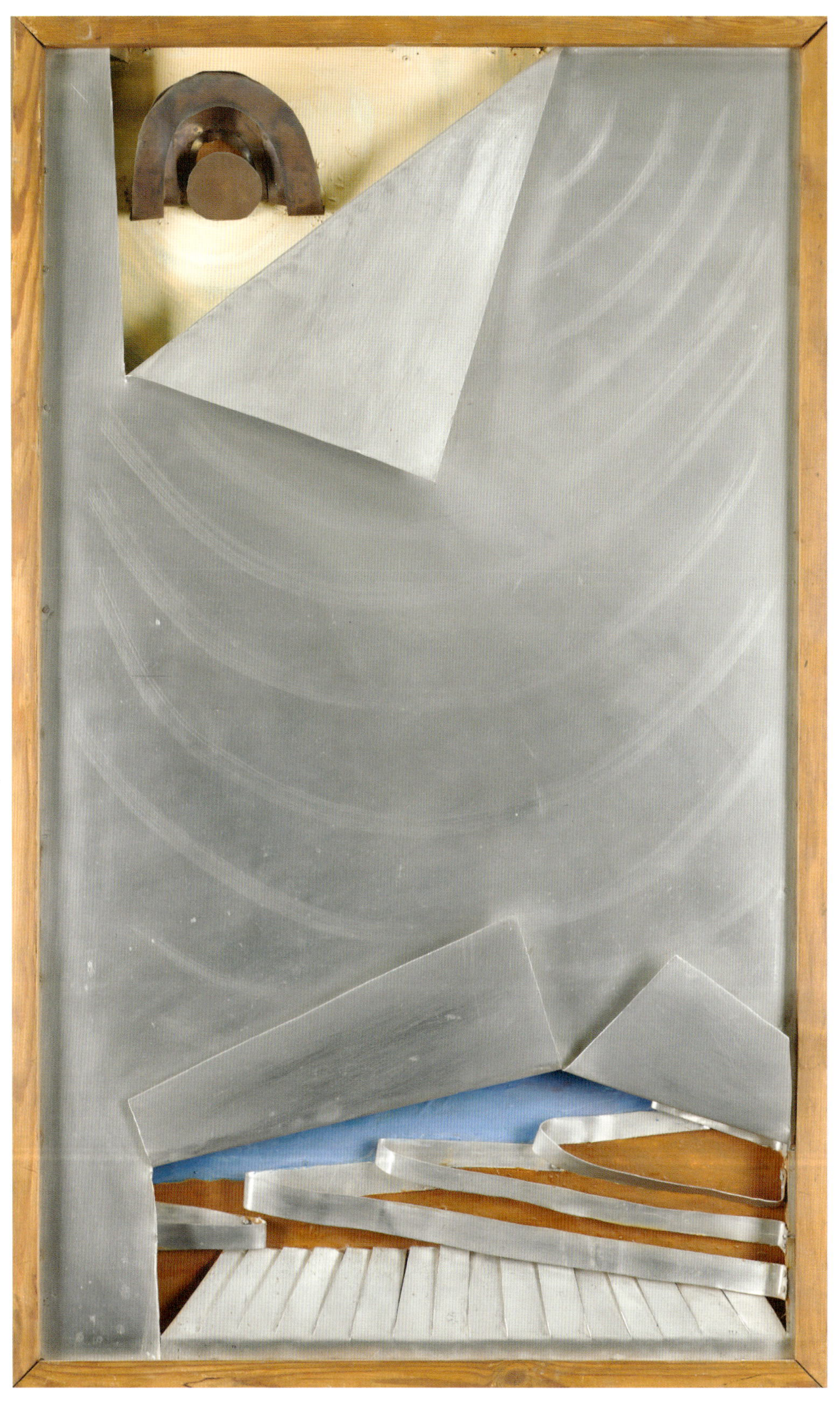

1 – **Rachel Reckitt** (1908-1995), *How high the heavens are*, late 1960s, wood and metal, 40 × 24 in. (101.6 × 61 cm).

Art,
Faith
&
Modernity

Edited by Sacha Llewellyn & Paul Liss

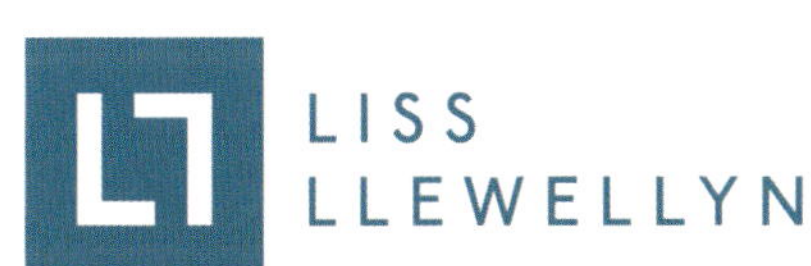

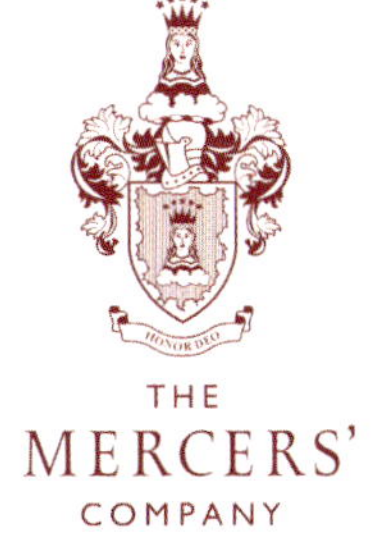

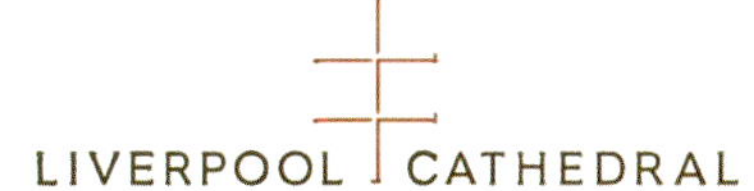

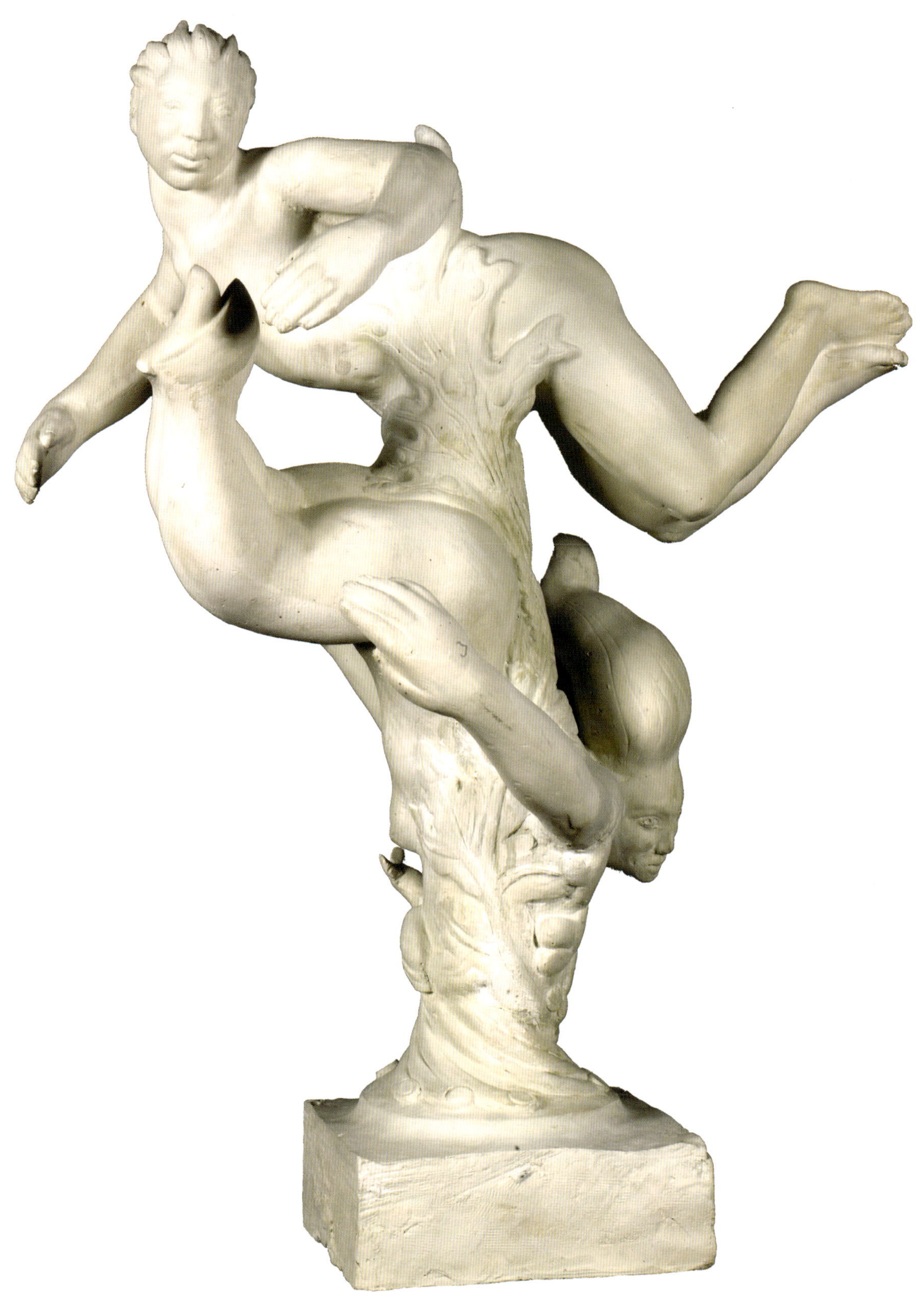

2 – James Woodford (1893–1976),
Nereid – fountain group, c.1947, signed in pencil on the base, the original plaster maquette, 30 in. (76 cm. high).

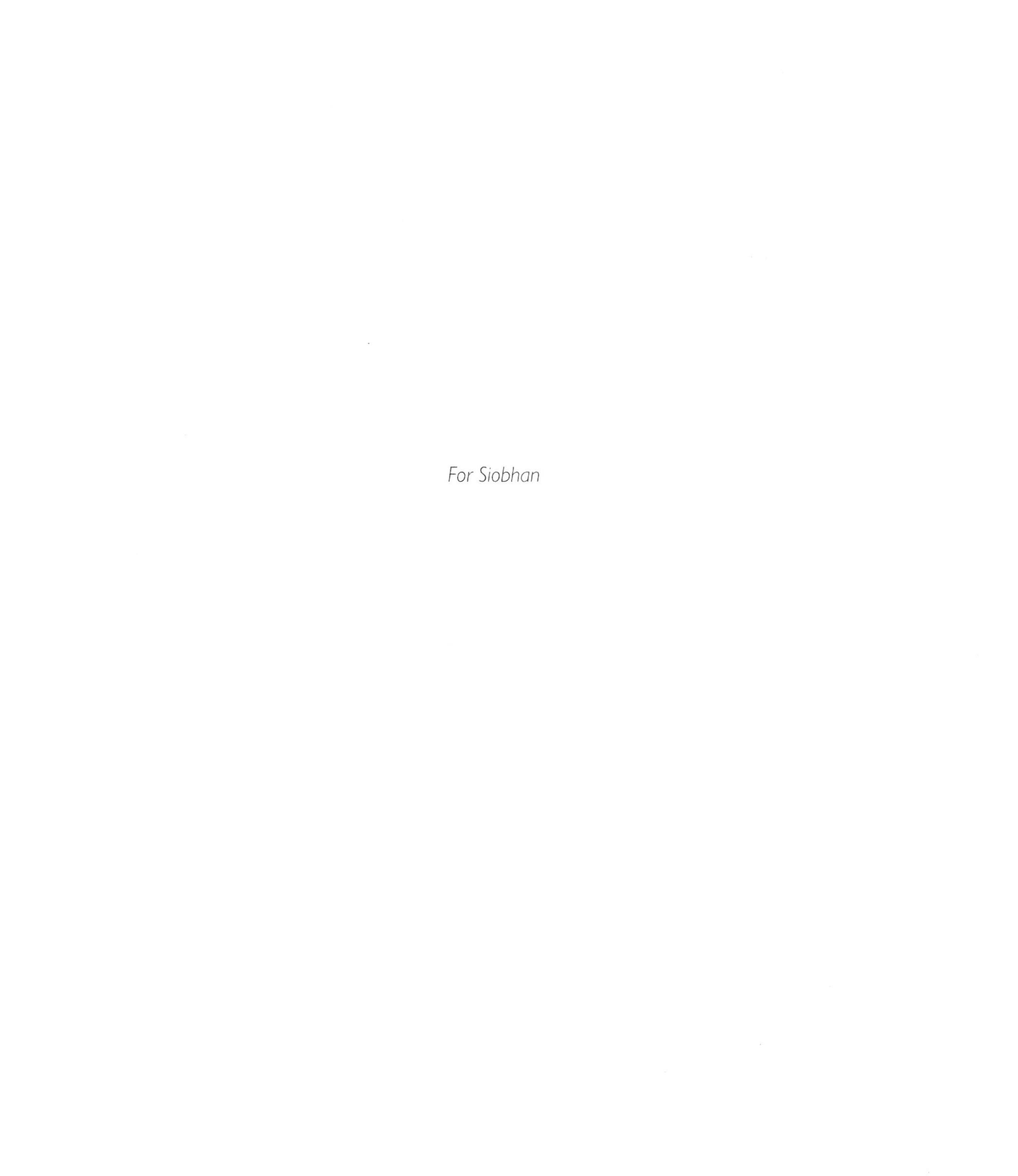

For Siobhan

ACKNOWLEDGEMENTS

We would like to thank

Paul Smith, Liverpool Cathedral
Stanley Spencer Gallery, Cookham
Wolverhampton Art Gallery
The Worshipful Mercers' Company
Nicholas Bagshawe
Robin Birley
Prudence & Rosalind Bliss
David Buckman
Elizabeth Bulkeley
Simon Brett (woodengraver@icloud.com)
Michael Campbell
Christopher Campbell-Howes
David Capps
Stephanie Chapman
Eleanor Chatterley
Frank Cohen
Andrew Cormack
Andrew Ellis
Jane England
Sarah Flynn
Charles Francis
Tigger Hoare
Tudor Hopkins

Glynn Hopkins
Libby Horner
Geoff Hassell at Artist Biographies
Neil Jennings
Shaun Kenny
Simon Lawrence
David Leighton
Pauline Lucas
Harry Moore-Gwyn
Tim Morel
Conor Mullan
Norma Rink
John Rooks
Peyton Skipwith
Stuart Southall
Simon Spear
Quentin Stevenson
Richard Thompson
David Thomson
Louise Walker
Grant Waters
Micky Wolfson

First published in 2019 by LISS LLEWELLYN

ISBN : 978-1-9993145-0-7

Text © Paul Liss & Alan Powers

Photography: Glynn Clarkson, Pierre Emmanuel Coste & Petra van der Wal

Design and Typesetting by David Maes
Printed by Zenith Media, June 2019

Contents

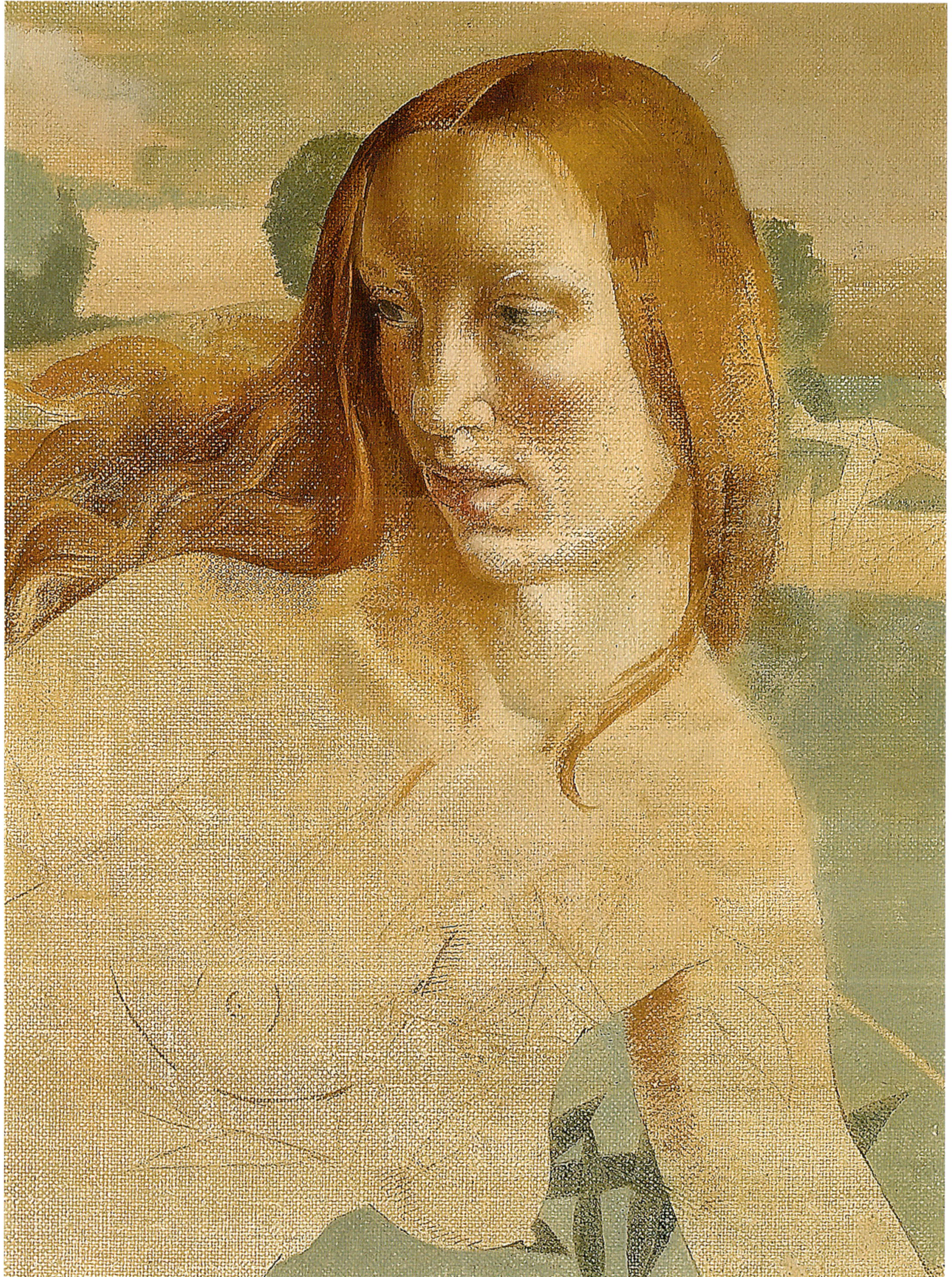

Religious Art in a Secular Age

In 1957, when asked by Tate to explain the meaning of his painting *Allegory* (1924) **(21-23)**, Thomas Monnington (1902-1976) replied that it was 'not overtly to do with the Garden of Eden,' but that it 'was an attempt to express in pictorial form my attitude to life – almost my faith'

Monnington's attitude was typical of his generation. Although religion was not a defining ingredient of his art, the search for meaning in a wider spiritual context, was.

The 172 works by 73 artists presented here, loosely grouped under the umbrella of religious art, draw attention to one of the richest – though under-researched – aspects of 20th century British visual culture. Anchored by Alan Power's defining essay, *Art Faith and Modernity* presents a poignant argument – both visual and cerebral – for a reassessment of the important place that religious art continued to occupy in 20th century Britain.

Art, Faith & Modernity is part of Liss Llewellyn's on-going programme of exhibitions, produced in partnership with museums and cultural institutions, which seeks to reappraise some of the unsung heroines and and heroes of Modern British art.

Paul Liss

3 – **Thomas Monnington** (1902-1976), Study for *Allegory* (detail), c.1925. (See page 42)

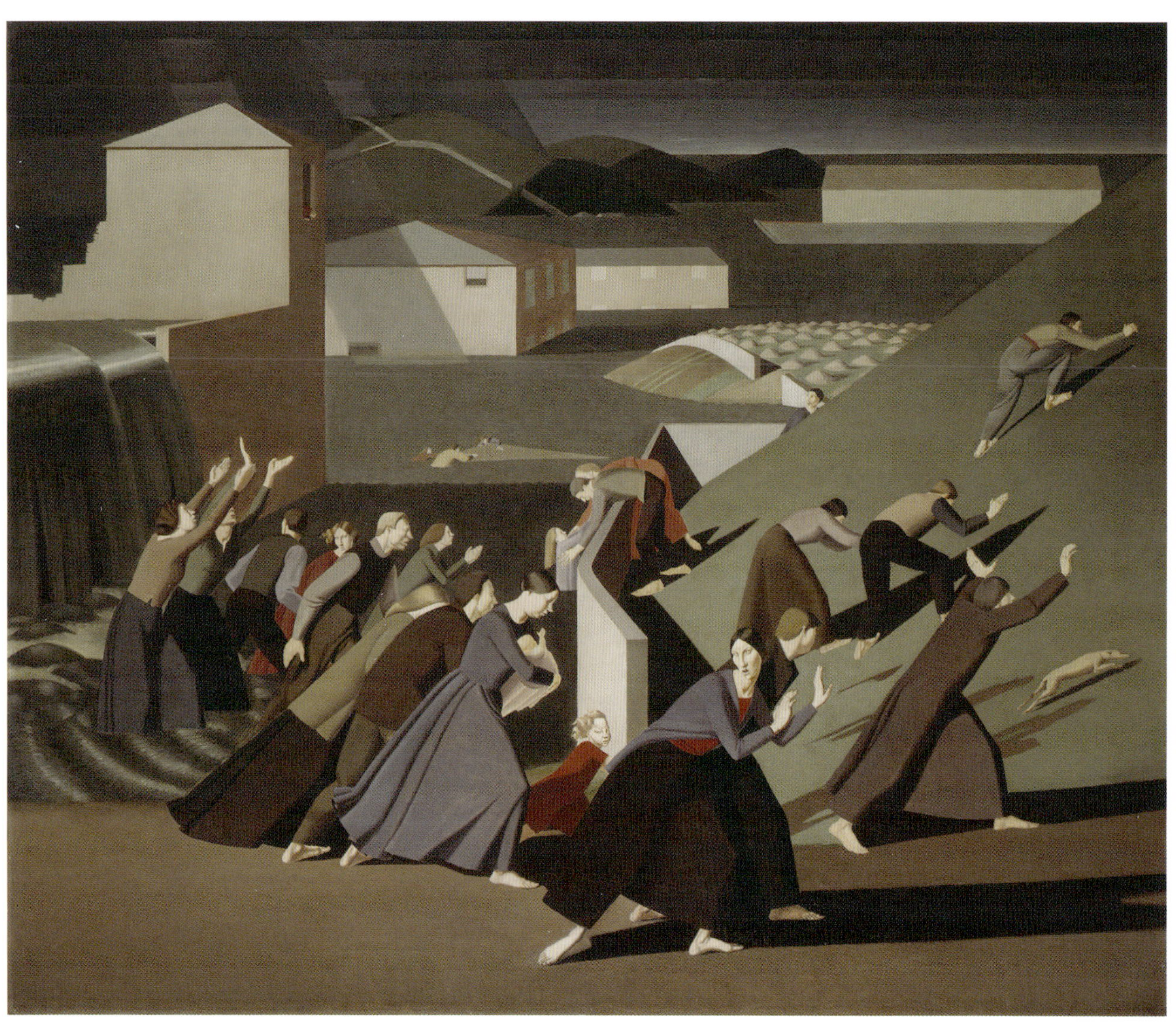

4 – Winifred Knights (1899-1947), *The Deluge*, 1920,
oil on canvas, 60 x 72 ¼ in. (152.9 x 183.5 cm). © The Estate of Winifred Knights / © Tate, London 2019.

Art, Faith & Modernity

Alan Powers

In putting together this unprecedented collection of work by artists both known and virtually unknown, a new window has been opened into British art history, encouraging redefinitions of the terms of its title. The period they cover is usually seen as sharply divided between 'progressive' and 'traditional' artists, but it has become apparent over the past 30 years that the old categories are a prison of sorts that shut out not just good work that lies outside but a deeper understanding of what has always been considered inside. John Christian's Barbican exhibition, *The Last Romantics: The Romantic Tradition in British Art, Burne Jones to Stanley Spencer*, 1989, introduced 'two generations of neglected British artists, whose abundant outpourings, full of religious and mythic quests, anguished lovers and tormented souls' who 'have suffered the critical ravages of time'.[1] It could be described as two exhibitions in one, since 'anguished lovers and tormented souls' belonged largely to the earlier part, before 1900, while the later part, including the sections on 'Slade School Symbolism' and 'Rome Scholars, Muralists and Others' challenged the finality of 'Last' in the title derived from a poem by W B Yeats. The public saw largely forgotten subject pictures outside the category of social realism or reportage that had a continued presence at least until the Second World War, and that without being 'progressive' in formal terms, were able to use the language of tradition to convey emotions of their own time.

Winifred Knights's *The Deluge*, 1920, (**4**) was shown at the Barbican in public almost for the first time since its completion as the successful competition entry for the Rome Scholarship. Recently sold at auction by the British School at Rome, it joined the collection of the Tate three years later, beginning a slow ascent to recognition and the reshaping of history that it quietly demanded. It has become in many ways the touchstone of a new evaluation of British art between the wars, a process that, it must be stressed, is still far from complete and often impeded by received opinion and hierarchies.

It should now be impossible to dismiss this painting as a minor version of a Stanley Spencer or a failed attempt at the summit of Modernism. In that alternative universe, Knights might have moved from here in the manner of one of her successors in the Rome Scholarship, Barbara Hepworth, to become a leader of abstraction in the 1930s, but she went the other way and so was forgotten. With the enthusiastic reception of a survey of her brief life's work at Dulwich in 2016, however, experts were challenged to make allowance for this opposite direction of travel, and perhaps to begin to recognise a whole cohort of artists who were travelling with her.

Art and the Church

'Art is the secret of the Church, as it is the secret of all noble forms of human fellow-ship. That is the reason for the strange fact that the credit of the Church to-day stands, not on the theological systems of the past, but on its architecture, its ceremonial, its music, crafts, sculpture, and painting. As we contemplate the world to-day, is it not clear that only by the recovery of beauty can Christendom itself be recovered?'[2] In 1926, this was the view of the Rev. Percy Dearmer (1867-1936), author of *The Parson's Handbook*, 1899, and co-editor with Ralph Vaughan-Williams and Martin Shaw of *The English Hymnal*, 1906. The son of an artist and a populariser rather than an original thinker, Dearmer did much to spread the acceptance of art in churches between the wars.

The outcome seen in churches in Britain tends to the populist and sentimental; departures from such norms are rare and were most often the subject of controversy. We may recall the raid carried out in 1932 at St Hilary church near Marazion in Cornwall by disgruntled parishioners abetted by their supporters from further afield, on account of the failure to secure Faculty permission for introducing works of art into the church by the vicar, Bernard Walke.[3] Fortunately, the most important, including the panels in the fronts of the choir stalls by Gladys Hynes, Ernest Procter and Alethea and Norman Garstin and others survived (**5**). Walke had an ally in George Bell, who in his enthronement

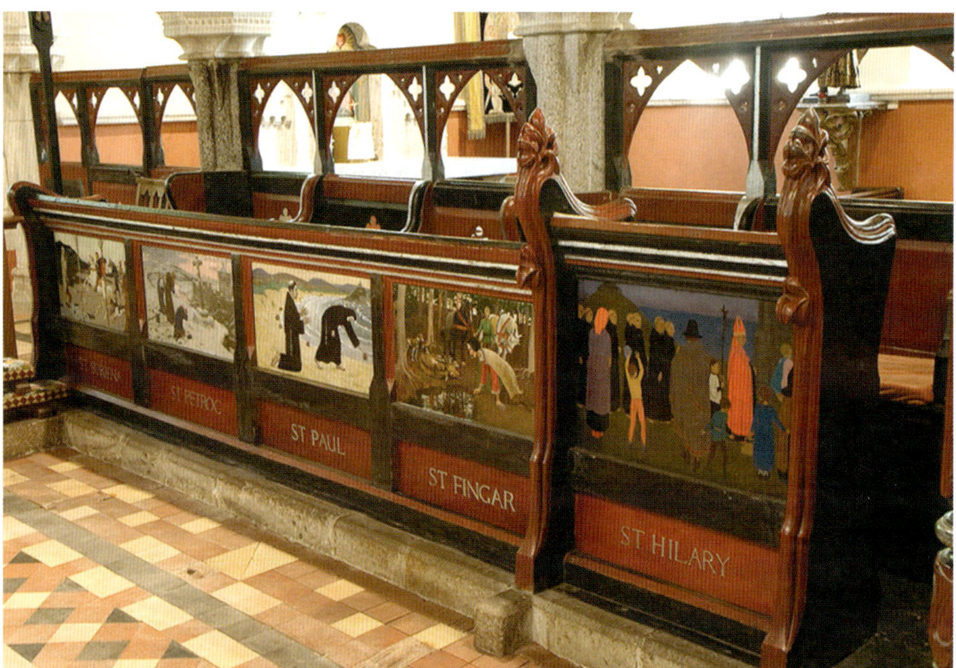

5 – **Saint Hilary Church**, panels in the fronts of the choir stalls.

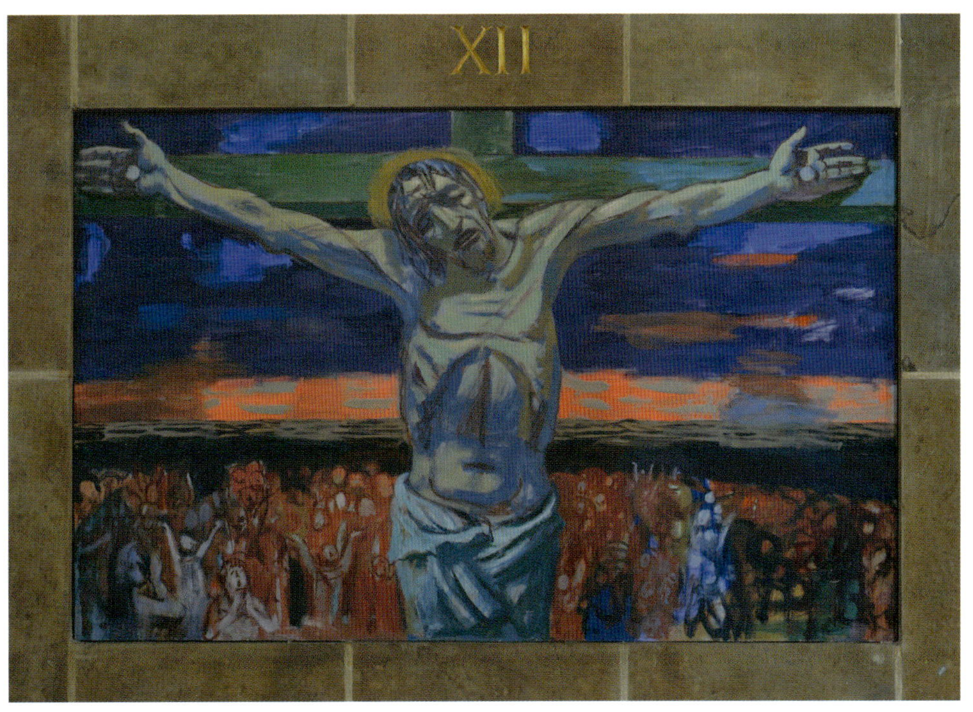

6 – Hans Feibusch (1898-1998), *Twelfth Station*, Church of St Alban's, Holborn, 1966.

address as Bishop of Chichester in 1930, expressed the hope of 'a re-association of the Artist and the Church; learning from him as well as giving to him; and considering with his help our conception alike of the character of Christian worship and of the forms in which the Christian teaching may be proclaimed.'[4] Walke and Bell were both as keen on drama as they were on visual arts – Walke pioneered Nativity Plays, which were regularly broadcast from his church, despite the lack of technical resources, while one of Bell's commissions was for T S Eliot's *Murder in the Cathedral*, performed at Canterbury in 1935, where he had previously been the Dean. In the visual arts, Bell is chiefly remembered for his mural commissions, especially his encouragement of Hans Feibusch (**6**). The German émigré artist's proposal for Christ in Majesty over the chancel arch of St Mary's, Goring-on-Sea (1954) was initially contested by the Chancellor of the Diocese partly on the grounds that Feibusch insisted on the right to change the work after permission was given. As Bishop, Bell made the final decision, setting a precedent for future latitude, with the words 'unless the Church is to be sterile in the fostering of creative art, it must be prepared to trust its chosen artists to begin their work and carry it through to the end as the fulfilment of a trust, the terms and circumstances of which they understand and respect.'[5] Bishop Bell and his advisory group at the foundation of the Sussex Churches Art Council, 1944, agreed that 'there was no need for an artist to be a professing member of the Church in order to paint for it.'[6]

Commissions for works of art in churches and cathedrals in Britain are now to some extent regulated by agreed processes of review and decision-making, but their systems are not foolproof. The distressing story of the St Martin's altarpiece in Canterbury Cathedral should stand as a warning, since two artists' lives and confidence were severely damaged by its mishandling. Presumably the power of the silhouettes in Glyn Jones's first version were too much for the committee – too modern in style, and perhaps too disturbing in mood for commemoration of Lord Milner, self-confessed 'British Race Patriot', and a controversial figure in the Imperial development of South Africa. The alternative commissioned from Winifred Knights, with clumsy interventions by Milner's friend, the architect Herbert Baker, could have been a work more consonant with the artist's instincts, as her studies for it show. Adding insult to injury, the cathedral later managed to mislay her side panel, an awkward requirement of the original commission, when the chapel was rearranged.

'Art' is probably the simplest of the triad of descriptive terms under which this collection has been assembled. 'Faith' of some kind is necessary to support the effort of making any work of art that is not a piece of hackery. An eighteenth-century patron of church art might have been as unconcerned as Bell's group about the artist's private beliefs, but during the intervening nineteenth century, faith and works were probably seen as a desirable coupling, and might tell in the artist's favour again today. In the twentieth century, 'Modernity' certainly played a role in removing the need for any explicit adherence to a faith. As a counter to the assumption that a world of trains, telephones and air travel irrevocably altered everyone's world view around 1900, we might have to assume a more gradual and unselfconscious change, or perhaps a more passionate search backwards in time for some solid bedrock. This bedrock was nearly always found in the Italian Renaissance, a conservative choice, perhaps, since this seam had already been mined by the Pre-Raphaelites, to whom many of the artists in this exhibition, as in *The Last Romantics*, were the conscious or unconscious successors.

In *Modern Painting and the Northern Romantic Tradition,* 1975, the American art historian Robert Rosenblum explored the alternative historical line of development that in the twentieth century produced Expressionism, 'based not on formal values alone … but rather on the impact of certain problems of modern cultural history, and most particularly the religious dilemmas posed in the Romantic movement, upon the combination of subject, feeling, and structure'.[7] At a time when the task of art history was seen, in part at least, as mapping the road towards Modernism as Abstraction, this was a valuable shift towards recognising pictorial content even when, as in the work of Mark Rothko, it was veiled by form.

This 'combination of subject, feeling and structure' is especially apparent in the case of Evelyn Dunbar. Beginning at the Royal College of Art as part of its neo-Renaissance revival, she moved towards what Rosenblum recognises in the message of the German pastor,

Friedrich Schleiermacher in the time of Caspar David Friedrich (1774-1830), 'a kind of personal unbosoming of subjective responses before the mysteries of divinity'. At the time of her death, *Jacob's Dream*, the culmination of a series of paintings, shows her becoming comfortable with a different pictorial language through which to depict the unpaintable idea of angels on a ladder. Had she, like the eight-year old William Blake, seen 'a tree filled with angels, bright angelic wings bespangling every bough like stars'? Her work makes this assumption quite plausible, even if she never saw fit to mention it. Dunbar is arguably the star of this show, not only for the skill of her drawing and the human warmth of her imagination, but her ability to keep 'the Divine Vision in Time of Trouble'.[8]

Paintings as Dreams and Subjects

In her study of the French painter Pierre Puvis de Chavannes, Jennifer Shaw credits him with revealing 'the possibility of imagining paintings as dreams'.[9] The American critic Margaret Steele Anderson wrote in 1914, 'the influence of de Chavannes is greater than the number of his followers', especially owing to his origination of 'a new ideal of decoration'.[10] In Britain, his influence is most directly seen in Frederick Cayley Robinson one of many artists once popular in a sentimental way, as the Medici Society print of his *Pastoral* indicates. Robinson's four large panels for the Middlesex Hospital (1916 and 1920, now in the collection of the Wellcome Institute) (**7**), were probably the best importations of the Puvis sensibility, with added elements of mystery in which modern life seems to touch on something more profound.

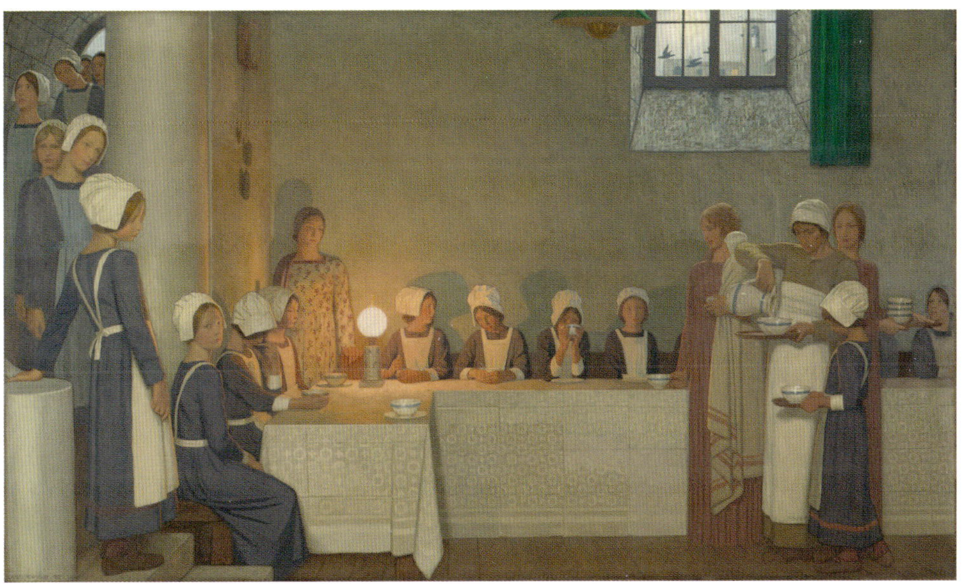

7 – Frederick Cayley Robinson (1862-1927), *Orphan girls entering the refectory of a hospital*, 1916-20, oil on canvas, 78 ¼ × 133 ½ in. (199 x 339 cm), Courtesy of the Wellcome Collection.

Stanley Spencer placed Bible stories in his home village of Cookham, without which it is hard to imagine how his work as an artist would have developed. 'Heaven lay all about me in my infancy' wrote Thomas Traherne in the seventeenth century, in words only made available twentieth, in fact in 1908, the year that Stanley Spencer enrolled at the Slade School of Fine Art in London.[11] Spencer shared Traherne's experience, finding the divine 'hidden or only half-glimpsed through fences or partly opened gates'.[12] His *Christ Carrying the Cross* (1920, Tate) is one of the most magical of his transpositions of Biblical events to Cookham, with the angels gathered at the windows of a house called 'The Nest' and the strange 'day for night' lighting effect. At the Sandham Memorial Chapel, Burghclere, 1928-9, Spencer had his opportunity to paint a place of worship, but it is more a chapel about himself, seen through his wartime experiences, than it is about the distant figure of Christ above the altar, overwhelmed by the number of crosses piled up by the resurrected soldiers (**8**).

Deep and inexplicable responses to place and nature are a feature of childhood more generally associated with later creativity.[13] Paul Nash recollected in later life the 'places' in Kensington Gardens, with 'a force, gentle, insistent', the scene of his childhood walks, that he considered special.[14] The experience of such places can be equated with a religious experience, and it has served several of the artists included in this exhibition as the counterpart to a Biblical subject. Typically, these are not the most theologically

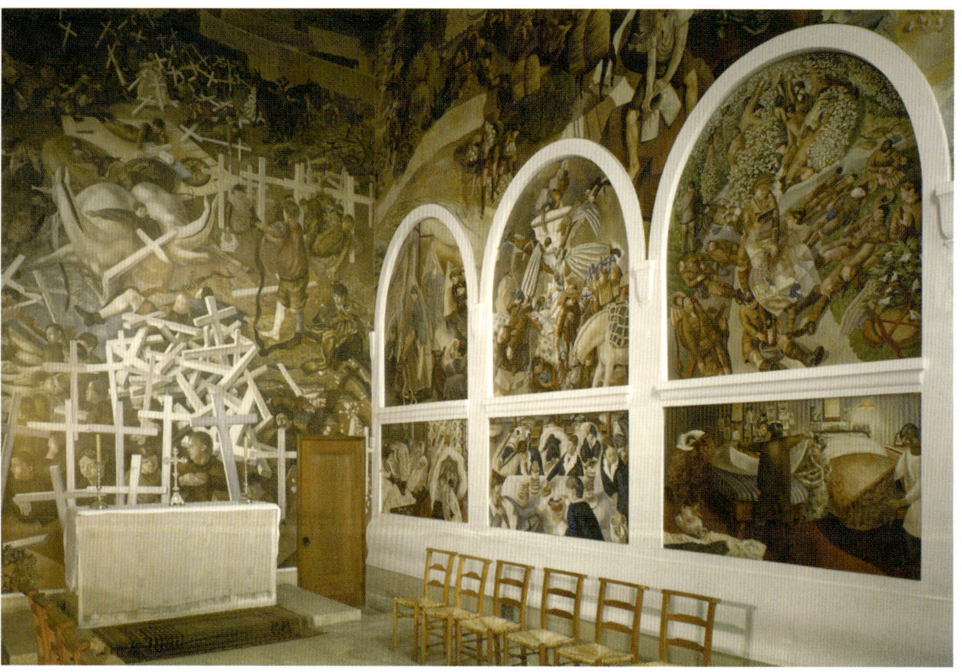

8 – Stanley Spencer (1891-1959), Resurrection Scene – Sandham Memorial Chapel, Burghclere, Hampshire, 1928-29. © The Estate of Stanley Spencer, © National Trust Images/A C Cooper, All rights reserved DACS 2019.

loaded episodes of the Bible or the Gospels, but the more anecdotal, incidental ones. One of Spencer's early subjects was *Zacharias and Elizabeth* (1913-14, Tate) the offering made by the elderly priest that summons the Angel Gabriel to foretell the birth of St John the Baptist to his elderly wife. Every figure and its actions illustrate the text from St. Luke's gospel, but the subject without its setting would produce a different and surely less magical effect.

Dora Carrington told her fellow Slade student, John Nash, of her desire to emulate Holman Hunt's *The Hireling Shepherd*, 1851, (Manchester City Art Gallery) (**9**), based on a parable of the Good Shepherd in St John's Gospel.[15] The Pre-Raphaelites, present in the engravings on the Spencer family's walls and in the unpurged public galleries of the Edwardian age, achieved a similar overlay of the natural and supernatural.[16] Part of the shock tactic of Holman Hunt's painting and some other Pre-Raphaelite works came from the use of contemporary clothes and physical human types (the 'coarse' countrygirl and the swaggering man), used in association with a religious message. Spencer was the master of this territory, but others pushed out its borders, such as Victor Moody with his *Judgement of Solomon* (**36**), apparently intended as part of a series of mural lunettes, unusual in its drab but eloquent urban setting, or Fyffe Christie's *Christ Feeding the People* (**72**), where the un-English departure from neo-Renaissance decorum evokes the style of American WPA murals from the Depression.

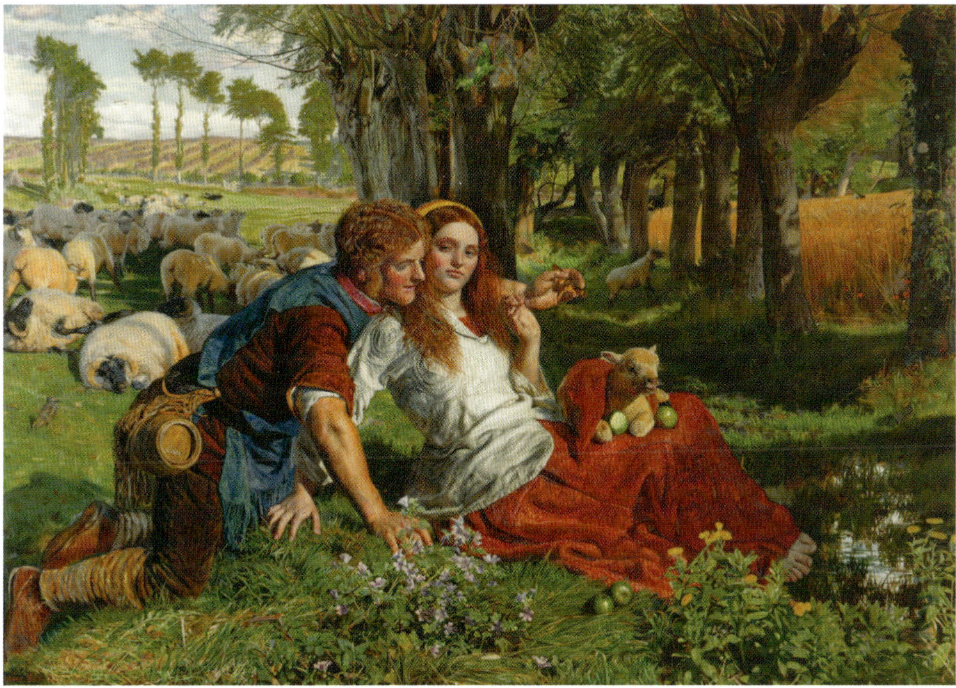

9 – **William Holman Hunt** (1827-1910), *The Hireling Shepherd*, 1851, oil on canvas, 30 × 43 in (76.4 cm × 109.5 cm). Manchester Art Gallery.

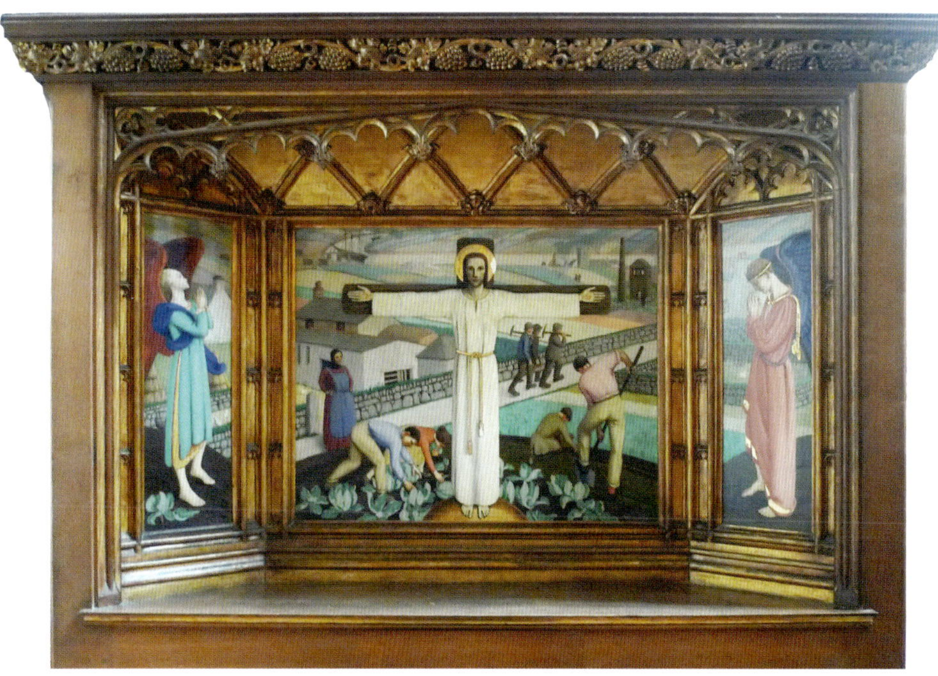

10 – **Annie Fearon Walke** (1877 -1965), *Christ the Worker*, 1923, Truro Cathedral.

The Christian Socialist movement, to which George Bell was an adherent, encouraged art, so that Keir Hardie, the founder and first leader of the Labour Party, was shocked to discover that the Rev Cuthbert Headlam, a prominent figure in this movement, 'divided his attention fairly evenly between socialism and the ballet'.[17] Surprising in view of the conventional assumption that most church-goers are social conservatives, this alliance was at times able to generate works such as the altarpiece in the Jesus Chapel at Truro Cathedral (1923) by Annie Fearon Walke (**10**), the wife of the vicar of St Hilary, showing the crucifixion with field workers planting cabbages while tin miners walk into the distance, and Archibald Ziegler's *An Allegory of Social Strife* (**83**), where 'bad' capitalists and a group apparently composed of socialists each stand at the foot of the cross on which the worker hangs in the public square.

The Rome Scholarship in Painting was set up, along with similar awards for Architecture and Sculpture, in 1912. While artists had been travelling to Italy for three centuries (if we count from Inigo Jones), this activity had lacked the official support on a national level that was taken for granted in France. The British scheme for combining these three arts was explicitly predicated on the idea of 'decoration', understood in terms of frieze-like figure compositions in idealised settings, of the type seen in many Renaissance works, but now given a new currency by Puvis. Paintings of 'noble simplicity and calm grandeur' (in the words of German father of art history, Johann Joachim Winkelmann) were to grace the walls of public buildings, as seen in the idealistic murals by Puvis himself and John Singer Sargent in Boston Public Library in the 1890s, a building by the architect Charles Follen McKim who had himself helped to found the American Academy in Rome in 1894.

The competition subjects for selecting Rome scholars reflected art school practice, trying to avoid banality (not that all competitors achieved this) and aiming instead for subjects that were high-minded but a little piquant. Anything religious was contained within this formula, so that when *The Deluge* (**11**) was set in 1920, Winifred Knights's winning entry might equally have been from any literary or mythological source. The summation of her time as a student drinking from Renaissance sources in Rome was *The Marriage Feast at Cana*, 1923 (**65-67**), a more devotional Biblical subject, more Puvis-like in its static serenity than the subject of *The Deluge* could ever have been. But although the narrative elements of Christ's first miracle were present, these are not the driving force of the work, any more than *The Fall of Icarus* was for Pieter Brueghel the Elder, for the painting seems really to be about Knights's own life, as is her unfinished panel, *Bathsheba*, 1923, set on the city walls of Orvieto with only a corner of sky and distant landscape completed.

Pastoralism and Symbols

Through their culture, where Neo-Platonism ran in parallel with Christianity, Italian Renaissance artists rediscovered a view of the world in which mythologies mingled,

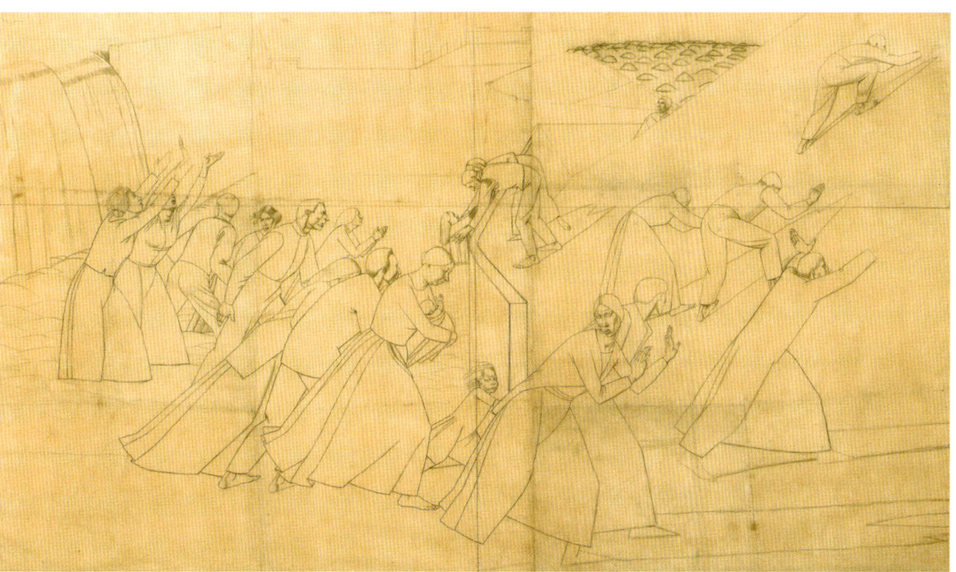

11 – **Winifred Knights** (1899-1947), Cartoon for *The Deluge*, 1920,
pencil on tracing paper, 60 ¼ × 72 ¼ in. (152.9 × 183.5 cm).

transcending the limits of any specific tradition of faith or doctrine. These provided ideal models in the twentieth century when a literal take on Church doctrine was falling out of favour. The artists of this period gravitated towards pastoral subjects which are often dismissed as retrogressive or nostalgic. Were they, however, looking for something different – a quality of strangeness and veiled meaning found in Renaissance emblem books and associated with the term 'imaginal', meaning something beyond the level of ordinary perception that obliquely and transiently conveys the sense of a universal reality? The richness of symbolic content in Renaissance art only began to re-emerge in the late nineteenth century, aided perhaps by the rediscovery of the *Hypnerotomachia Polifili* by Francesco Colonna, the intriguing symbolic engravings from which were reprinted by the Government-funded Department of Science and Art in 1888 and thus were, presumably, available to students in most city art schools across the country.[18]

In a similar spirit, the writer and artist David Jones refreshed the understanding of the sacraments of the Church through his universalising of 'The Sign', finding this less in the poetry of place than in the knowledge of an older symbolic order. In *He Frees the Waters in Helyon*, 1932, (**12**) his last unfinished wood engraving, the source was the *Itinerarium* of Johannes de Hesse, 1500, giving an account of the unicorn (a symbol of Christ) that comes at dawn to purify a polluted stream 'so that the good animals can drink there during the day'. For Jones, a veteran of the trenches, the shattered trees were

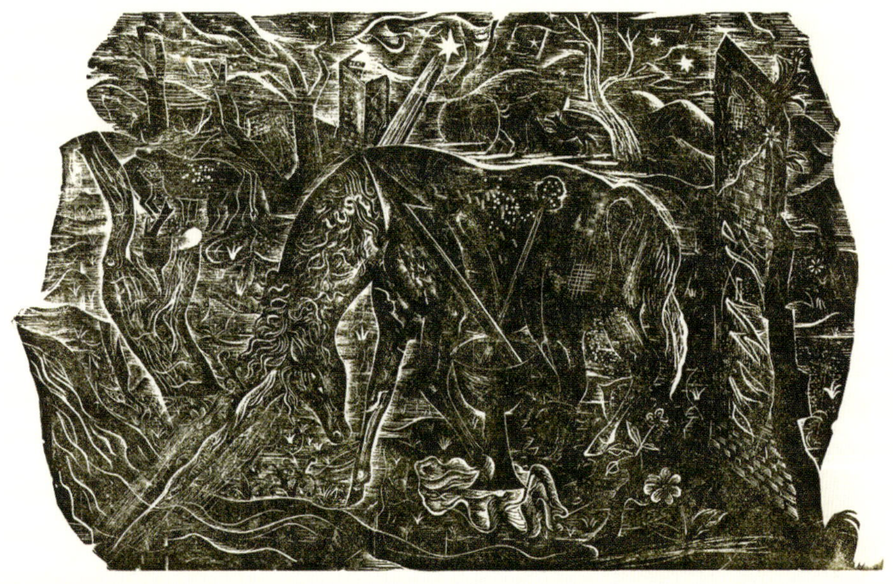

12 – **David Jones** (1895-1974), *He Frees the Waters in Helyonn*, 1932,
wood engraving on paper, block: 6 x 9 ¾ in. (15.2 x 24.6 cm), paper: 11 ¼ x 15 in. (28.7 x 38 cm).

those of the battlefields of Flanders, although spiritual connotations aside, the image has far more universal relevance to our own time.

It may have been in a similar spirit that Charles Mahoney composed the frieze-like altarpiece in the Lady Chapel at Campion Hall, Oxford, (**47, 48, 101-104, 140, 141**) with its Tower of Strength, its Lily and Thorn, and its Garden Enclosed. Choosing Mahoney for this commission in place of Spencer, whose personal eccentricities repelled the Jesuit community, Father Martin D'Arcy overlooked the fact of Mahoney's anti-religious feelings, but was rewarded nonetheless by a confession of faith in love of cultivated nature what Richard Davey has called 'spiritual innuendo' – a term that could describe the avoidance of explicit religious content in many of the works presented here.[19] Anne Newland's *The Legend of Ceres*, could most easily pass as an actual renaissance drawing, on the other hand, and it is fascinating how its subject and title seem to have oscillated between Christian and Pagan subject matter much as Botticelli or Piero di Cosimo might have done, demonstrating perhaps the narrow gap between them.

Pastoral is usually interpreted as a comforting and perhaps self-deceiving *genre*. It is deeper and subtler than this in its operation, however, with the potential to speak politically. In such cases, the predictable expectations of content can be deliberately subverted. Eric Gill's overtly sexual imagery for Powys Mather's *Procreant Hymn* (**20**) may strike us as being, in the current phrase 'too much information', but in its time, regardless of what we may think of revelations about Gill's personal behaviour, it was, even in its 'polite' versions, a recognition of a human universal. After all, what else were all those nymphs and shepherds up to in Arcadia? And what other motive was in King David's mind when he saw Bathsheba at her open-air bath?

More striking as a subversion of pastoral content is George Warner Allen's *The Rubbish Dump, A Black Country Altarpiece* (**86**), an extraordinary discovery with its own fascinating story of commissioning as an item that should have been one of many paintings of social and ecological protest in churches in an alternative universe where 'conventional' technique would be allied to explicit social criticism, with a quality of vision in its execution that lifts it above the rather low expectations attached to the term 'social realism'. Dorothea MacLagan is another remarkable discovery and *An Allegory: Truth and Beauty* (**91**) comforting each other, a protest picture with an even more direct message.

In Mahoney's obsessively repeated depictions of Adam and Eve (**17-19**), or at other times simply of a standing nude woman in a garden, are both personal and universal in meaning, as well as being the extension of the discipline of the nude coupled with the painting of leaf and flower forms. They are reminiscent of the lush landscape settings of Adam Elsheimer in early seventeenth-century Rome. Nothing could be more different than the depiction of 'our first parents' in

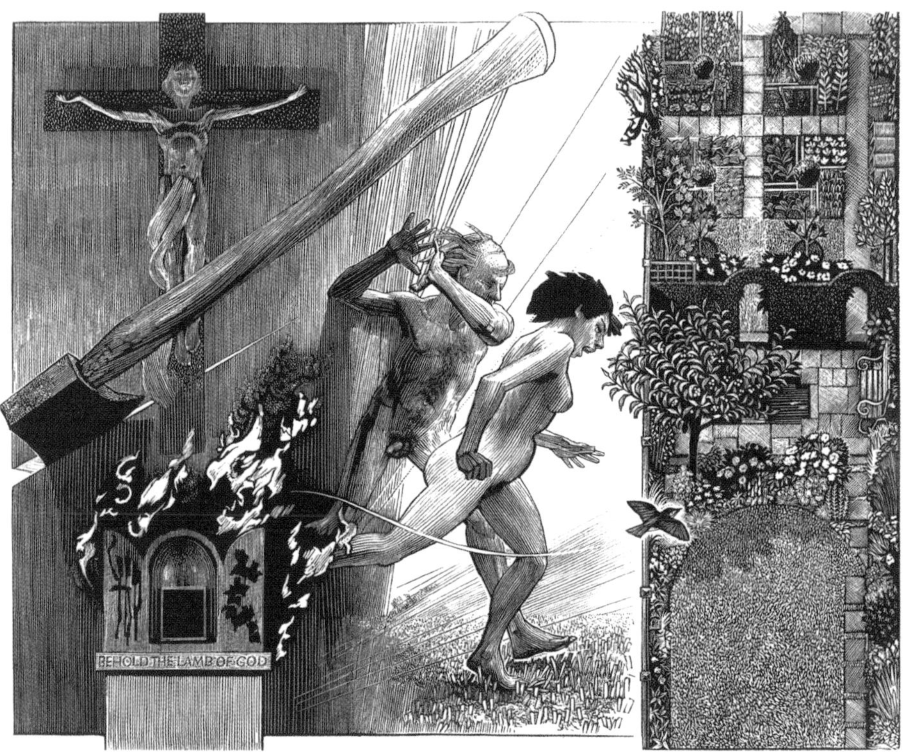

13 – **Simon Brett** (b.1943), *Garden Plan*, 1995, from *The Axe of God*, 1983-2016,
wood engraving, 8 × 10" in. (20 × 25 cm).

Garden Plan in Simon Brett's series of wood engravings, *Axe of God*, 1983-2016, (**13**) is
not just a depiction of shame, as the moving drawing by Evelyn Gibbs shows us, but the
violent and shattering force of the universe. The axe has similarly fallen in Helen Blair's
Scene from the Book of Job (**39**), a subject taken from the one of the most hermeneutically
dense books of the Old Testament which experienced a revival at this time through
the ballet based on Blake's engravings and its score by Ralph Vaughan Williams of 1931.

Wood engravings encouraged a more Expressionist emotional register than paintings,
perhaps because they were aimed at a more tolerant and limited audience of collectors.
An outstanding example was the set of near-abstract wood engravings by Paul Nash for
Genesis, published by the Nonesuch Press in 1924. The Golden Cockerel Press *The Four
Gospels*, 1931, on the other hand, with Eric Gill's series of 'black line' engravings, has been'
judged by many the great twentieth century book', but may now seem too smooth and
accomplished.[20] Frank Brangwyn benefited from the discipline of printmaking, which
arguably drew on his strengths of design rather than his uneasy colour palette, and his idea
of lithographing The Stations of the Cross (**77**) onto wooden panels, as a potential alternative to the conventional imagery of the church furnishing trade, was an inspired one.

Somewhere between these extremes comes a 'problem picture' such as Monnington's *Allegory* (**21-23**), another product of the Rome School in its prime that works to undermine and destabilise its required monumental scale as public art, suggesting an unwillingness to commit to completion or specific meaning. Here, despite the extreme and loving academic treatment, is a work that could be considered post-modern. The Faculty of the Rome School required its students to make multiple studies, as if to 'show their workings', and this and other products of the same regime may legitimately be considered as collective multiple works rather than single canvases.

A parallel instance of multiplicity is the body of work made by Barbara Jones based on the human head re-imagined as a forest of symbols. Her surviving large scale mural panels, *Man at Work, a century of technical and social progress* (**94**) was made for the British government Central Office of Information, for an exhibition in Turin in 1961. It is a very seventeenth-century 'conceit', resembling the famous frontispiece of Thomas Hobbes' *Leviathan,* 1651, with its figure of the superhuman ruler made up of the multitude of individuals. Comic and occasionally sinister, Jones finds equivalents for the senses that hold the eye in exploring and interpreting the image. A second version appeared as the Philips mural *Man and his Senses* (**93**), for the electrical goods company's headquarters at Eindhoven in the Netherlands, completed in 1966 (but also dated to 1971).[21] It seems to have gone through several iterations, and one related study has retained its explanatory key, made as an overlay on tracing paper. These and no doubt other related studies are really a single composite work. Whether they illustrate 'Faith' in any conventional sense may be questioned, but they do explore the human condition in terms that relate the symbolism of the past to the technological order of the present.

Other works in this collection go further in stretching the symbolic language. Rachel Reckitt's *How high the heavens are* (**1**) strips away the veil of the visible to find an inner reality, with the perennial assumption that it must lie beyond the clouds in the sky. The shimmering zinc sheet rises from what may be a flat landscape and folds above to reveal a dreamlike found object. John Tunnard's two pastels are not immediately recognisable in terms of the spatial 'constructions' for which he became best-known. There is something closer to Rothko about them, a more sober and perhaps self-revealing quality from an artist whose work sometimes verges on the glib and formulaic.

Abstraction is pushed even further in Valentine Dobree's *The Event* (**70**), whose triptych form suggests a religious content that is, nonetheless, hard to decipher. 'Threeness', that fundamental principle of the western Church, recurs in the works of Allan Milner and Victor Reinganum (**81, 84**). It is so inbuilt in the culture that a religious theme is always latent.

The large watercolour paintings by David Evans add a different dimension, shifting the focus from the human action back to the setting. In taking *The Tower of Babel* (**30**) as his subject, Evans could be mistaken for the late Edward Burra in his savage satires, also in watercolour, on the landscapes of extraction and industry. Although Evans's work was closer in character to that of the Rome Scholars of an earlier generation, one should also recall John Napper (1916-2001), who was similarly out of step with his times but recognised by a few as an artist of integrity and quality, able to reinterpret old themes with a skilful deployment of anachronism, as in his mysterious, Piero della Francesca-like composition, *The Night that Pontius Pilate Died* (**14**) and the Poussin-derived *The Adoration of the Golden Calf*, both of 1991.

In an interview with William Parente for the catalogue of his exhibition in 1991, Napper seems to have summarised much of what this exhibition is saying:

Parente: When the idea for a subject comes along, as you say, do you have to go back to the source, say the Bible, to read up about it, or is that material fairly accessible in your memory?

Napper: it is in my memory because I was brought up on all this … it's part of one's folklore.

Parente: That many people have forgotten.

Napper: Which is a pity, because it's an enrichment. I'm not talking about religion as religiosity but I am concerned with the eternal truths that exist in the imagination. Only in the imagination, perhaps there can be a synthesis of past, present and future. One of the functions of painting is to give concrete expression to such imaginative thoughts.[22]

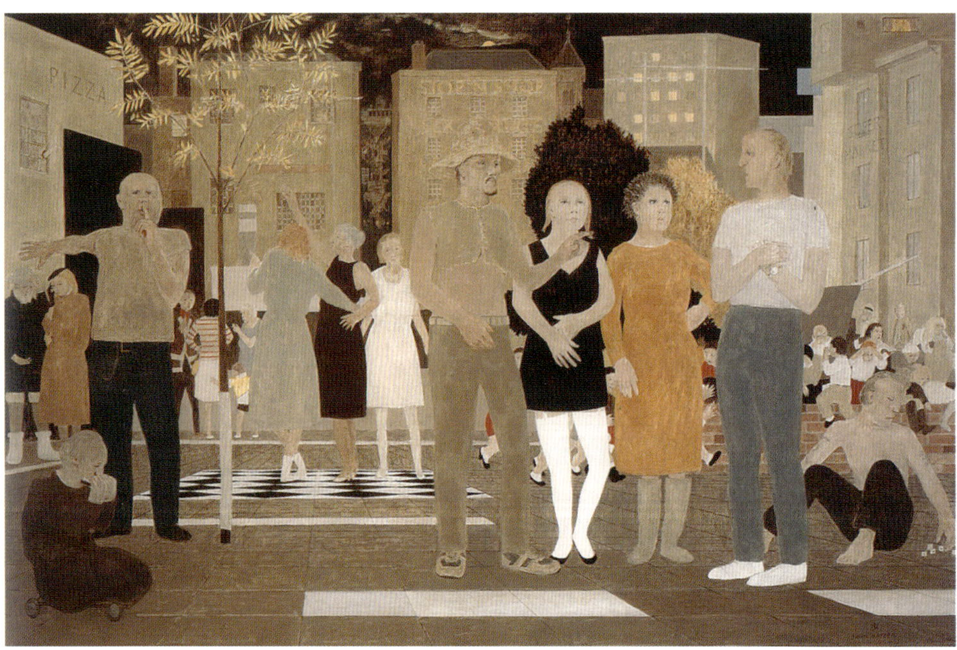

14 – **John Napper** (1916-2001), *The Night That Pontius Pilate Died,* 1991, oli on canvas, 34 x 51 in. (86.5 x 129.5 cm).

ENDNOTES

1   John Hoole, 'Foreword' in John Christian, ed., *The Last Romantics* (London, Lund Humphries, 1989), p.7

2   The Rev. Percy Dearmer, speaking at the Church Congress, Southport, *The Times*, 8 October 1926, p.17

3   See Bernard Walke, *Twenty Years at St Hilary* (London, Anthony Mott, 1935)

4   Quoted in Ronald C D Jasper, *George Bell, Bishop of Chichester* (London, Oxford University Press, 1967), p.121

5   Quoted ibid., p.133

6   Ibid, p.130

7   Robert Rosenblum, *Modern Painting and the Northern Romantic Tradition* (London, Thames & Hudson, 1975), p.8

8   William Blake, *Jerusalem The Emanation of the Giant Albion* (1804-20), Plate 44, Line 15, 'Therefore the Sons of Eden praise Urthonas Spectre in Songs / Because he kept the Divine Vision in time of trouble.'

9   Jennifer L. Shaw, *Dream States: Puvis de Chavannes, Modernism and the Fantasy of France* (New Haven and London, Yale University Press, 2002), p.190

10   Margaret Steele Anderson, *The Study of Modern Painting* (New York, The Century Co., 1914), p.52

11   Traherne's writings were discovered in manuscript in 1898 and *Centuries of Mediation*, containing his best-known passages, was published in 1908.

12   Gilbert Spencer, *Stanley Spencer* (London, Victor Gollancz, 1961), pp.110; 113

13   See Edith Cobb, *The Ecology of Imagination of Childhood* (New York, Columbia University Press, 1977)

14   Paul Nash, *Outline, an autobiography and other writings* (London: Faber & Faber, 1949), pp.35-37

15   Carrington to Nash, July 1913 (Tate Archive), printed in Ronald Blythe, *First Friends: Paul and Bunty, John and Christine – and Carrington* (Huddersfield, The Fleece Press, 1997), p.40

16   According to Gilbert Spencer, op.cit., p.111, an engraving of *Ecce Ancilla Domini* (1850, Tate) by Dante Gabriel Rossetti hung in the nursery at Fernlea, Cookham.

17   Quoted in P d'A Jones, *The Christian Socialist Revival 1877-1914* (Princeton, Princeton University Press, 1968), p.146

18   J. W. Appell, ed., *The Dream of Poliphilus etc.* (London, Department of Science and Art, 1888 and subsequent editions)

19   Richard Davey, 'Charles Mahoney and Christian Art', in *Charles Mahoney 1903-1968* (London, The Fine Art Society with Paul Liss, 1999), p.44

20   Christopher Skelton, *The Engravings of Eric Gill* (Wellingborough, Christopher Skelton, 1983), p.xxii

21   1966 is given by Ruth Artmonsky in 'The Murals of Barbara Jones', in Paul Liss et. al., *British Murals and Decorative Painting 1920-1960* (Bristol, John Sansom, 2013); 1971 in Ruth Artmonsky, *A Snapper up of unconsidered trifles: a tribute to Barbara Jones* (London, Artmonsky Arts, 2008)

22   John Napper, *Recent Paintings*, Albemarle Gallery, London, 1991, p19

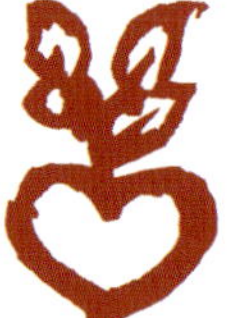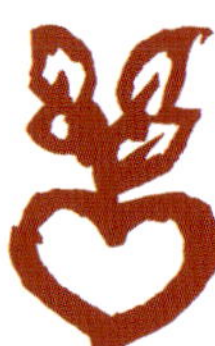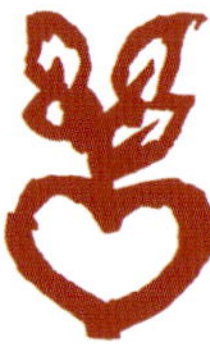

 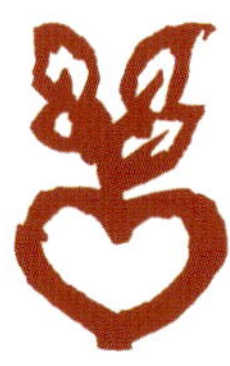 # CATALOGUE

''There is a time for everything,
and a season for every activity under the heavens...'

Ecclesiastes 3:1

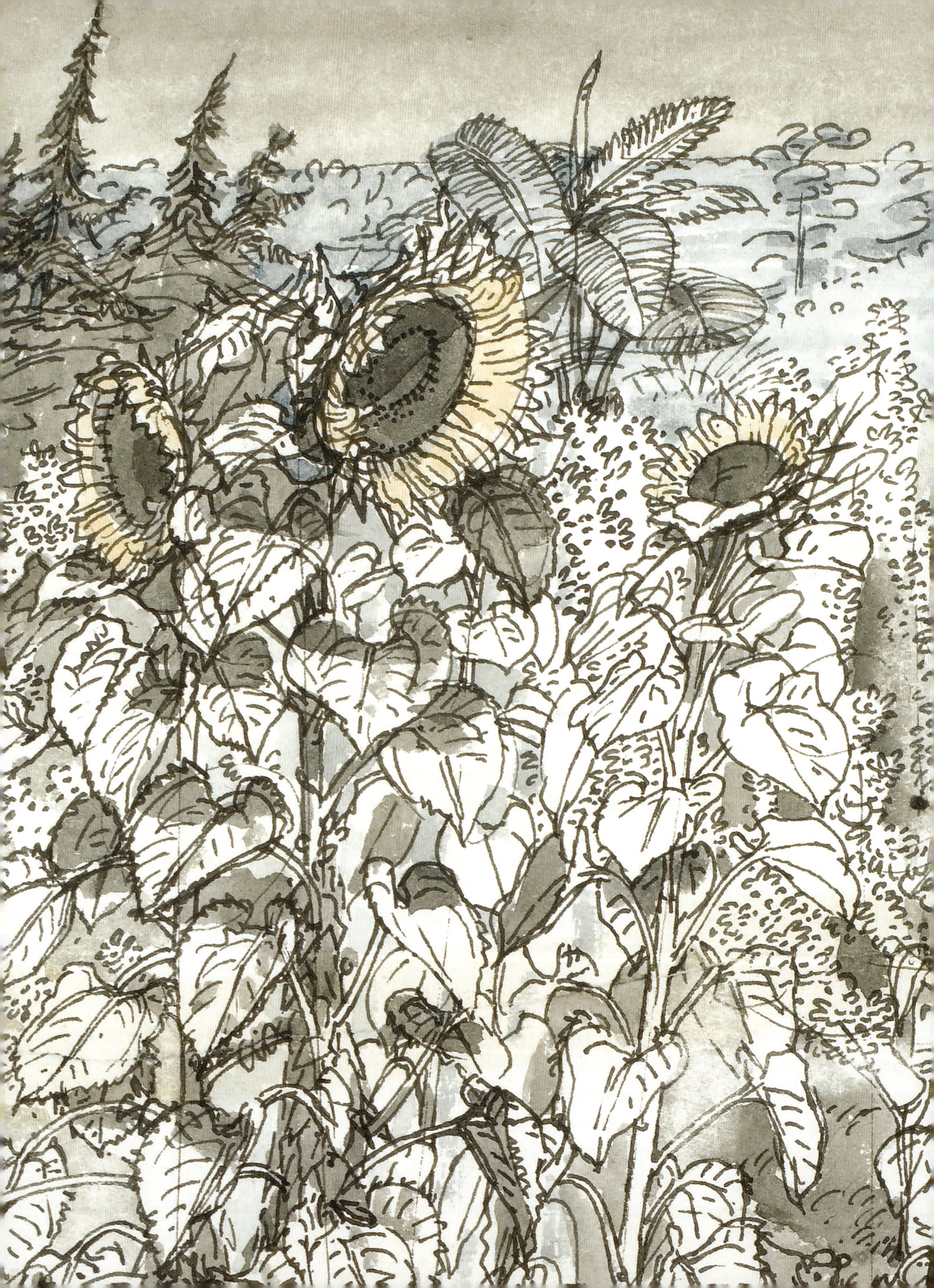

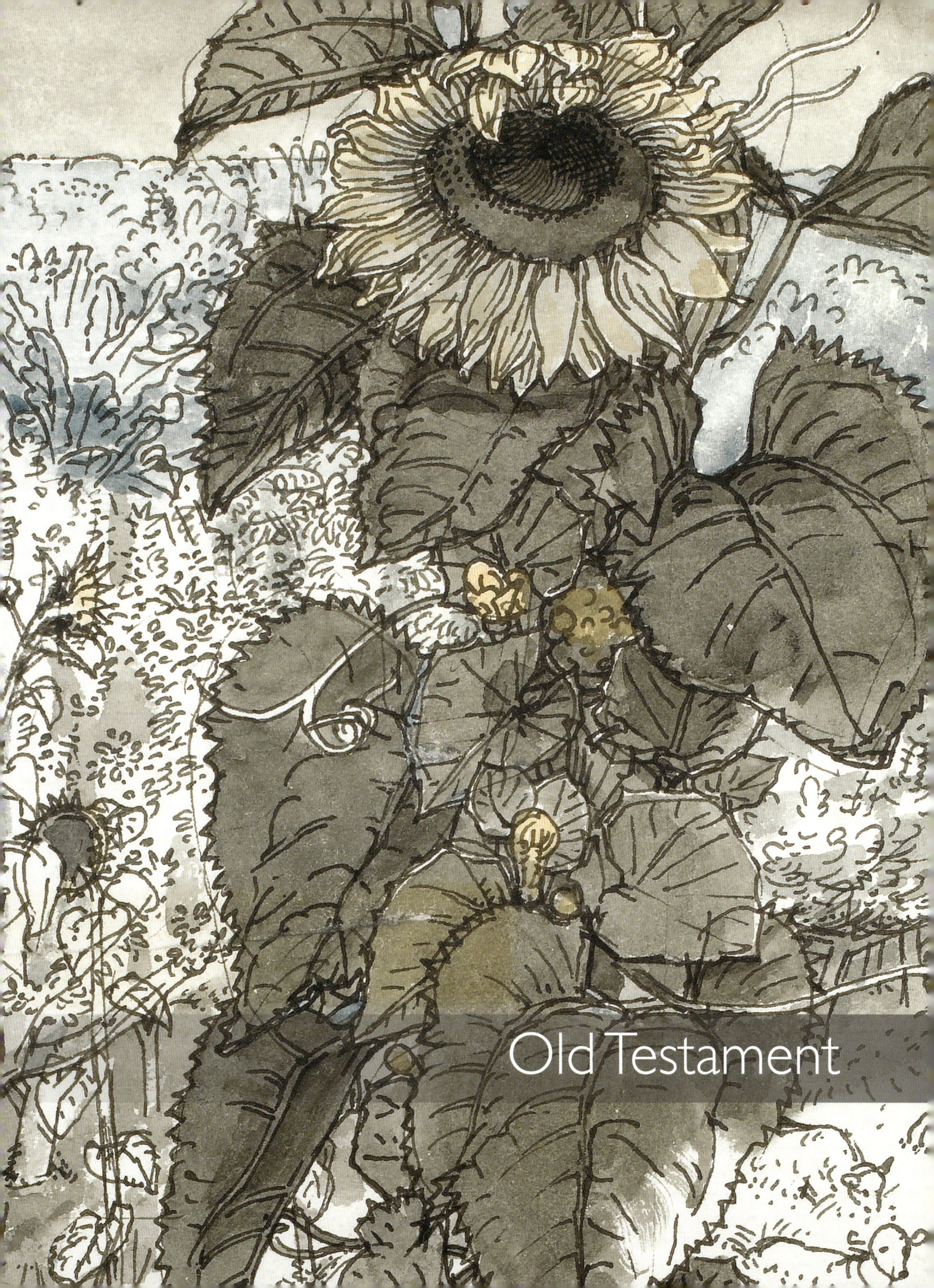
Old Testament

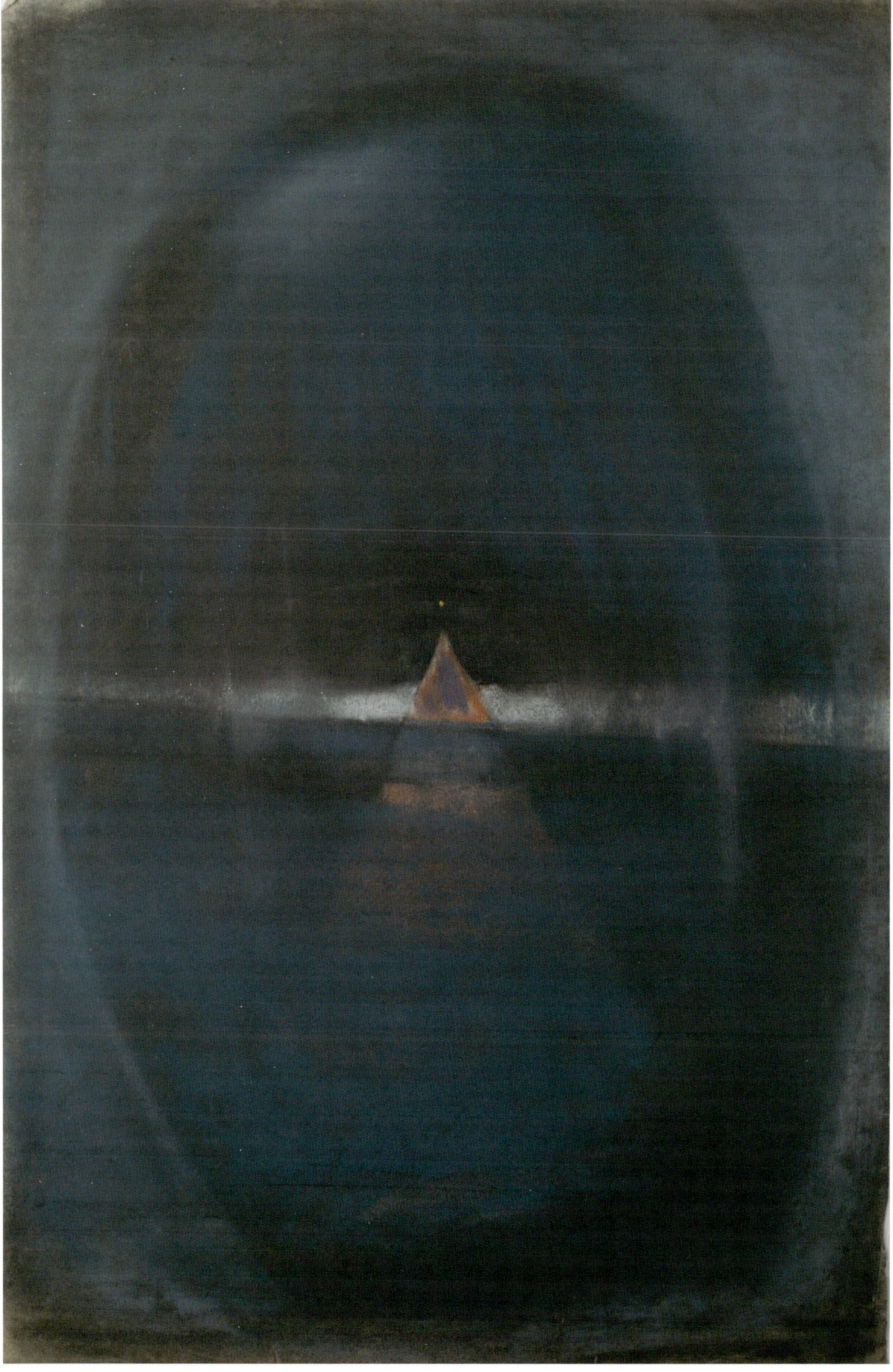

16 – John Tunnard (1900-1971), *Orange Flame*,
pastel on paper, 21 ½ × 14 ¾ in. (54.6 × 37.4 cm).
Provenance: Private collection.

15 – John Tunnard (1900-1971), *A point on the horizon line*,
pastel on paper, 22 × 15 in. (54 × 38 cm).
Provenance: Private collection.

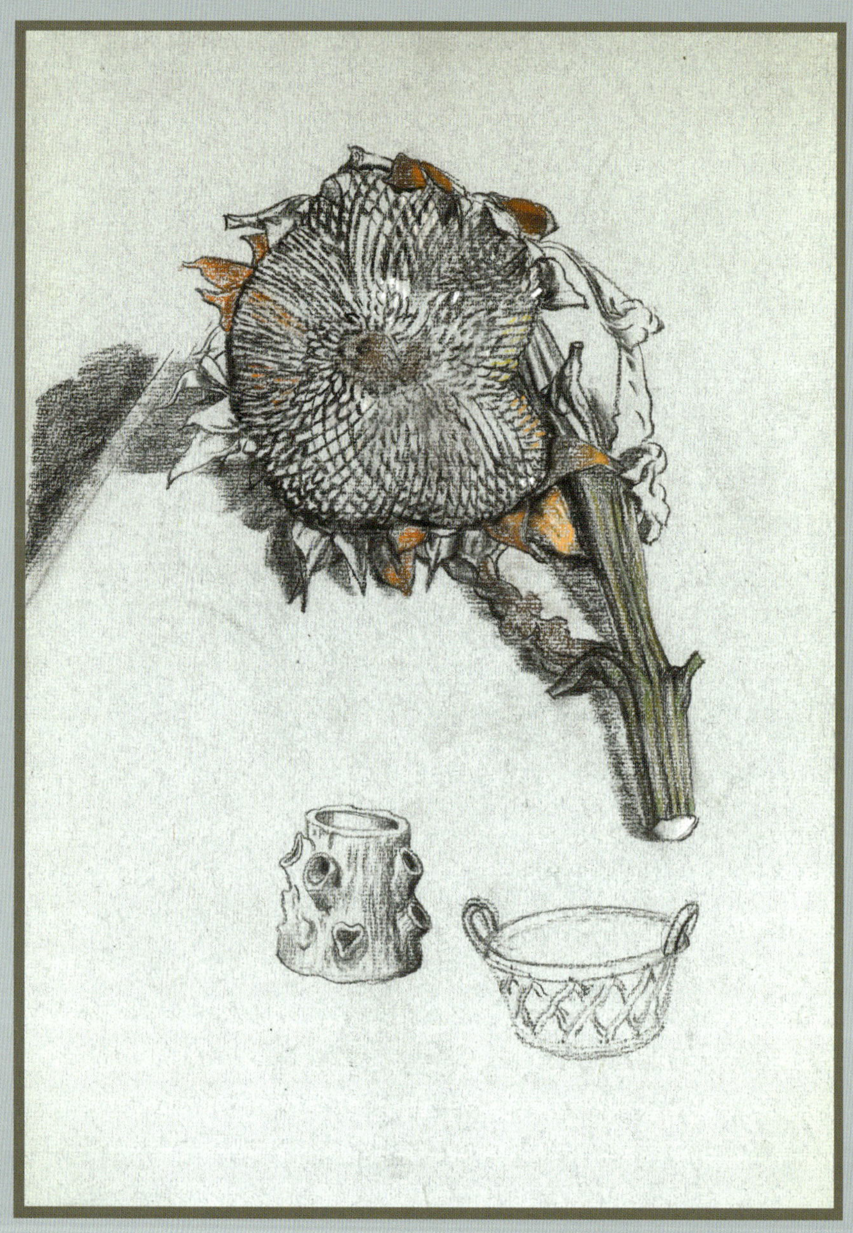

17 – **Charles Mahoney** (1903-1968), Study of a sunflower,
black chalk and pastel on paper, 19 x 12 ½ in. (48.5 x 31.5 cm).

Mahoney was particularly fond of the giant sunflower, Helianthus annuus, capable of outgrowing a man within a season. He made many studies of this species, capturing the convoluted energy of their rough stems and massive heads, and the ragged angles of their great leaves.

18 – **Charles Mahoney** (1903-1968), *Adam and Eve in the Garden of Eden,
pen & ink, wash and colour on paper, 19 x 12 ½ in. (48.5 x 31.5 cm).*

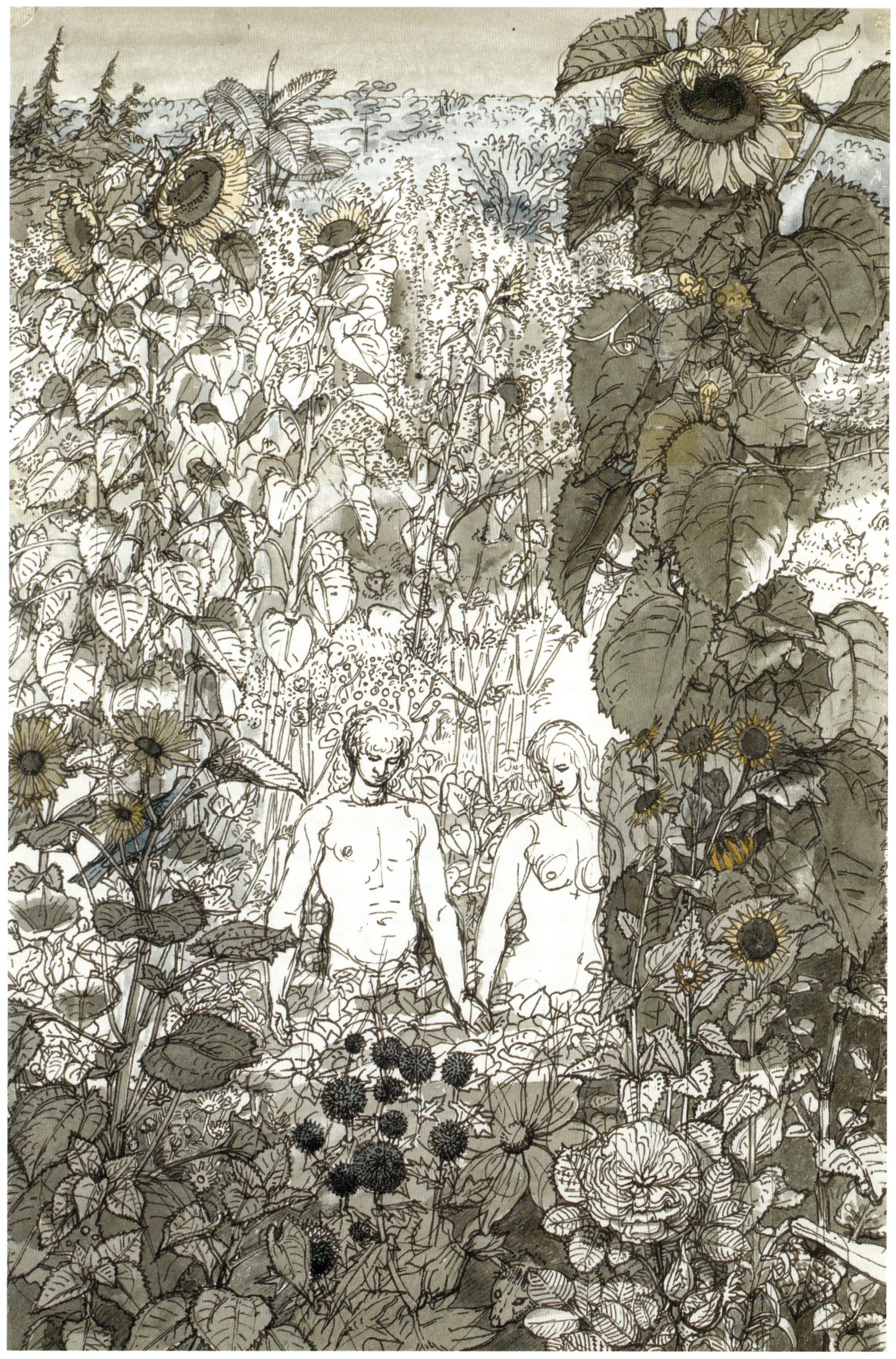

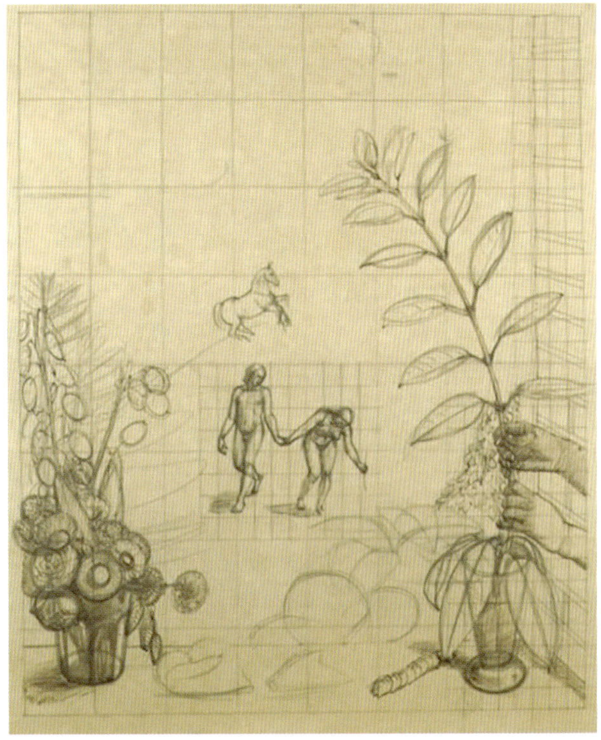
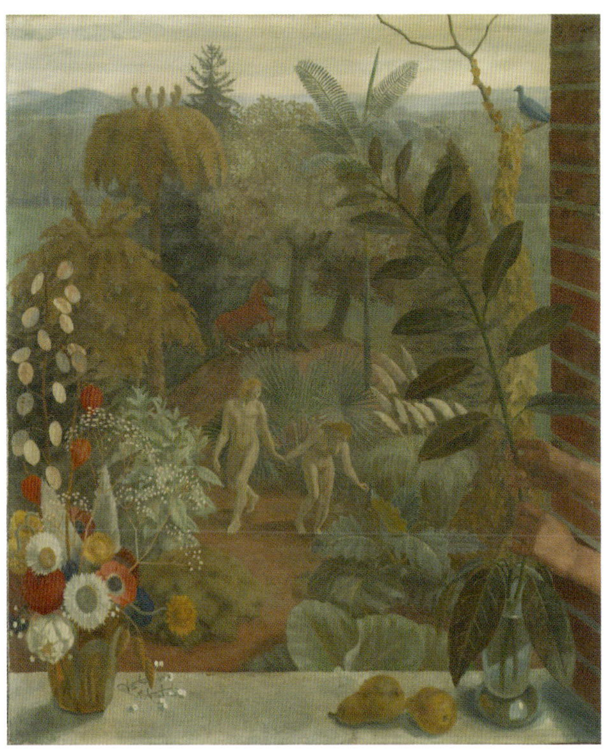

a

b

19 – Charles Mahoney (1903-1968),
Adam and Eve in the Garden of Eden,

a Study for *Adam and Eve in the Garden of Eden* c.1935, pencil, pen and brown and black ink on paper, squared, 22 × 18 ½ in. (56 × 47 cm).
b *Adam and Eve*, oil on canvas, 40 × 30 in. (91.4 × 76.2 cm). © Tate (N05323).
c Study for *Adam and Eve in the Garden of Eden* c.1935, pencil, pen and brown and black ink on paper, squared, 22 ¼ × 19 in. (56.4 × 43.6 cm).

Literature: Herburt Furst, 'Standards of Criticism', *Apollo*, XXXVI, 1942, p. 15.

Mahoney exhibited Adam and Eve (now in tye collection of Tate Britain) at the New English Art Club in 1936 (199). Mahoney, who at this time was collaborating with Evelyn Dunbar on the illustrated book *Gardeners' Choice* (1937), alluded to their blossoming romance through the story of Adam and Eve, the subject of several paintings and illustrated letters to her.

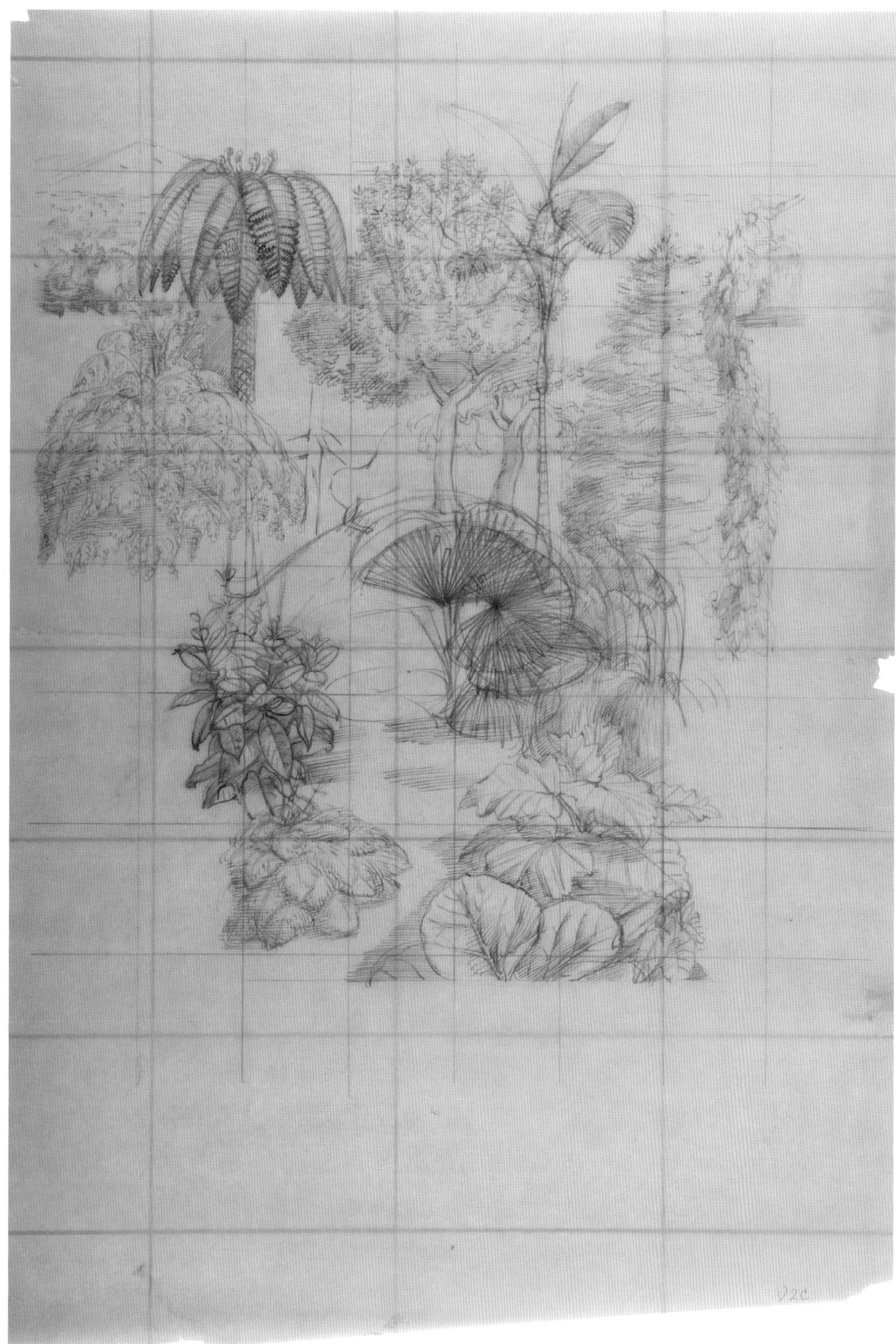

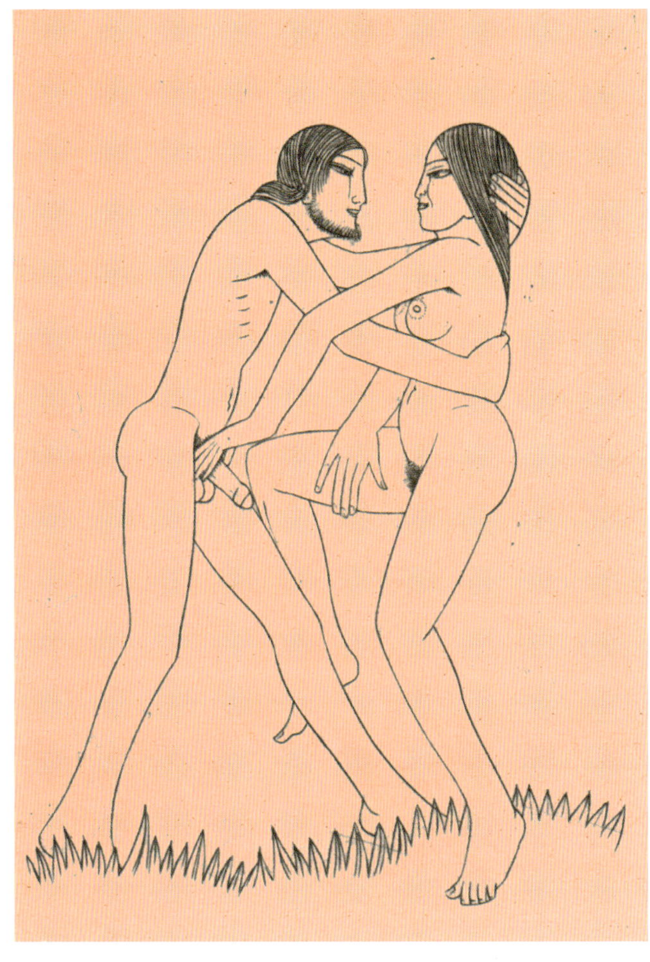

20 – *Earth Inviting* (Alternative), plate: 5 × 3 ½ in. (12.5 × 8.8 cm).

Eric Gill (1882-1940), *Procreant Hymn*, 1926
Nine copper plates and prints for the 'Procreant Hymn' by E. Powys Mathers, originally published by The Golden Cockerel Press in 1926.

In the 1926 publication there were just five illustrations – 'God Sending', 'Earth Waiting', 'Earth Inviting', 'Dalliance' and 'Earth Receiving'. However the publisher included an advertisement for alternative plates available to subscribers individually. These alternative plates follow the composition of the published versions but the male and female figures are presented in a state of self evident sexual arousal which would clearly have been unexpected (and, in many quarters, unacceptable) at that time.

Plates comprise:
a   *God Sending* (P.359)
b   *Earth Waiting* (P.360)
c   *Earth Inviting* (P.361) – this plate has a second design on the reverse, *Yahoo* (P.411)
d   *Dalliance* (P.362)
e   *Earth Receiving* (P.363)
f   *God Sending* (Alternative) (P.364)
g   *Earth Inviting* (Alternative) (P.365)
h   *Earth Wrestling* (P.366)
i   *Earth Receiving* (Alternative) (P.367)

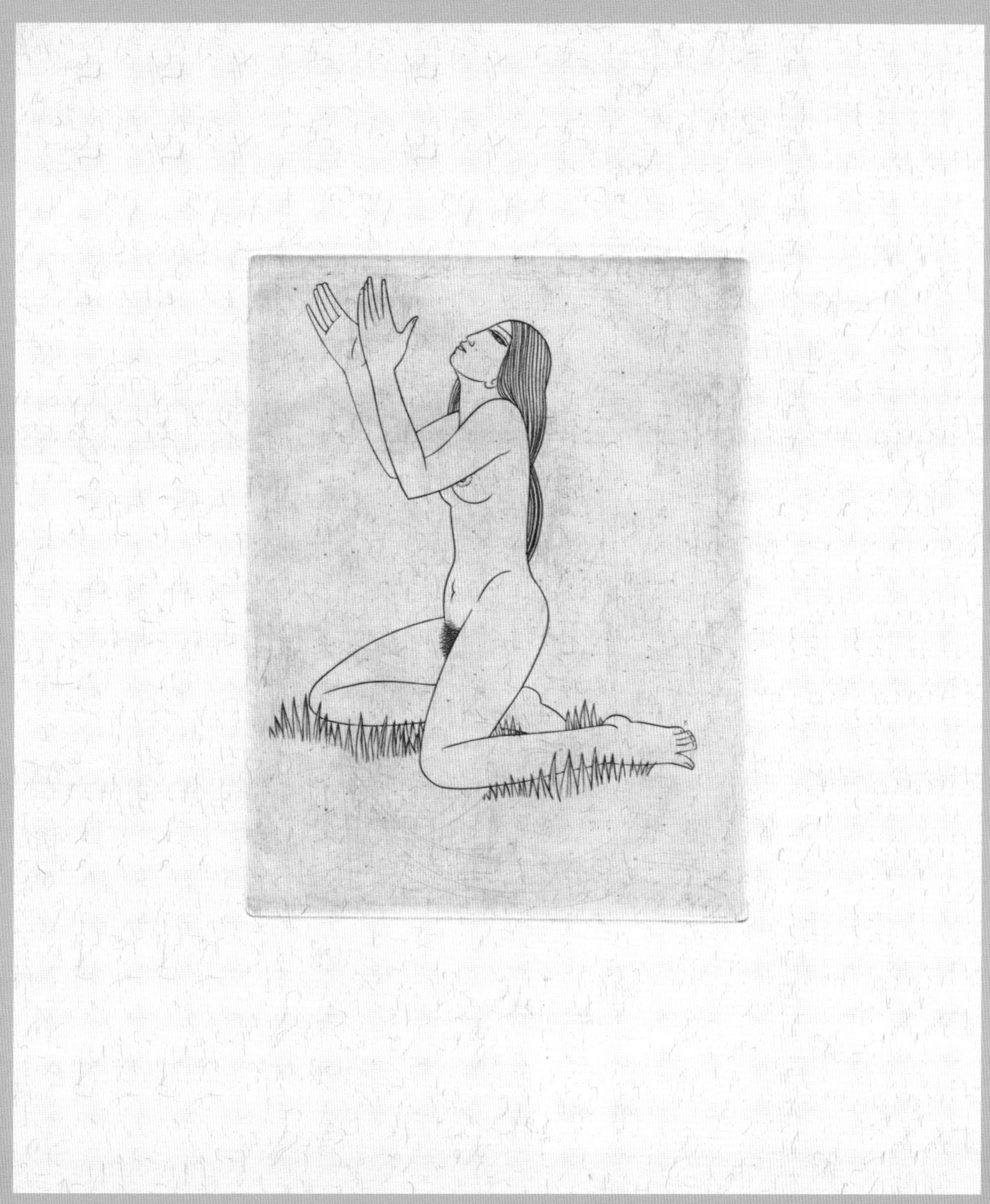

a   *Earth Waiting*, plate: 4 ¼ × 3 ½ in. (11.1 × 8.8 cm).

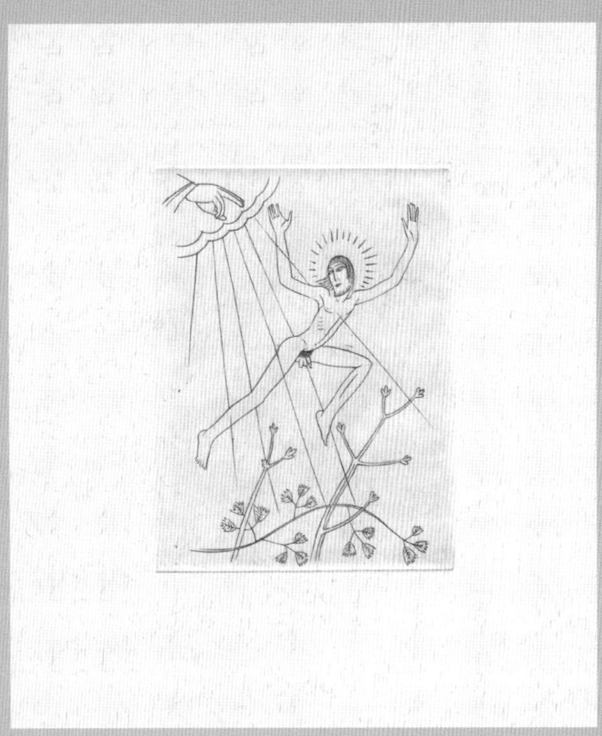

b   *God Sending*, plate: 4 ½ × 3 ½ in. (11.3 × 8.8 cm).

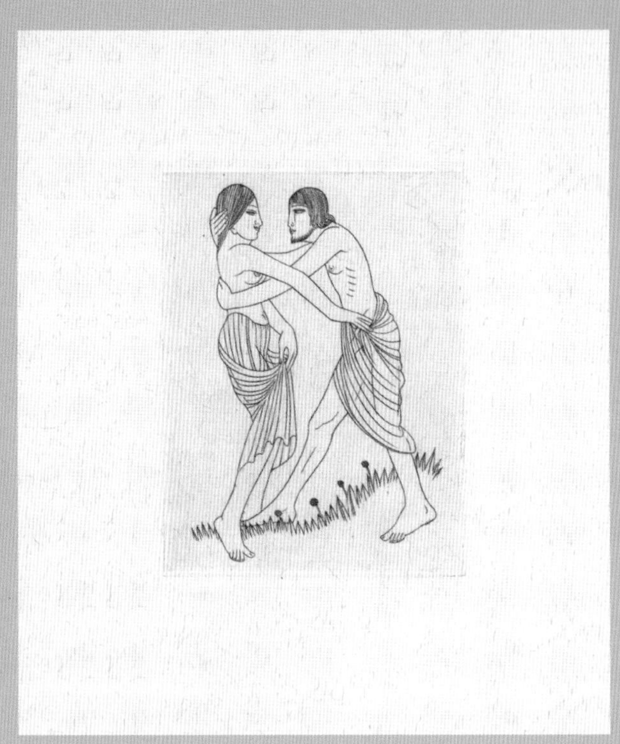

c   *Earth Inviting*, plate: 4 ½ × 3 ½ in. (11.3 × 8.8 cm).

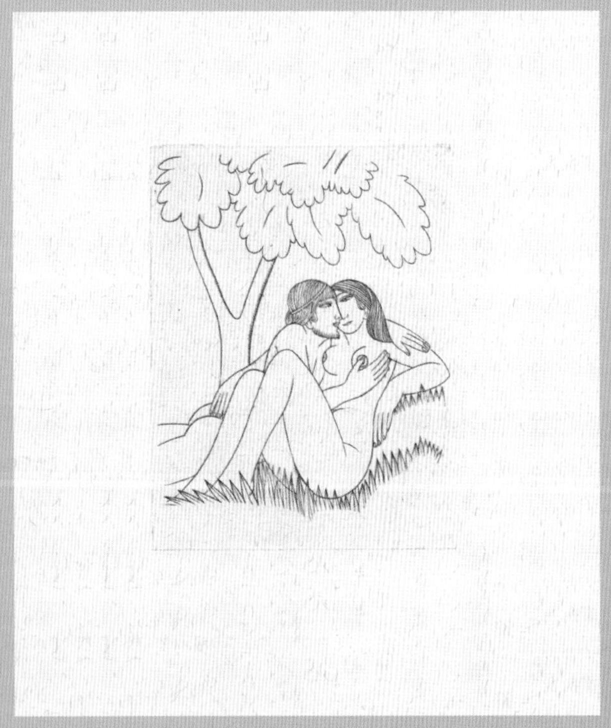

d   *Dalliance*, plate: 4 ½ × 3 ½ in. (11.3 × 8.8 cm).

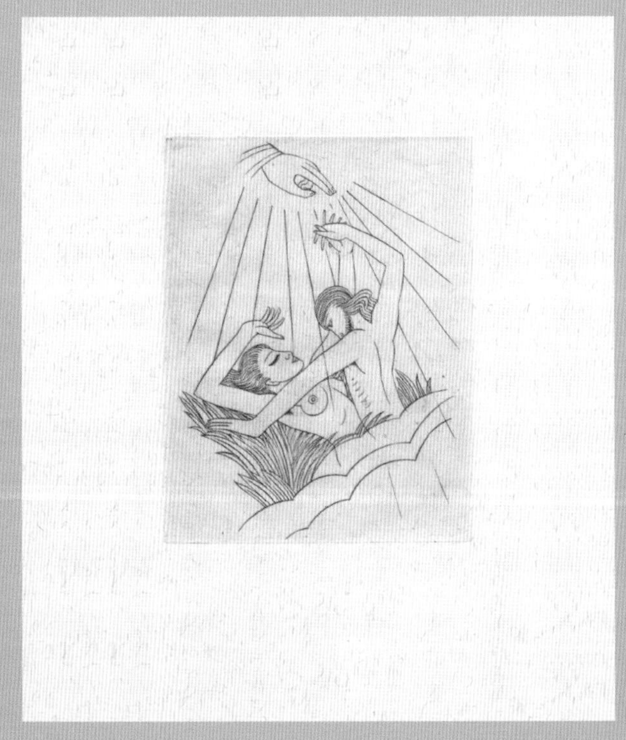

e   *Earth Receiving*, plate: 4 ½ × 3 ½ in. (11.3 × 8.8 cm).

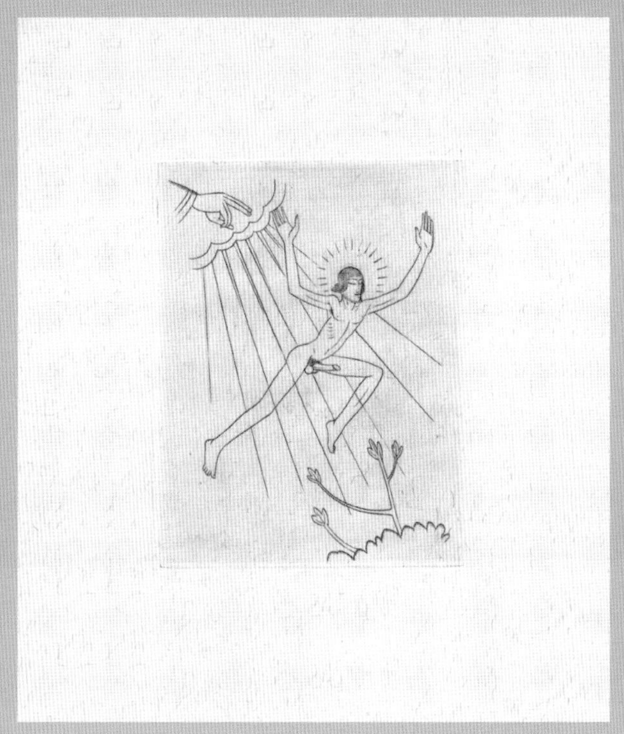

f   *God Sending* (Alternative), plate: 4 ½ × 3 ½ in. (11.3 × 8.8 cm).

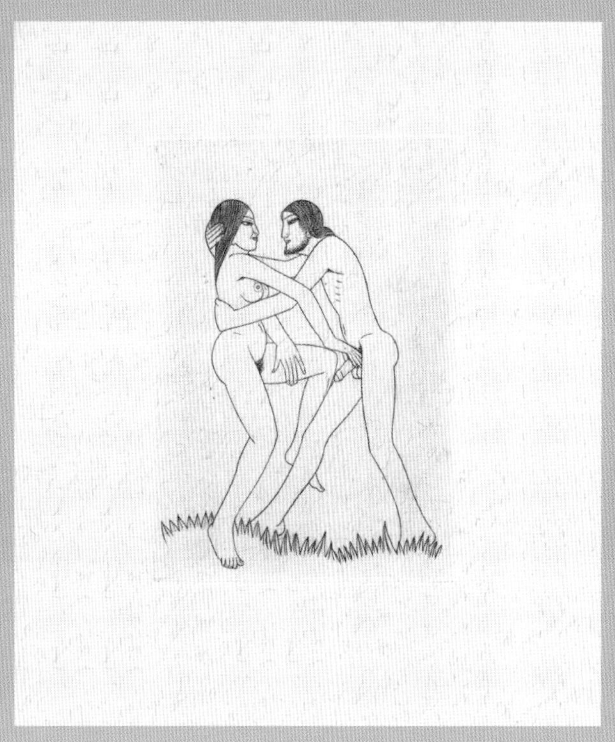

g   *Earth Inviting* (Alternative), plate: 5 × 3 ½ in. (12.5 × 8.8 cm).

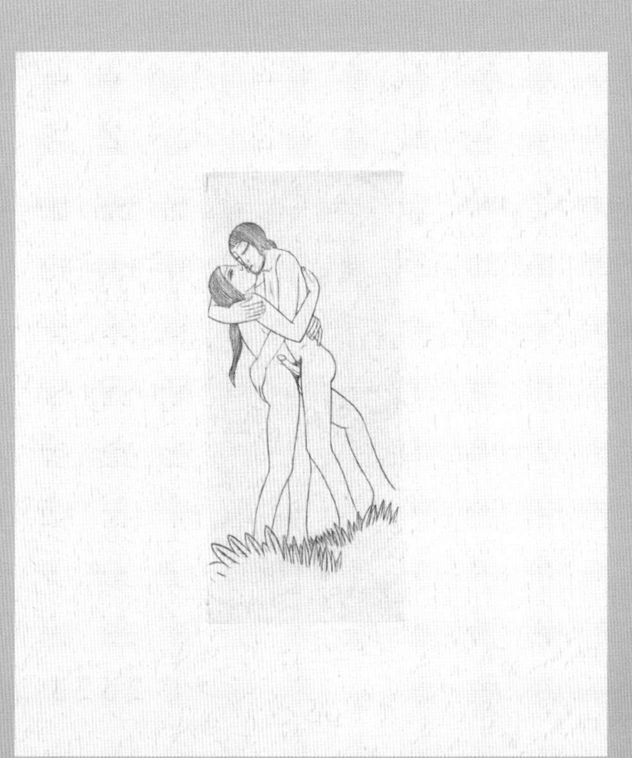

h   *Earth Wrestling*, plate: 5 × 2 ¼ in. (12.5 × 5.8 cm).

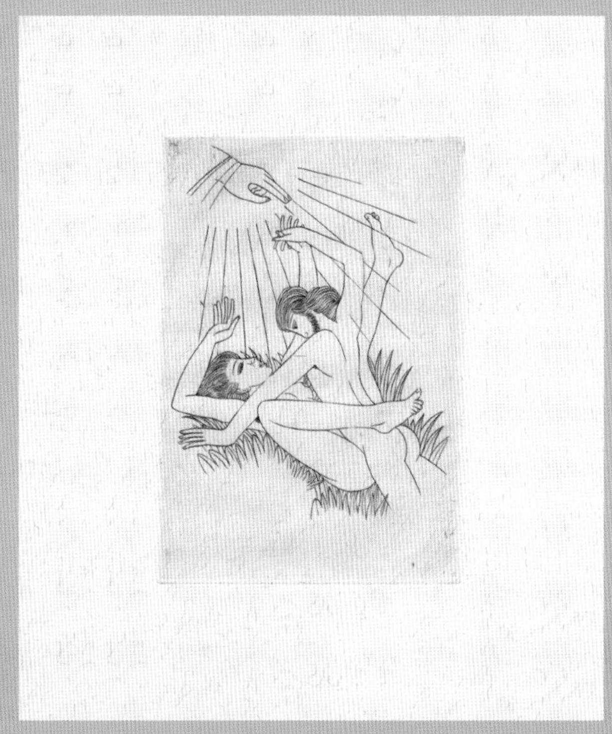

i   *Earth Receiving* (Alternative), plate: 5 × 3 ½ in. (12.5 × 8.8 cm).

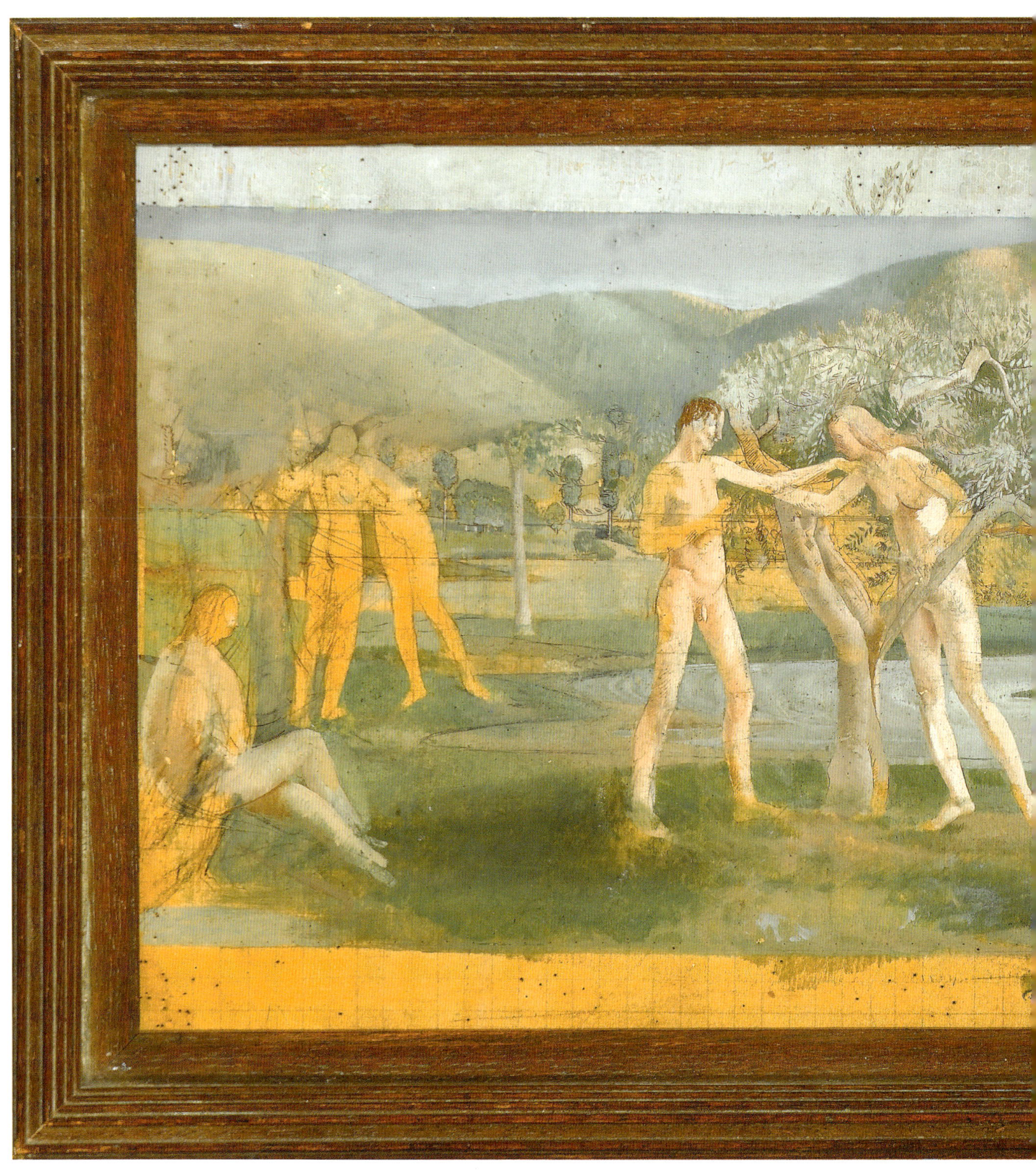

21 –Thomas Monnington (1902-1976), Study for *Allegory*, c.1924,
Oil on tracing paper, laid on board, squared for transfer, 12 ½ x 22 ½ in. (31.7 x 57.2 cm).
Exhibited: *Inspired by Italy*, Exeter Museum and Art Gallery, August-September 1996, (21).Exhibited: *Inspired by Italy*, Exeter Museum and Art Gallery, August-September 1996, (19); *Thomas Monnington*, The Fine Art Society, 1997, no 23.
Literature: *Inspired by Italy*, Exeter Museum, 1996; *Thomas Monnington*, The Fine Art Society, 1997.
British Murals & Decorative Painting 1920-1960, Sansom & Co, 2013, pp.170-171.

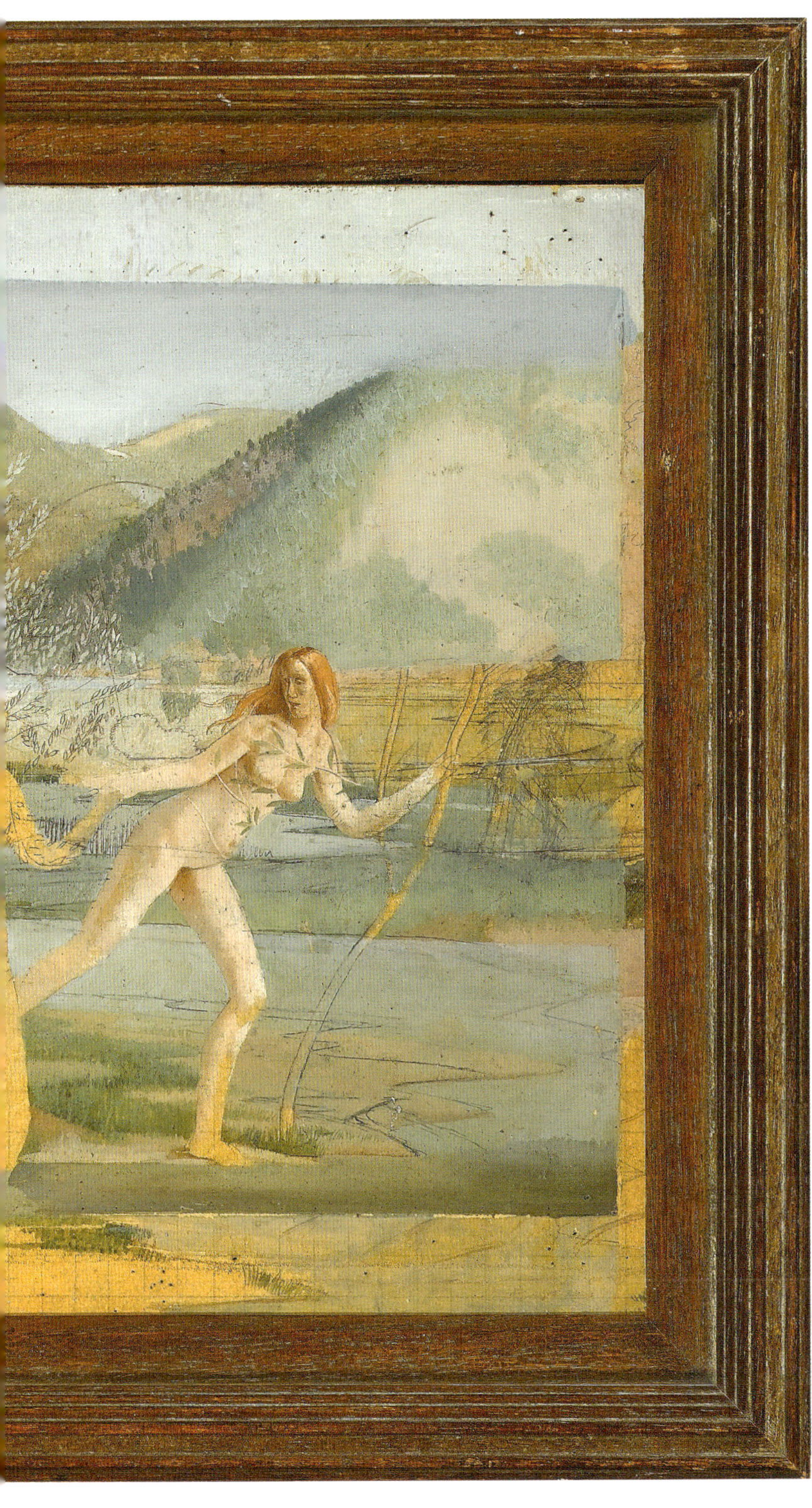

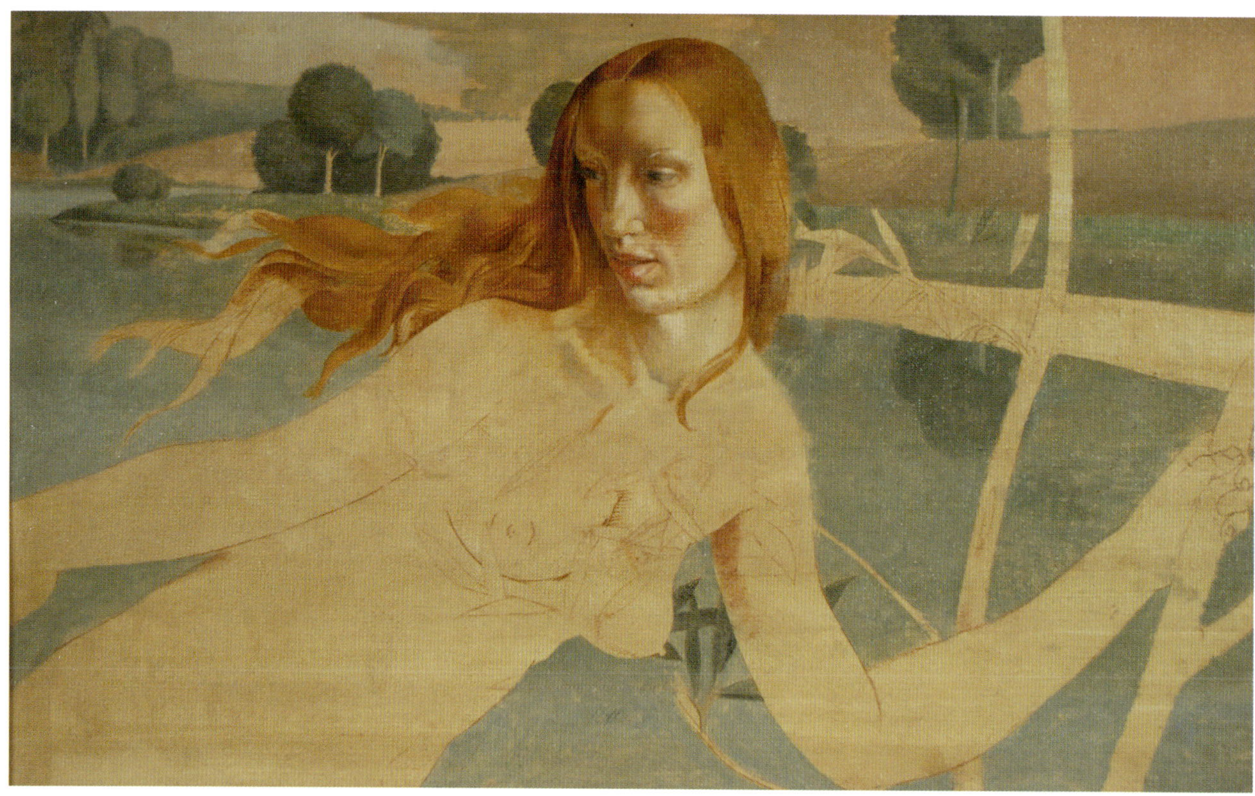

22 – Thomas Monnington (1902-1976), Study for *Allegory* (head of woman to the right), c.1925, oil on canvas, 11 x 19 in. (28 x 48.2 cm).
Provenance: Lady Monnington; Nicholas Bowlby.
Exhibited: *Inspired by Italy*, Exeter Museum and Art Gallery, August-September 1996, (19); *Thomas Monnington*, The Fine Art Society, 1997, no 23.
Literature: *Inspired by Italy*, Exeter Museum, 1996, reproduced on front cover; *Thomas Monnington*, The Fine Art Society, 1997, p. 38
British Murals & Decorative Painting 1920-1960, Sansom & Co, 2013, p.173.

The exact meaning of the *Allegory* is unclear and Monnington himself remained elusive about it; invited by the Tate to explain it, he replied, "The idea is a bit complex and was based on the story of the Garden of Eden, but rather a personal interpretation of it" (letter of 17 May 1953). When pressed, a few years later to elaborate, he answered, "I don't think this picture has anything to do with the Garden of Eden story, but I am no more able to explain its exact meaning now than I was at the time I painted it. The whole design certainly had a very particular meaning and purpose and was an attempt to express in pictorial form my attitude to life – almost my faith (2nd April 1957). Having to be content with this, the Tate Gallery retitled the picture *Allegory* – Monnington having always referred to it simply by the title *Decoration*. Iconogrpahically it contains elements of several myths but most obviously The Garden of Love; specific episodes within the painting are reminiscent of Adam and Eve; Apollo and Daphne; The Fountain of Youth. Luciano Chelles has pointed out that the composition is to some extent an adaptation of Piero della Francesca's *Death of Adam* (San Francesco, Arezzo). Ricketts and Shannon, asked by the Faculty of Painting at the British School to report on Monnington's progress commented that they found Monnington, "keenly alive to the merit of the masterpieces he had seen in Italy and alive to the technical practises of the Masters." (12.1.25)

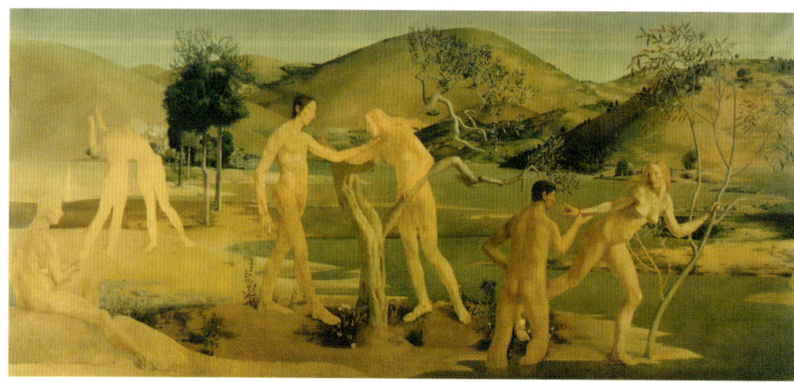

23 – Thomas Monnington (1902-1976),
Allegory, c. 1924,
egg tempera on canvas,
49 ½ x 109 in. (125.7 x 276.8 cm).
© Tate, London 2019

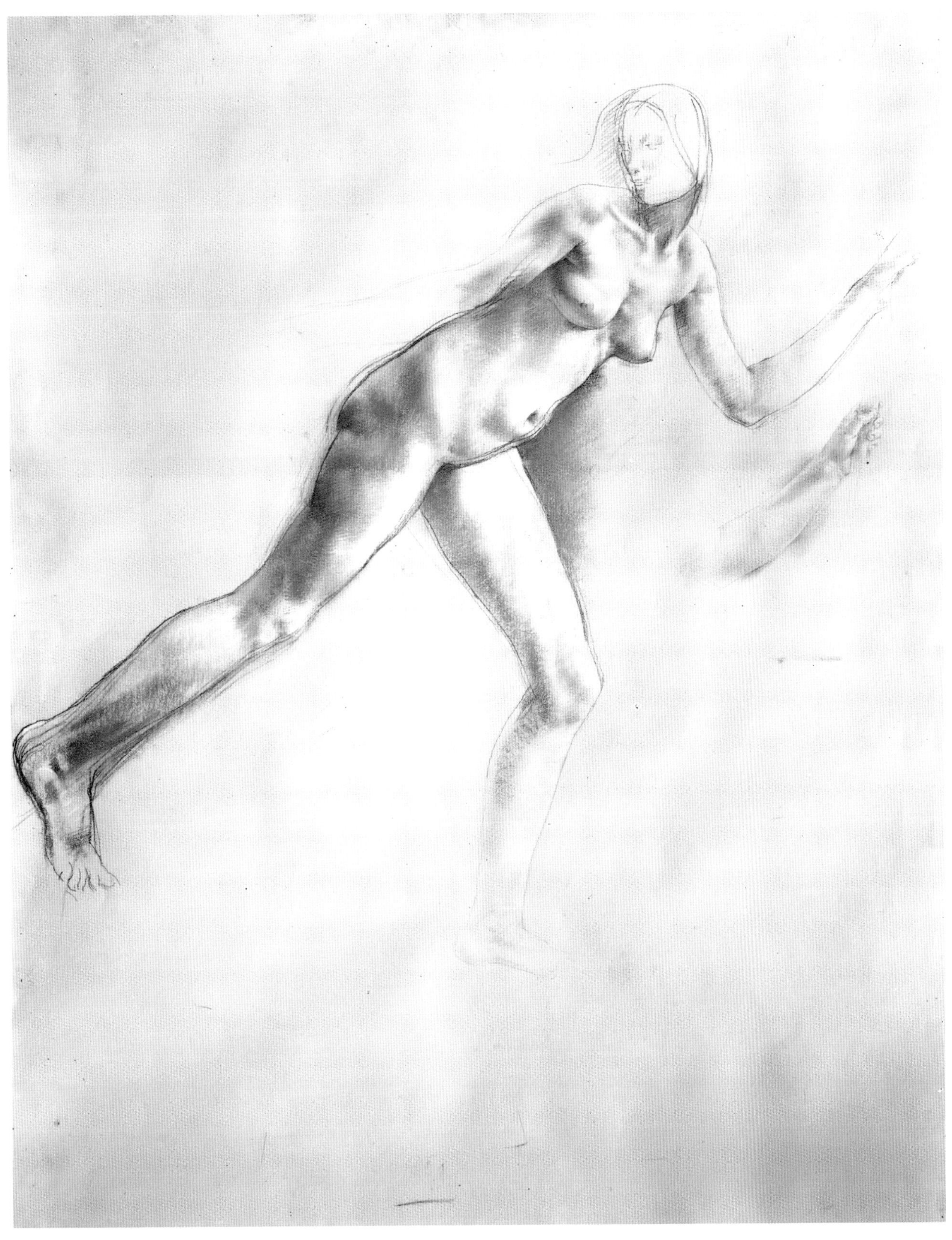

23 b – Thomas Monnington (1902-1976), Preparatory drawing for *Allegory*, photographed c.1924, pencil on paper, whereabouts of drawing unknown.

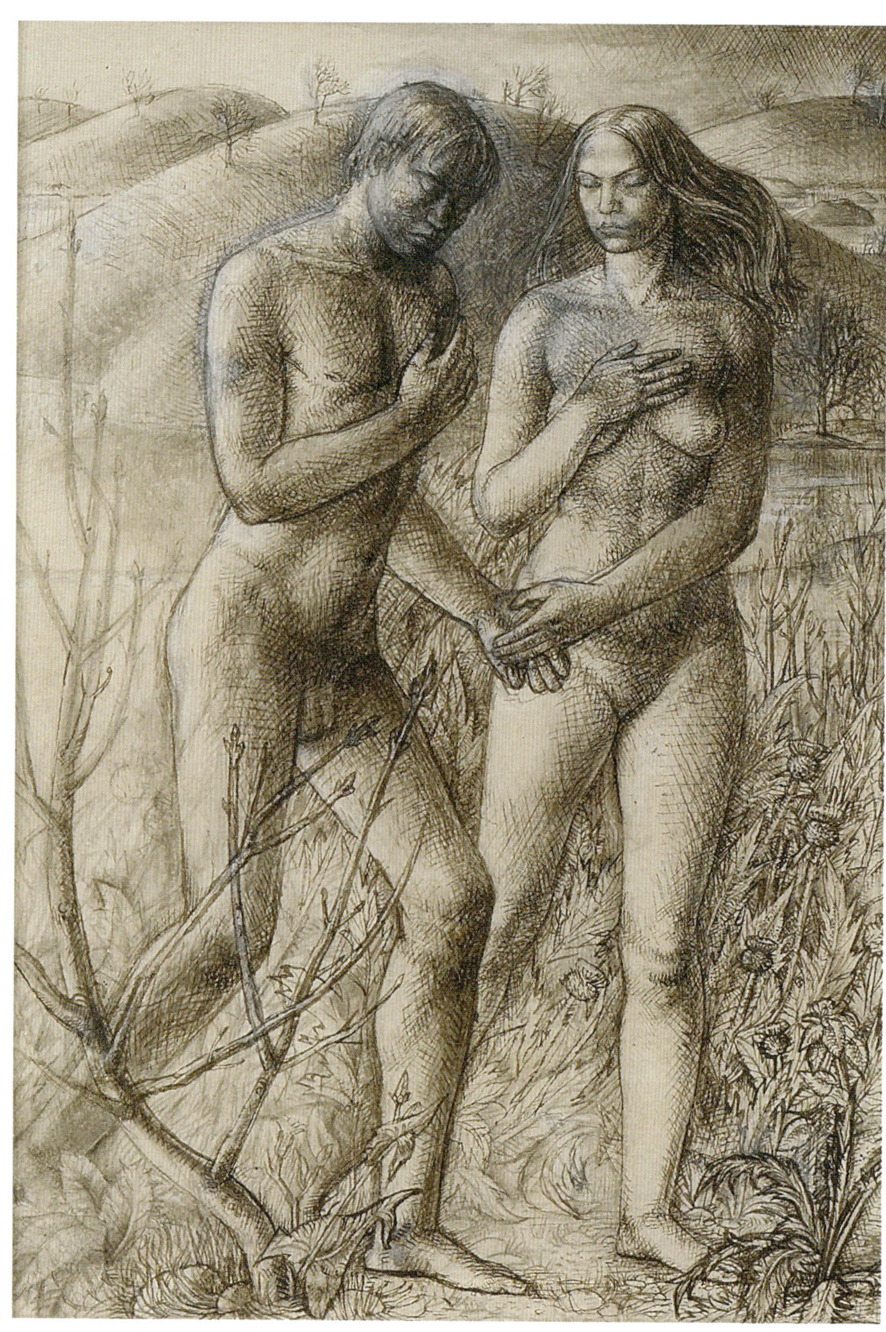

24 – Evelyn Gibbs (1905-1991), Study for *The Expulsion*, 1929,
ink and gouache on paper, 6 x 4 in. (15 x 10.5 cm).

The Expulsion was produced during Gibbs' last year at the Royal College of Art – the year she was awarded the Rome Scholarship in Engraving. Her prints of this period are amongst the most outstanding produced by any of the Rome Scholars. Like so many of her colleagues in Rome, she was, ironically, more influenced by the Northern Italian quattrocento artists than by either the Classical or Baroque tradition of Southern Italy. *The Expulsion* is recorded as having been produced in an edition of 40, though its scarcity suggests not all were printed.

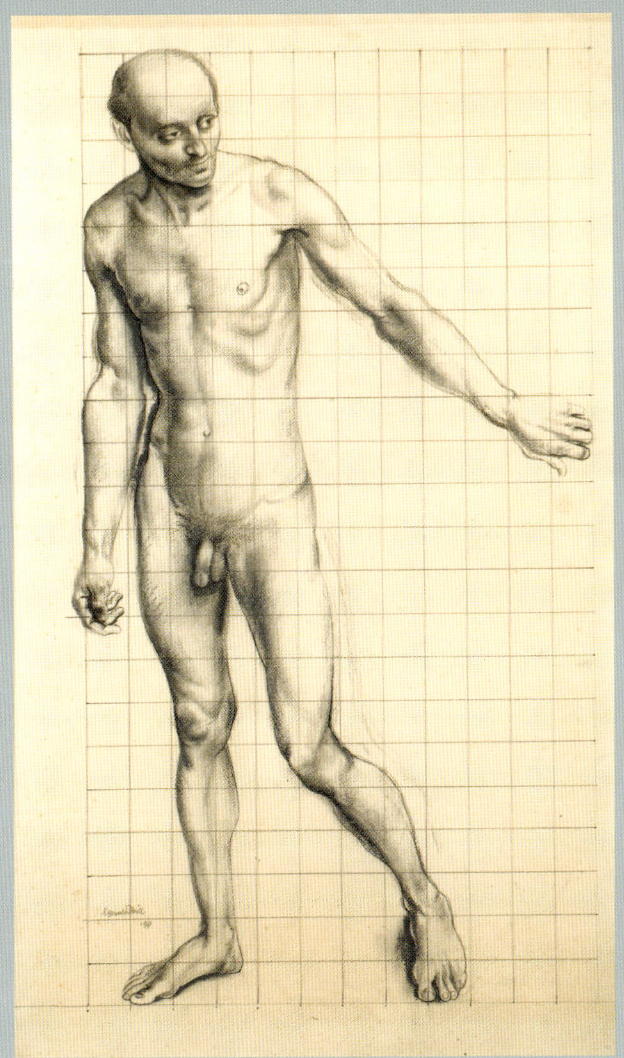
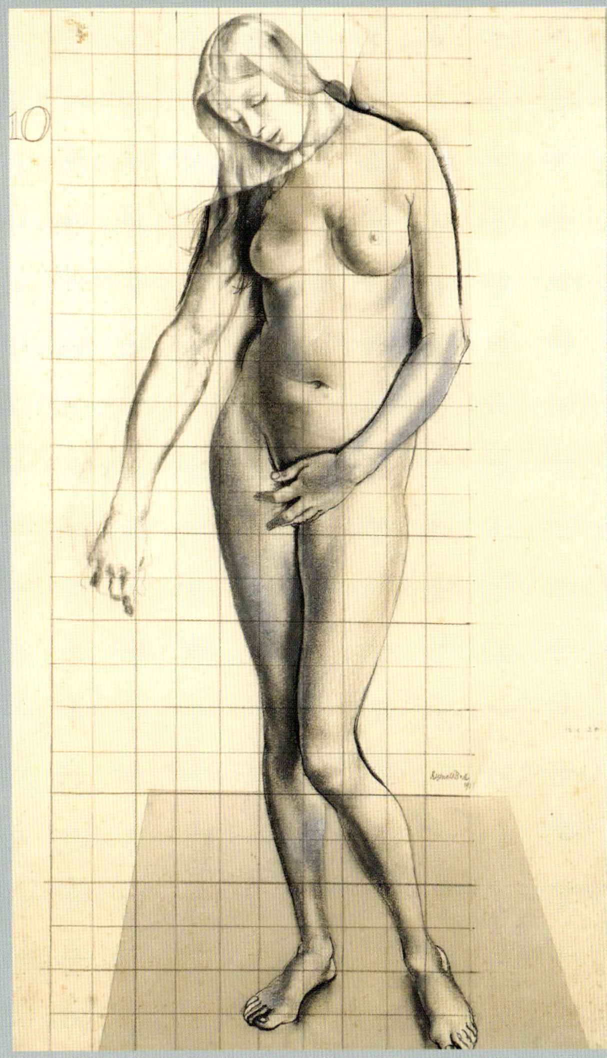

a

b

25 – Reginald Brill (1902-1974),

a   Study for the *Expulsion*, *Adam*, 1927, signed and dated, inscribed with title to the reverse,
black chalk on paper, squared in pencil, 25 × 16 in. (62 × 40 cm).

b   Study for the *Expulsion*, *Eve*, 1927, signed and dated, titled on various lables to the reverse,
black chalk with white highlights on paper, alteration to the head in collage, squared in pencil, 25 ½ × 15 in. (62 .3 × 38 cm).

Provenance: Richards/Webb.
Exhibited: Kingston University, (Permanent loan 13th July 1998)

Adam and Eve was the painting with which Brill won the 1927 Rome Scholarsip in Painting.

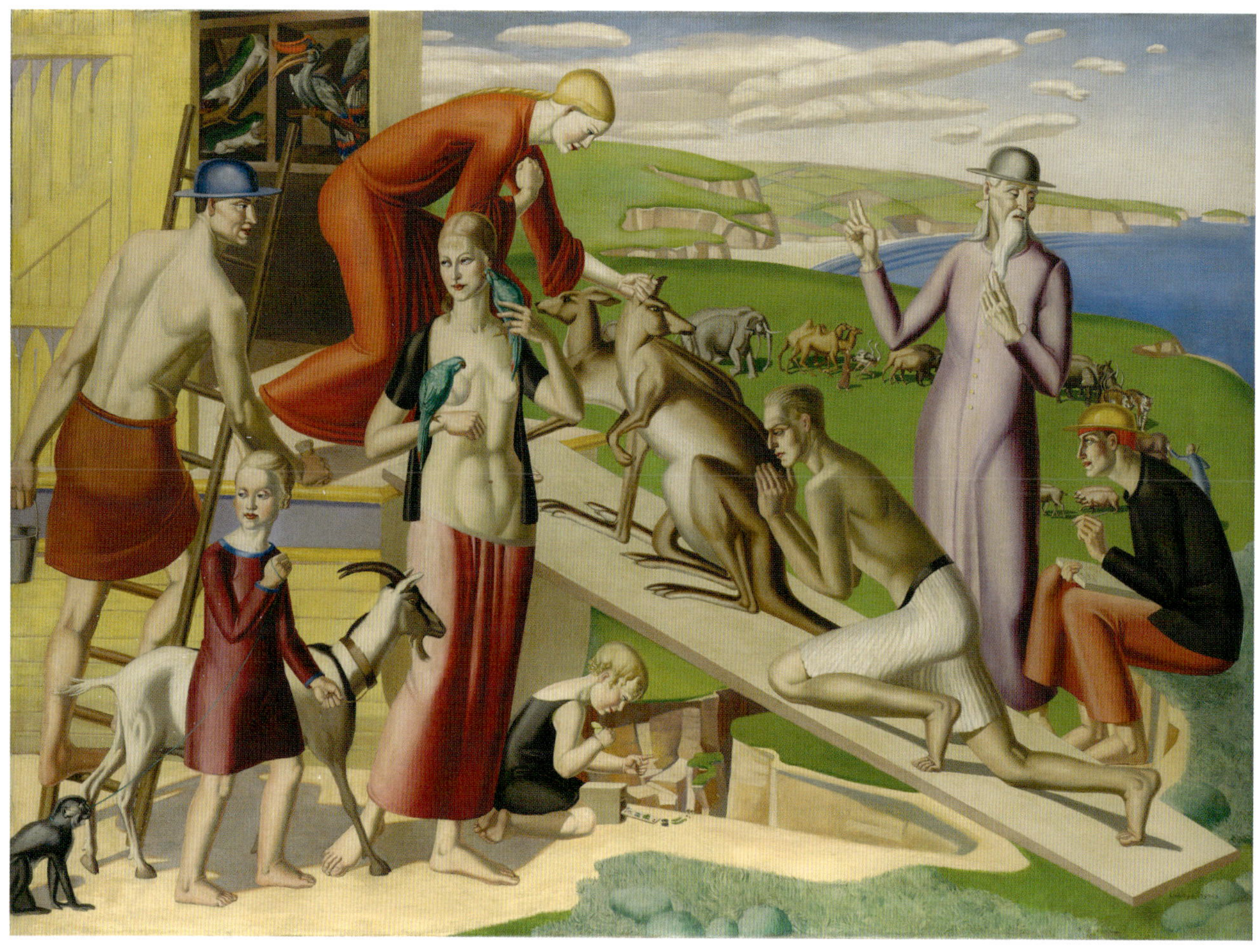

26 – Gladys Hynes (1888-1958), *Noah's Ark*, 1919, signed and dated, oil on canvas, 39 ¼ x 59 in. (100 x 150 cm).
Provenance: Julian Hartnoll, mid 1970's; John Anderson; Godrey Pilkington, mid 1980's Whitford and Hughes, late 1980's; private collection Switerland until 2013; private collection London.
Exhibited: Daily Express Young Artists' Exhibition at the Galleries of the Royal Society of British Artists in Pall Mall in June 1927,
　　　　The National Galleries of Scotland, True to Life, 2017,
Literature: *The Sphere*, June 18th 1927;
　　　　Patrick Elliot & Sacha Llewellyn; *True to Life, British Realist Painting in the 1920s & 1930s*, July 2017, Cat. 49, page 95.

With its well defined outlines, and clearly delineated areas of bold, vigorous colour and sideways dynamism, *Noah's Ark* shows the influence of Vorticism. Hynes was friends with Ezra Pound, the American poet and critic who gave the name Vorticism to the movement in 1913. *The Observer*'s critic P G Konody also saw the influence of the Italian Renaissance in Hynes' work, writing in 1922, 'Miss Gladys Hynes uses the language of the Primitives...her assured naivete, backed by consummate draughtsmanship, is perfectly delightful'.

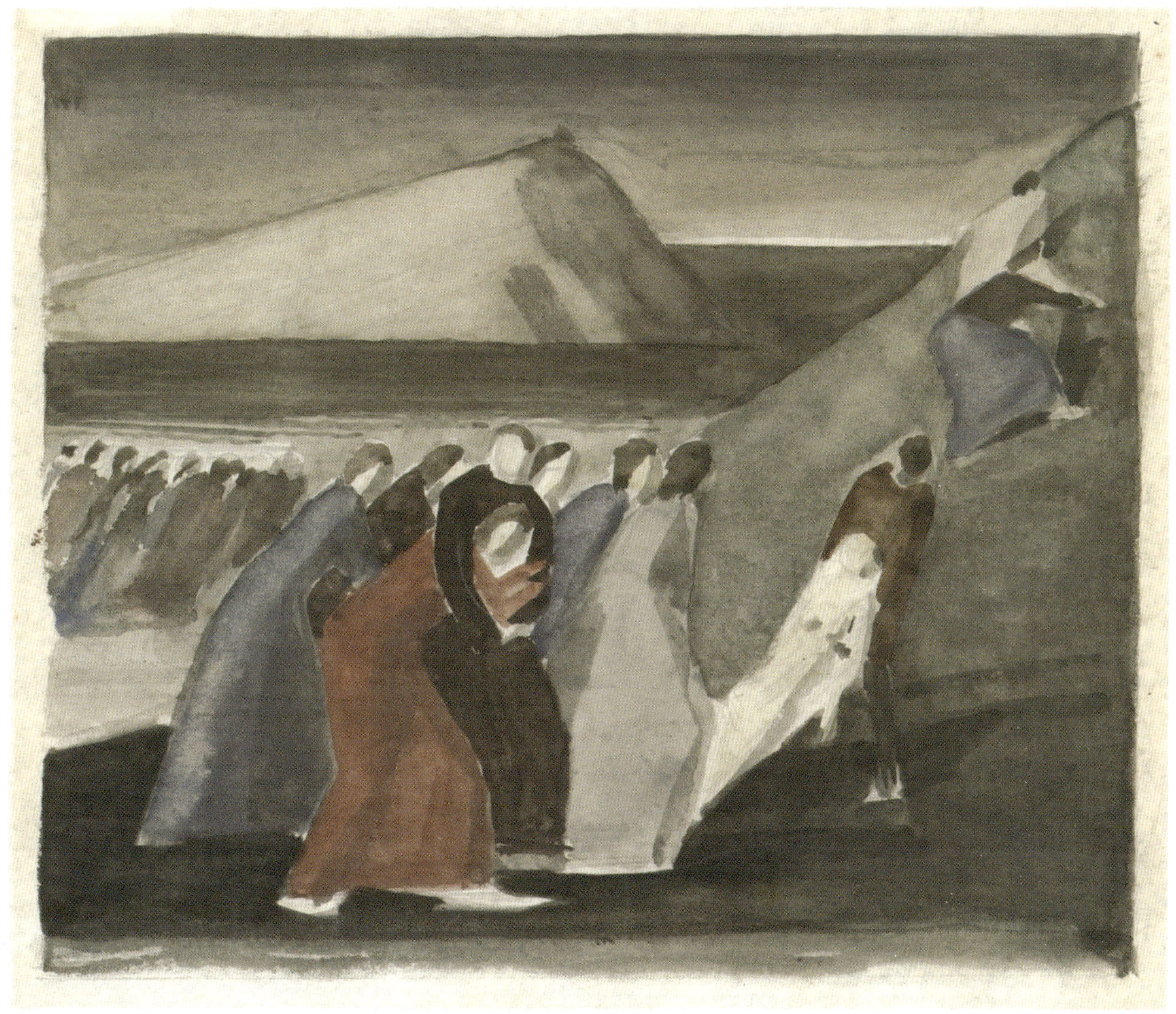

27 – Winifred Knights (1899-1947), Early compositional study for *The Deluge*,
watercolour on paper, 5 x 7 ½ in. (12.5 x 19 cm).
Provenance: Private Collection

'The Deluge' was the prescribed subject for the 1920 British School at Rome Scholarship in Decorative Painting. The Scholarship rules required that the painting was produced in oil or tempera, together with a cartoon, both of which were to be executed in eight weeks. Winifred Knights commenced work on July 5th 1920 and despite losing time through illness was judged the winner, news of which she received on September 21st 1920.

The artist's mother modelled for the central figure carrying the baby and Arnold Mason for the male figure beside her and the man shinning up the hill. The artist portrayed herself as the figure to the centre right of the foreground.

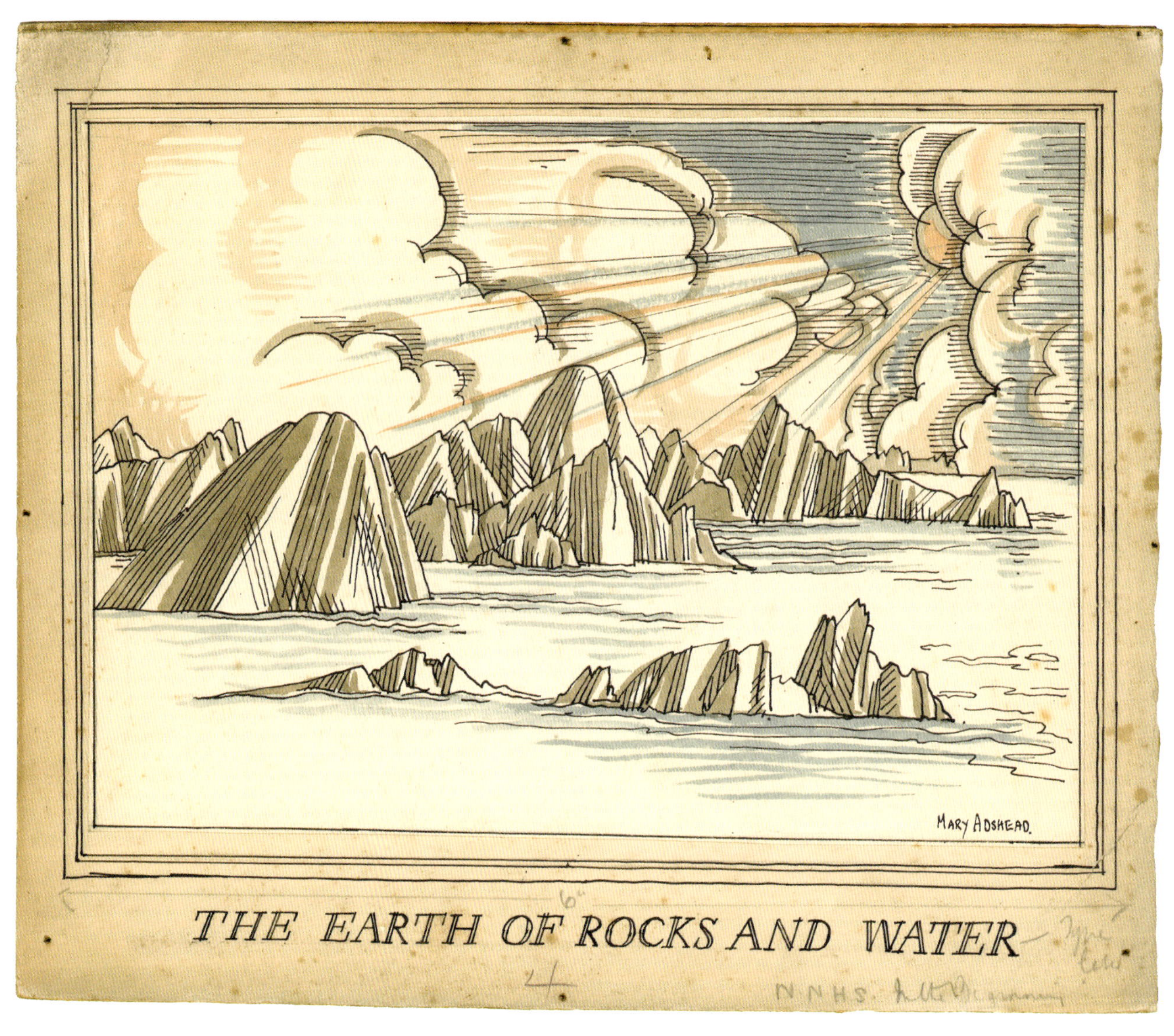

28 – Mary Adshead (1904-1995), *The Earth of Rocks and Water*, c.1930, signed and titled, inscribed with pencil, pen and ink and watercolour on card, 9 x 10 ½ in. (22.8 x 27 cm).

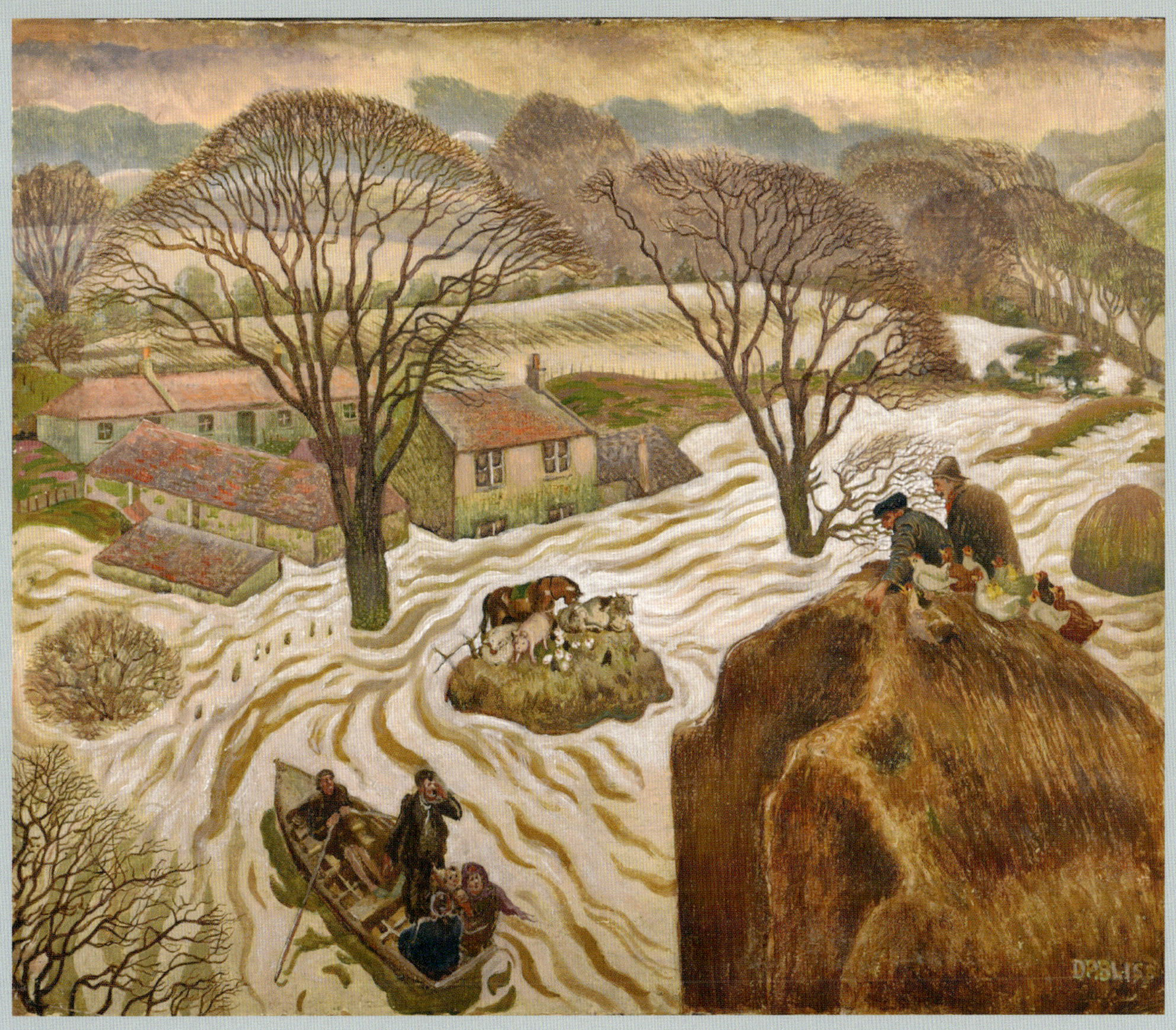

29 – **Dougas Percy Bliss** (1900-1984), *The Flood*, c.1933, inscribed on verso "Painted at Lambeth later Blackheath",
oil on board, 19 ¾ × 23 ¾ in. (50.5 × 60.5 cm).

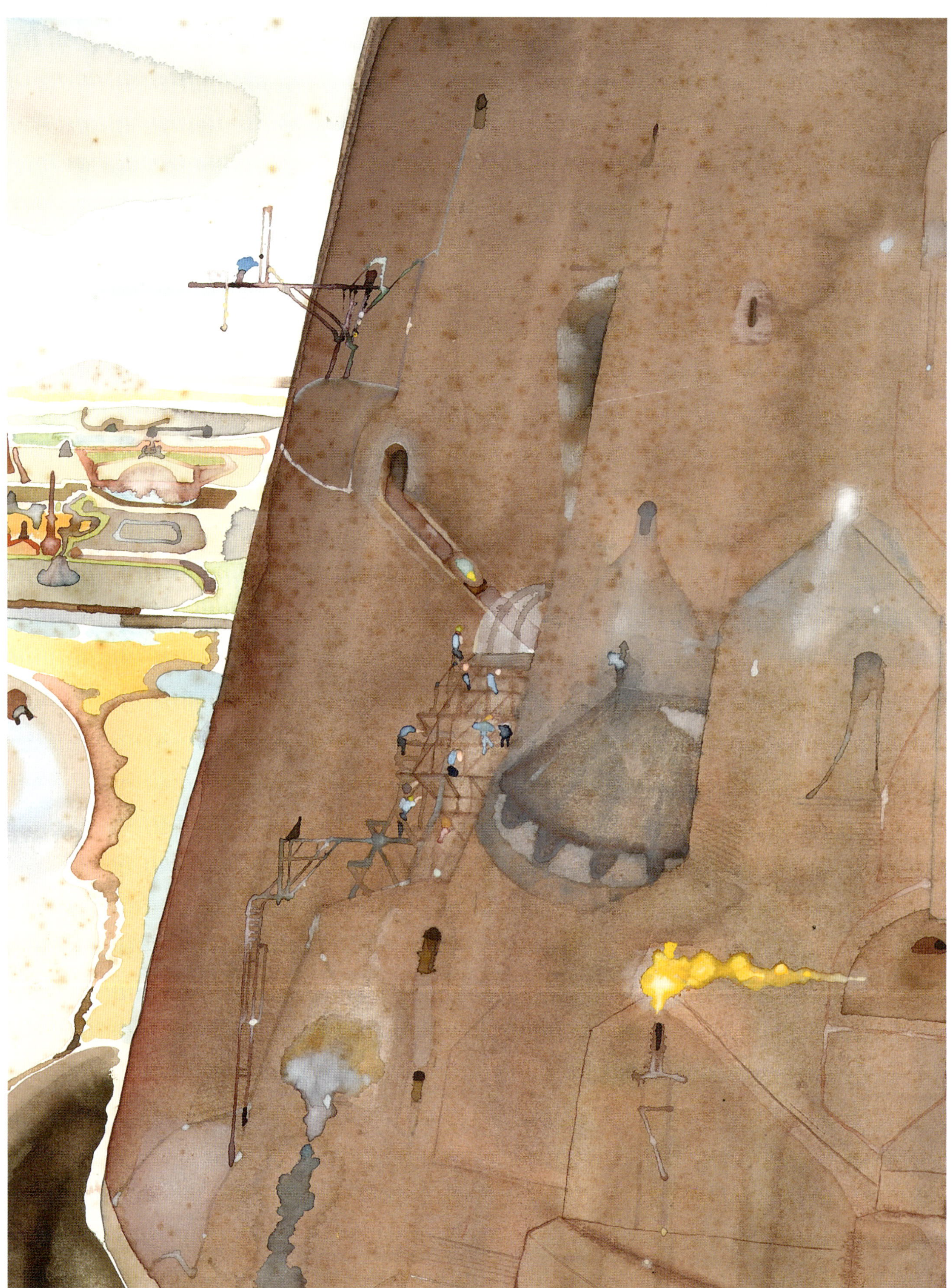

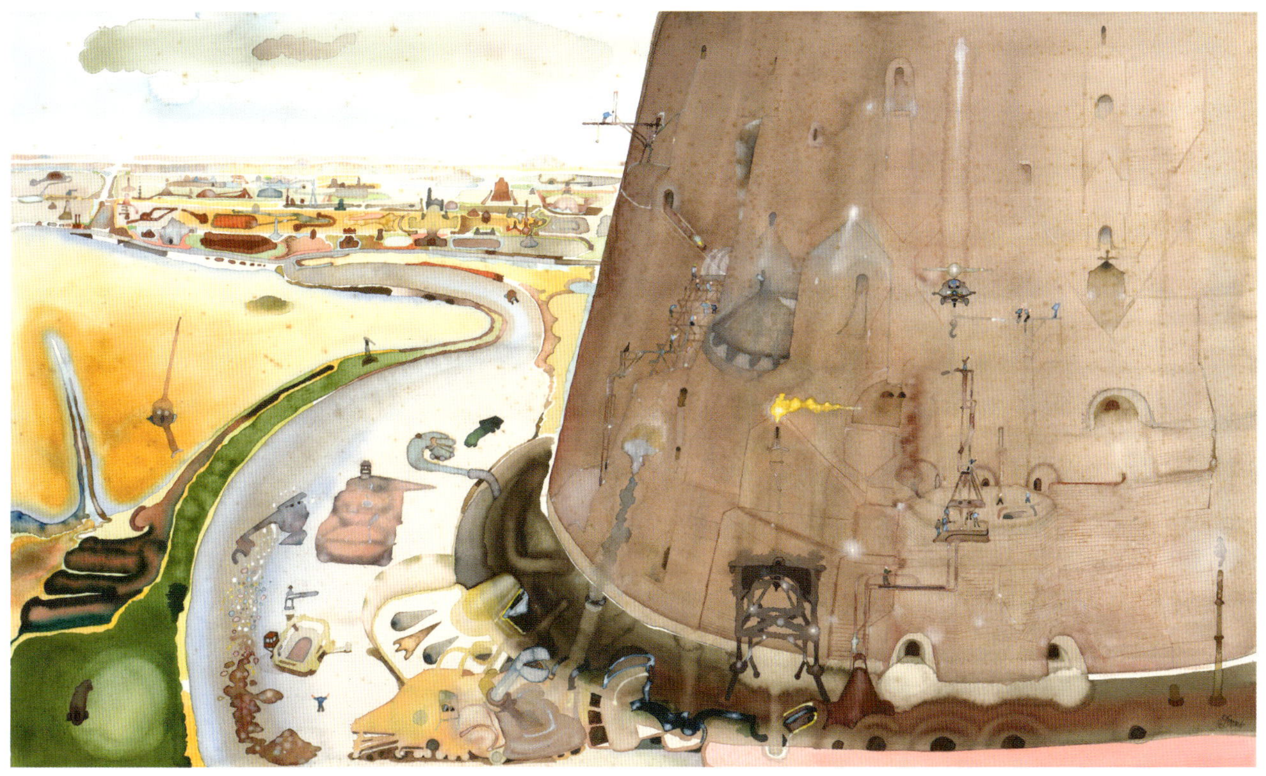

30 – David Evans (1929-1988), *Tower of Babel*, 1982, signed, watercolour on paper, 30 × 49 ½ in. (76 × 126 cm).
Provenance: The artist's studio
Literature: *David Evans (1929-1988)*, edited by Sacha Llewellyn & Paul Liss, published by Liss Llewellyn Fine Art, 2017, page 128-129.

Painting the landscape of his native Suffolk, where he settled (near Woodbridge) in 1969, Evan's brightly coloured compositions, which typically measure 30 × 50 inches, fused his local habitat with vivid fantasies inspired by imagery from contemporary life.

He was a ardent campaigner and environmentalist and the effects of pollution in the form of landfill, industrial plants and roads encroaching into his landscape are regular motifs. He was also drawn to metropolitan subjects – rock bands, cafeterias, excursions to museums and days out to the beach. *Tower of Babel* was inspired by the early 19th century Martello town on Shingle Street, a small coastal hamlet in Suffolk where Evans liked to spend time on beach.

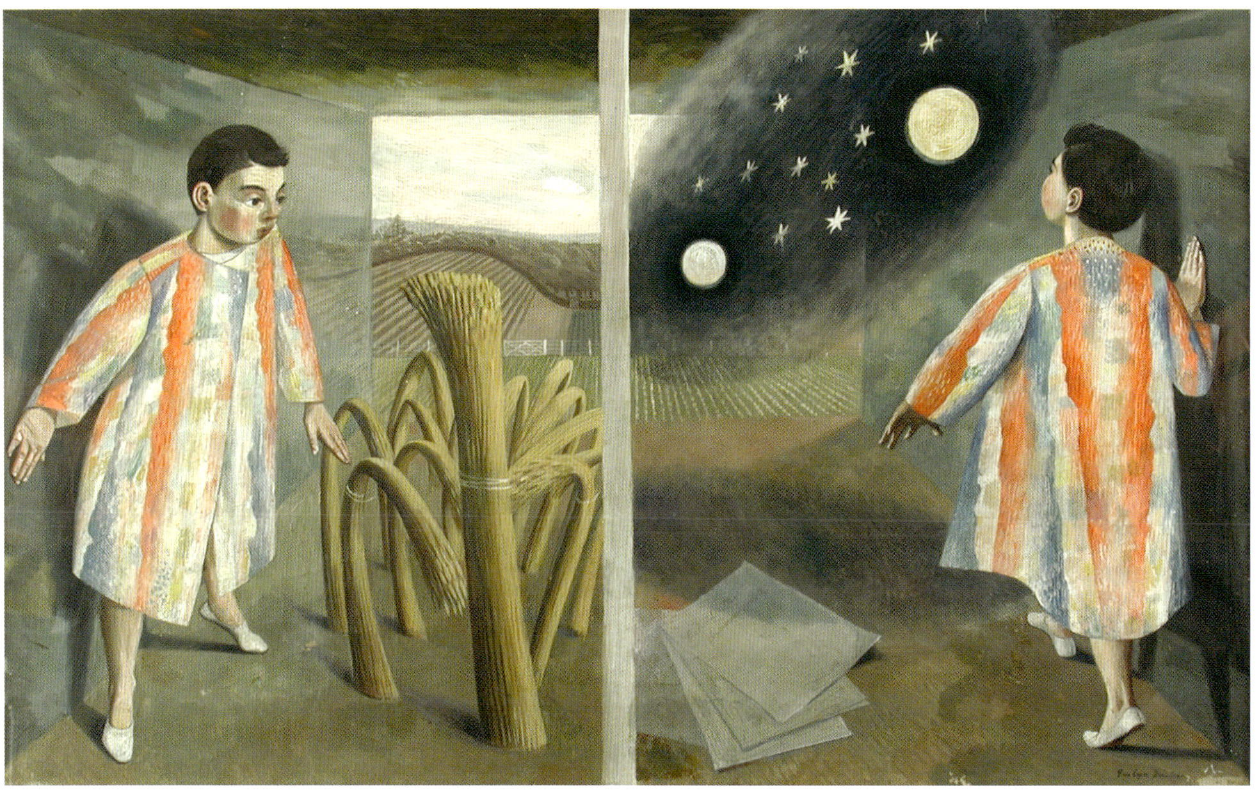

31 – Evelyn Dunbar (1906-1960), *Joseph's Dream*, 1938-43,
oil on canvas, 18 x 30 in. (46 x76 cm).
Provenance: Cambridgeshire County Council
Exhibited: NEAC, 1943,
       Derby, 1945,
       Painting for Schools, Whitechapel, 1948,
       Evelyn Dunbar – Paintings and Drawings 1938–1953, Withersdane, 1953.

In 1938 Dunbar conceived the idea of painting the most significant moments in the Old Testament account of the life of Joseph (Genesis 37-41). She selected *Joseph's Dream*, *Joseph in the Pit* and *Joseph in Prison*. World War 2 and Dunbar's appointment as awar artist interrupted this project, but after the war she took it up again, completing *Joseph in the Pit* and *Joseph in Prison* in 1949-50, when she was living in Enstone, Oxfordshire.

32 – Evelyn Dunbar (1906-1960), *Joseph in Prison*, 1949-50, signed with initials,
oil on canvas, 18 x 14 in. (46 x 35.5 cm).
Provenance: Mr L F Herbert.
Exhibited: Oxford, 1949-50,
Evelyn Dunbar – Paintings and Drawings 1938-1953, Withersdane, Wye, Kent, 1953.

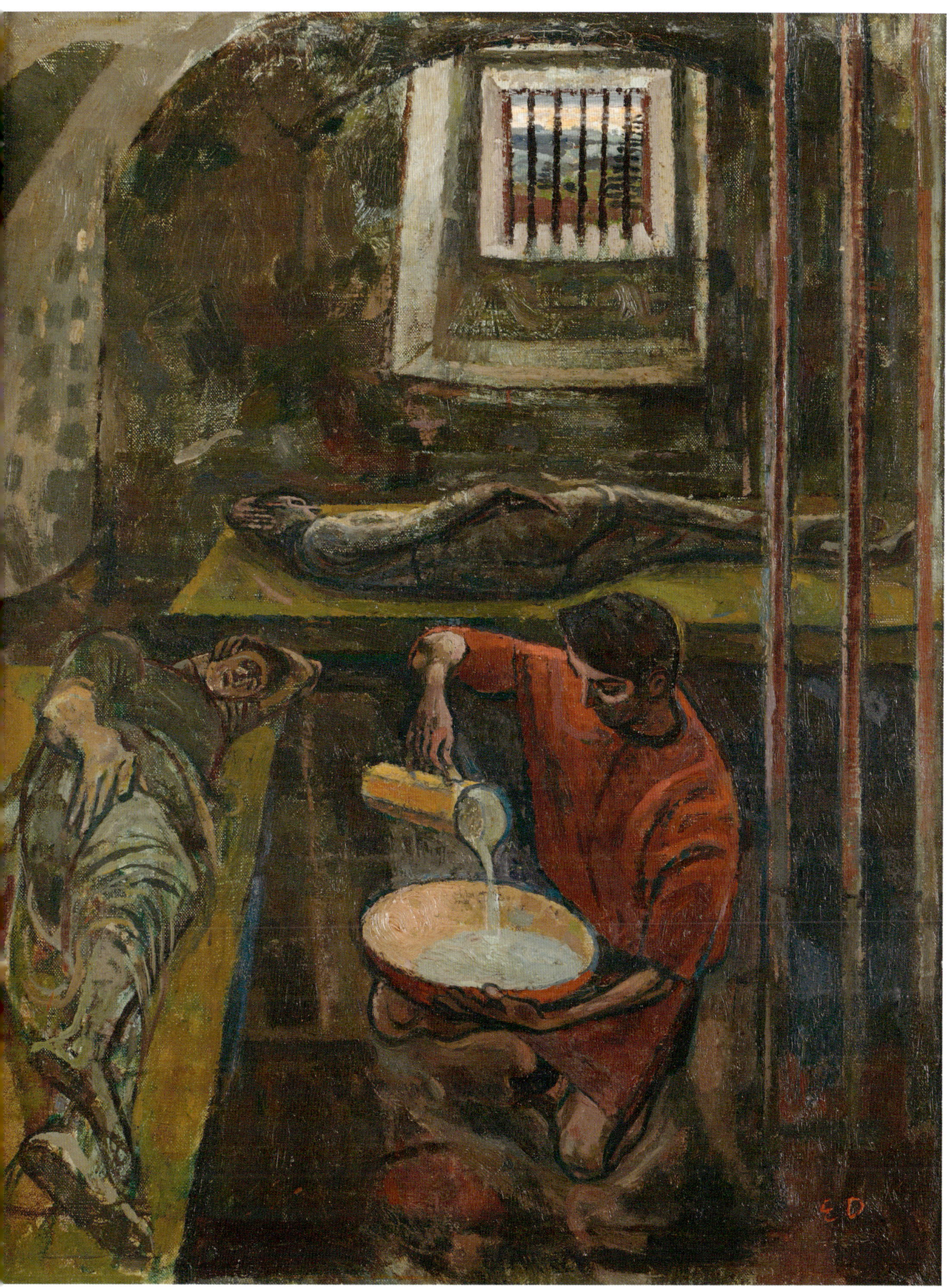

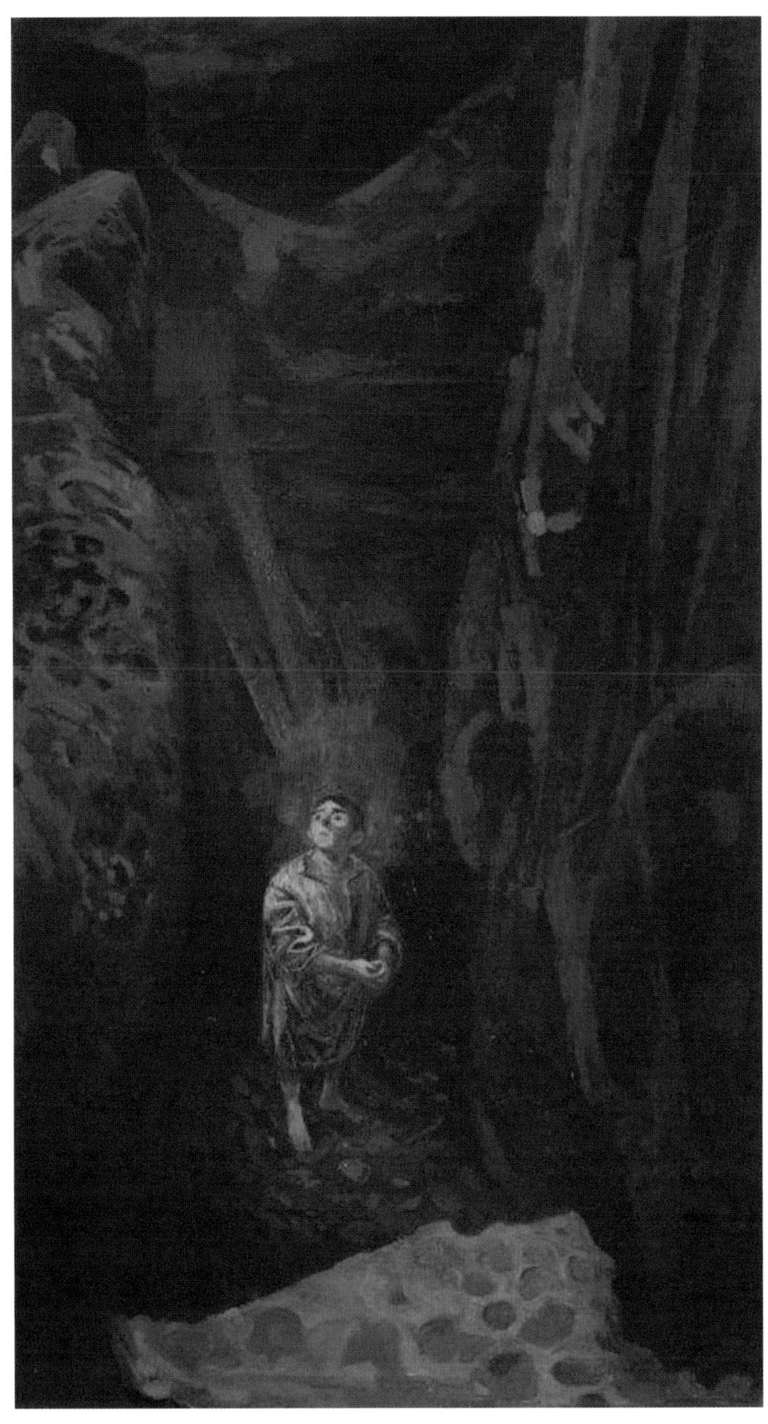

33 – Evelyn Dunbar (1906-1960), *Joseph in the Pit*, 1947,
oil on canvas, 18 x 10 in. (46 x 26 cm).
Provenance: Dunbar family; private collection.
Exhibited East Kent Art Society, Canterbury, 1960.

34 – Evelyn Dunbar (1906-1960), *Jacob's Dream*, 1960, signed with initials,
oil on canvas, 20 x 12 in. (50.8 x 30.5 cm)
Private collection..

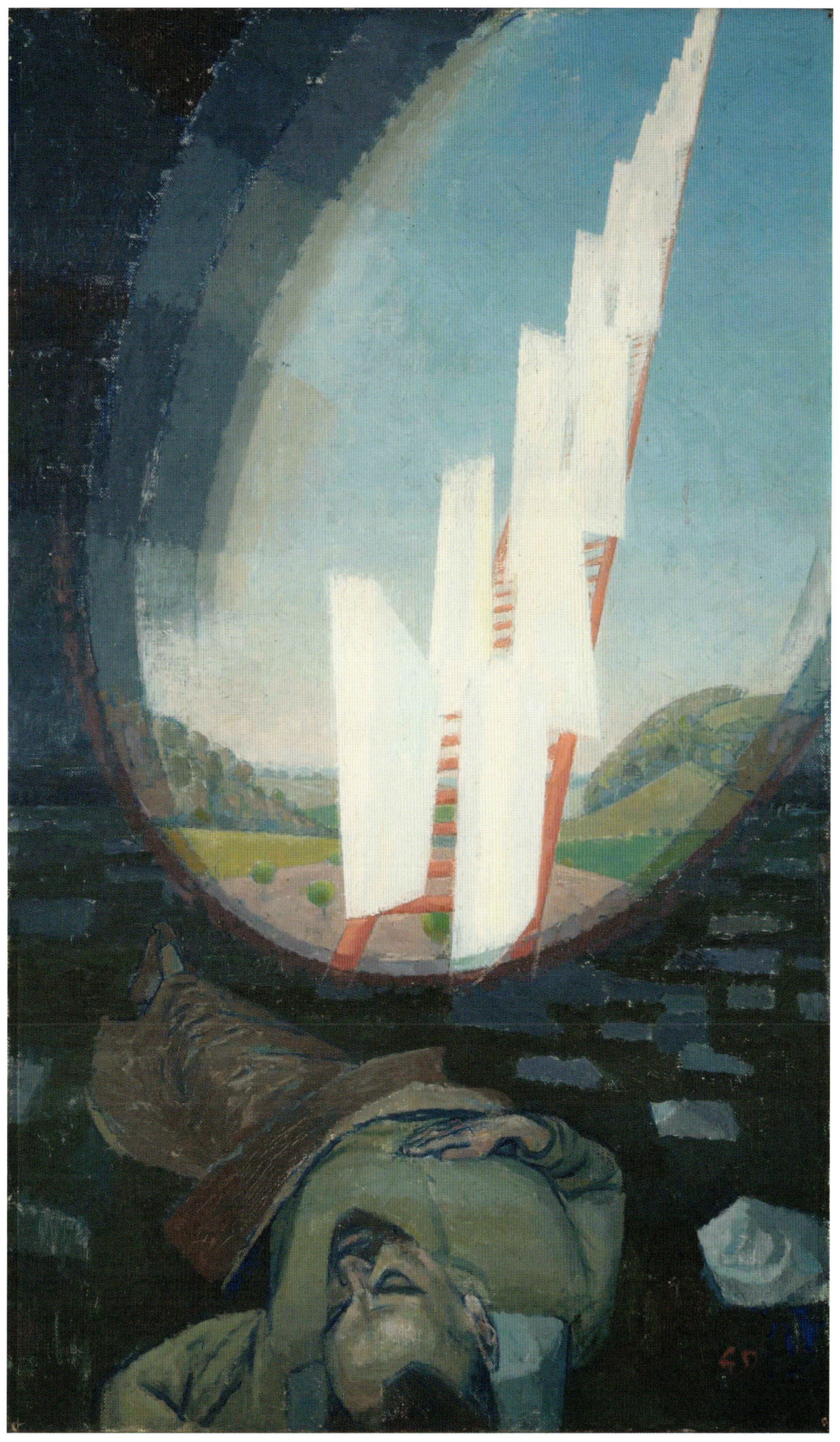

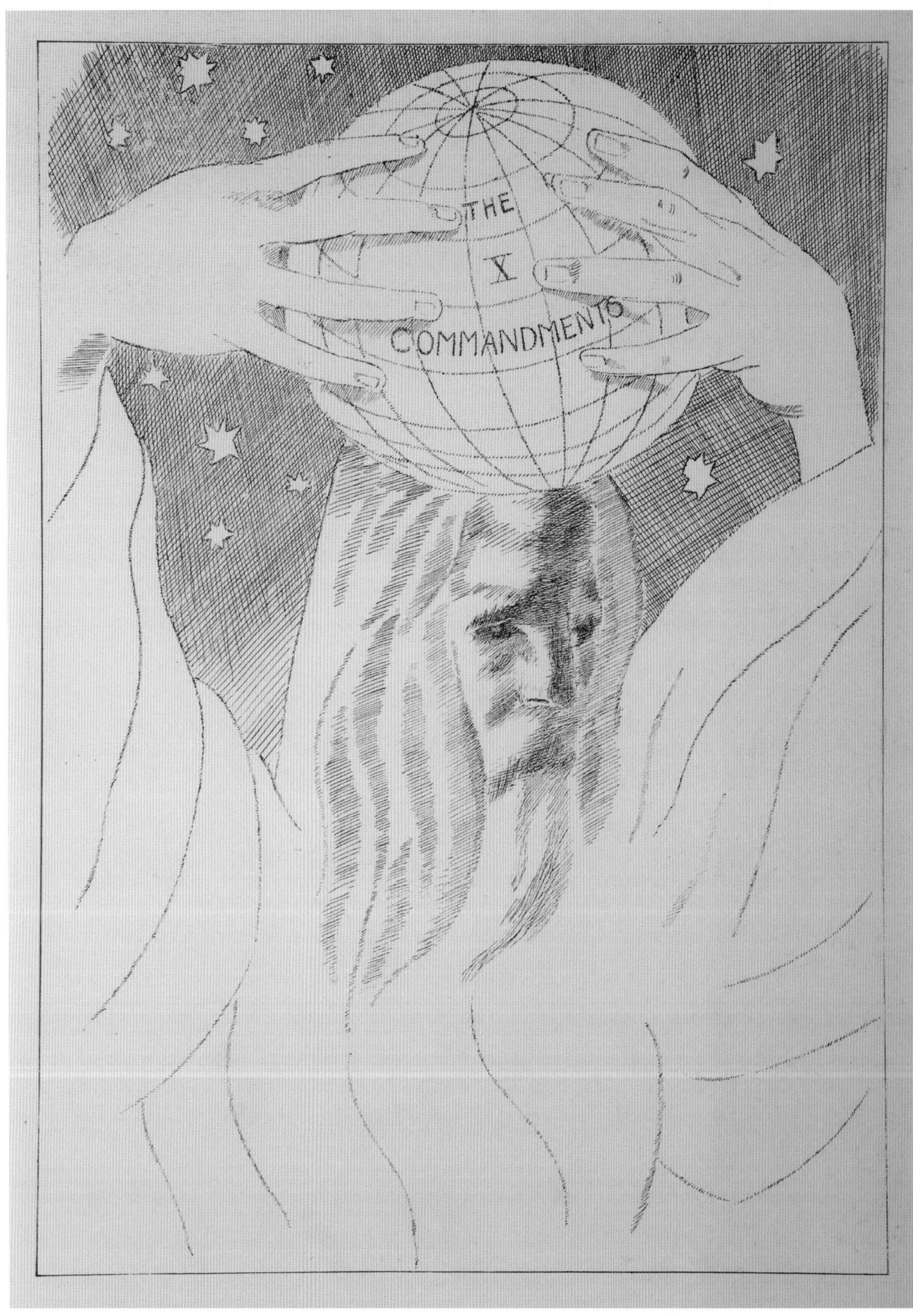

The Ten Commandments, title page 15 × 10 ½ in. (38.5 × 27 cm).

35 – Gilbert Spencer (1892-1979), *The Ten Commandments*, plates from a limited edition published in 1938, squared with notes.

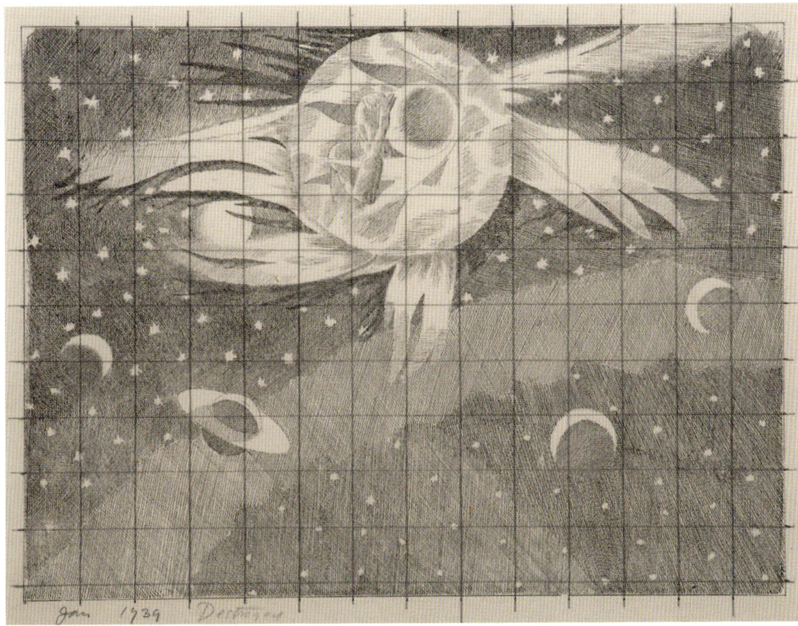

I I am the Lord your God, you shall have no other Gods before me, 10 ½ × 14 ½ in. (27 × 37 cm).

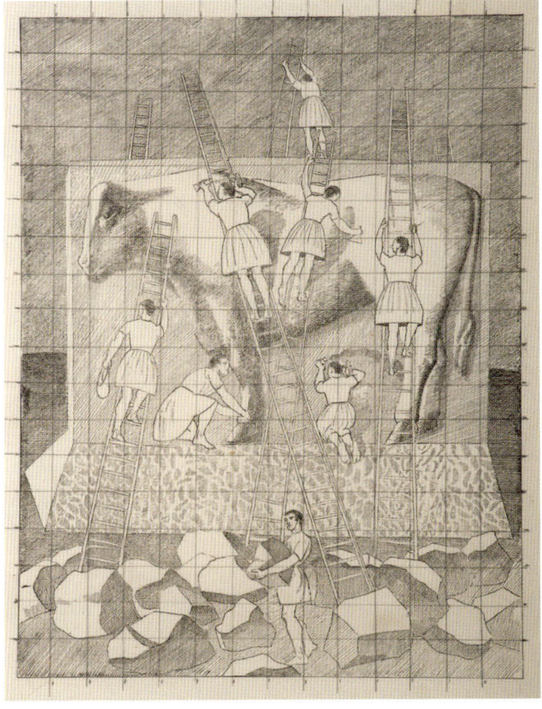

II You shall not worship false Gods,
14 × 10 ½ in. (35.5 × 26.5 cm).

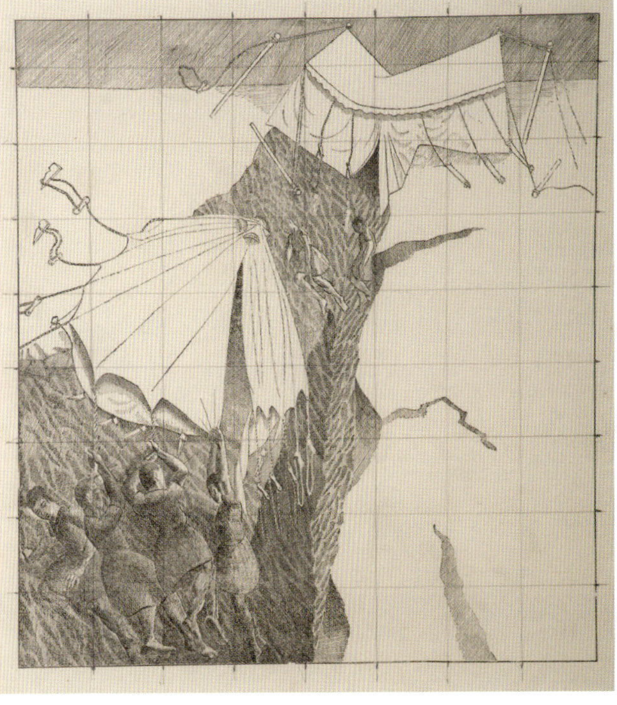

III YYou shall never take my name in vain,
12 × 10 in. (30.5 × 25.5 cm).

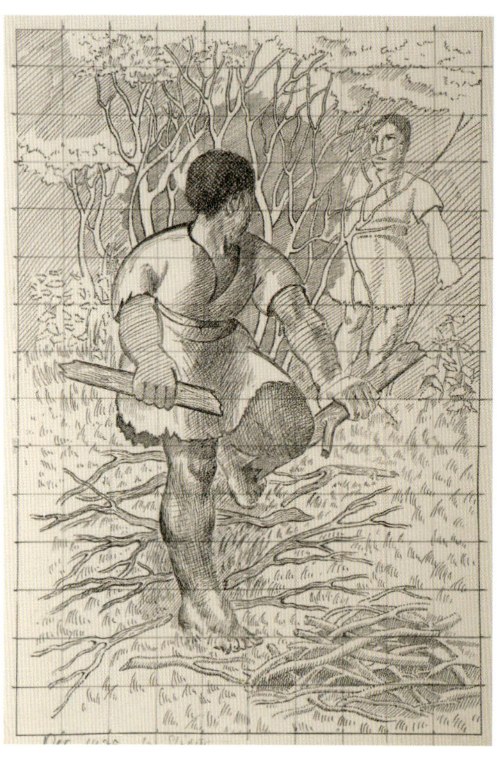

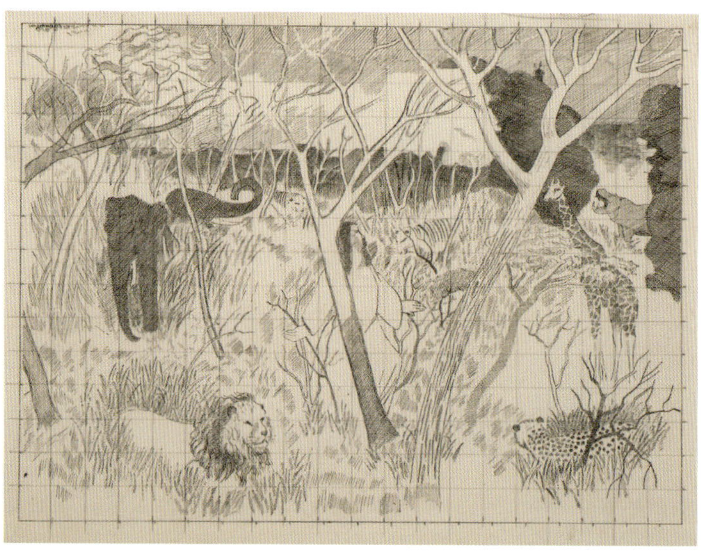

IV *You shall keep the sabbath day Holy,*
15 ½ × 10 ¼ in. (40 × 26 cm).

V *Honor your Father and Mother, 10 ½ × 14 ½ in. (27 × 37 cm).*

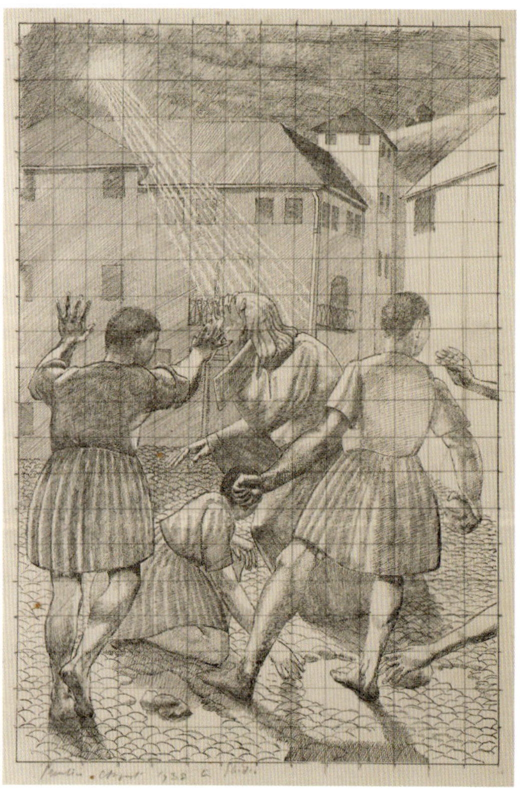

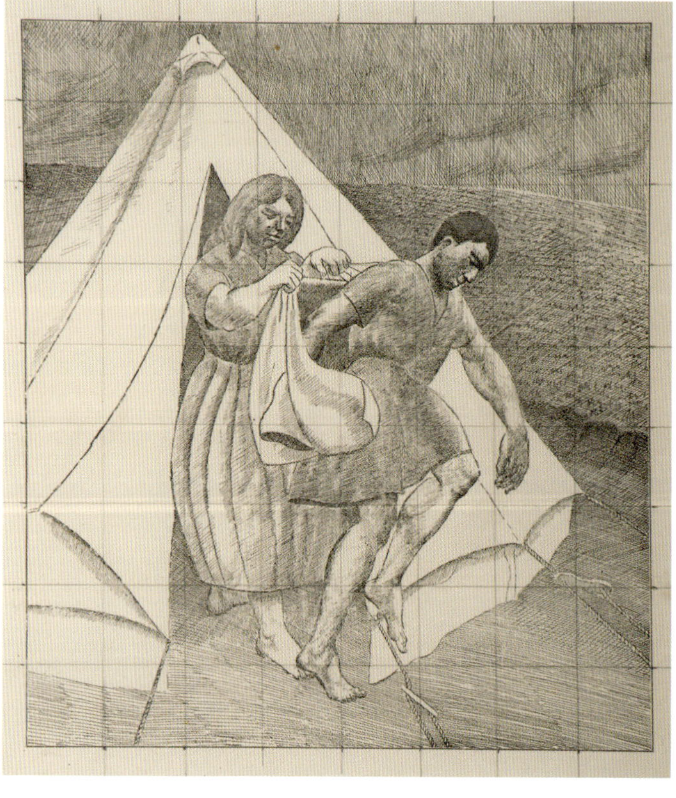

VI *You shall not murder,*
15 ½ × 10 ¼ in. (40 × 26 cm).

VII *You shall not commit adultery,*
12 ½ × 10 ½ in. (32 × 26.5 cm).

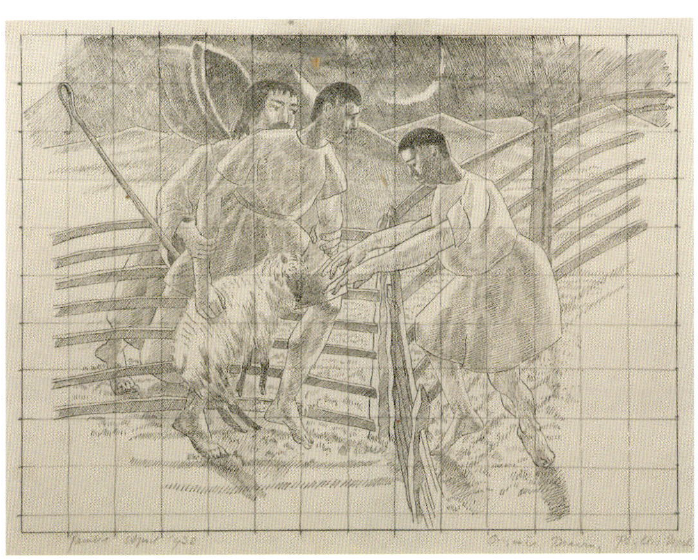

VIII You shall not steal, 10 ¾ × 14 ¾ in. (27.5 × 37.5 cm).

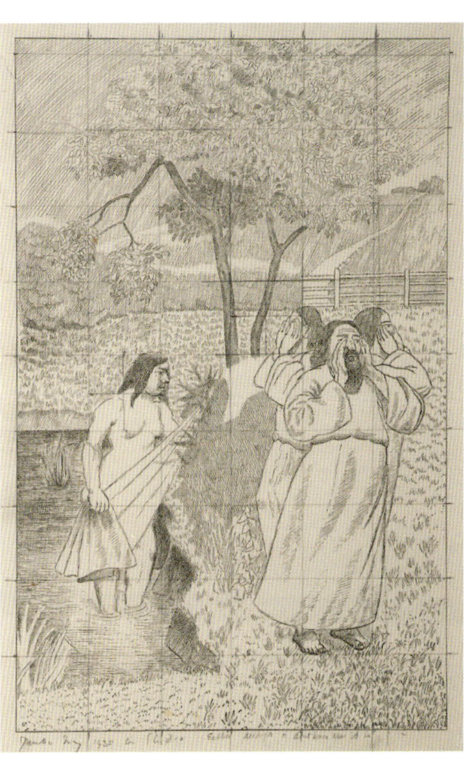

IX You shall not give false evidence against your neighbour, 15 ½ × 10 in. (40 × 25.5 cm).

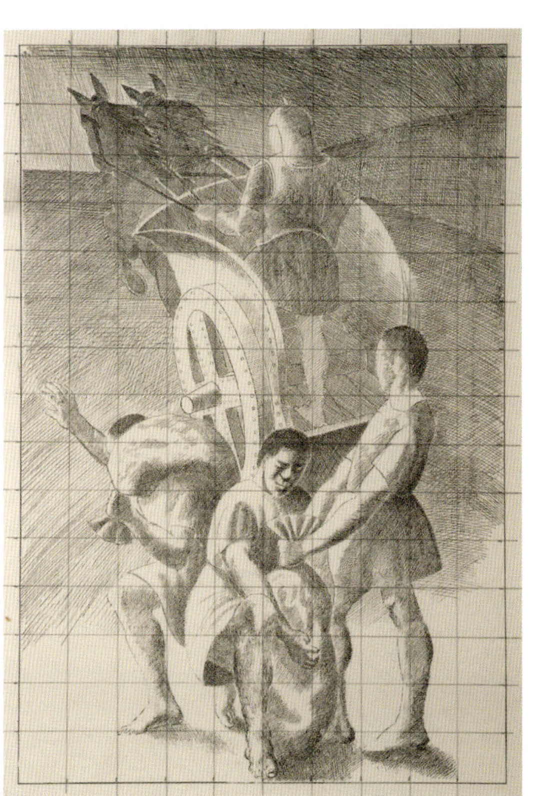

X You shall not be envious of your neighbour's house nor his wife, 15 ½ × 10 ¼ in. (40 × 26 cm).

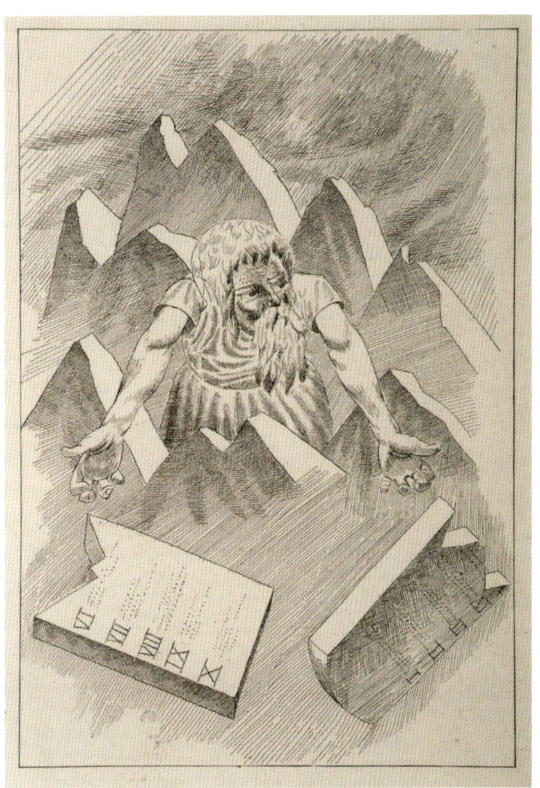

God, in His rage, broke the tables, 15 × 10 ½ in. (38.5 × 27 cm).

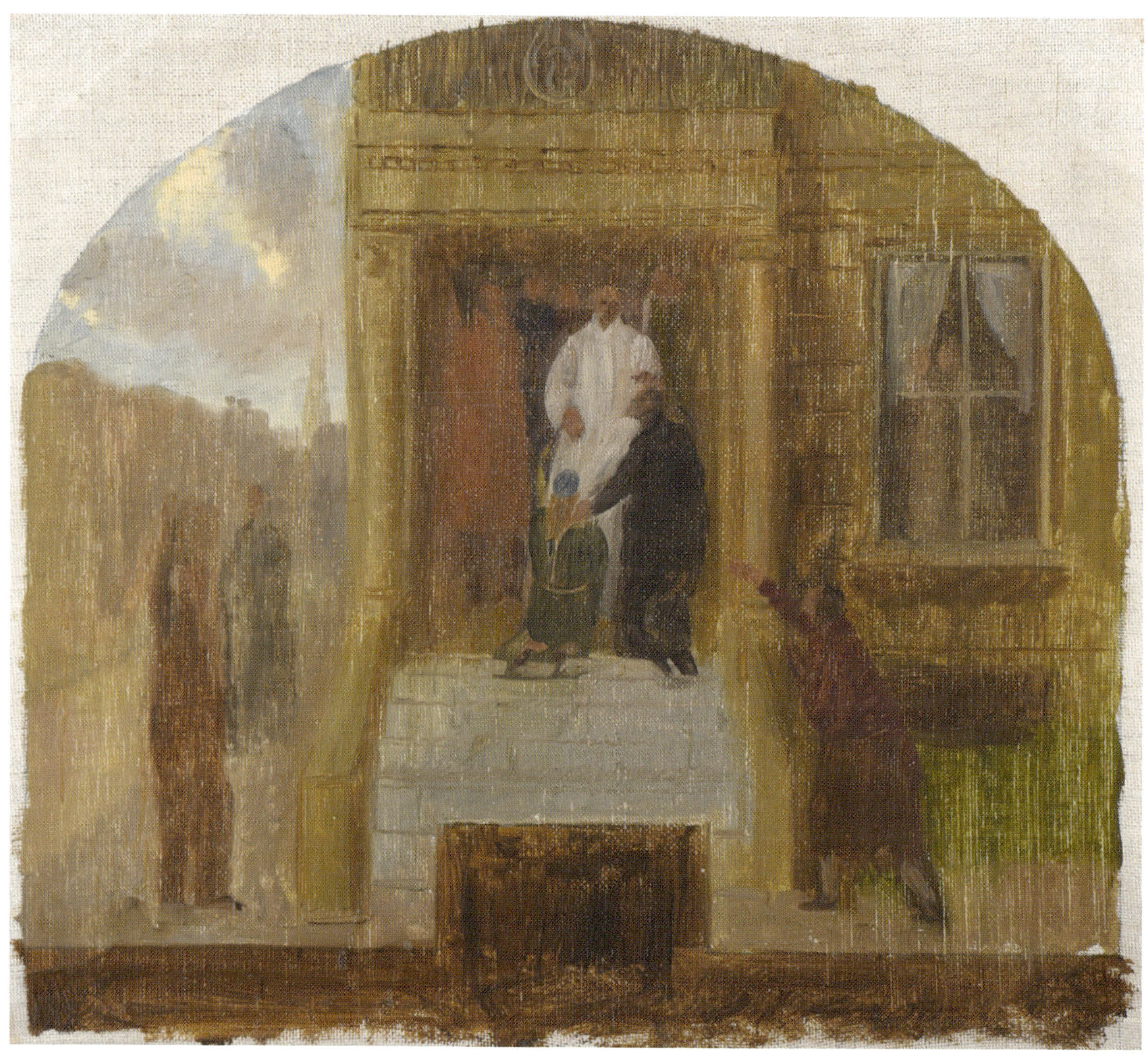

36 – Victor Hume Moody (1896-1990), *The Judgement of Solomon*, c.1930, oil on canvas, 10 × 11 ½ in. (25.5 × 29.3 cm).

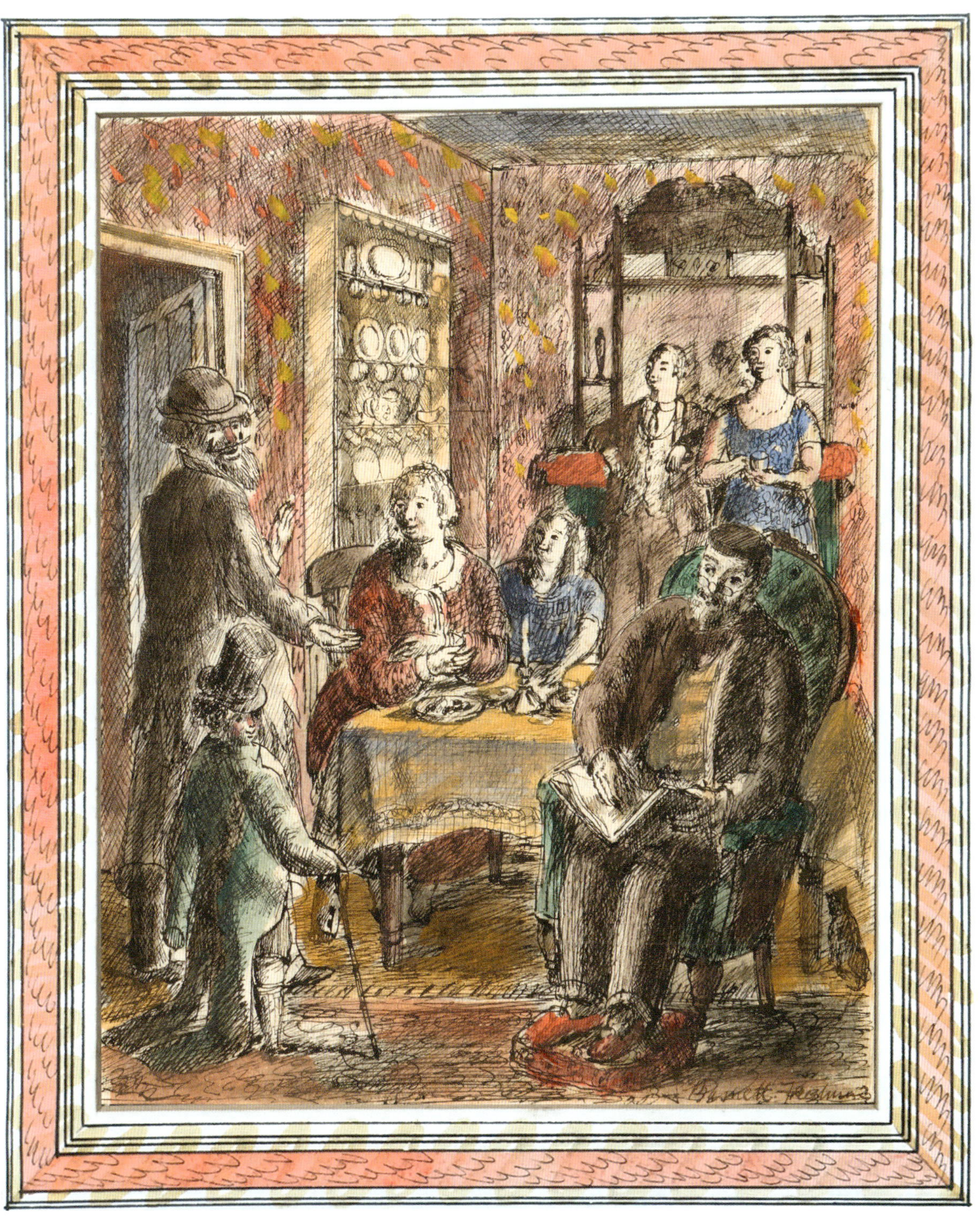

37 – **Barnett Freedman** (1901-1958), *Purim Party*, (window mount decorated by the artist), signed, Gouache, pen and ink on paper, 8 x 6 ½ in. (20.8 x 16.5 cm).

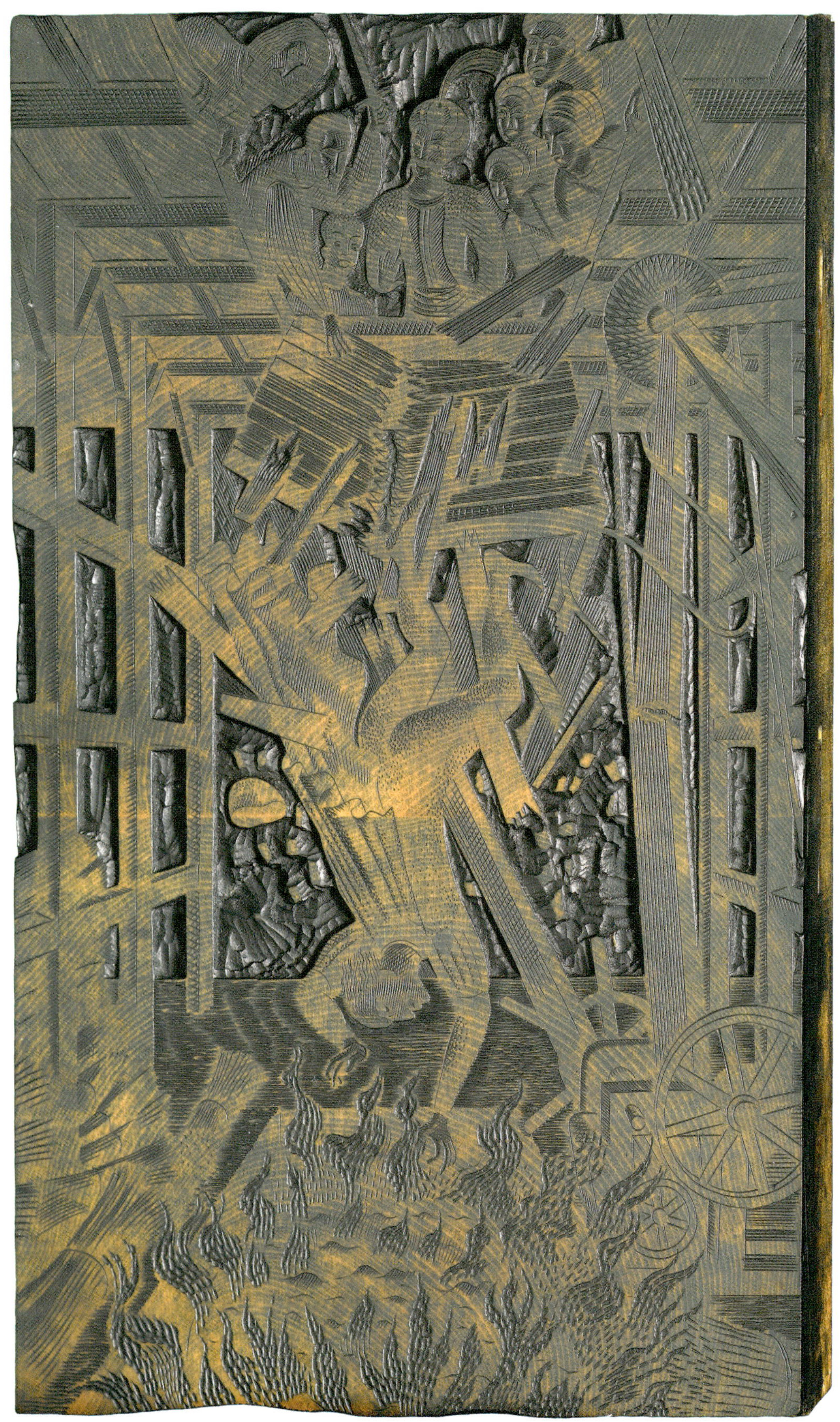

a

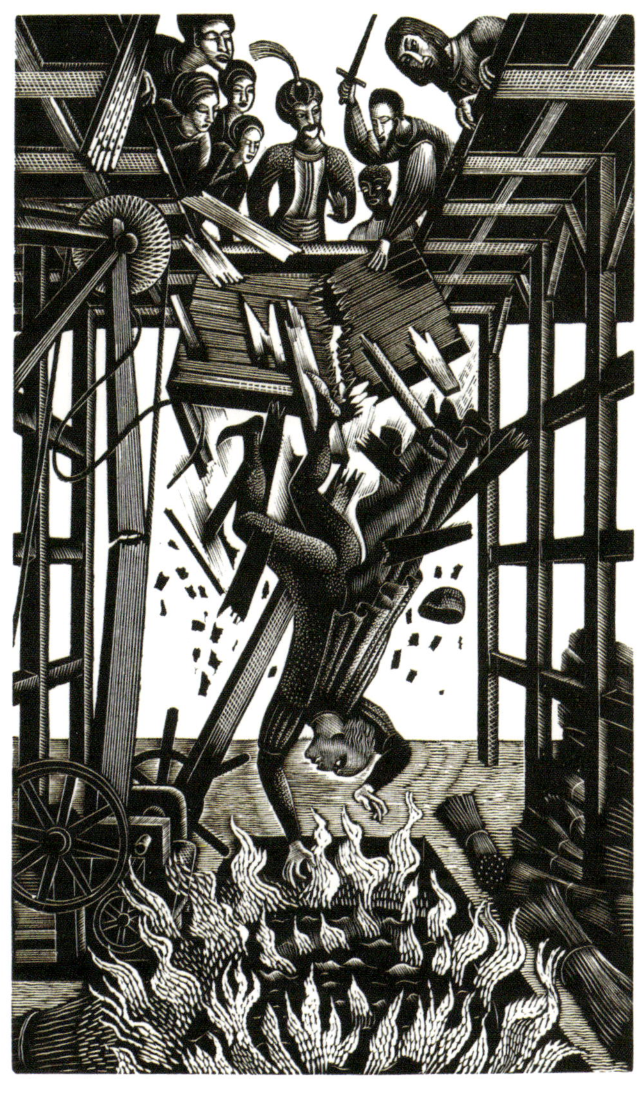

38 – Eric Ravilious (1903-1942), *The Famous Tragedy of the Rich Jew of Malta,* 1933,
a   original woodblock, engraved by Ravilious,
inscribed in ink on reverse to face p 84, and stamped T. Lawrence, end-grain box wood, 7 x 4 ¼ in. (17.8 x 10.7 cm)
b   print pulled from the original woodblock by Simon Lawrence, Fleece Press, 1998.

Ravilious contributed four wood engravings to this illustrated edition of Christopher Marlowe's celebrated book
 of 1589-90. These are the largest woodblocks that Ravilious produced.

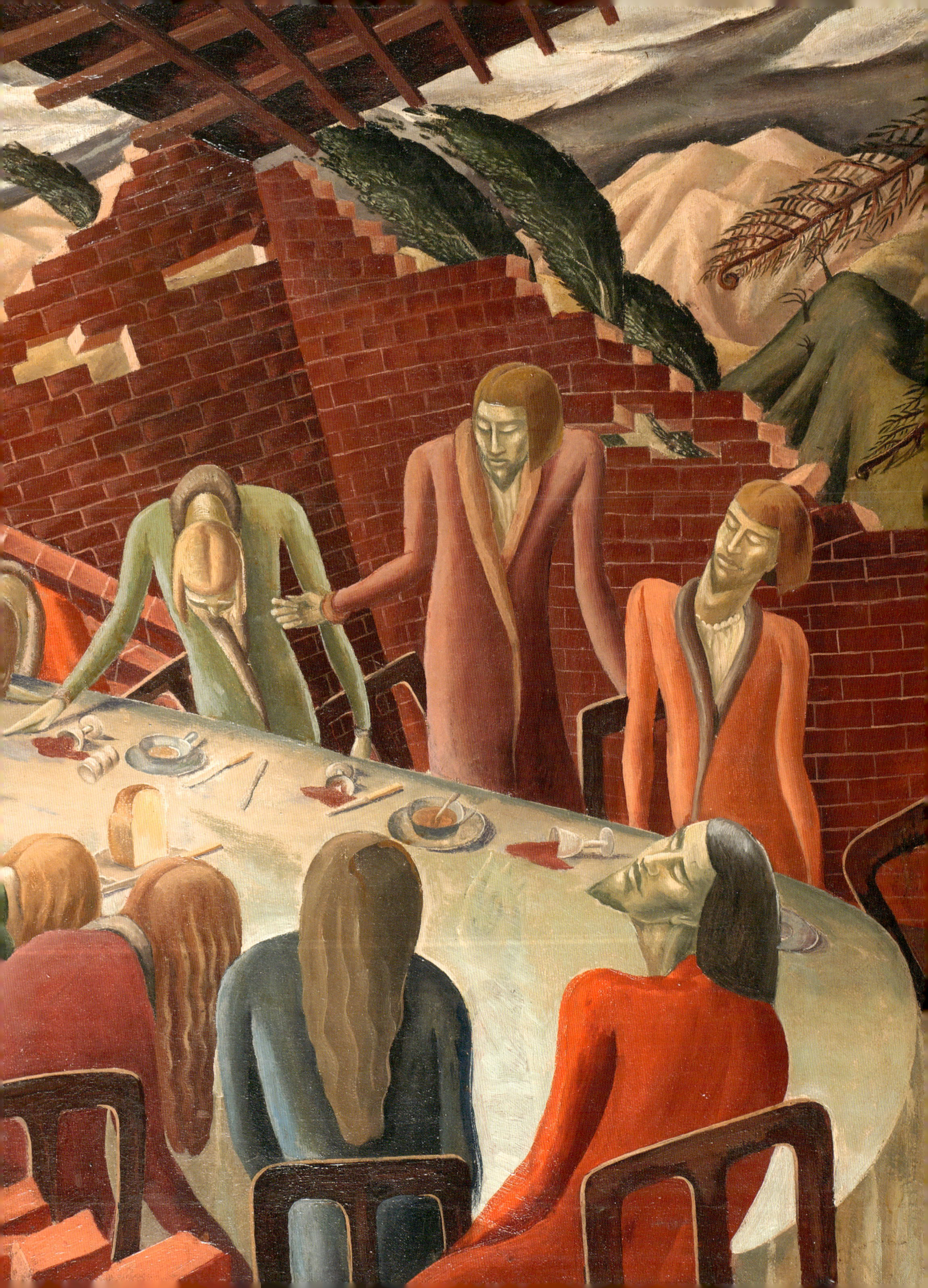

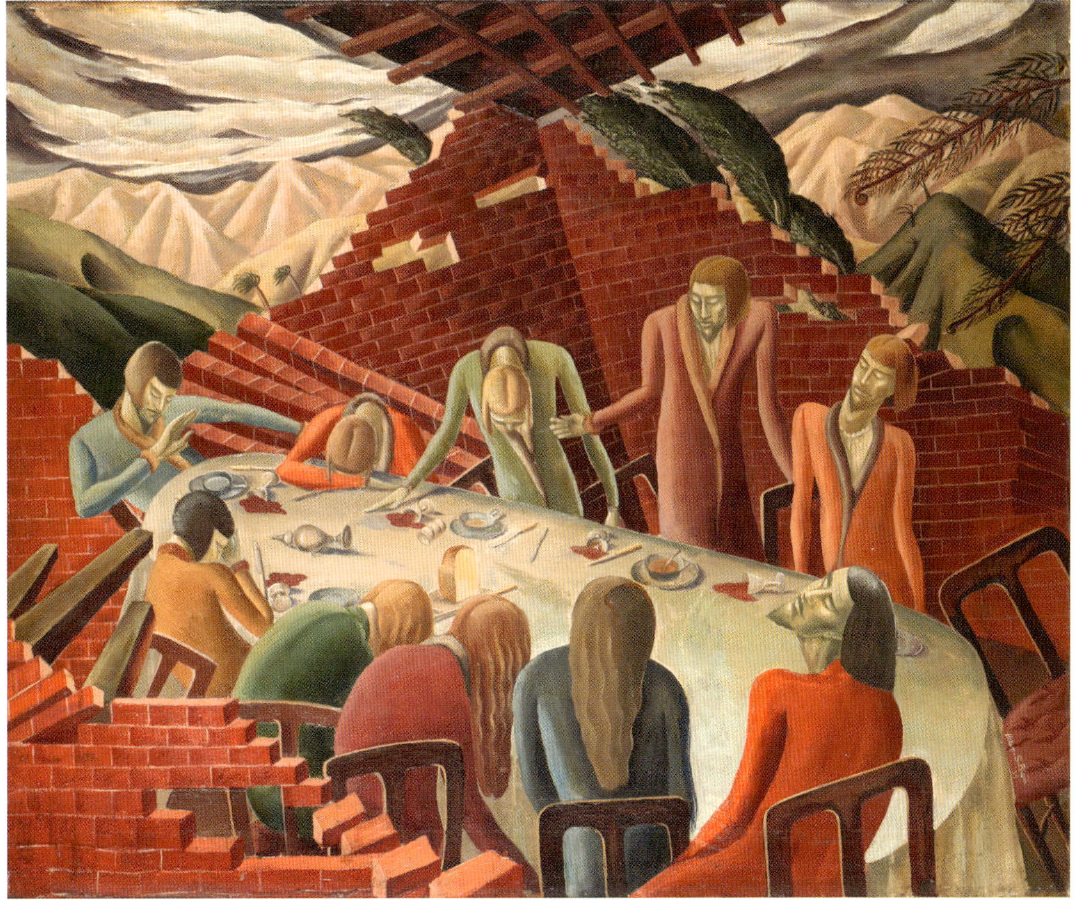

39 – Helen Blair (1907-1997), *Scene from the Book of Job,* c.1935, oil on canvas, 24 x 30 in. (61 x 76.2 cm).
Provenance: With the artist when she moved to England in March 1936;
Private Collection since November 1992.
Exhibited: Kirkcaldie and Stains, Wellington, 1936.

Blair's composition depicts *The Book of Job,* chapter 1 verse 18/19: '…*Thy sons and thy daughters were eating and drinking wine in their eldest brother's house. And, behold, there came a great wind from the wilderness, and smote the four corners of the house, and it fell upon the young men, and they are dead.*'

Before Blair and her husband, the glass engraver John Hutton, left New Zealand for England in March 1936, they mounted an exhibition at Kirkcaldie and Stains, Wellington's leading department store, in which *Scene from the Book of Job* was described: '… one of several works shown … in the modern idiom, … *Job* is a Biblical allegory expressed in terms of [Blair's] native background-New Zealand. [It] shows a formalization of New Zealand landscape more structurally interpreted.' (*Journal: Art in New Zealand,* 1936.)

Another local paper described *Job* as amongst, some 'very striking examples of modern art … by … artists who make no excuses for their exploration of modern methods in the art of painting. … Helen S Blair is distinctly intriguing with her scene from the *Book of Job* and with her 'Abstractions' while some of her landscapes … bear a distinct resemblance to the stark formality found in some of the landscapes painted by old masters as backgrounds to their figure subjects'. (*The Evening Post,* January 31, 1936.)

THE BOOK OF PSALMS

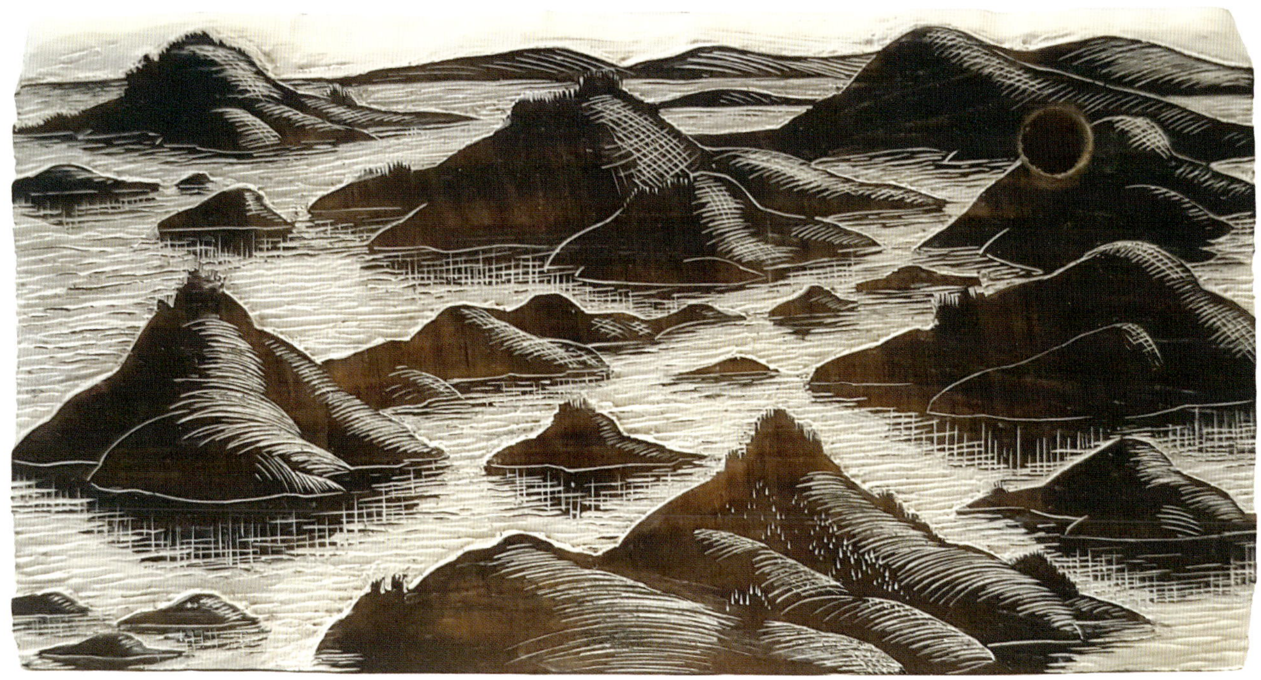

40 – Clare Leighton (1898-1989), Psalm 97:1, *The Lord Reigneth*, BPL 655, 1952, original woodblock (cancelled), 2 x 4 in. (5.1 x 10.2 cm).

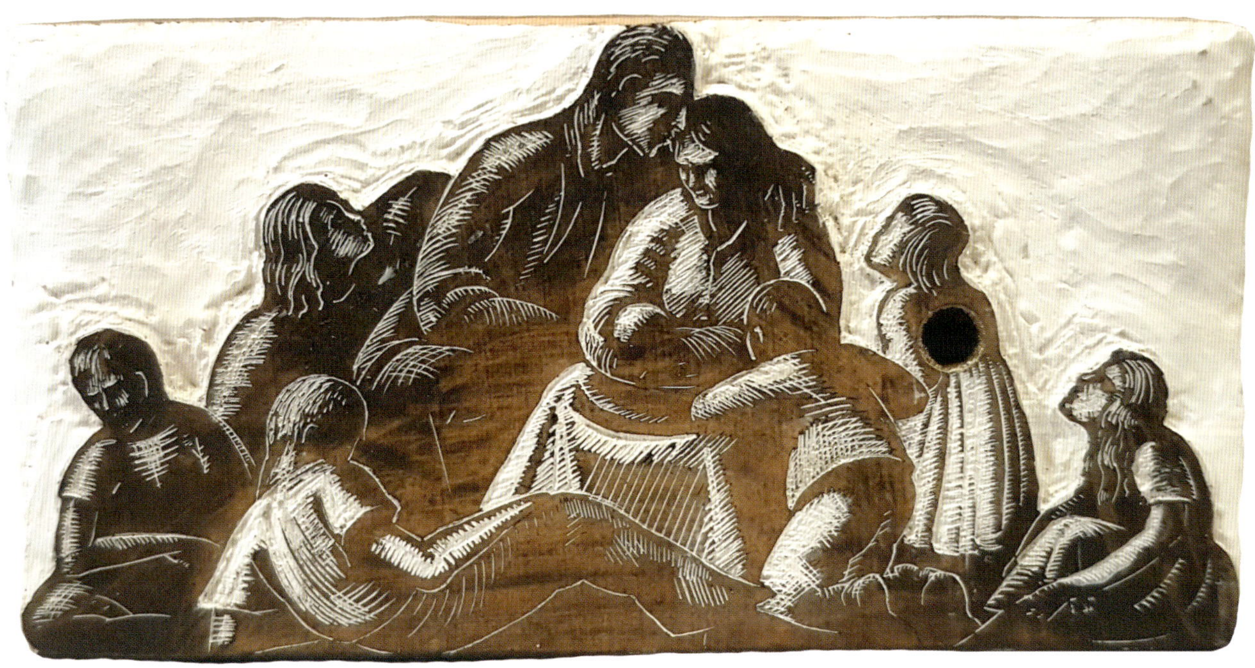

41 – Clare Leighton (1898-1989), Psalm 127:3-5, *Lo, children are an heritage of the Lord: and the fruit of the womb is his reward*, BPL 660, 1952, original woodblock (cancelled), 2 x 4 in. (5.1 x 10.2 cm).

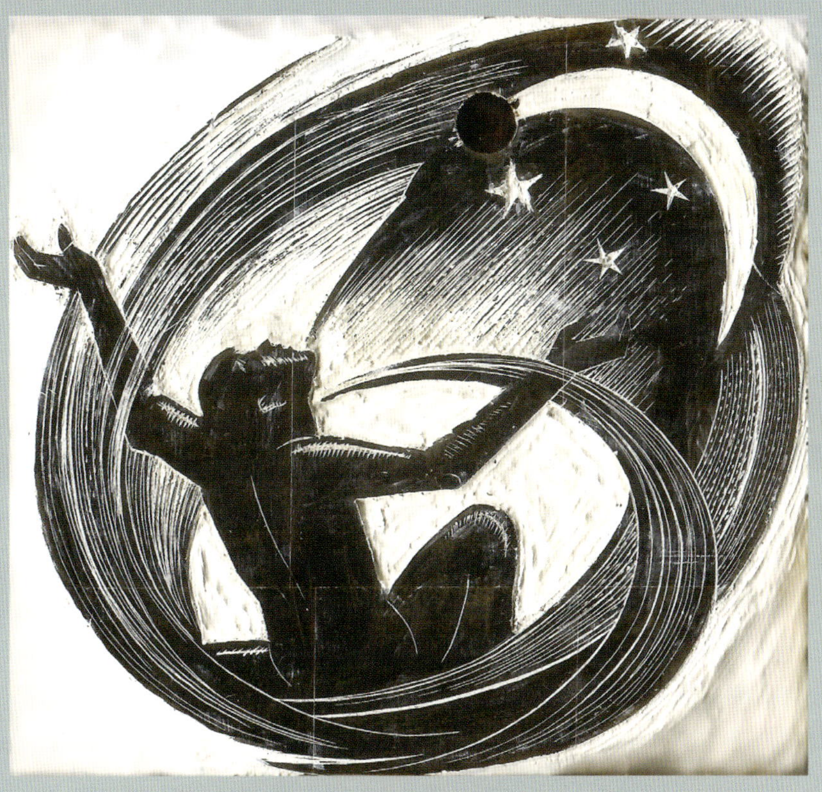

42 – **Clare Leighton** (1898-1989), Psalm 137, *By the Rivers of Babylon,* BPL 661, 1952, original woodblock (cancelled) 3 x 3 ¼ in. (7.8 x 8.5 cm).

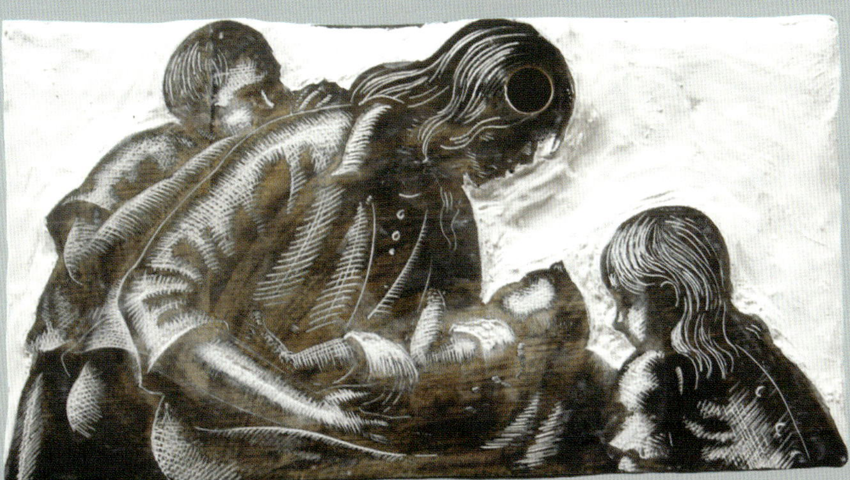

43 – **Clare Leighton** (1898-1989), Psalm 113:9, *He Maketh the Barren Women,* BPL 658, 1952, original woodblock (cancelled) 2 x 4 in. (5.4 x 10.2 cm).

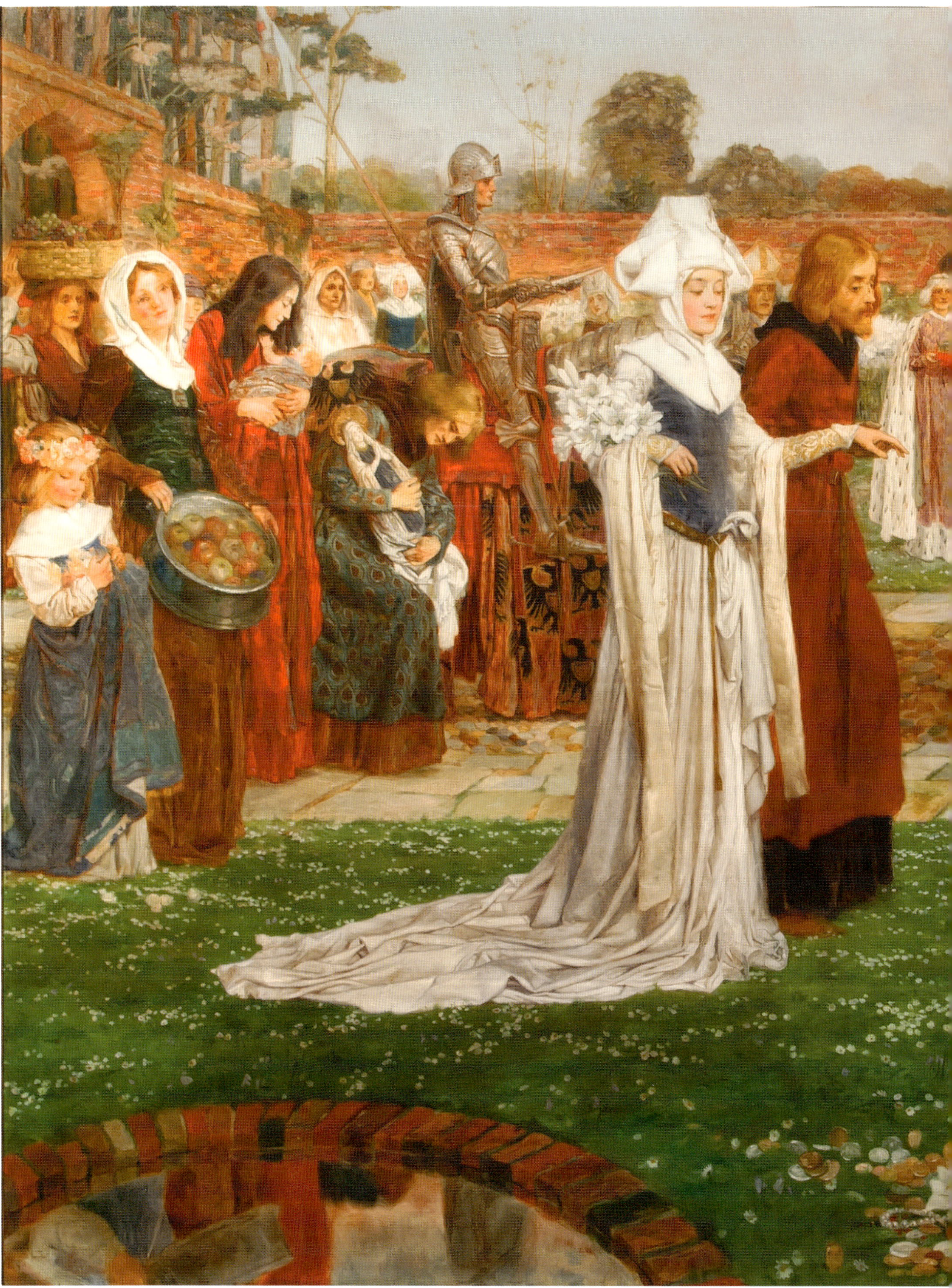

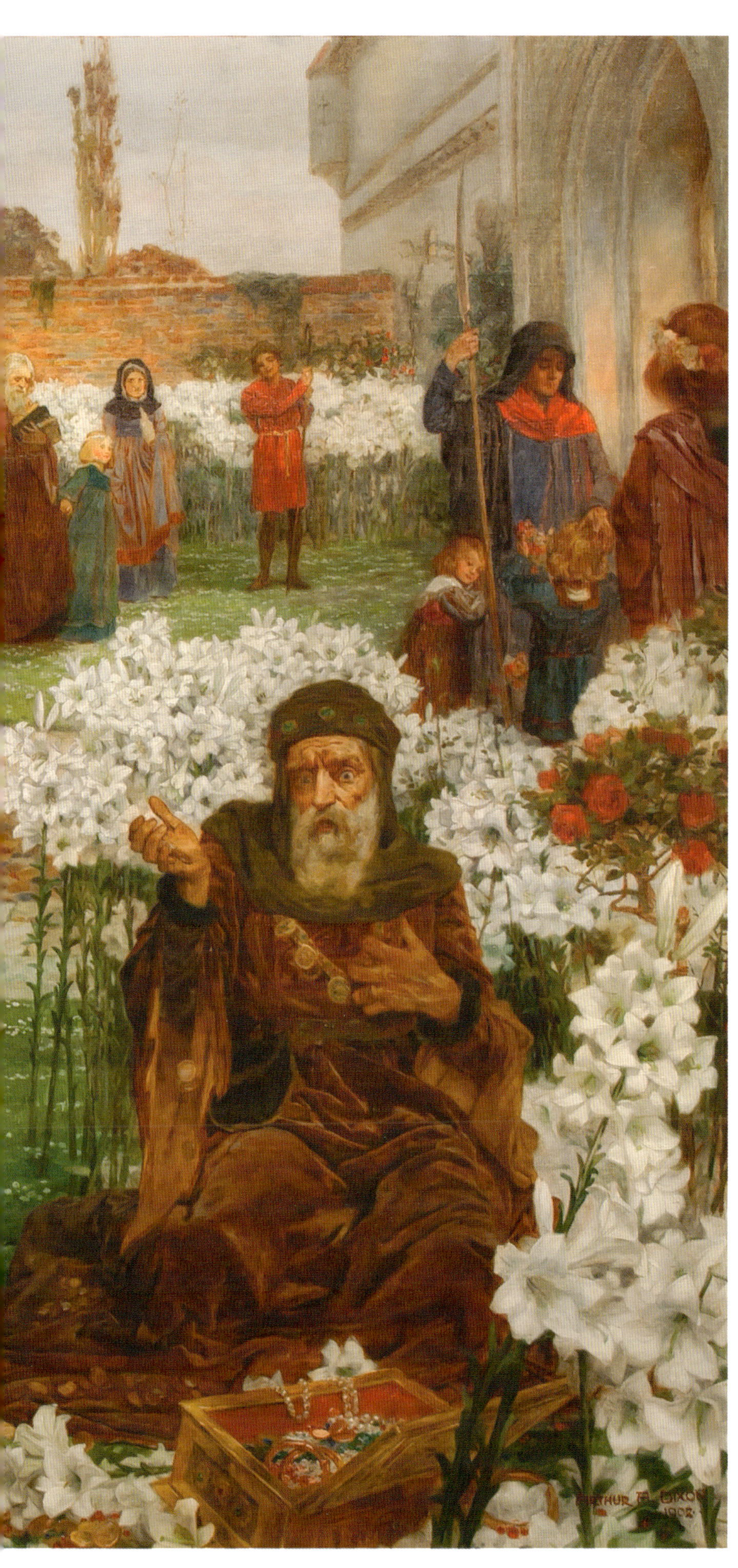

44 – Arthur A. Dixon (1872-1959),
Offerings, 1902, signed and dated,
Inscribed on artist's label on reverse :
'Bring an offering and come into His Courts',
oil on canvas, 44 x 60 in. (111.8 x 152.4 cm.)
Exhibited : London, New Gallery, 1903.

This work interprets the incantatory ambit of Psalm 96, and specifically line 8: 'Give unto the LORD the glory due unto his name: bring an offering, and come into his courts'.

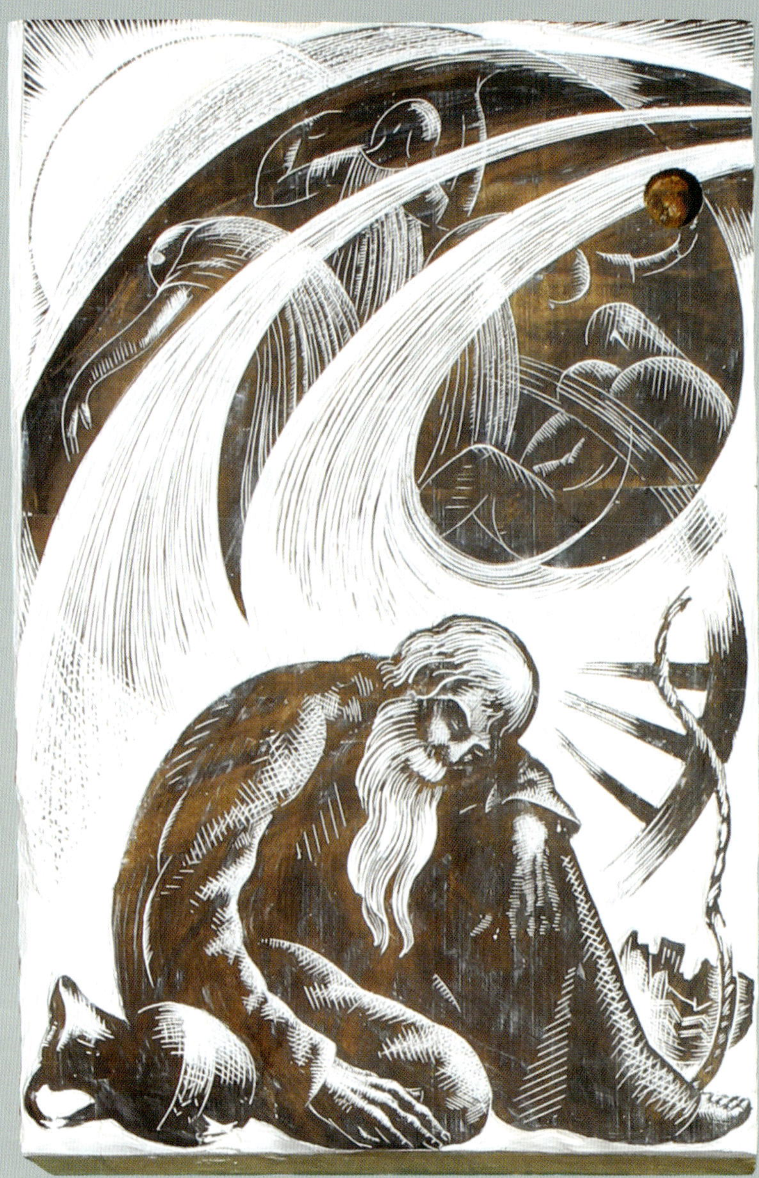

45 – Clare Leighton (1898-1989), *The Book of Ecclesiastes*, BPL 669,
original woodblock (cancelled), 6 x 4 in. (15.3 x 10.2 cm).

Clare Leighton attended the Brighton School of Art (1915), the Slade School of Fine Art (1921–23) and the Central School of Arts and Crafts. Despite her childhood nickname 'The Bystander', she became a hugely visible artist on both sides of the Atlantic, and her vast oeuvre – she wrote twelve books and made 840 prints – includes engravings, paintings, bookplates, illustrations and stained glass. Her twelve plates for Wedgewood, *New England Industries*, 1952, are amongst her best-known work.

When tasked with creating the windows for St Paul's Cathedral in Worcester, Massachusetts, Leighton commented: "I knew ... that I was asked to do no ordinary, temporary thing but a work that must endure to the glory of God; and I thought of the motto of Sir Basil Spence when he was designing the new cathedral at Coventry: 'Only the very best will do for God.'"

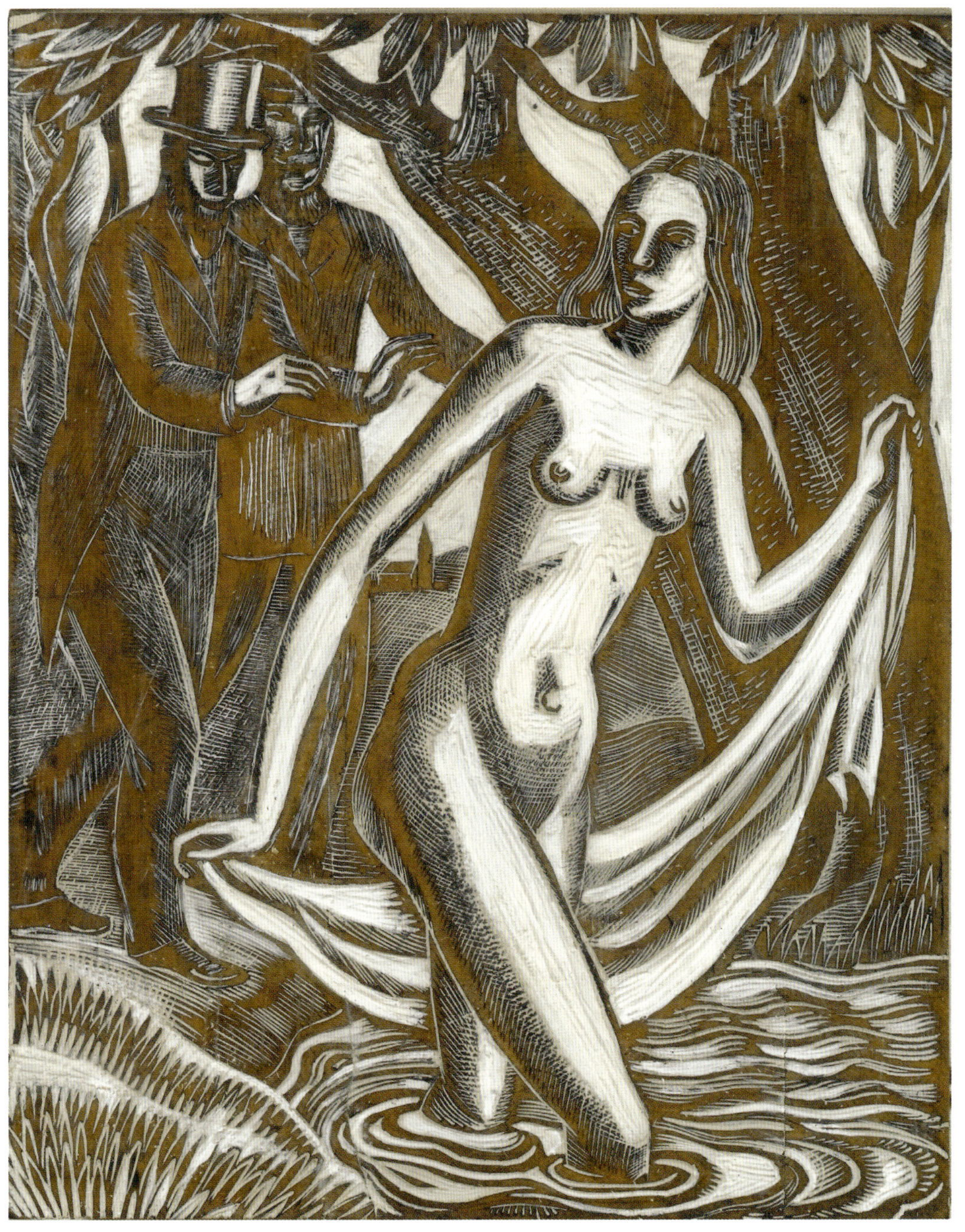

46 – John A. Austen (1920s), *Susanna and the Elders*, c.1920,
original woodblock, 3 ½ x 4 ½ in. (9 x 11 cm).

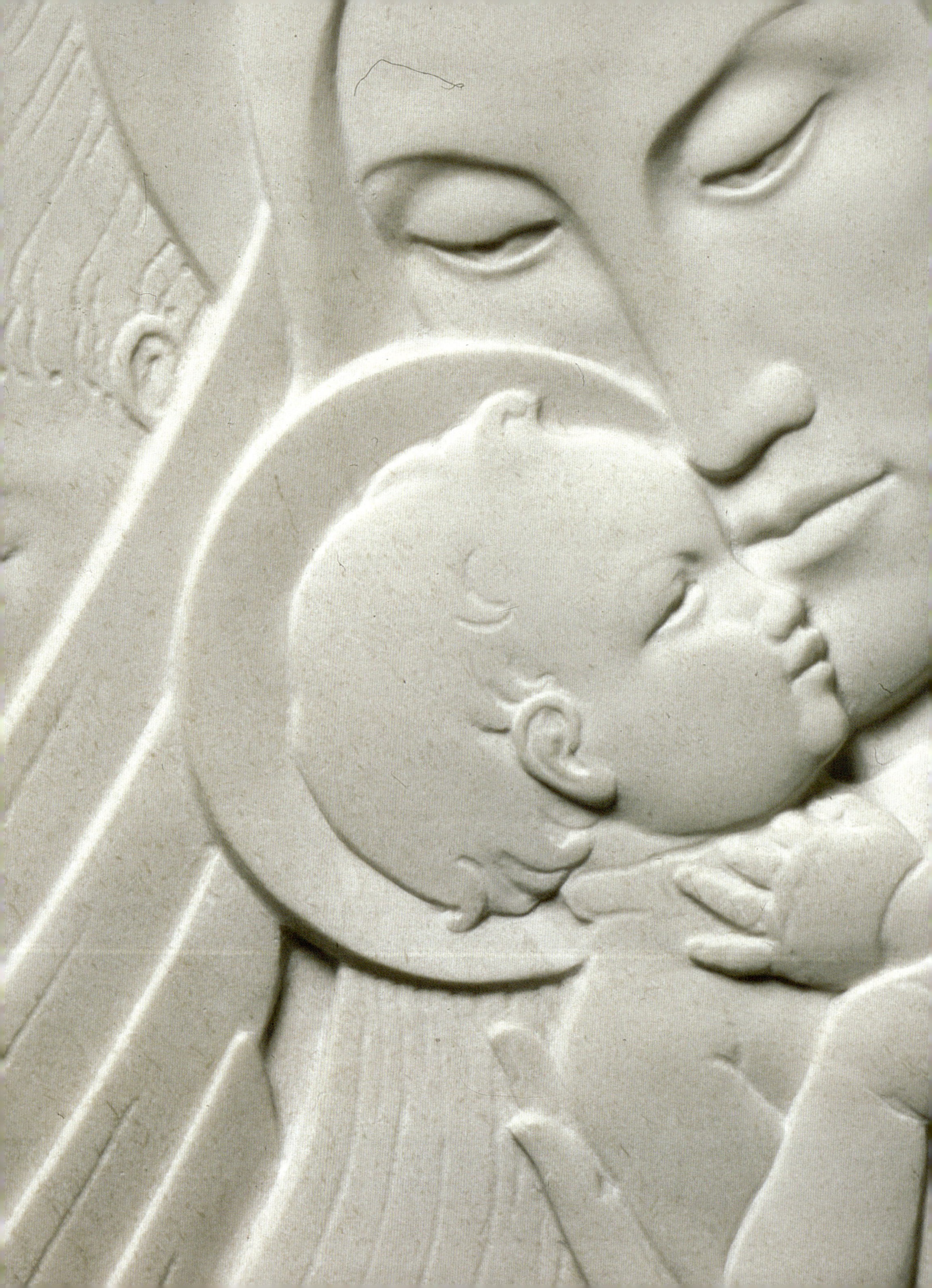

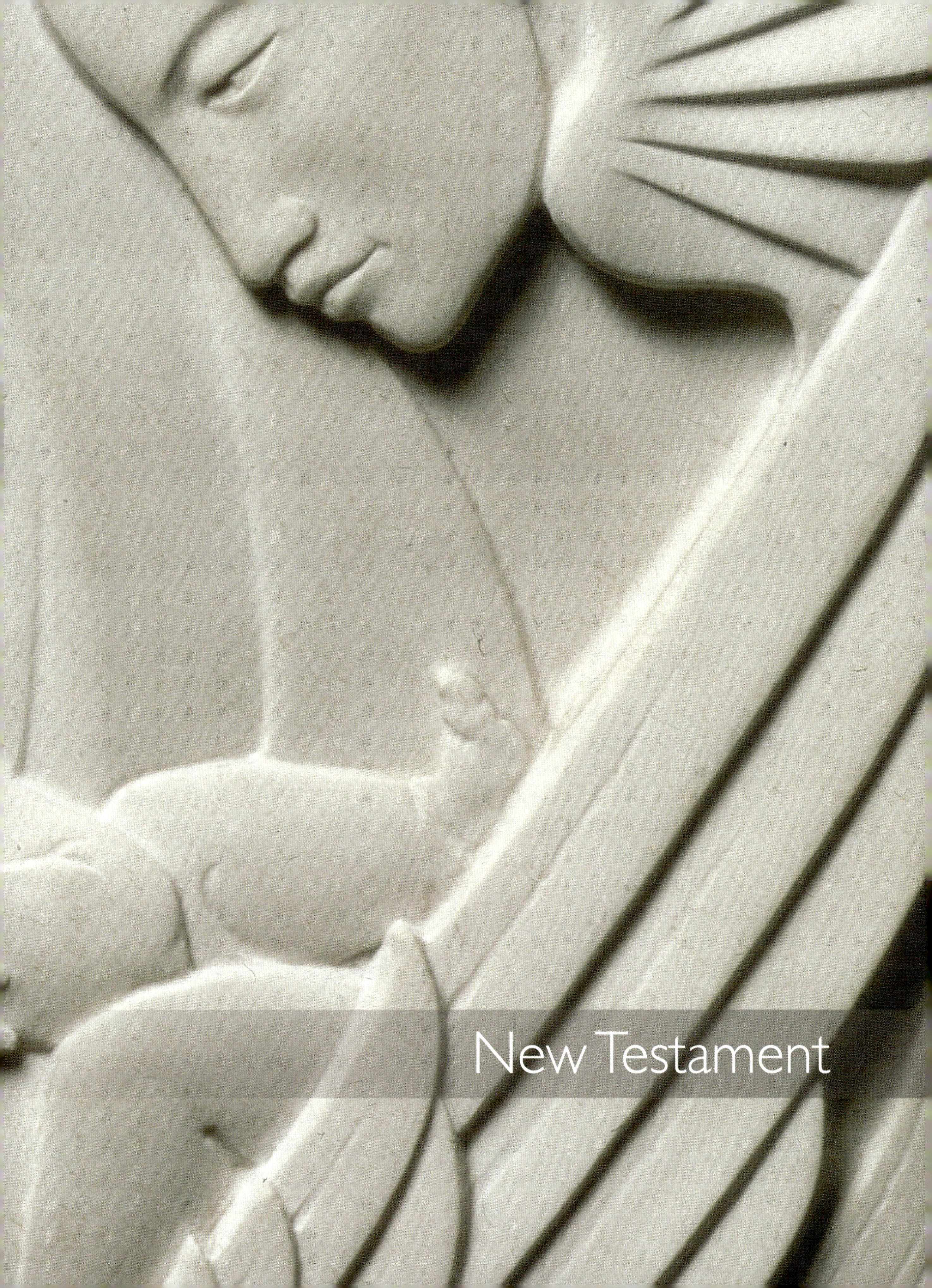
New Testament

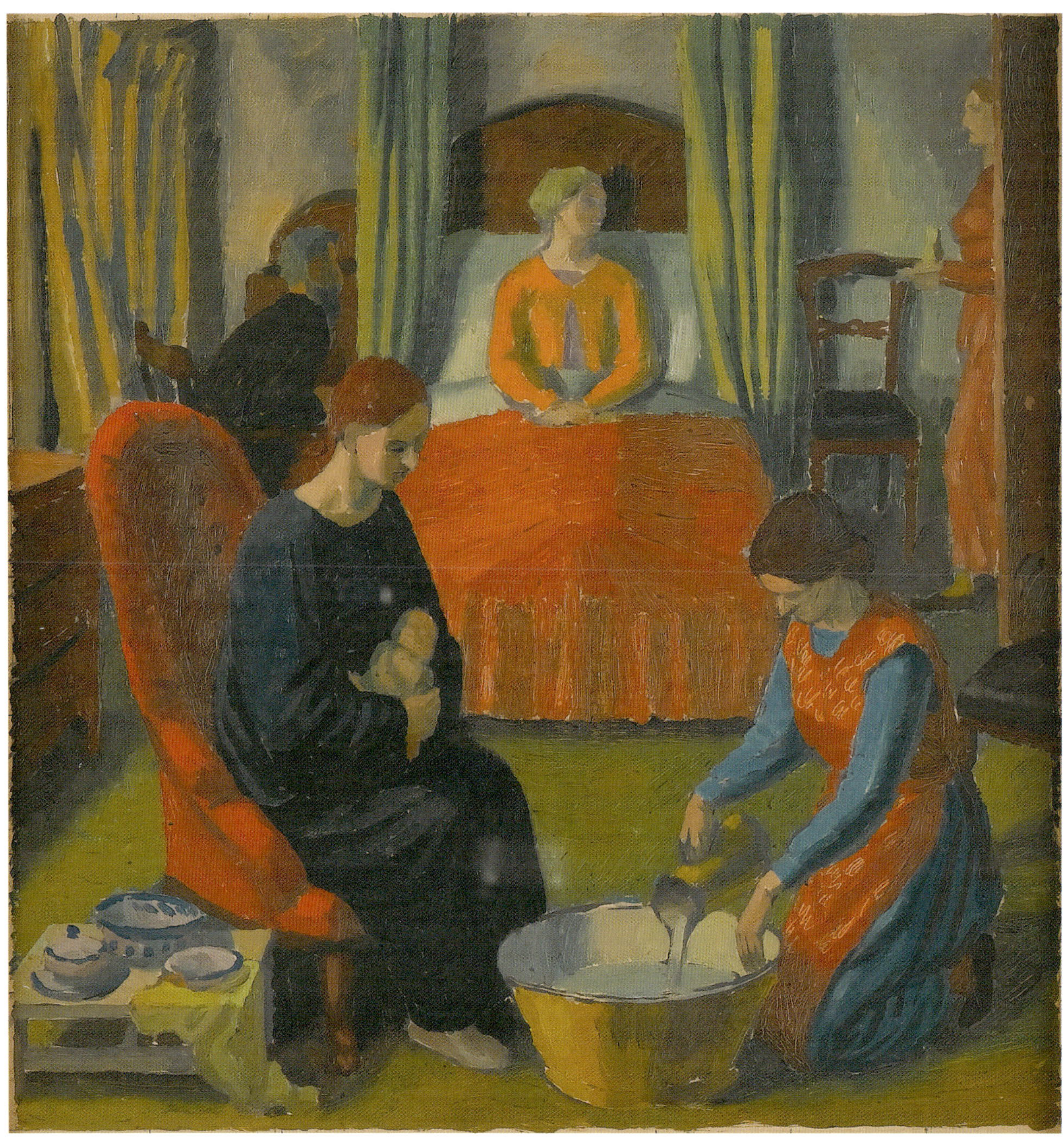

47 – Charles Mahoney (1903-1968), Study for *The Birth of the Virgin*, c.1942,
oil on paper; 11 ½ x 11 in. (29.2 x 28 cm).
Provenance: The Artists Daughter; thence by descent.

Mahoney was commissioned to produce a mural scheme for the Lady Chapel at Campion Hall in 1941, made up primarily of three large panels: the Nativity and Adoration of the Shepherds, the Coronation of the Virgin, and Our Lady of Mercy. In detail and composition the paintings owe much to early Italian example. Electing to paint directly onto canvas fixed to the walls and by daylight hours only, the project inevitably became drawn out and Mahoney could only work *in situ* during the Easter and summer vacations when he was not teaching. The project continued into the following decade and coincided with a serious decline in the artist's physical health. In spite of these problems, Sir John Rothenstein was moved to describe the scheme as as second ...only to that by Stanley Spencer at Burghclere.

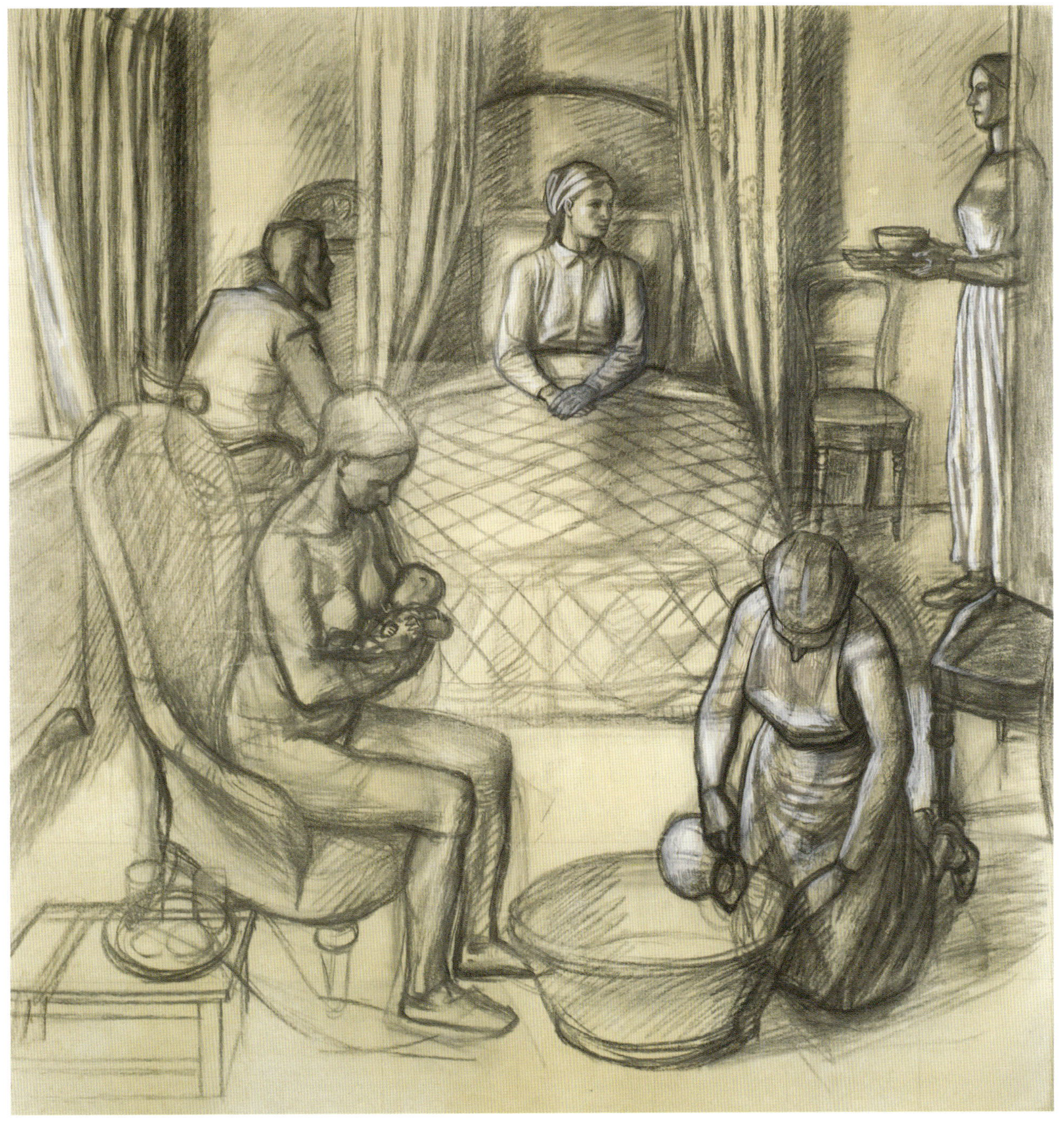

48 – Charles Mahoney (1903-1968), Full size preparatory cartoon for *The Birth of the Virgin, Campion Hall*, c.1941,
charcoal and pencil with highlights in black on paper, 34 ¼ × 35 in. (87 × 89 cm).
Provenance: Provenance: The Artist's Estate
Exhibited: Preston, Canterbury, London, Charles Mahoney, The Fine Art Society, no 74,
Literature: *Charles Mahoney*, Liss Fine Art, 1999, pp.40-41 and pp.56-57;
British Murals & Decorative Painting 1920-1960, Sansom & Co, 2013, pp.85-86 and pp.232-243.

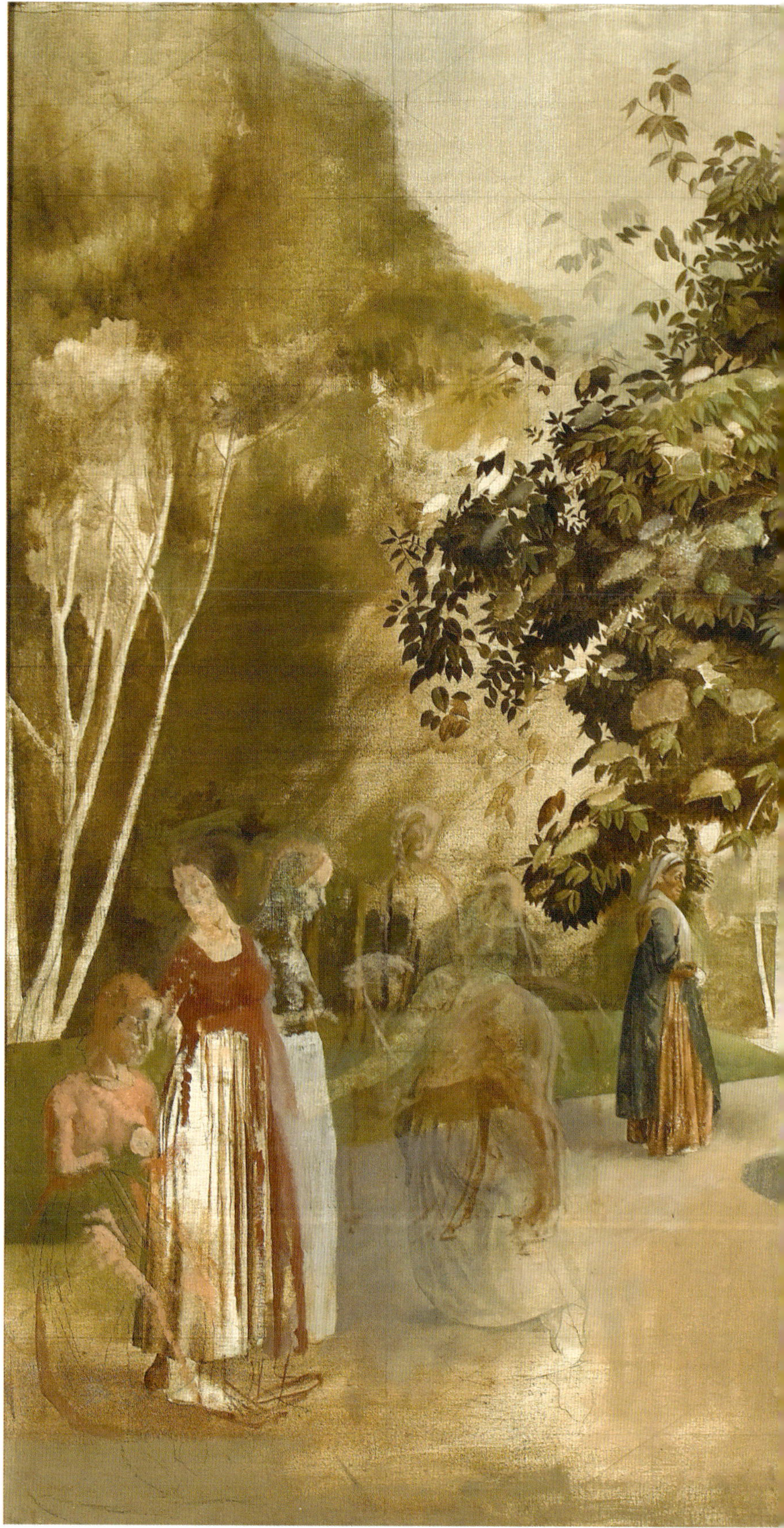

49 – Thomas Monnington (1902-1976),
The Annuciation, c.1924-25,
oil on canvas, 39 x 57 in. (99 x 145 cm).
Provenance: the Rt. Hon. F. Leverton Harris;
Anthony Mould; Jonathon Clark;
Private collection.

Exhibited: *Exhibition of Works Submitted in
the Preliminary Competitions for the Rome
Scholarship of 1926, together with Some
Examples of the Work of Rome Scholars*, Royal
Academy, March 1926;
Inspired by Italy, Exeter Museum and Art
Gallery, August - September 1996, (no. 21);
Thomas Monnington, The Fine Art Society,
1997, cat no. 15.

Literature: Paul Liss, *Thomas Monnington*, The
Fine Art Society, 1997, pp 27 & 36;
Sam Smiles, *Inspired by Italy*, Exeter Museum
and Art Gallery, August - September 1996;
*British Murals and Decorative Painting 1920-
1960*, Sansom & Co, 2013

Although the subject of this painting
is unclear it is most likely to be the
Annunciation exhibited at the Royal
Academy in March 1926. A reference by
Monnington in December 1924, of his
intention to paint, in addition to his *Allegory*,
"another smaller picture, some work for
which I have already done." may relate to
this painting. In another letter, from Jim Ede,
the British School at Rome is informed that
Mr. Leverton Harris – listed as the owner
of the painting when exhibited at the Royal
Academy – thought of going to see the
picture but it seems that as yet it is hardly
begun (23.3.1925). The painting appears to
be set in the Borghese Gardens, the setting
Knights used for her *Marriage at Cana*,
(1923-26). (See pages 94-95.)

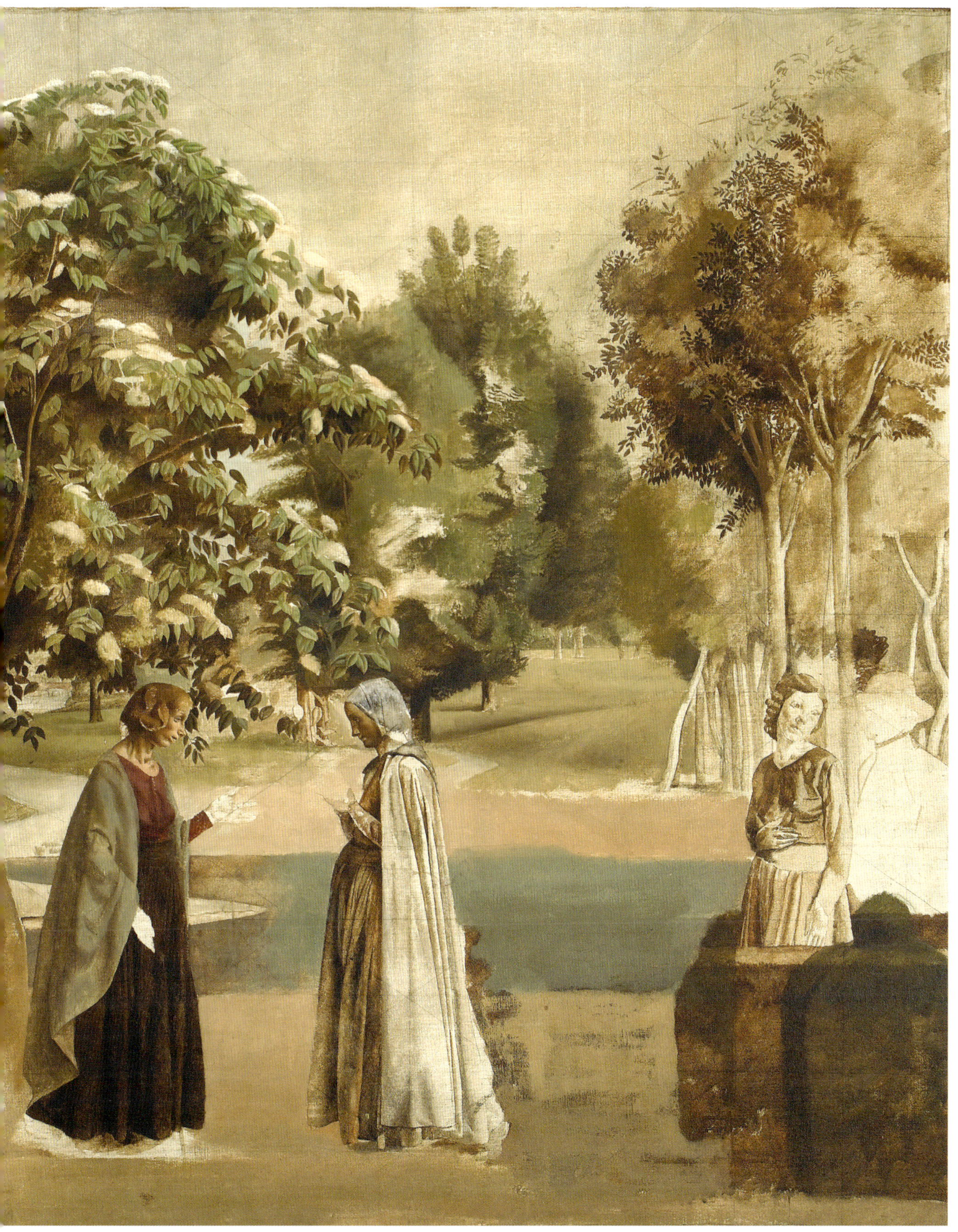

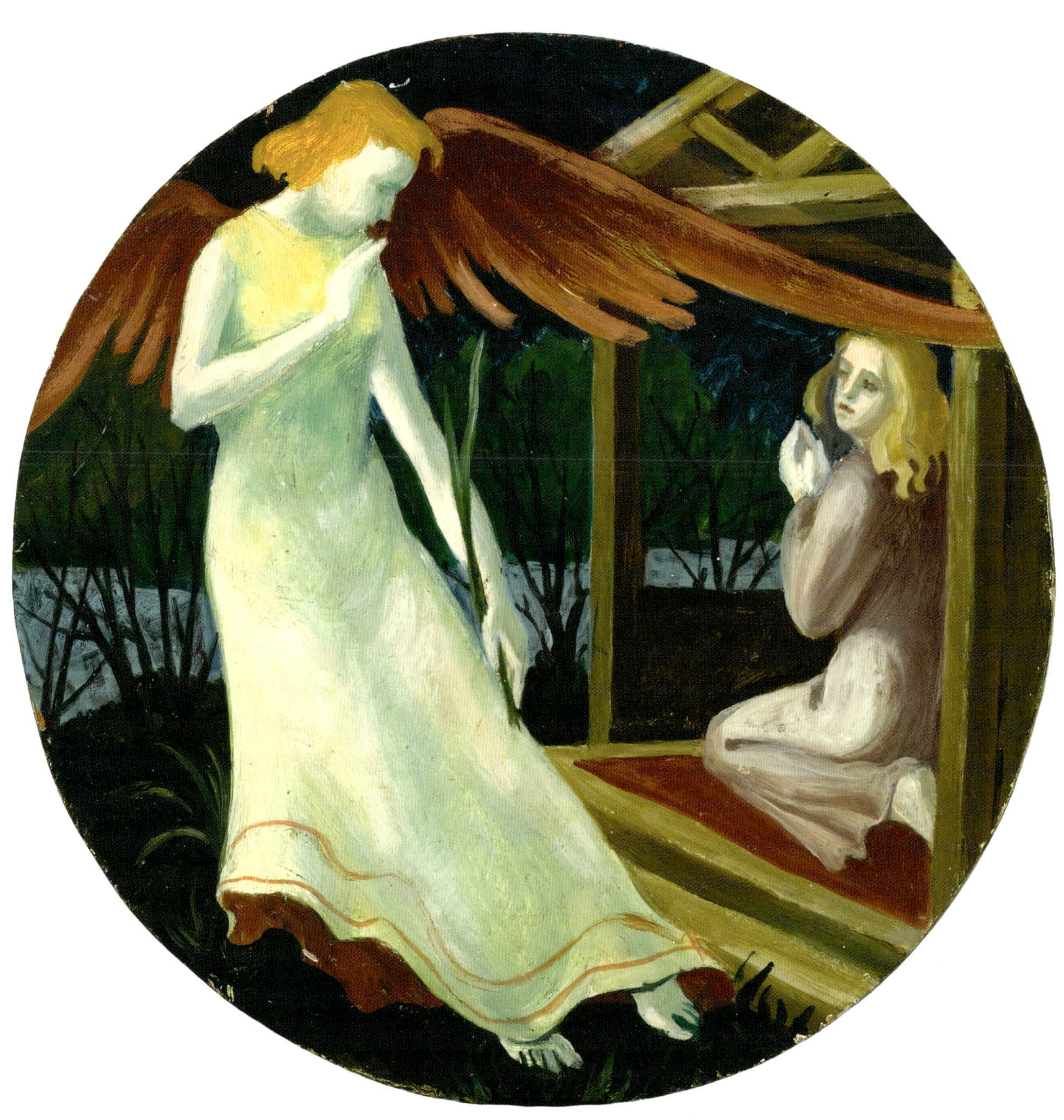

50 – **Fyffe Christie** (1918-1979), *Annunciation,* c.1960, oil on wood, tondo 10 in. (25.5 cm) diameter.
Provenance: in the artist's possession until 1979; thence with his wife Eleanor Christie-Chatterley until 2012.
Literature: Buckman, David, *Nature and Humanity, The Work of Fyffe Christie, 1918-1979,* Sansom & Co, 2004.

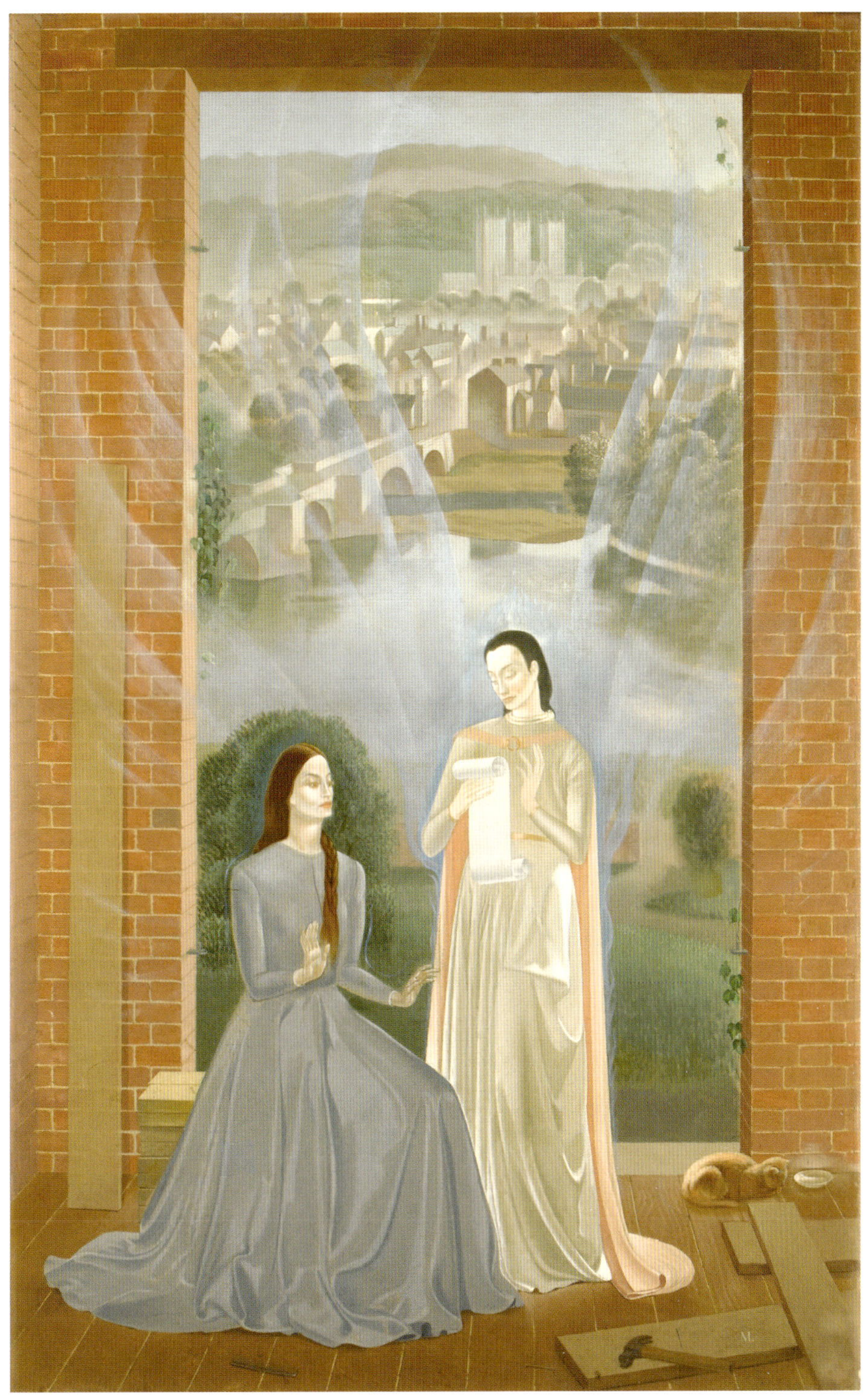

51 – **M. L.**, *Annunciation with Lincoln Cathedral in the background*, c.1925, signed with initials M.L.,
'Orpington' printed on an incomplete exhibition label to the reverse,
oil on canvas, 55 ¼ × 35 in. (140.5 × 89 cm).

This Annunciation scene is set against a backdrop of Lincoln with its distinctive 11th century Cathedral.
The author of this work, and its complex iconography, has yet to be deciphered. It has been suggested
that this is the work of Miss Mary Long (of Swinderby Rectory) who was a member of the Lincolnshire
Drawing Club. Another possibility is that it is the work of Margaret Little (b. 1901).

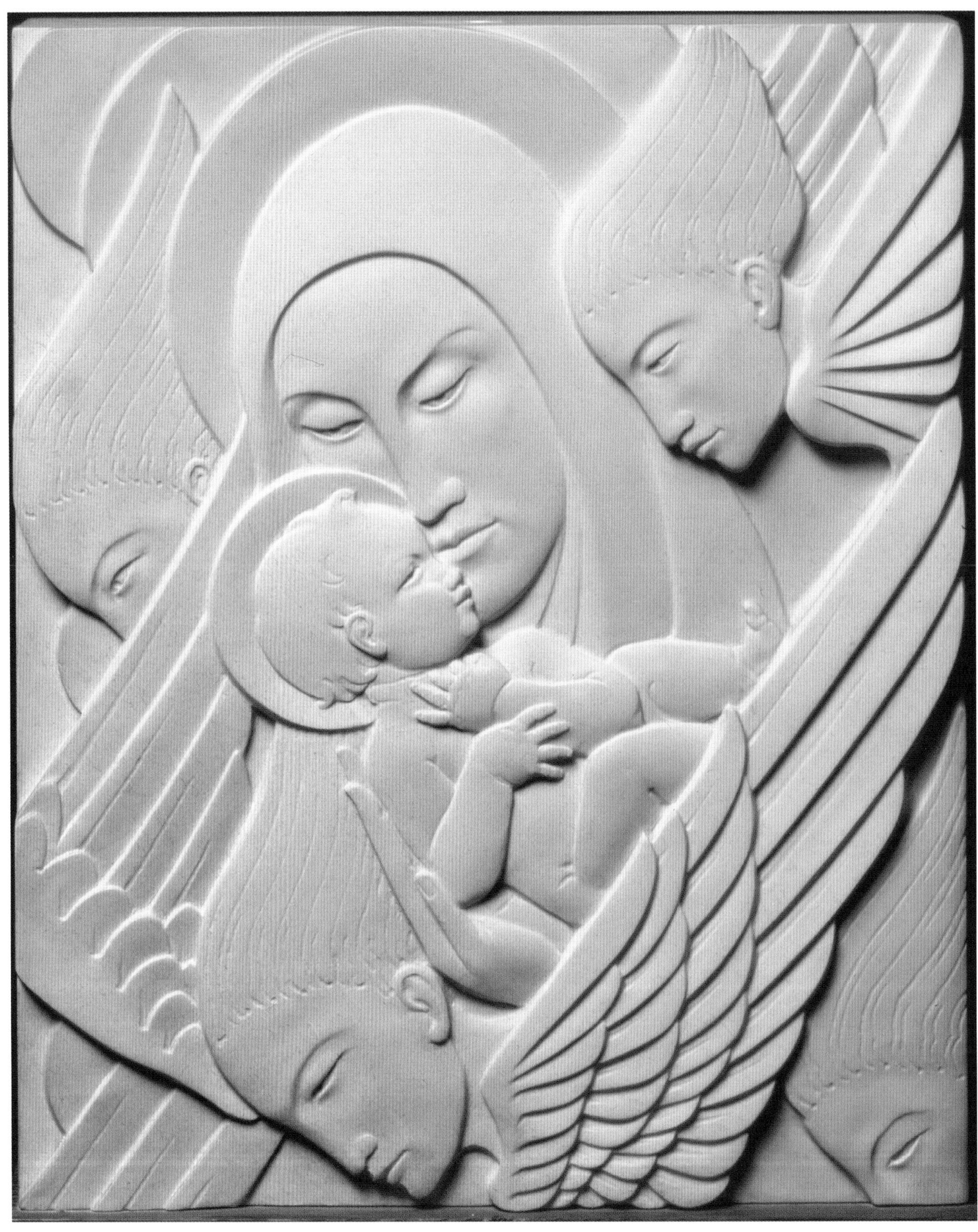

52 – Daisy Teresa Borne (1906-1998), *Madona of the Adoring Angels*, c.1929,
Palomino marble, (38.1 x 31.7 x 7.6 cm).
Provenance: Collection of Peyton Skipwith.

Madonna of the Adoring Angels was the second of Daisy Borne's artworks exhibited at the Royal Academy, where she debuted in 1932. The 1939 piece was her first in Palomino marble and first religious subject (a theme in which she would specialise). Together with Joyce Bidder, with whom she shared a studio for fifty years, Borne's sculpture interlaced Neo-Classical and Modern elements.

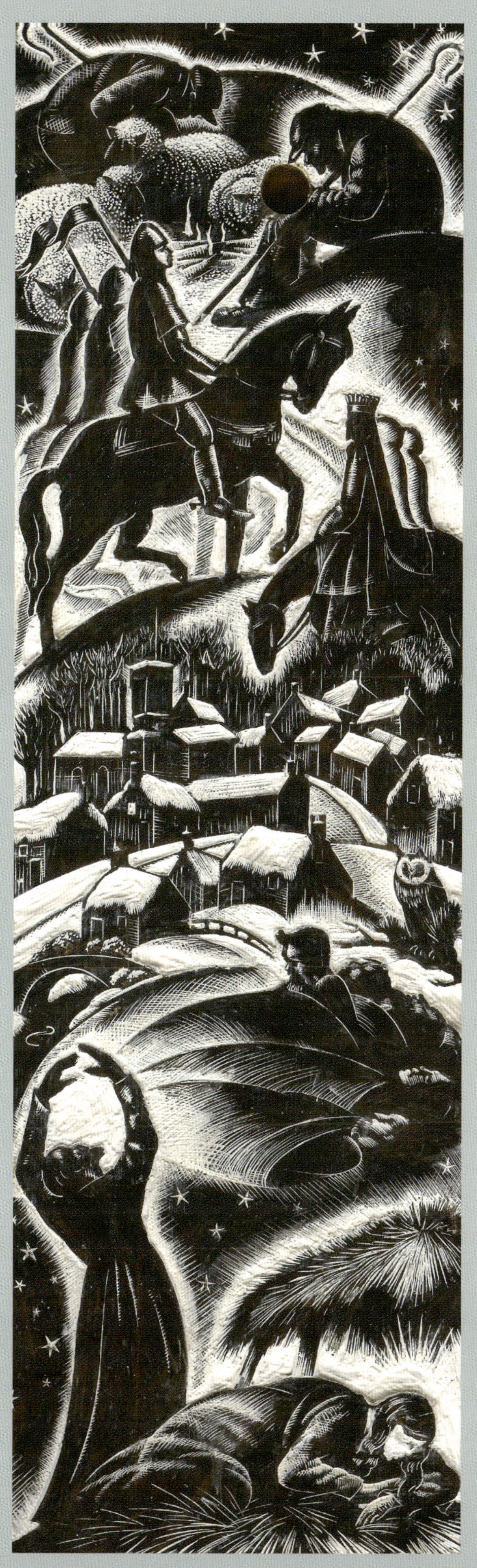

53 – Clare Leighton (1898-1989),
The Nativity,
original woodblock (cancelled),
12 x 3 ½ in. (30.5 x 8.9 cm).

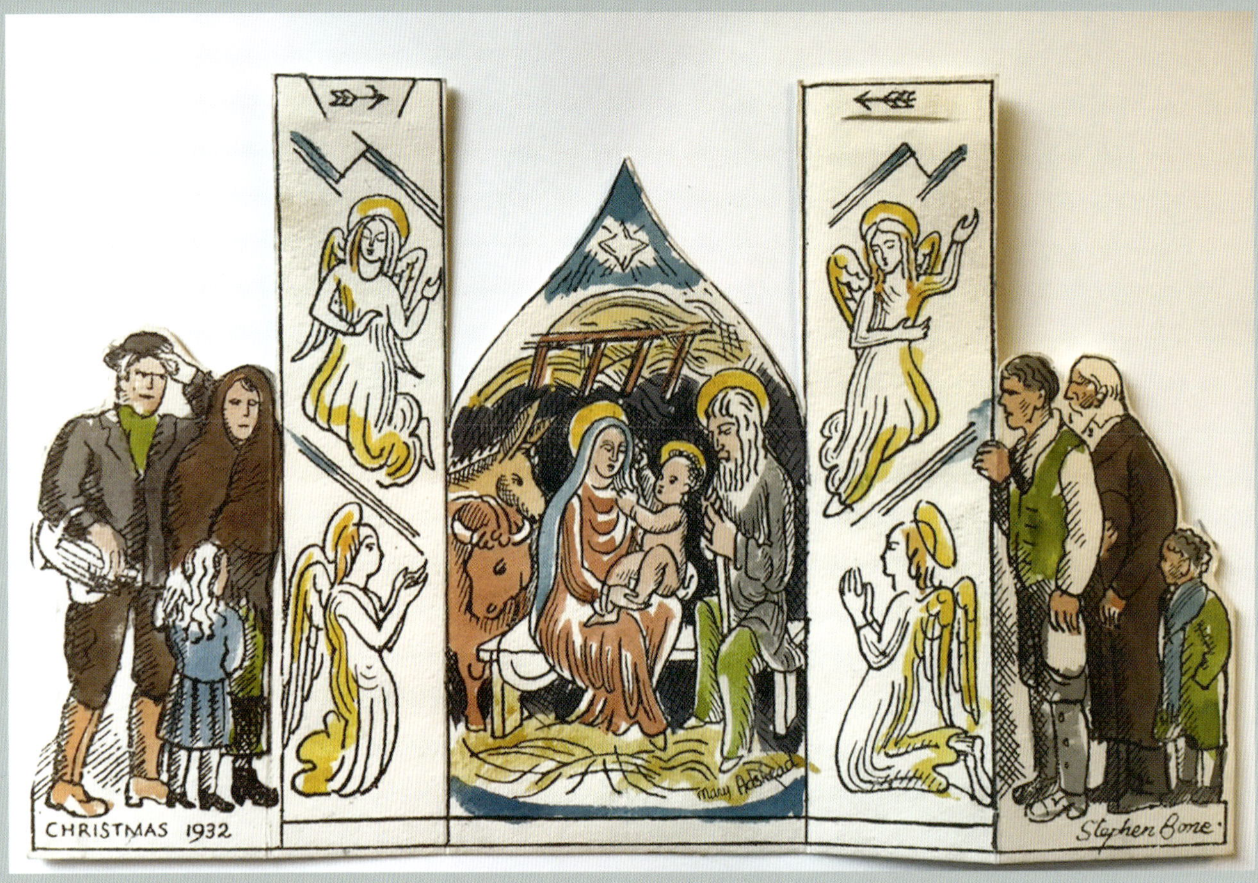

54 – Mary Adshead (1904-1995), *The Bone Family partaking in the Nativity*, 1932, signed, wayercolour over a lithographic base, 4½ x 7 in. (11.4 x 17.8 cm).
Provenance: The Artist's Family

Like so many artists of her generation Adshead took great pleasure in making her own Christmas cards, especially to exchange with fellow artists. In an often jovial spirit she frequently included portraits of herself and Stephen Bone together with other members of her family

55 – Peter Wright (1919-2003), *Madonna and Child*, signed on base with monogram, fired porcelain, broken black and white glaze, 11 ½ x 5 ½ in. (29 x 14 cm).
Provenance: acquired directly from the artist, 1963.

Wright was inspired by " . . . looking at clay images of very early Mediterranean cultures and at the bronze Etruscan votive figures; both of these groups of images have always fascinated me." (Letter to Barrie Liss, 7 December 1962)

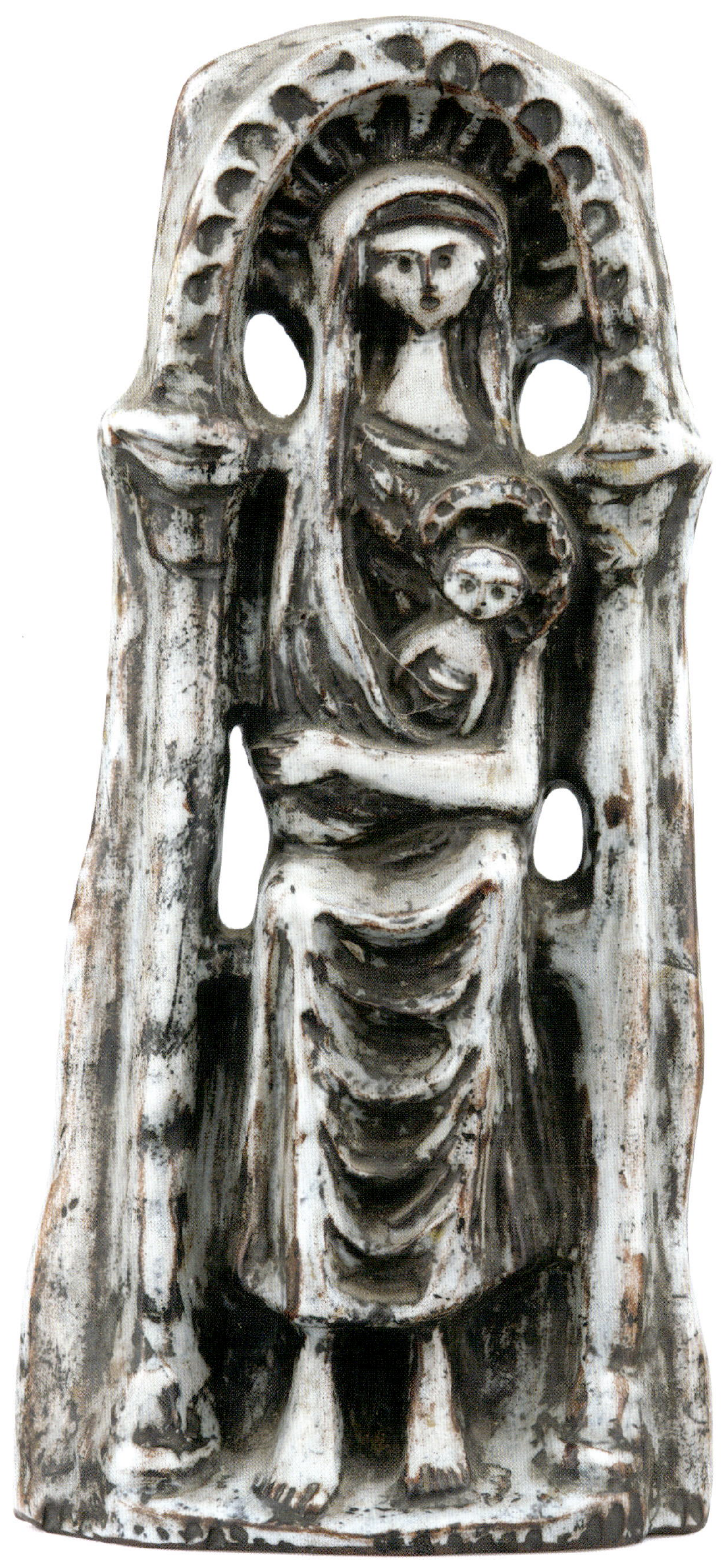

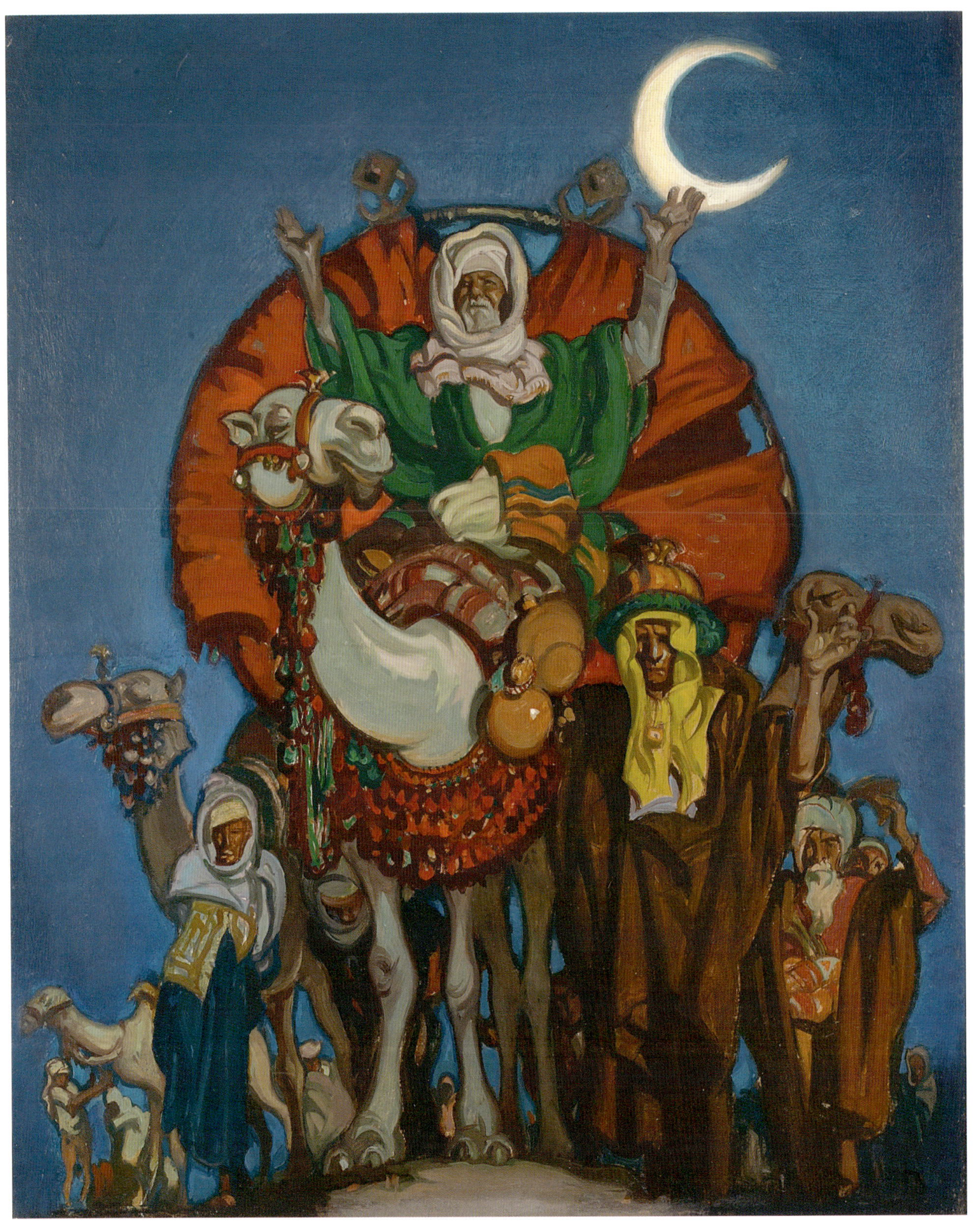

56 – **Frank Brangwyn** (1867-1956), *The Three Kings*, 1934, oil on board, 29 × 24 in. (74 × 61 cm).

The Three Kings was used as the cover design of the 1934 Christmas edition of *The Radio Times*.

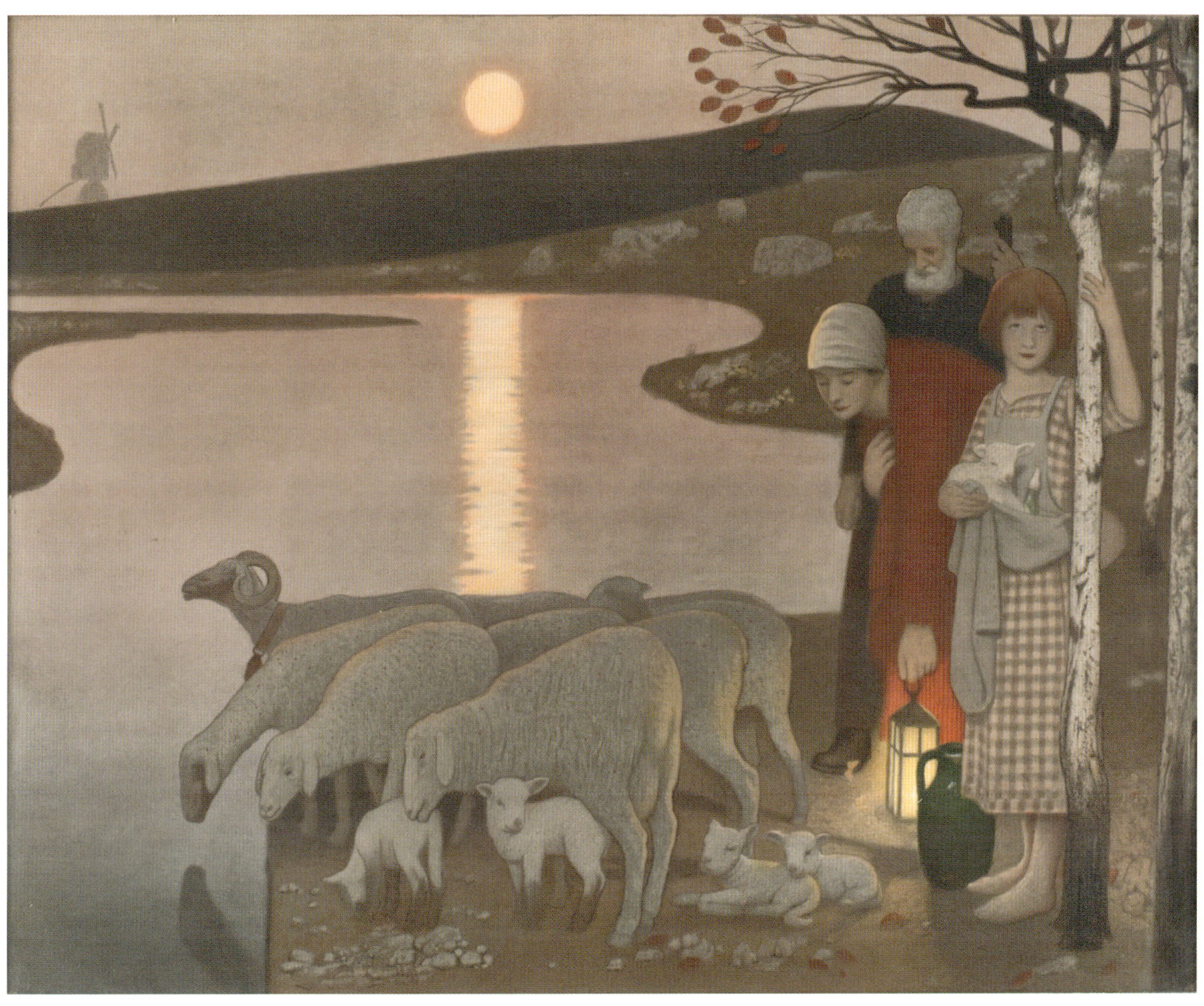

57 – Frederick Cayley Robinson (1862-1927), *Pastoral – A Medici Print in a Rowley Gallery frame, c.1930,*
Medici colour reproduction, 16 ½ × 21 in. (42 × 53.3 cm).

Exhibited at the Royal Academy in 1924 Pastoral, one Cayley Robinson's best known images, was acquired directly from the artist in the same year. It was reproduced as a Medici Gallery print in the late 1920's. The Medici Society was founded in 1908 to bring art to a wider public through high quality colour reproductions provided, "for the lowest price commercially possible" to members who paid a subscription.

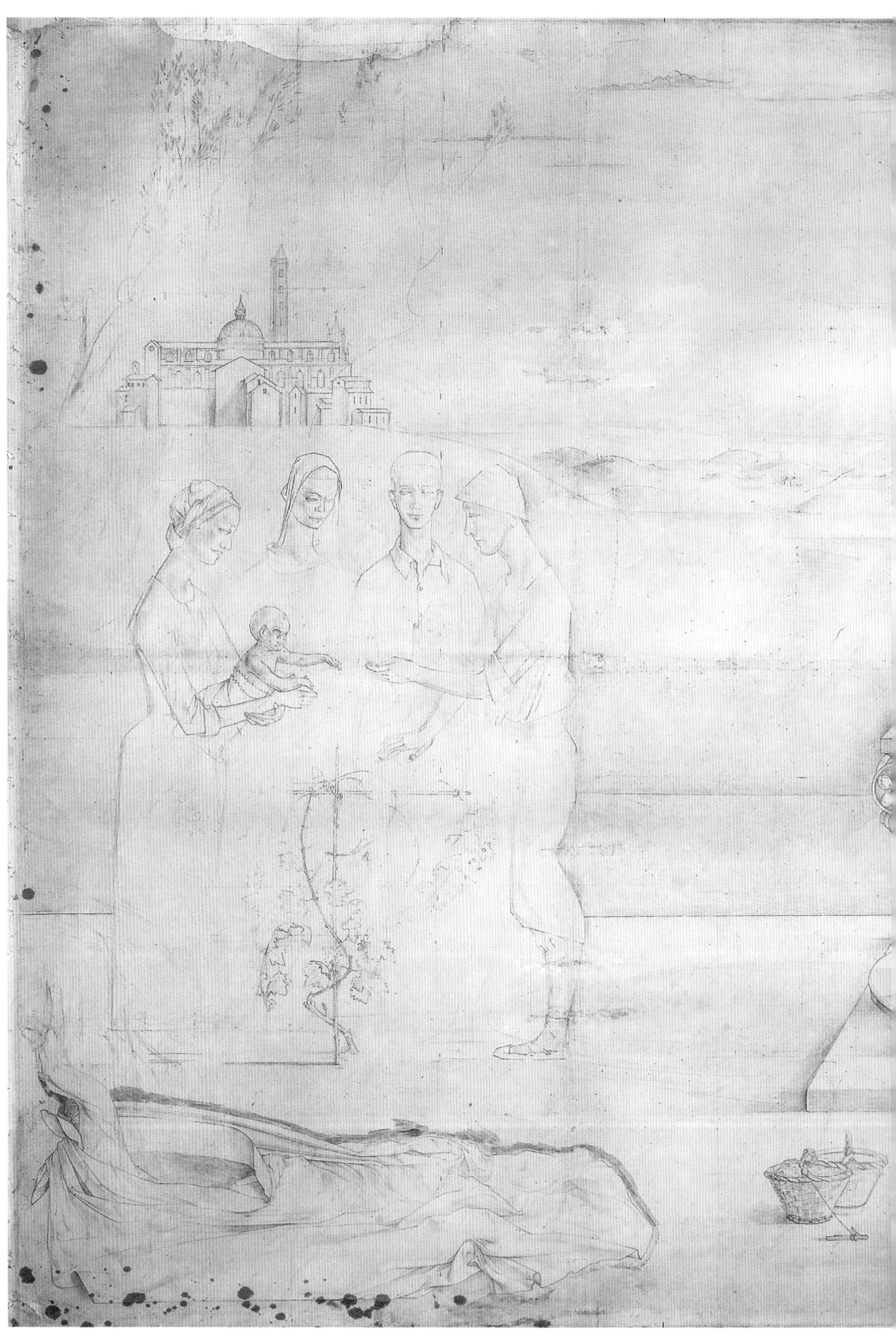

58 – **Anne Newland** (1913-1997), Study for *The Legend of Ceres*, c.1938-39, pencil on tracing paper, 45 ¼ x 75 in. (114.5 x 191 cm).

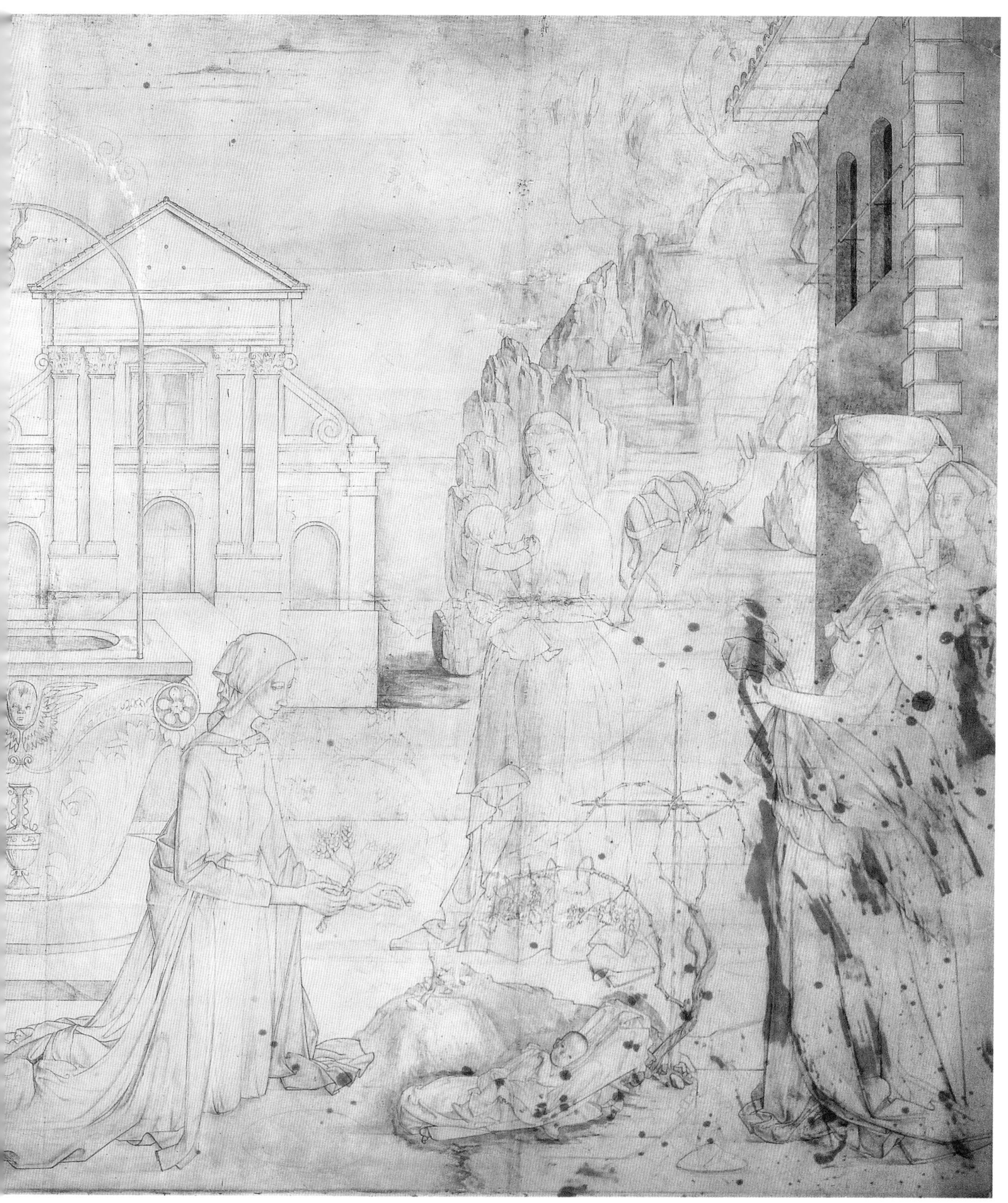

This cartoon was Newland's principal work of her scholarship at The British School at Rome. Ceres, in Ancient Roman mythology, was the goddess of agriculture, grain crops, fertility and motherly relationships. In 1950 at the Royal Academy Newland exhibited a variation on the theme, entitled *Three Marys*, which was loosely inspired by this earlier decorative composition.

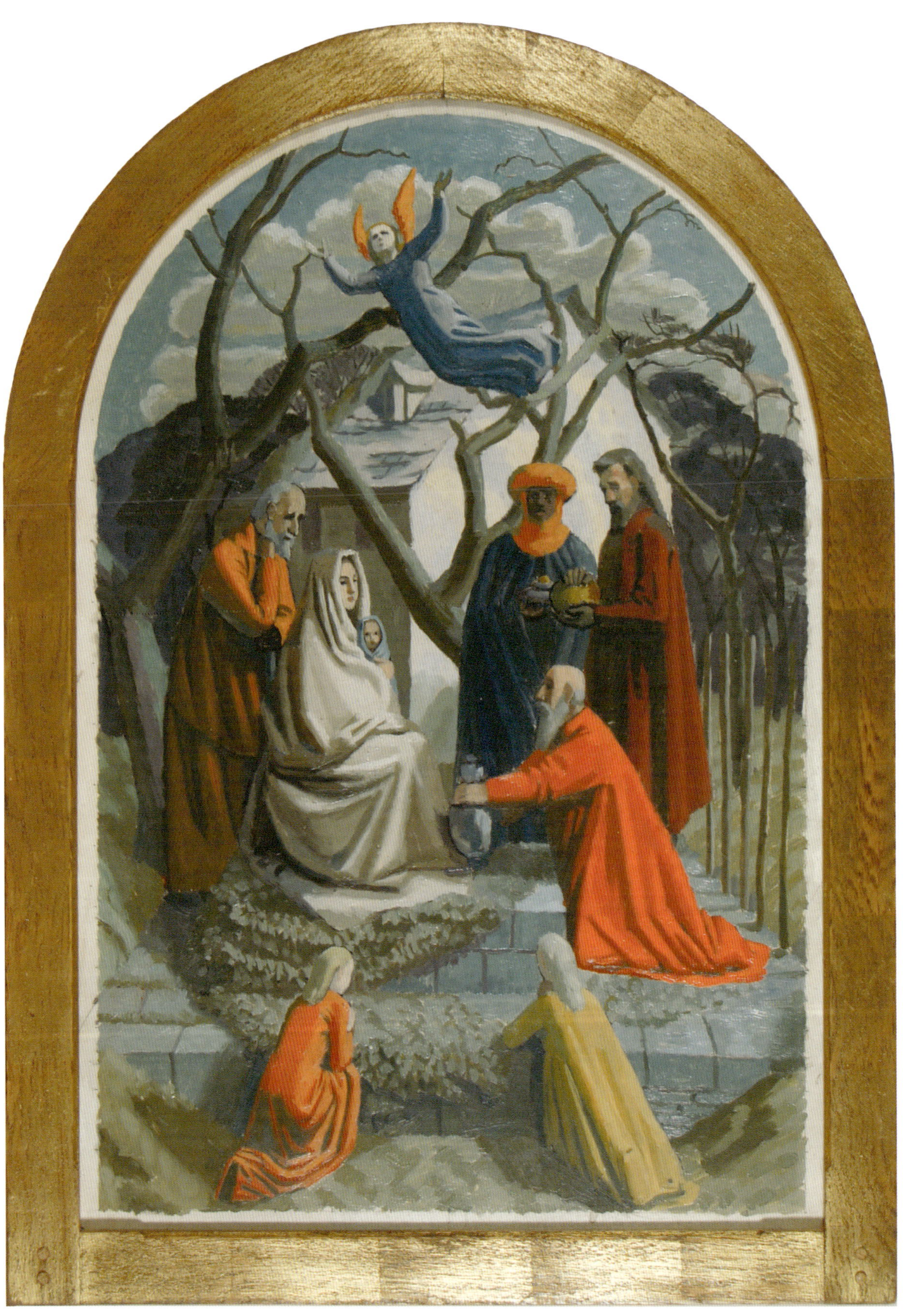

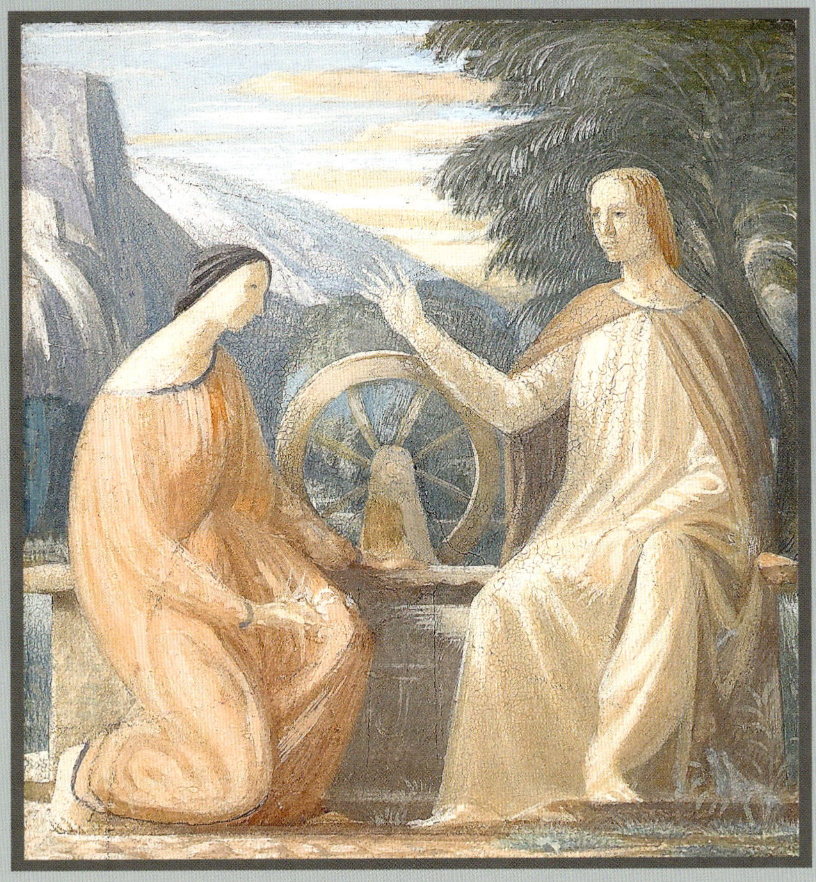

60 – Thomas Monnington (1902-1976), Study for *Christ meeting the Woman of Samaria at the Well,* for Kippen Kirk, c.1930, studio stamp to the reverse,
tempera, 3 ¾ x 3 ¾ in. (10 x 9.5 cm).
Provenance: Lady Monnington

Between 1924 and 1936 Kippen Church was transformed from being an unremarkable Presbyterian Kirk into one of the most beautiful of Scotland's religious buildings. The reconstruction of the building was undertaken in celebration of its centenary, and largely funded by Sir David (D.Y.) Cameron (1865-1945), who was at the time a member of the Kirk Session. A Director of both the National Gallery of Scotland and the Tate Gallery, Camerons influence extended throughout the artistic community of his day and he commissioned works from many of his favourite artists, including Monnington who was asked to produce a painting for one of the three chapels. The chosen subject shows Jesus on the way to Galilee passing through Samaria: It was noon when he reached the beautiful Vale of Shechem. At the opening of this valley was Jacob's well. Wearied with His journey, he sat down here to rest while his disciples went to buy food.

59 – Charles Mahoney (1903-1968), *Adoration of the Shepherds (Winter),* c.1942, signed and inscribed on label to the reverse, oil on paper (arched top), 17 ¾ x 11 ¾ in. (45 x 30 cm).Provenance: The Artist's Estate.
Exhibited: The Whitworth Art Gallery, 1957; Preston, Canterbury; London, *Charles Mahoney,* The Fine Art Society, (cat 81).
Literature: *Charles Mahoney,* Liss Fine Art, 1999, pp.40-41 and pp.56-57;
British Murals & Decorative Painting 1920-1960, Sansom & Co, 2013, pp.85-86 and pp.232-243.

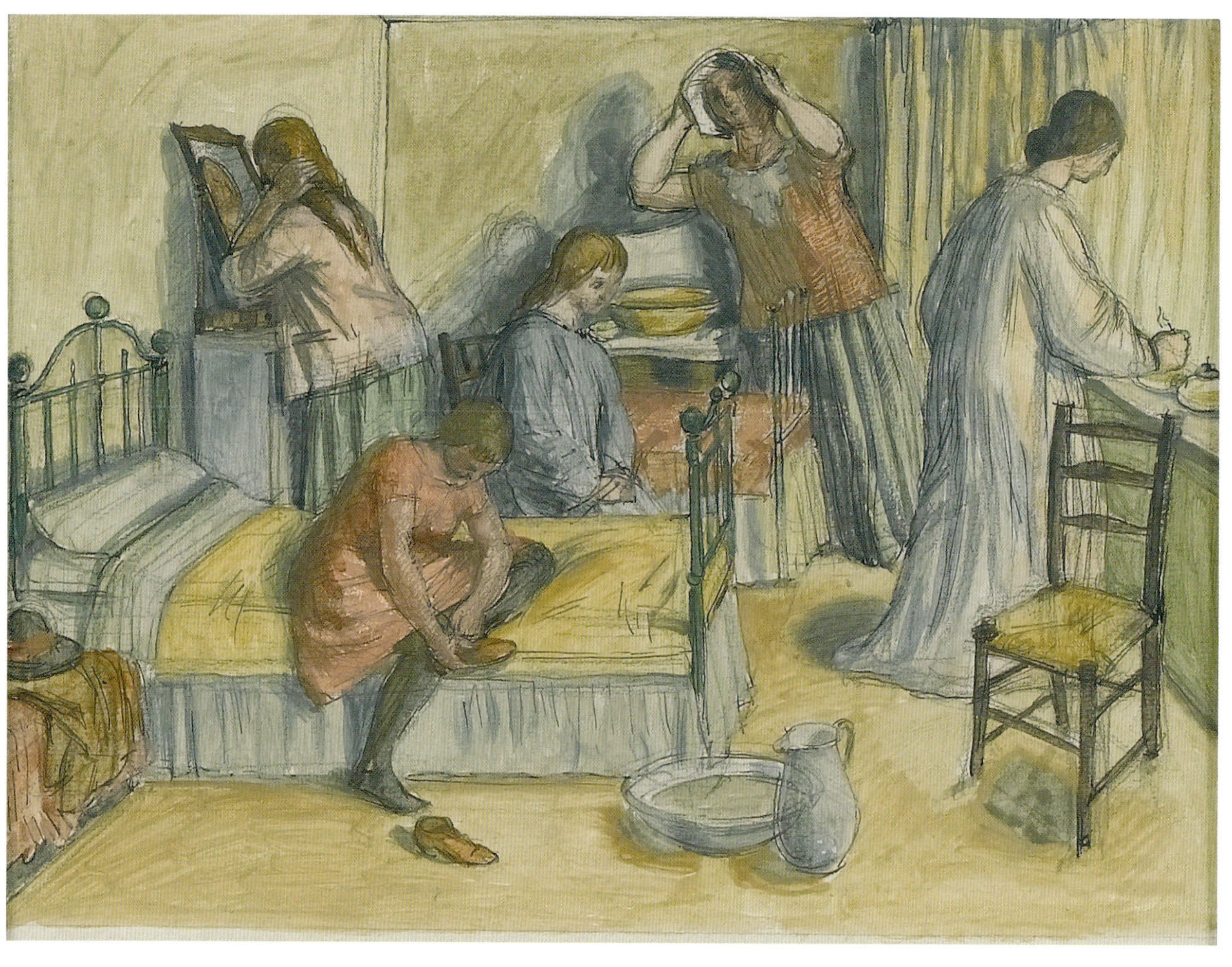

61 – **Charles Mahoney** (1903-1968), *The Wise and Foolish Virgins*, c.1928,
thinned oil over pencil on paper, 8 ¾ × 11 ¾ in. (22 × 30 cm).
Provenance: The artist's daughter; thence by descent

62 – **Winifred Knights** (1899-1947), Illustration to Algernon Blackwood's *The Centaur*, 1915,
pen & ink and watercolour on paper, 9 ¾ × 7 ¼ in. (24.7 × 18.4 cm).
Provenance: Private collection.

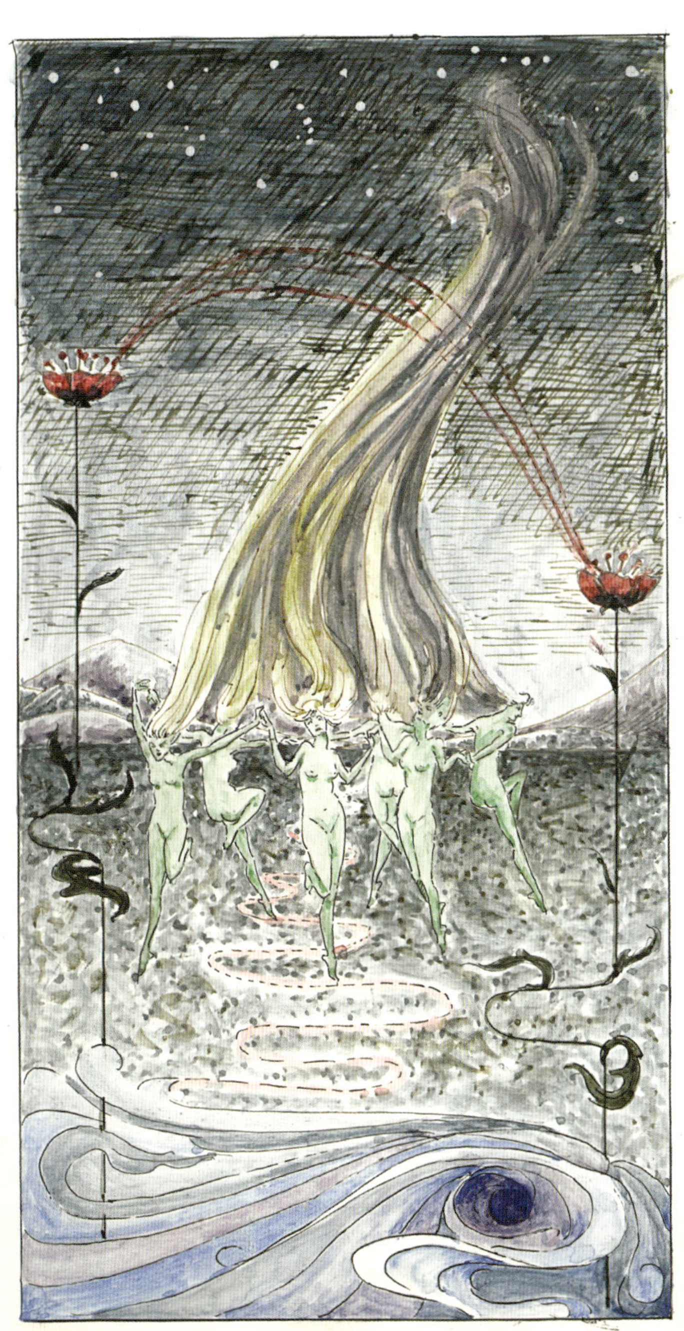

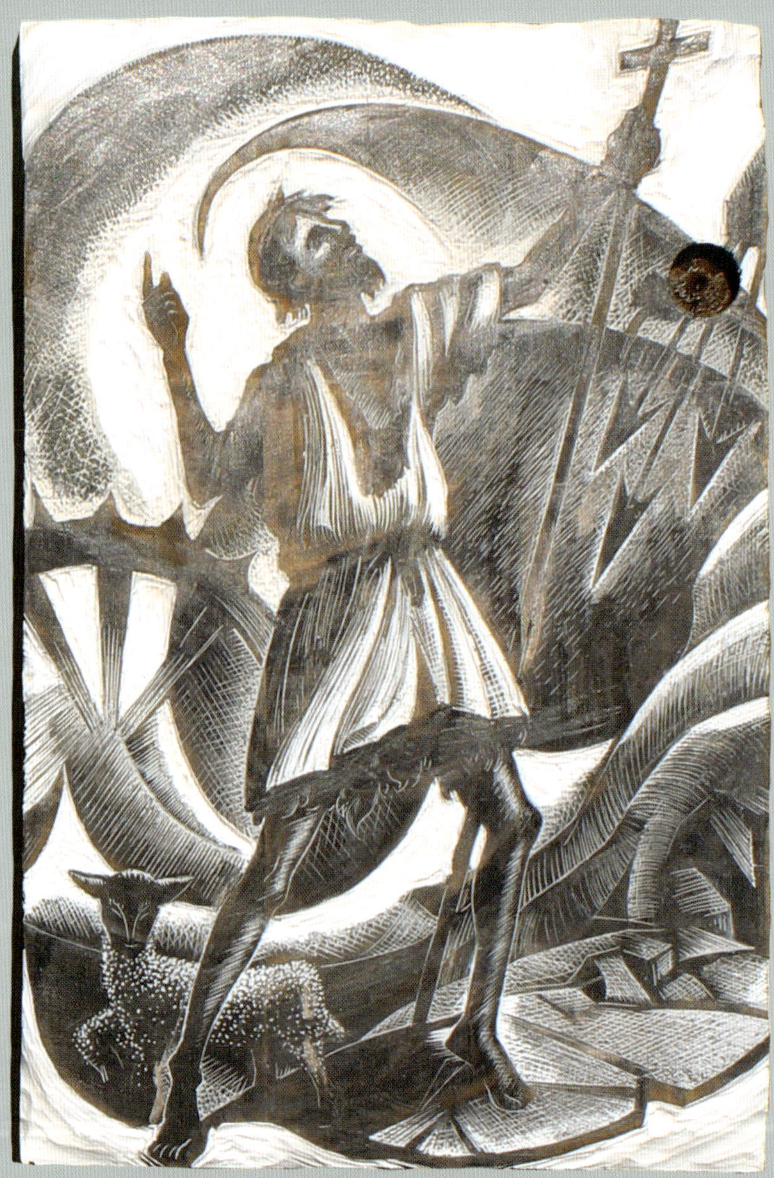

63 – Clare Leighton (1898-1989), *St John the Baptist*, BPL 765, 1965,
original woodblock (cancelled) 6 x 4 in. (15.3 x 10.2 cm).
From *The Earth is the Lord's: Poems of the Spirit*, 1965
by Helen Plotz (Compiler), Clare Leighton (Illustrator).

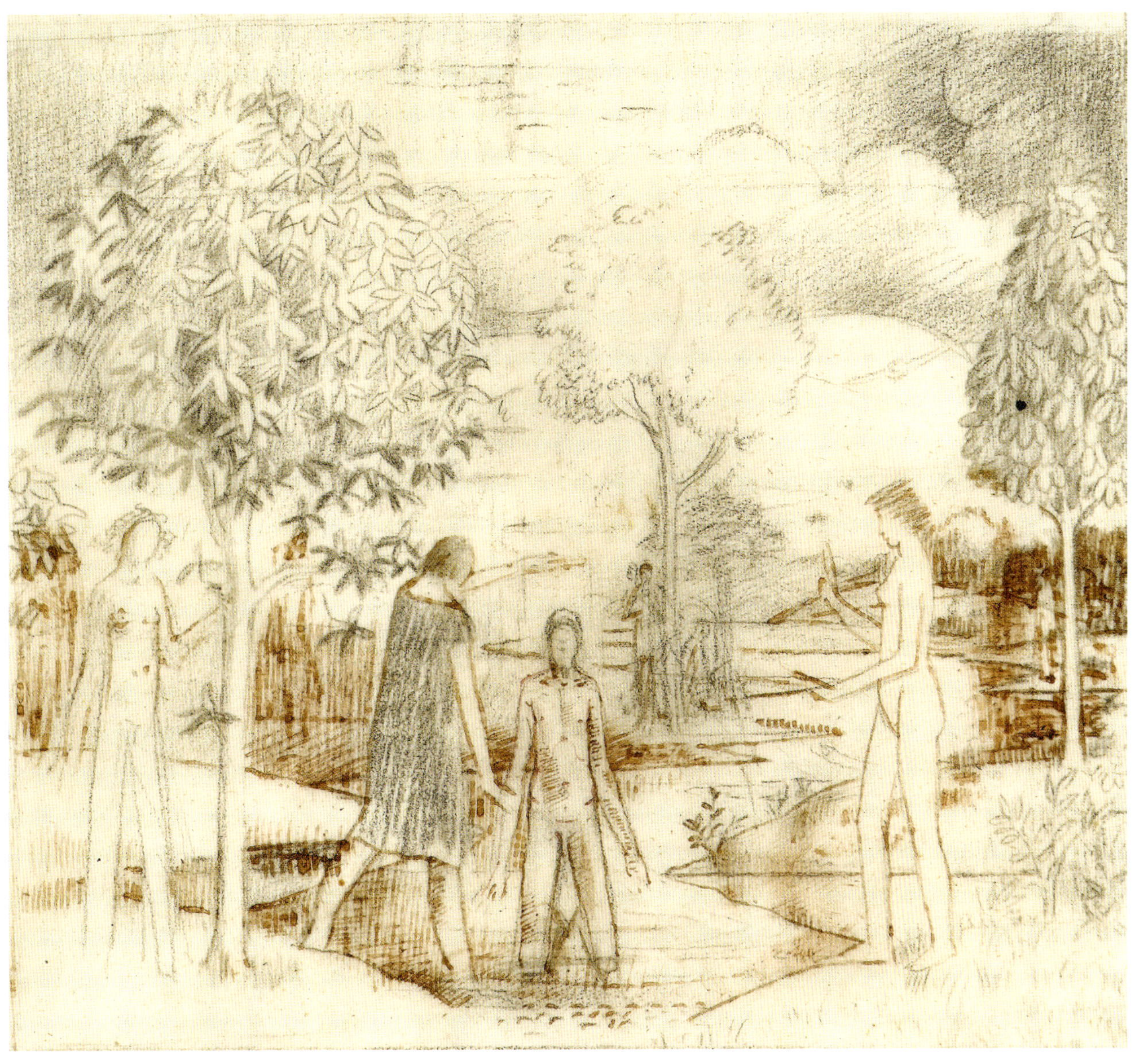

64 – Thomas Monnington (1902-1976), *Baptism*, c.1924, inscribed,
pencil and brown ink on tracing paper, 6 × 6 in. (15.1 × 15.1 cm).

This compostion is clearly indebted to Piero della Francesca's *Baptism of Christ* (1450s, National Gallery, London). The National Gallery *Baptism* had a special significance for Monnington – it was, he later recalled, on first seeing this work as a young teenager, that he decided his vocation was to be an artist.

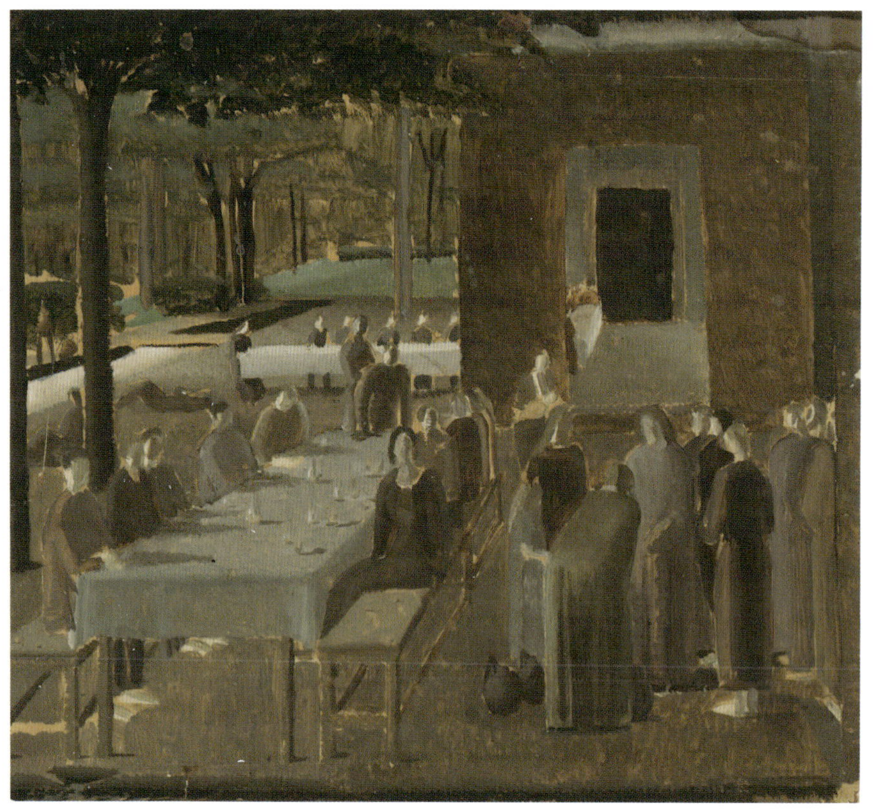

65 – **Winifred Knights** (1899-1947),
Study for the *Marriage at Cana*, c.1922,
oil on tracing paper,
11 ½ x 12 ¾ in. (29 x 32,5 cm).
Exhibited: Winifred Knights, Dulwich
Picture Gallery, 2016, curated by
Sacha Llewellyn
Literature: Sacha Llewellyn, *Winifred Knights 1899-1947* (London: Lund Humphries in association with Dulwich Picture Gallery, 2016); *Winifred Knights 1899-1947* (exh. catalogue The Fine Art Society PLC and Liss Fine Art in Association with the British School at Rome 1995, p. 53).

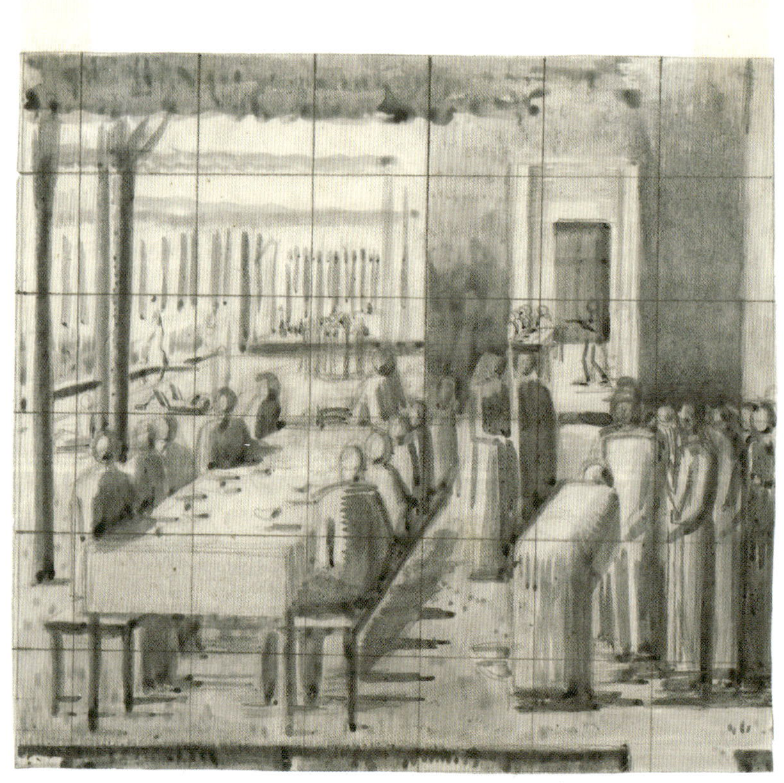

66 – **Winifred Knights** (1899-1947),
Compositional study for
The Marriage at Cana, c.1922,
wash on paper, squared,
6 x 6 ½ in. (15 x 16.5 cm).

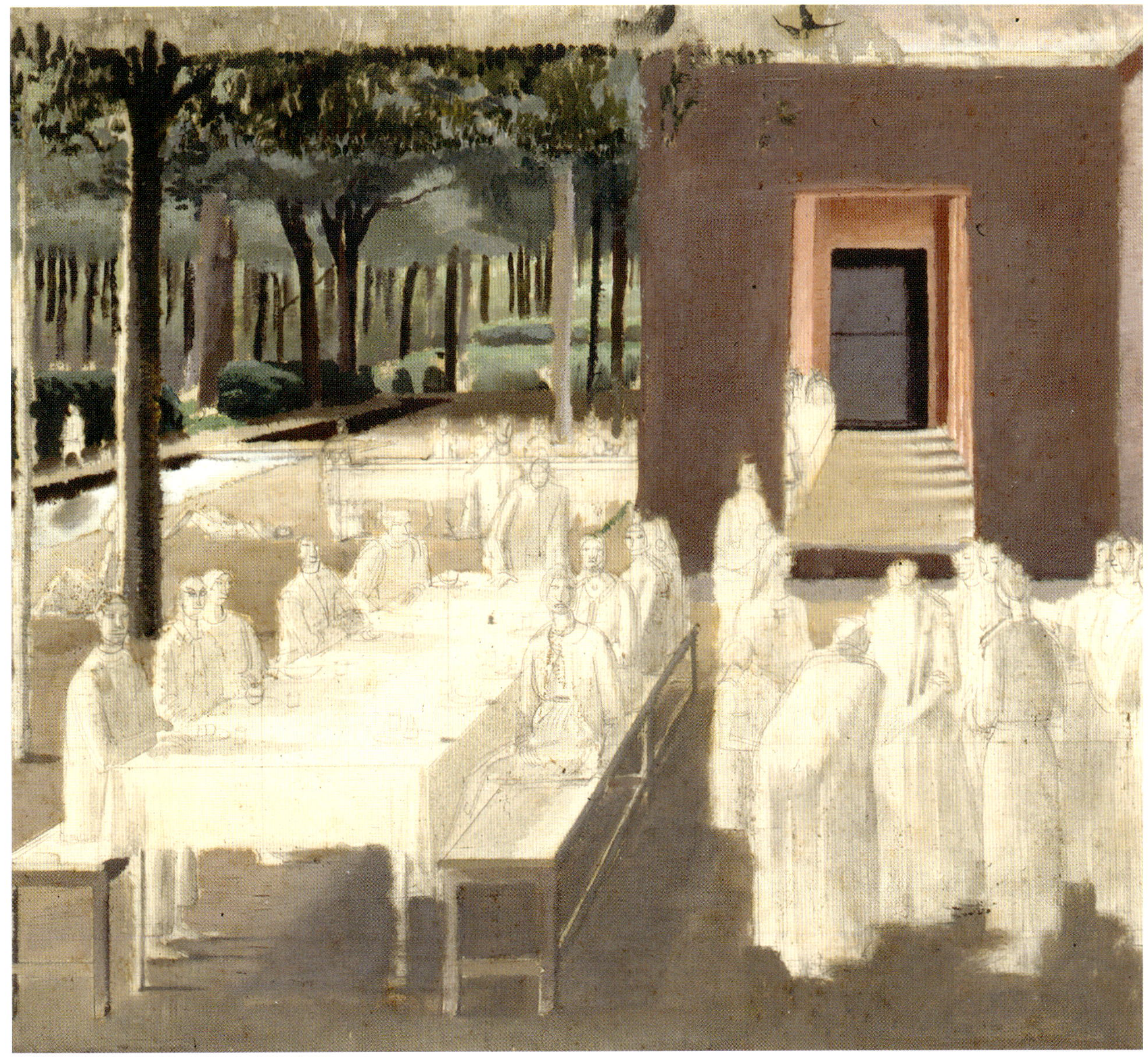

67 –Winifred Knights (1899-1947), Compositional study for the *Marriage at Cana*, c.1922,
oil on paper, squared, 12 ¼ x 13 ¾ in. (31.1 x 35 cm).
Provenance: John Monnington up to 1996; Private collection; David Thomson 2000.
Exhibited: *Winifred Knights*, Dulwich Picture Gallery, 2016, curated by Sacha Llewellyn.
Literature: Sacha Llewellyn, *Winifred Knights 1899-1947* (London: Lund Humphries in association with Dulwich Picture Gallery, 2016);
Winifred Knights 1899-1947 (exh. catalogue The Fine Art Society PLC and Liss Fine Art in Association with the British School at Rome 1995, p. 53).

The 'Marriage at Cana', started in 1922, is the principal painting produced by Knights during her time at the British School at Rome. It depicts the miracle of the water turned into wine, (related in John 2:1-12). The setting for the painting is the Borghese Gardens adjoining the British School at Rome. The setting is also reminiscent of the background devised by Piero delta Francesca for the fresco of 'The Adoration of the True Cross' in the Church of S.Francesco in Arezzo, visited by Knights prior to starting work on her own composition. The artist includes herself among the guests, along side, in the earliest studies, Arnold Mason. Tom Monnington, who did not arrive at the British School at Rome until 1923, is included in later studies at the far end of the table, in effect next to Mason. As known rivals over Knights they clearly made an ill-suited pair for a marriage feast and Mason is subsequently omitted from the final composition. The existence of numerous pencil, watercolour and oil studies demonstrate the meticulous thought and care that Knights put into the conception of this painting. In 1922 she wrote to her mother:' I have drawn 11 plates of melon, pink melon, 9 glasses of wine some empty, because they have run out, and 38 people.'

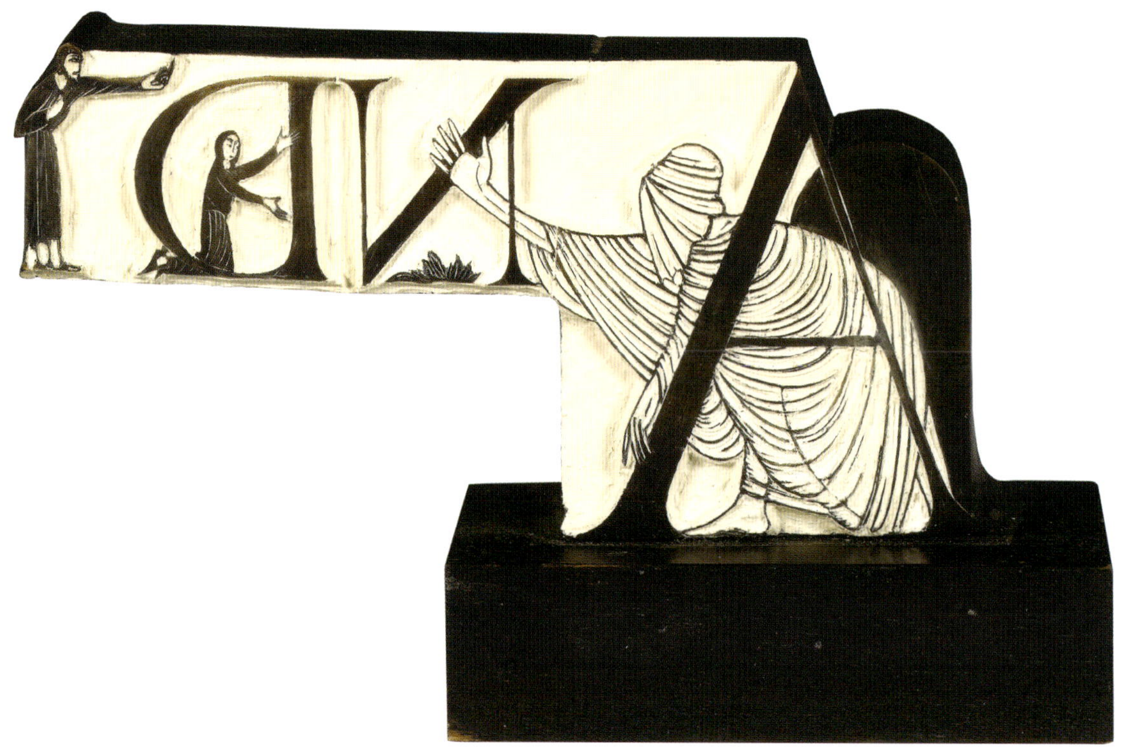

68 – Eric Gill (1882-1940), *'And'* Initial letter for *The Four Gospels,* Golden Cockerel Press, 1931, *Physick 818* on lable to the base, the original block, 4 x 7 in. (10.2 x 17 cm).

Eric Gill greatly prized his woodblocks – he bought them back from the Golden Cockerel Press, ran gesso into them, carved them into silhouettes and mounted them on pedestals as free standing objects.

The Four Gospels, designed by The Golden Cockerel Press and with engravings by Eric Gill, printed as an edition of 500, was the culminating achievement of the private press movement. Robin Gartin, in British Printmakers 1855-1955, has described it as 'being among the greatest book productions between the Wars'

Robert Gibbings, the owner of The Golden Cockerel Press, was responsible for setting the type, leaving appropriate spaces for which Gill designed the initial letters and words. Leaves curl into the space between paragraphs, swords hang down into the margin, and the symbols of the evangelists each hold up the title of their gospel. It was a marriage of image and text that recalls the best of medieval illuminated manuscripts, yet is suited perfectly to the modern age and flawless in its execution.

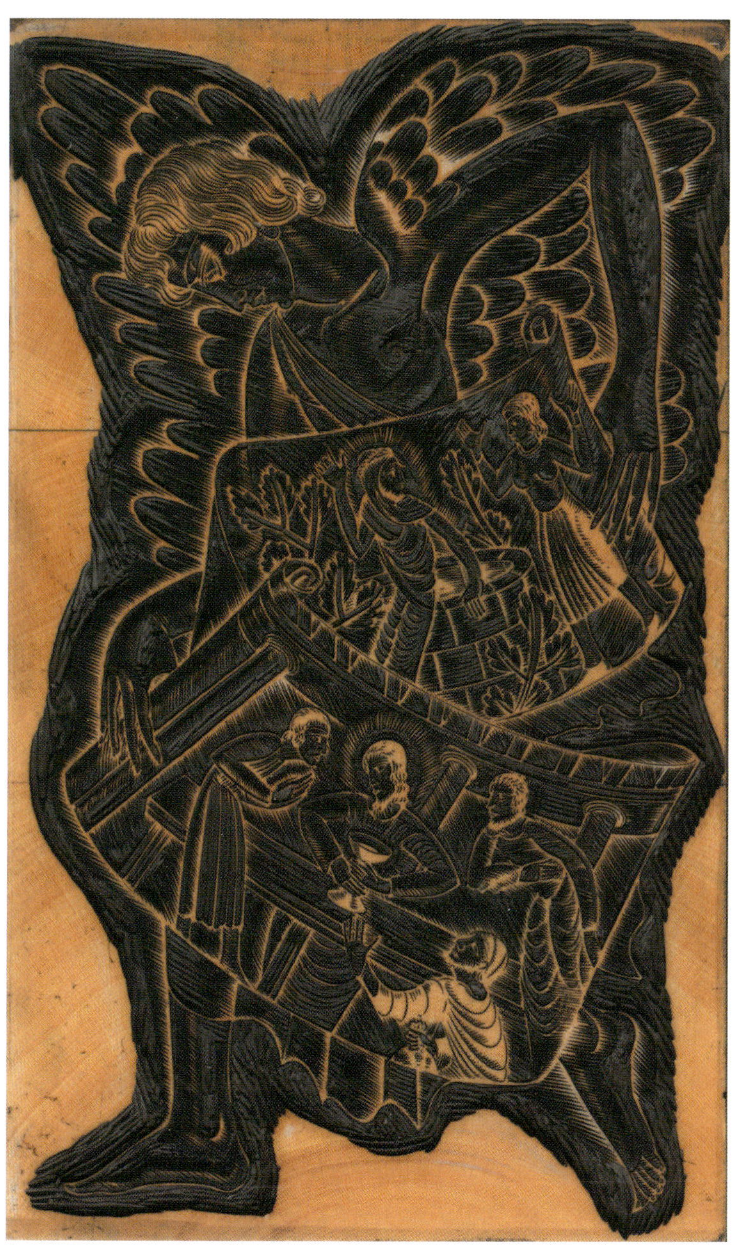

69 – **Eric Gill** (1882-1940), *Saint John, The Aldine Bible*, 1934-36, the original woodblock, 6 ½ × 4 in. (16.5 × 10 cm).

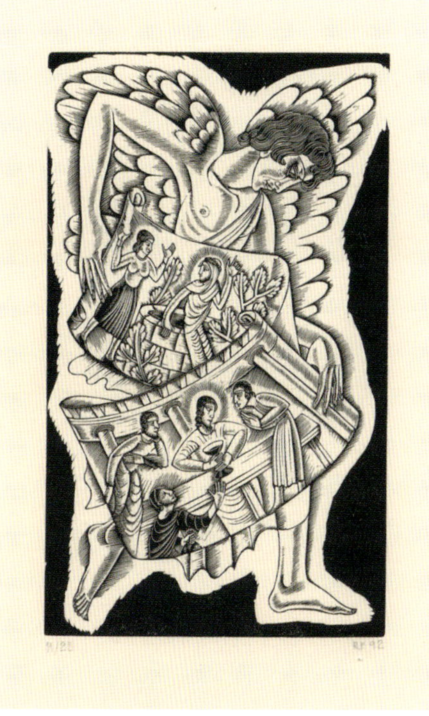

69 a – *Saint John, The Aldine Bible*, 1934-36, print pulled from the woodblock.

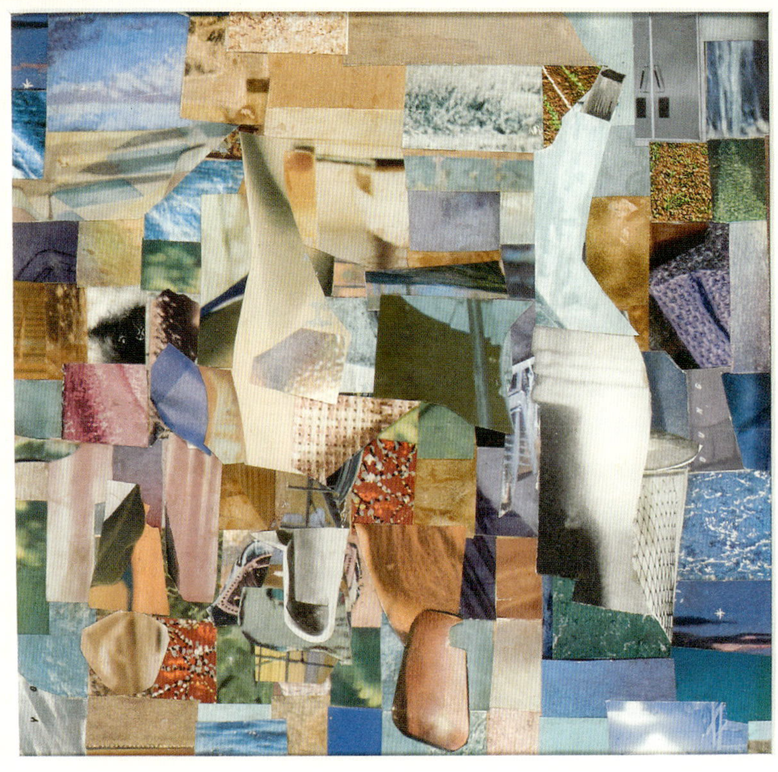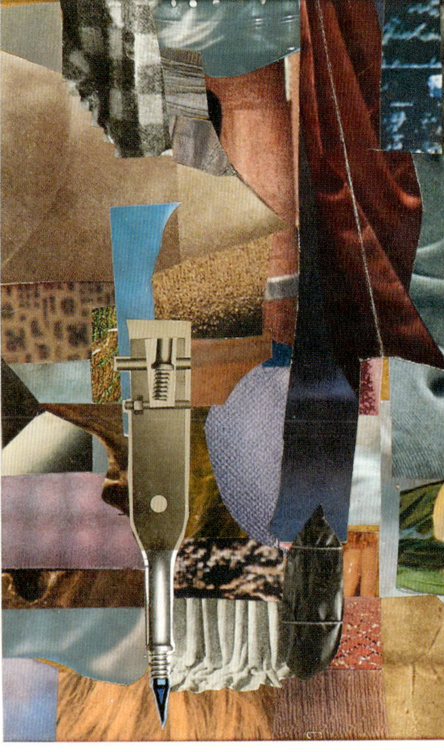

70 – Valentine Dobree (1894-1974), *The Event*, collage, triptych: 2 × 7 ¼ × 7 ½ in. (18.5 × 19.5 cm) and 1 × 7 ¼ × 11 ½ in. (18.5 × 29 cm).Exhibited: London, Claridge Gallery, Valentine Dobrée, December 1931.
Literature: Hilary Diaper, *Valentine Dobrée*, The University Gallery, Leeds, 2000, pp. 8-11.

Although the choice of a triptych format traditionally has a religious connotation, it is unclear to what the 'Event' refers – it is however typical of Dobree's preference for enigmatic subjects.

The use of collage as fine rather than decorative art was one of the most significant innovations of the twentieth century and Dobrée was one of its most talented practitioners in Britain during the late 1920s and early 1930s.

Most of the thirty-four works shown in her pivotal Claridge Gallery show of 1931 remain untraced. The art critic of *The Times* reviewed this work in the following terms:

'*Her designs, mostly cut out of patterned wallpapers, are definitely and very intelligently "cubist". Indeed the first response to them is the feeling that here at last is the proper application of an artistic formula that is never quite satisfactory in painting. The chief attraction is in colour, Mrs Dobree producing enchanting effects in the schemes of grey-blue and buff. There is a lively invention in the designs, and they are carried out with the most subtle logic in tone relation and a happy use of textures.*' (9 Dec. 1931).

Dobree was much praised by her friend and fellow artist Dora Carrington: "She has given so much of herself to the world, lived so fiercely it is splendid..." The influential Modernist art critic Herbert Read, whose collection included work by Dobrée, was also amongst her admirers.

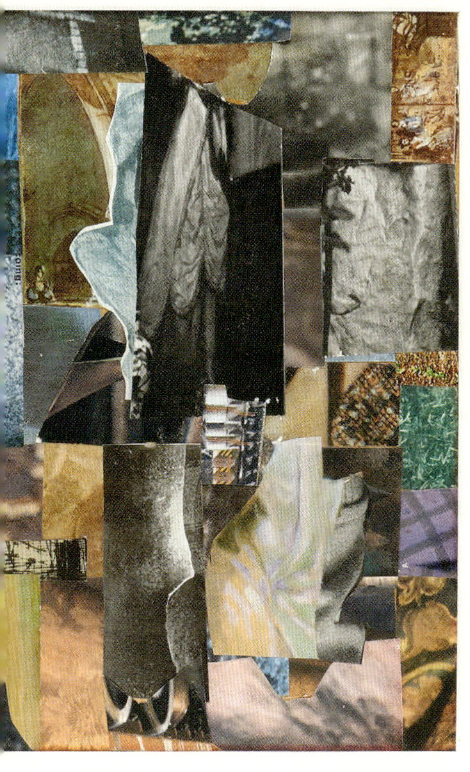 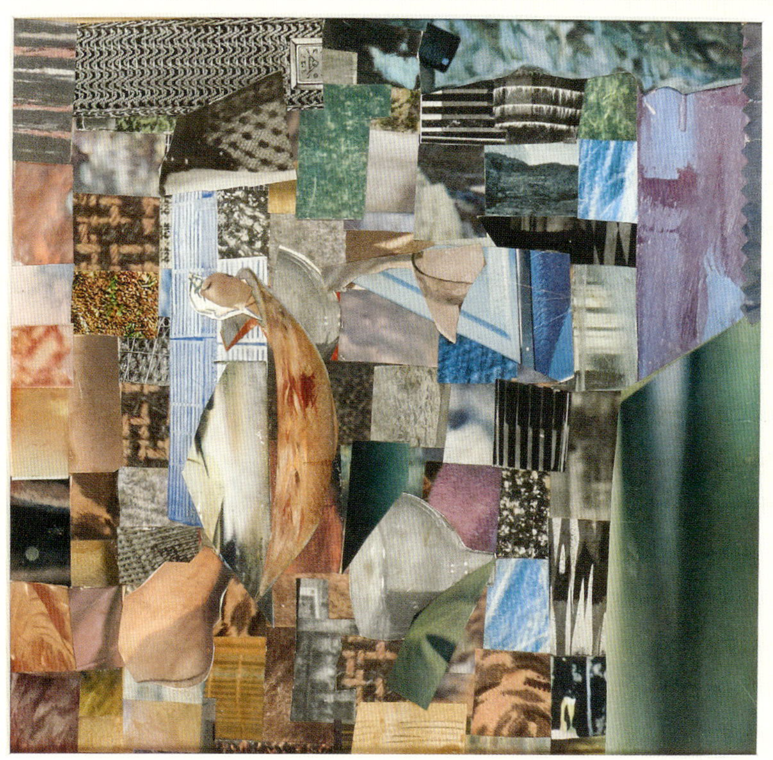

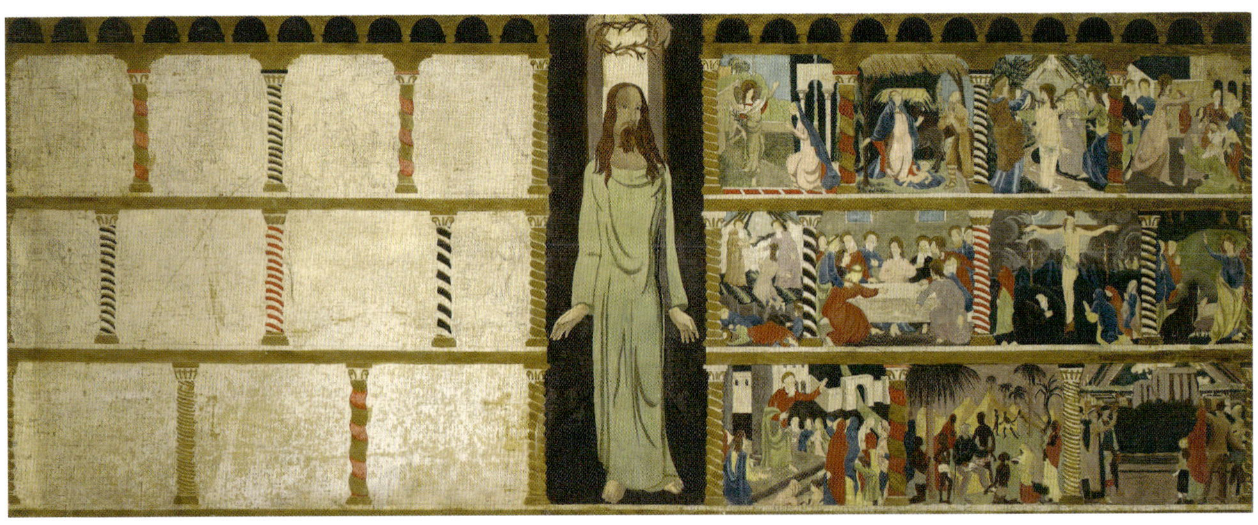

71 – Mary Adshead (1904-1995),
Scenes from the Life of Christ, Teaching the Gospel, mid 1920s,
oil on canvas, 20 × 51 in. (51 × 130 cm).

This unfinished reredos is likely to date to the period in which Adshead produced her first mural, *The Joys of the Country*, Shadwell (1924), painted in collaboration with her fellow Slade student Rex Whistler. The scenes from the Life of Christ follow a conventional iconography until the last two panels which include a scene with a missionary reading the scriptures in Africa and figures in contemporary dress apparently admiring a Neo-Classical building.

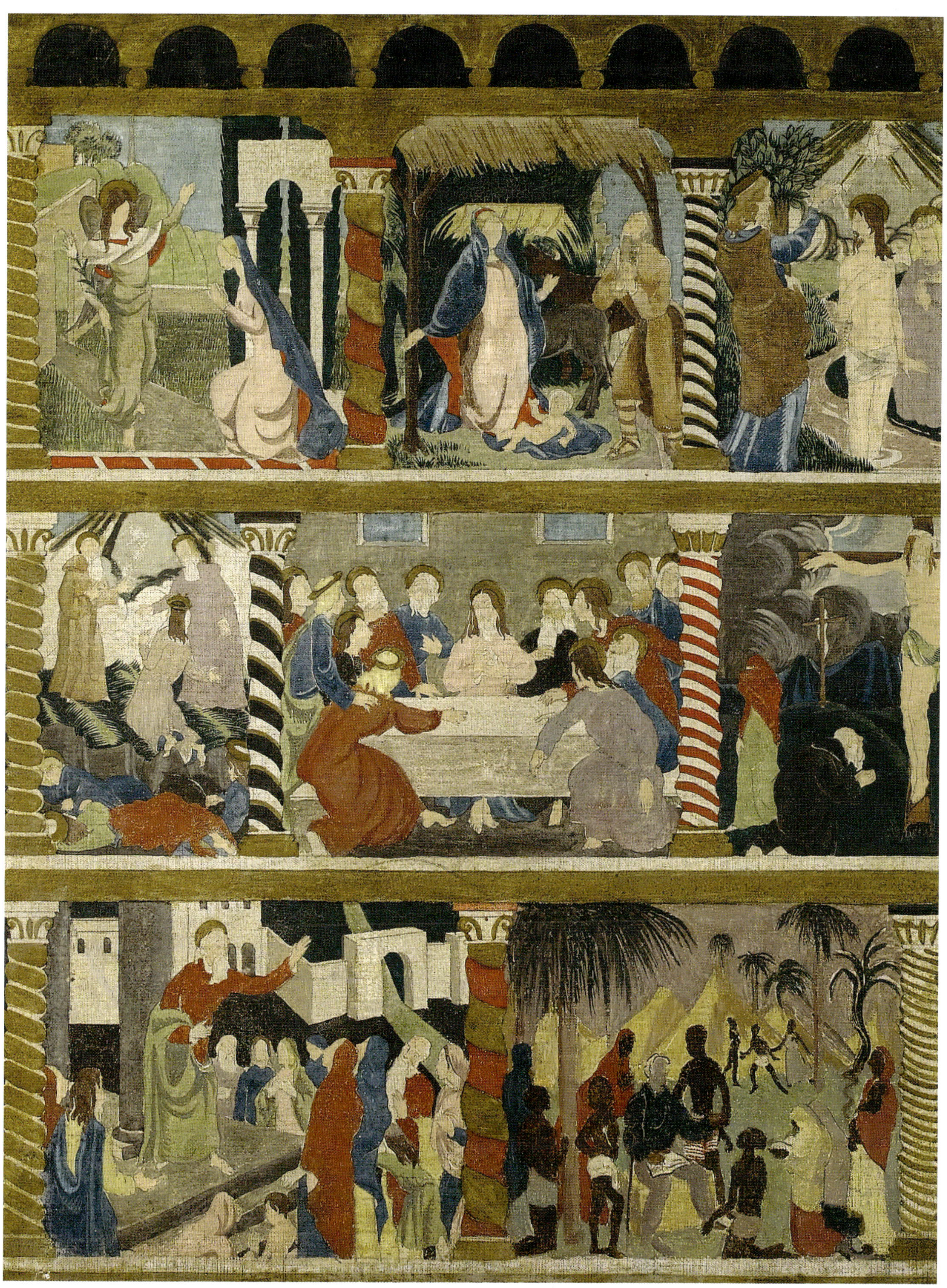

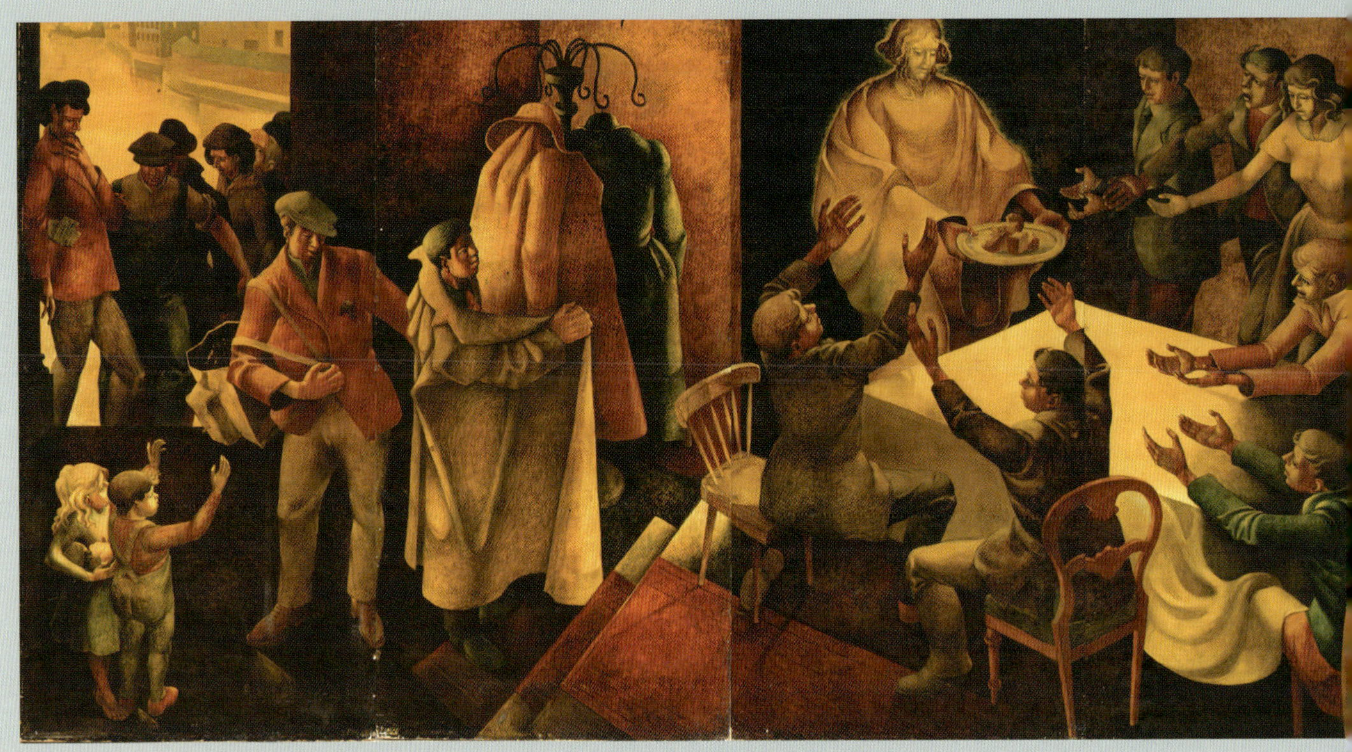

72 – Fyffe Christie (1918-1979), *Christ Feeding the People*, 1951, signed and dated,
oil on board, 8 panels, 96 × 384 in. (243.8 × 975.2 cm).
Literature: British Murals and Decorative Painting 1920-1960, Sansom & Co, 2013, pp 88-89.
Exhibited: St Mungo Museum of Religious Life and Art 1999.

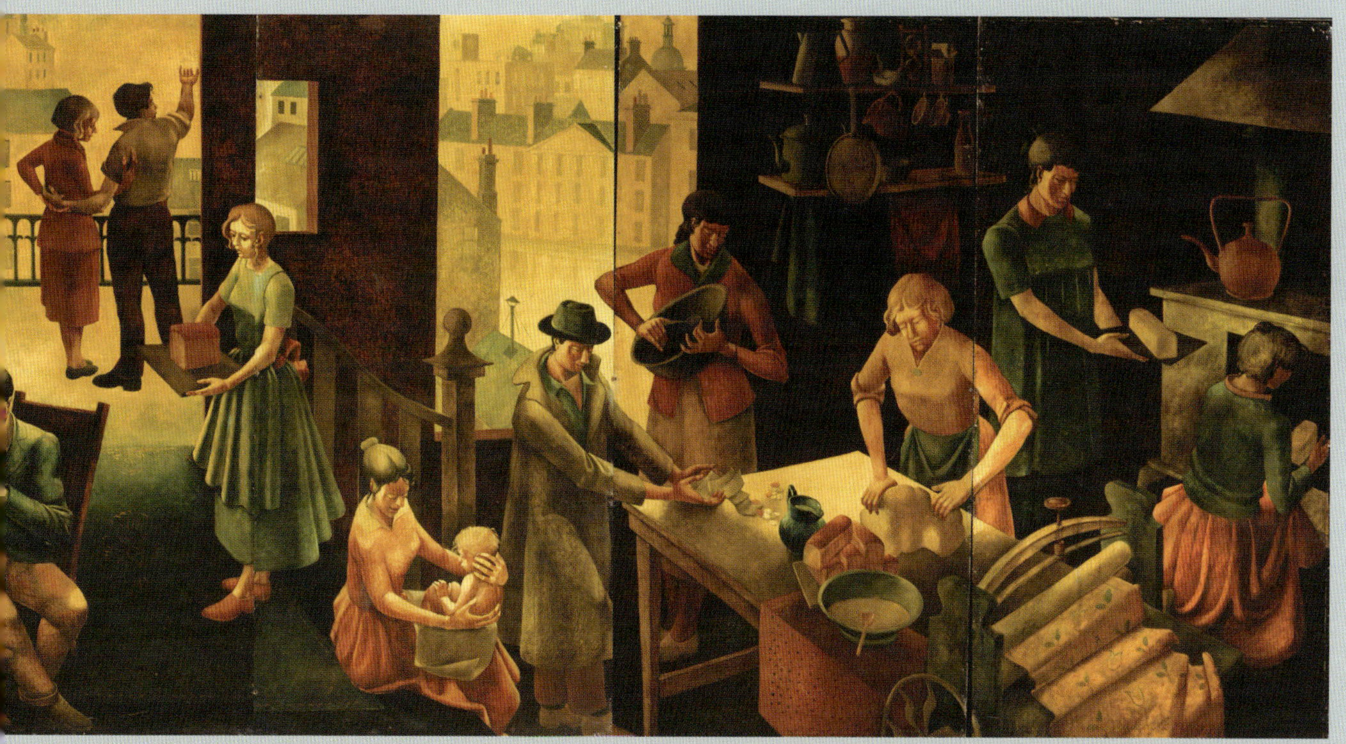

In the post-diploma year of 1950-1 Christie painted the mural of *Christ Feeding the People* for the Iona Community. The work was commissioned by the dynamic founder and leader of the community the Reverend George MacLeod who had been responsible for the reconstruction of Iona Abbey on the Island of Iona off Scotland's west coast. The 35 foot long mural painted on eight panels covered the walls of the community centre cafe on Clyde Street, Glasgow which was open to the public as a community centre and to provide cheap and nutritious food to visitors and the city's homeless. Christie depicted the huge scene of an interior with ordinary folk, men returning from work and women baking and bathing children, while the figure of Jesus was placed at the centre of the activity and the act of the breaking of bread placed at the heart of community life. The work was intended to be in accord with the community's declared aim of "rebuilding the common life" and it arguably achieved this by depicting ordinary community life in a contemporary Glasgow setting. Robert Radford wrote "The allegorical references to the labour of men and women and to community and service are, in essence, biblical but also universal, expressing the potential for transcendence of normality which this work shares with Spencer's Memorial Chapel at Burghclere. The mural became familiar to the generations of Glaswegians who frequented the centre. Shortly after completion of the work the newspaper The Glasgow Herald ran an article on mural art in Scotland and the work of the muralists Walter Pritchard, William Crosbie and Christie, the "powerful simplicity" of Christie's Iona Community mural drawing particular praise. Christie preferred to paint directly onto the wall but the Iona Community specified that the commission was completed on panels. Fortunately this allowed the work to be saved following the closure and demolition of the centre in the late 1970s.

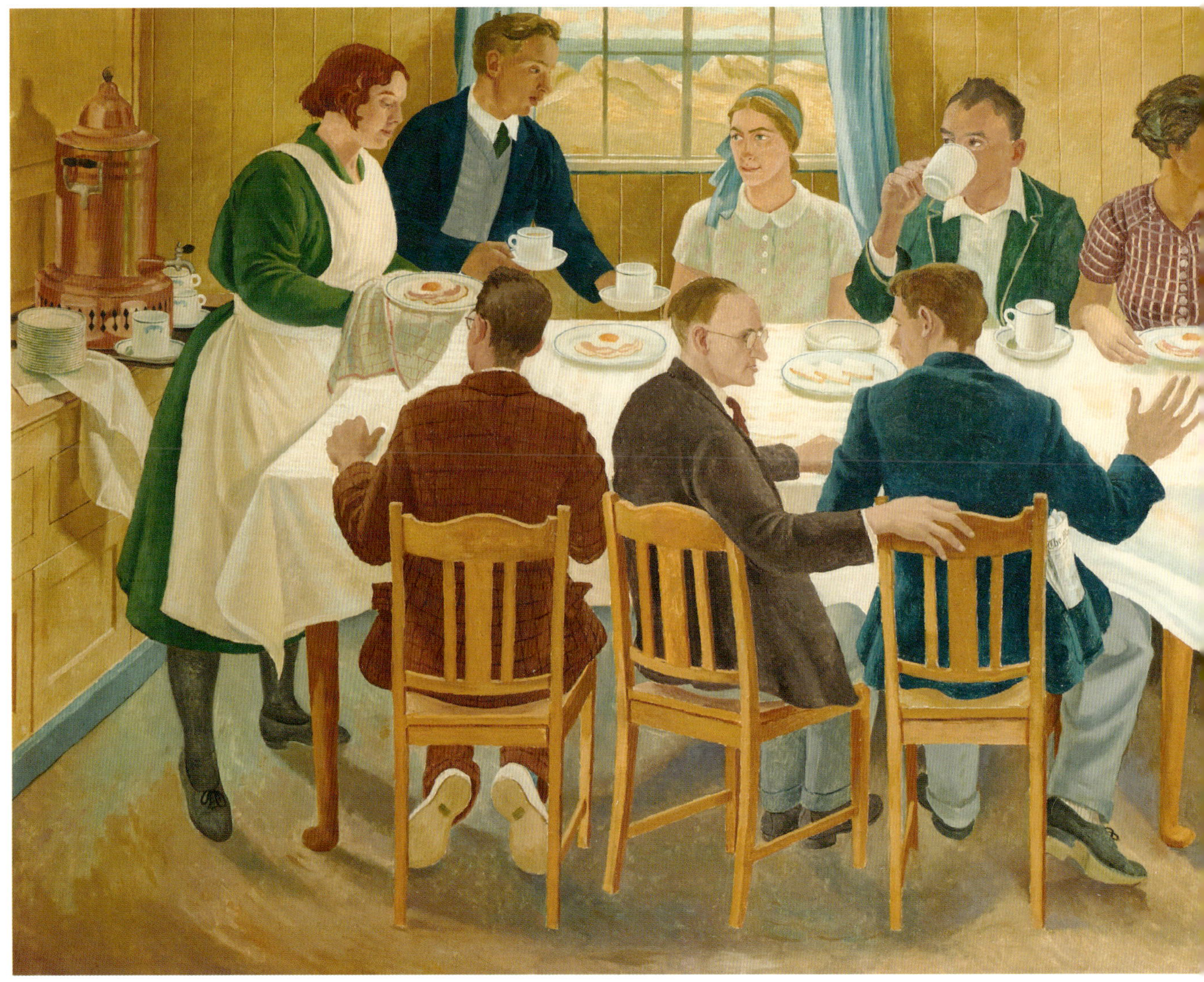

73 – Robert Baker (1909-1992), *Breakfast at Harlech College* (otherwise known as *Eggs & Bacon*), c.1935,
oil on board, 47 x 119 in. (119.4 x 302 cm).
Provenance: Coleg Harlech, Wern Fawr; Private collection.

Robert Baker received a commission to produce murals for Coleg Harlech in the mid 1930s, at the instigation of the powerful political insider Dr. Thomas Jones. As a Workers Educational Association, the College was the largest provider of adult community learning in Wales. The scheme comprised a series of panels showing everyday life at the College together with a cycle of murals in the student common room of landscapes with portraits of Welsh 'types'. The largest mural was a modern rendition of *The Last Supper, Breakfast at Harlech College*. The setting for this was the college canteen, with views of the Cambrian coast, glimpsed through the windows behind. Although all the figures have yet to be identified it is likely that Baker included a self portrait, and cast fellow students in the guise of Christ and his disciples. The picture is bursting with symbolism: the Crucifixion is alluded to by the glazing bars of the window behind Christ, (the figure who offers the bread to Judas). The three greengages on the plate in front of him might also be read as a sign of the Trinity. The bread signifies the communion. The cloth the shroud. Judas refuses to look Jesus in the eye, but rather averts his gaze. Judas has his knife and fork the wrong way round – a traditional reference to the fact that he is left handed (*sinister*). In common with Christ he is the only character to have buttons on his cuffs but to Christ's trinity of three he only has two. Jesus sits next to Peter on his left and John on his right. John was

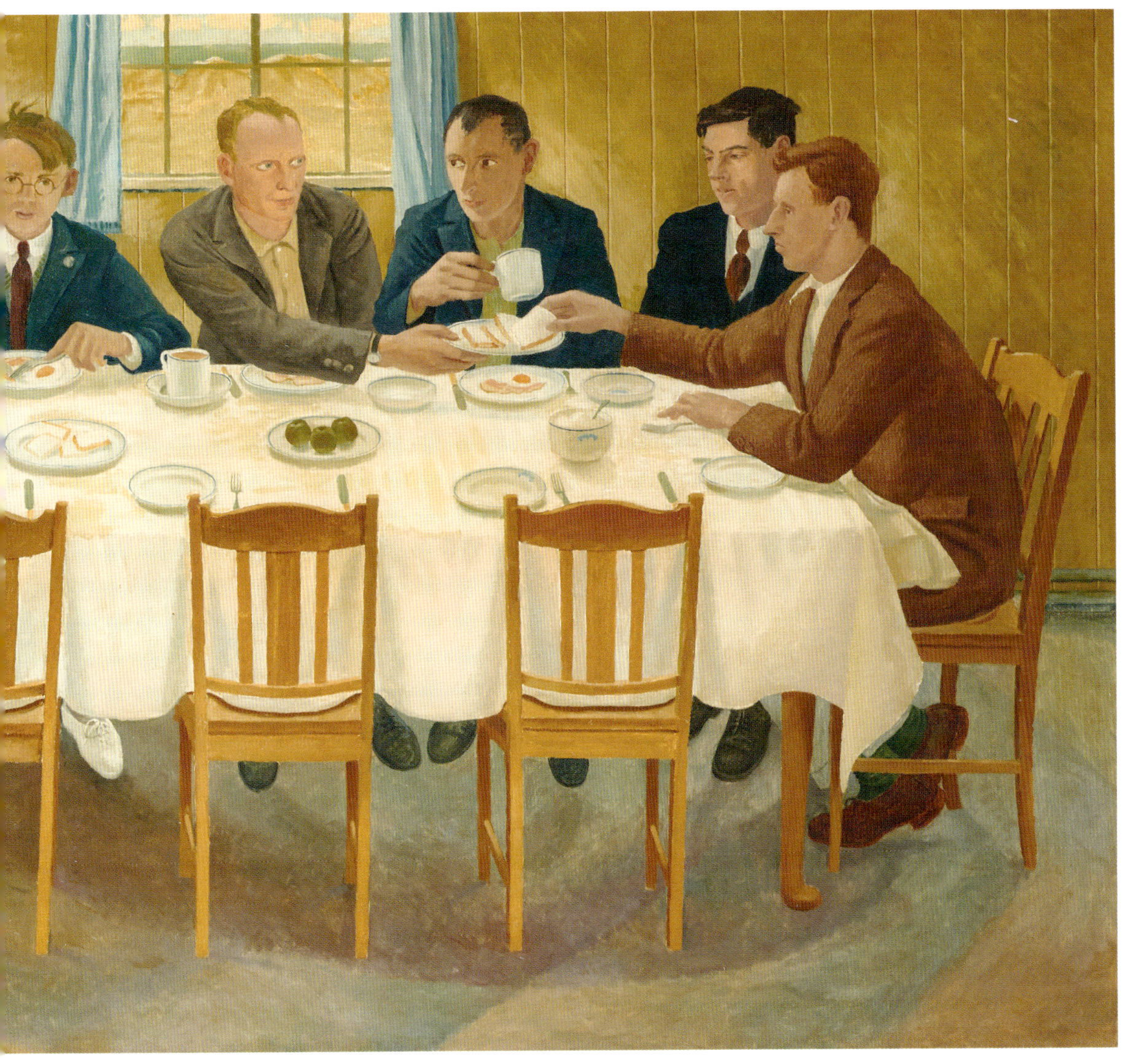

a favourite of Jesus, younger than the other disciples and considered naive (qualities suggested by his boyish looks). Traditionally women were not at the Last Supper – in this painting the Virgin wears blue and a headscarf, and Mary Magdeline is seated next to John. Three empty chairs invite the spectator to fill the places of the three missing (male) disciples. The older figure, turning and gesturing is Thomas (the doubter).

The composition makes interesting comparison with other contemporary paintings which might have been a source of inspiration for Baker – Lotte Laserstein's (1898-1993) *Abend über Potsdam*, 1930, Nationalgalerie, Staatliche Museen zu Berlin and *The Last Supper* by Mark Lancelot Symons (1887-1935), c. 1933, (Reading Art Gallery).

74 – Francis Spear (1902-1979),
Christ Derided, Nov 1942, 1942, signed with monogram and dated,
inscribed: *All they that see me laugh me to scorn, I was derision to all my people, Hail King of the Jews*,
black ink and gouache on paper, collage, 28 × 18 ½ in. (71 × 47 cm).
Provenance: Simon Spear, the artist's son.
Exhibited: *WW2 – War Pictures by British Artists*, Morley College London, 28 October -23 November 2016, cat 134.
Literature: *WW2 – War Pictures by British Artists*, Edited by Sacha Llewellyn & Paul Liss, July 2016, cat 134, page 177.

During the war Spear ceased teaching at the RCA (which was evacuated to Ambleside in 1940) and served for three years as a fire-fighter in Shepherds Bush. This wartime period was not a completely redundant time for Spear from a professional point of view – he assisted on the removal, for protection, of windows at Canterbury Cathedral. He also experimented with new designs which were more modern in feel, a change that he hoped would 'give the feeling of the subject with the greatest simplicity and with the elimination of all details.' and devised his distinctive monogram of an interlocking S with a sideways F. When the War ended Spear gained so many commissions – to replace stained glass windows destroyed during the Blitz.- that by 1947 he was employing four assistants.

Francis Spear is an important figure in twentieth century English stained glass. His working career covers 50 years, from 1922 when he began working with Martin Travers, to 1972, when he ceased teaching at Reigate School of Art. During his career, he designed windows for over 130 locations; and a short list of notable designs include his earliest window, at Warwick School (1925), St. Olave's in the City (1929), Snaith (1936), Beckenham (1948), Canterbury (1949), Glasgow Cathedral (1951, 1953, 1958), Highbury (1955), Westgate (1960) and Penarth (1962).

The collection of the Prints and Drawings department of the Victoria & Albert Museum own all of the surviving cartoons for the 300 extant windows he produced over his fifty year long career.

TO SCORN
LAUGH ME
ALL THEY THAT SEE ME
NOV
I WAS
DERISION
TO ALL MY PEOPLE
HAIL, KING OF THE JEWS
1942

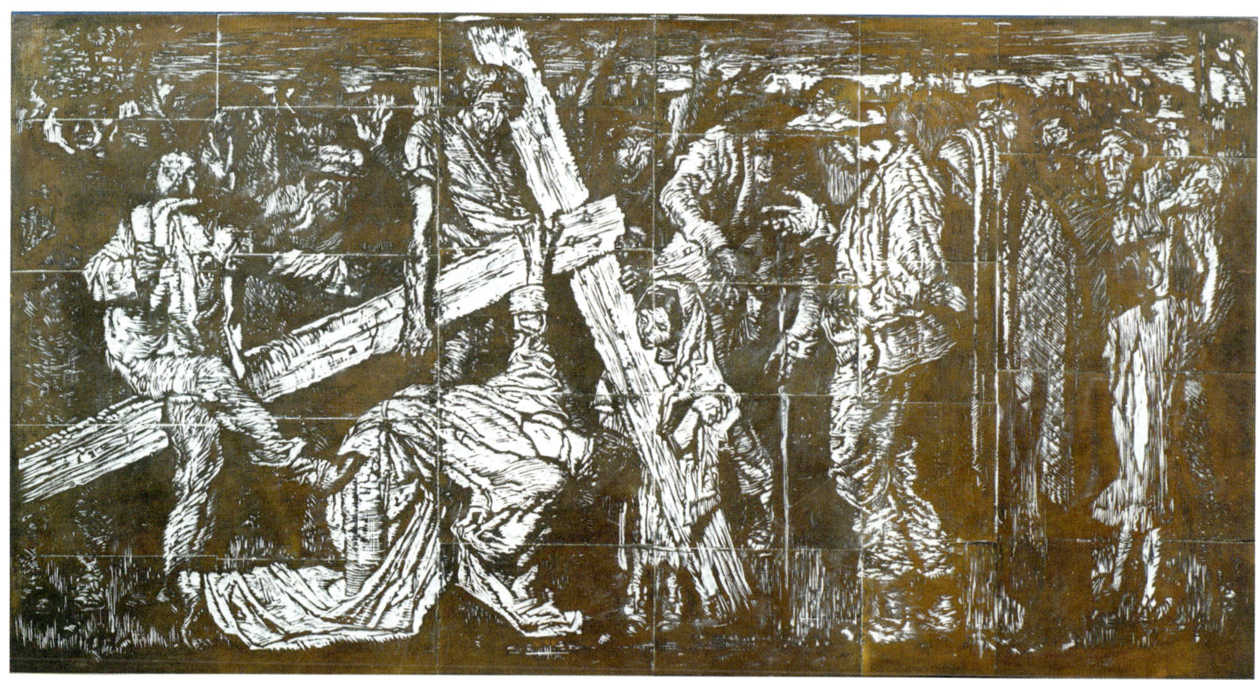

75 – **Frank Brangwyn** (1867-1967), *Jesus Falls Below the Cross*, 1916, original woodblock, 7 ¾ × 15 ¼ in. (19.7 × 38.7 cm).
Literature: Cat. 12, *Frank Brangwyn, Stations of the Cross*, Liss Fine Art 2015, page 24-25.

Also known as *Via Dolorosa No 1*, this was not one of a series of Stations of the Cross, but a stand alone work that may have been inspired by Brangwyn's sadness at the devastation that his native Belgium suffered during World War One. The on-lookers wear contemporary clothes.

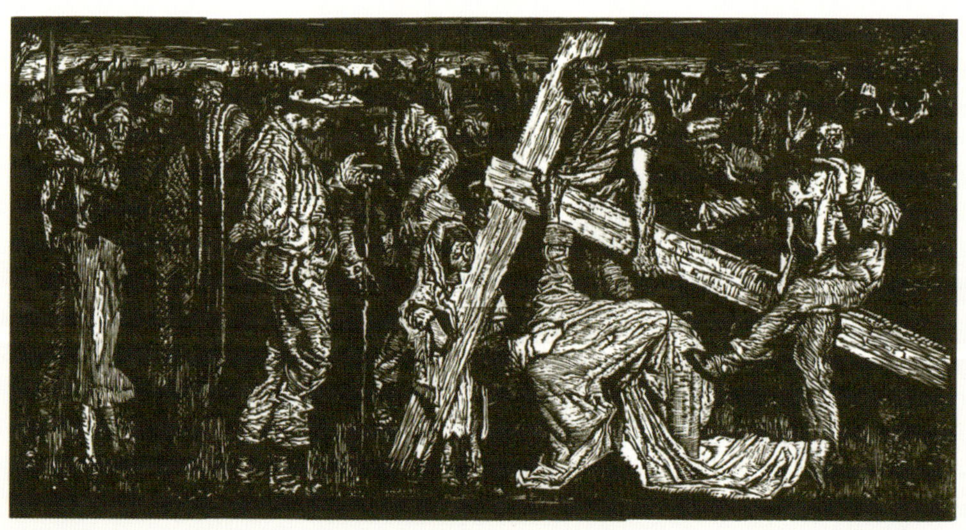

75 a – **Frank Brangwyn** (1867-1967), *Jesus Falls Below the Cross*, 1916, wood engraving.

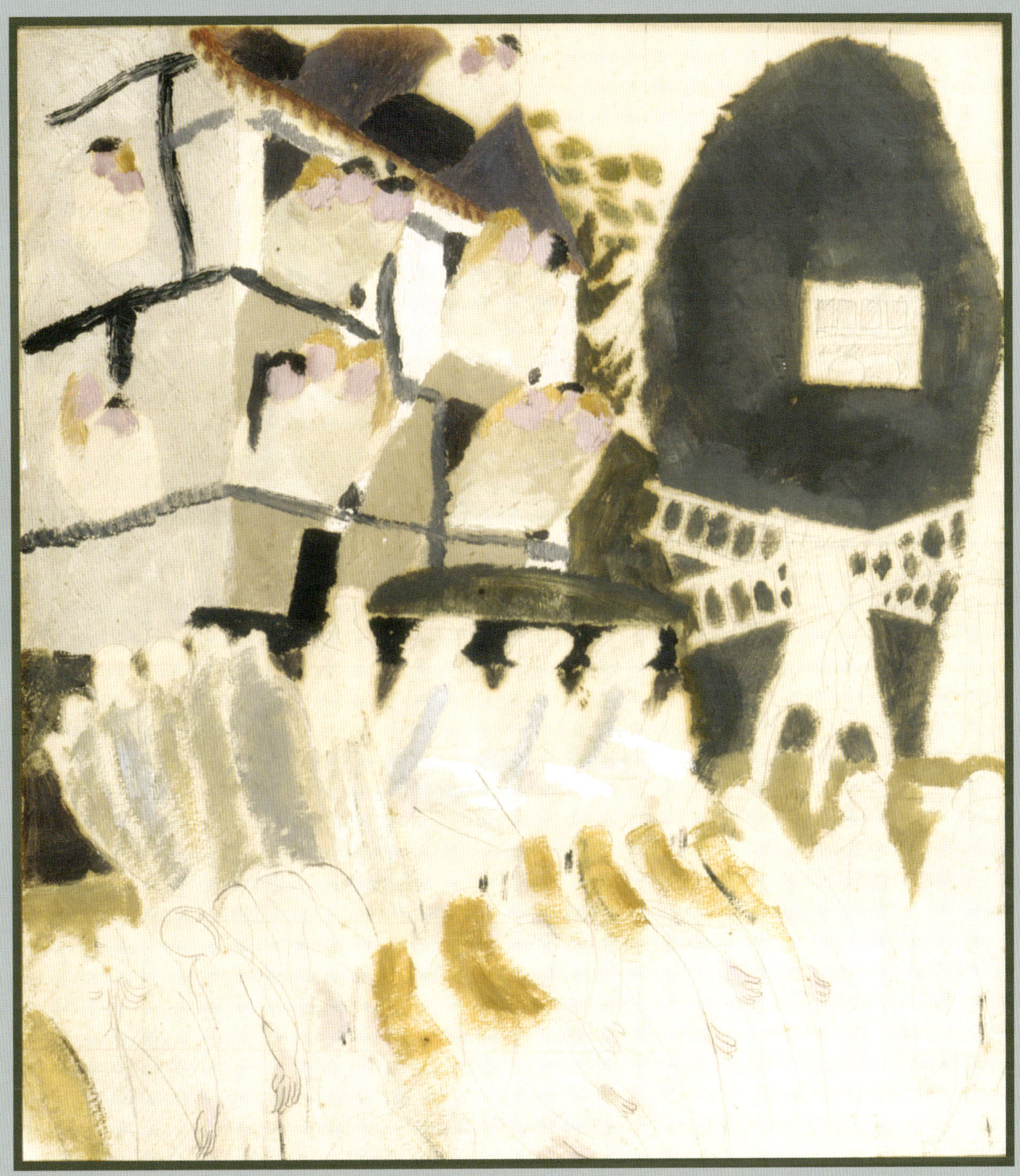

76 – Stanley Spencer (1891-1959), Study for *Christ Carrying the Cross*, 1920, oil and pencil on paper; 14½ x 13 in. (37 x 33 cm).
Provenance: Sir Hugh Walpole; Christie's 1947; Christie's 1996. Collection Stanley Spencer Gallery, acquired from Liss Llewellyn.

This is one of the final studies for the painting *Christ Carrying the Cross*, purchased by the Contemporary Art Society for the Tate collection in 1921. The events depicted were inspired by Spencer's memories of Cookham in childhood, when he watched the people pass by in the High Street on Sundays and in the evenings. He used the street as the setting of several of his religious paintings. In this one, the house shown was the artist's home, Fernlea, and the workmen carrying ladders are passing the Nest, the ivy-clad home of his grandmother. Spencer commented that he had made several drawing attempts of the cross and disciples ranged somewhat procession-wise either side of it, some of the soldiers helping in the carrying of the cross, some escorting them. Spencer was a devout Christian and believed God resided in all things and the miraculous could be found in everyday events.

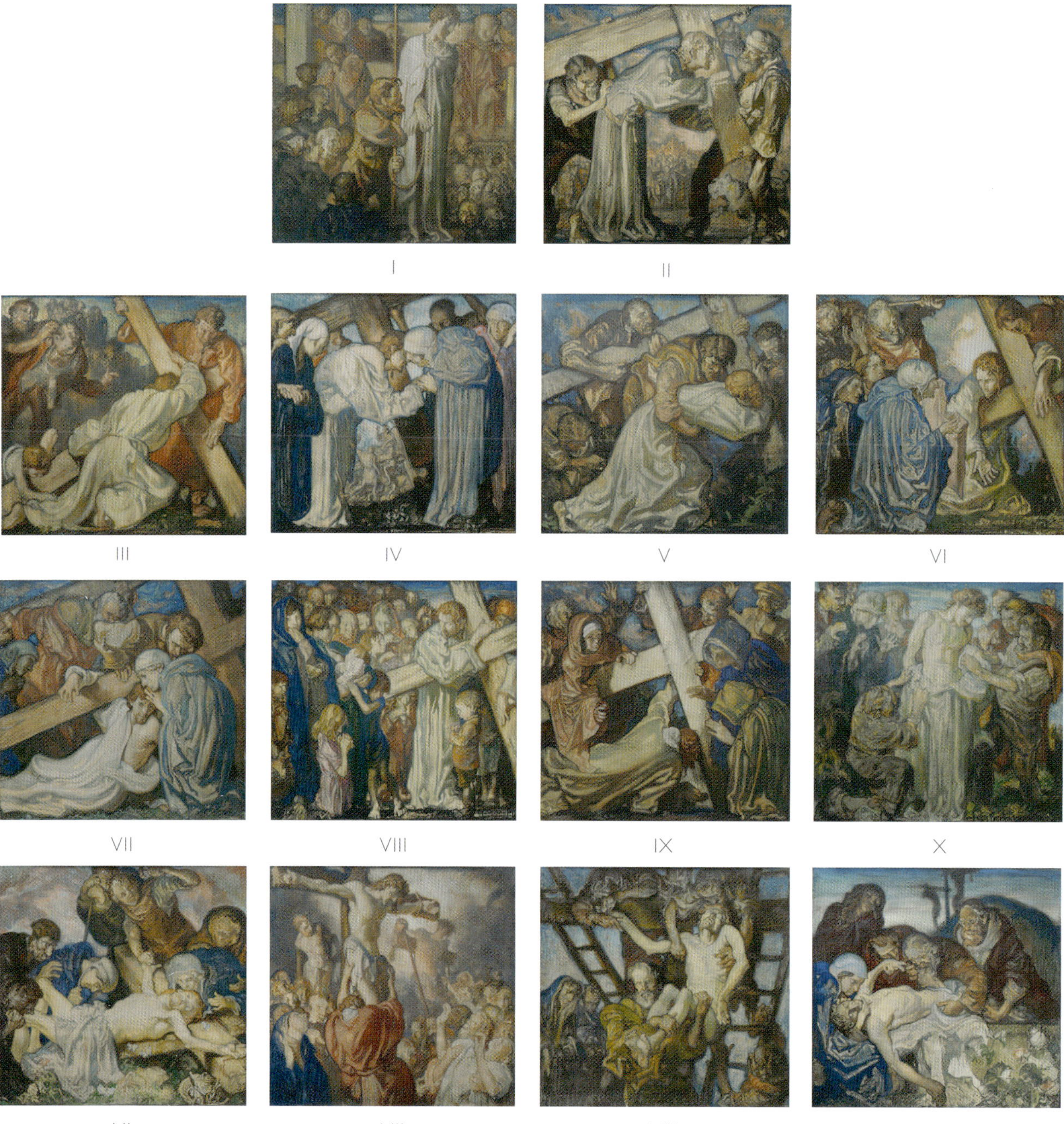

I   II

III   IV   V   VI

VII   VIII   IX   X

XI   XII   XIII   XIV

77 – Frank Brangwyn (1867-1956), *Stations of the Cross*, 1934-35,
oil over lithograph, laid on board, 33 ½ × 35 ½ in. (85 × 90.5 cm).

In the early 1930s Frank Brangwyn told William de Belleroche that he had been 'thinking of making a set of the *Stations of the Cross* in lithography. A subject I've had at the back of my mind all my life. . . . I've always wanted to do this, and have thought about it for years.' He thought that lithography was a 'medium which would suit the work and lend itself to dramatic treatment – would make people realise the great tragedy – stir up their religious beliefs, their emotions'. Brangwyn began the series in 1934, drawing his designs on tracing paper. The drawings were then transferred to zinc lithographic plates by rubbing the back of the paper with red conté and tracing the outline of the image. Brangwyn worked on the zinc plates using a combination of lithographic chalk and etching tools, employing a variety of different methods to gain the exact effect and tonality he required.

The series was printed in February 1935. Appreciating that *The Stations of the Cross* would be placed on damp church walls, and having always been keen on innovatory techniques, Brangwyn chose to print two sets on sycamore which are now in the Chapter-Hall of the Benedictine Abbey of St André, Zevenkerken, Bruges and in the Chapel of the Jesuit College, Campion Hall, Oxford where they form an integral part of the wood panelling. A further 16 sets were printed on paper and in 1935 the series was reproduced in a smaller format in *The Way of the Cross. An Interpretation by Frank Brangwyn RA*, with a commentary by Gilbert Keith Chesterton, who termed Brangwyn 'one of the most masculine of modern men of genius'. As far as is known only one of the 16 lithographic sets was coloured and this was presented to St Michael's Abbey, Farnborough in the 1950s, de-accessioned in 2012.

The *Stations of the Cross* follow the tradition of the Flemish painters with whose work Brangwyn would have been familiar having been born in Bruges. e clothing is contemporary which gives the work immediacy, suggesting that the tragedy of the Calvary is never-ending. One is drawn into the story by the strength and proximity of the characters – the viewer is made to 'feel the tragedy as if he were an eye-witness'. As Chesterton points out, 'every face is different; and every face is vigorous, with an ugly energy that is more attractive than vulgar beauty'. The man holding the cross in the 5th Station has almost simian features, the praying girl and toddler in the 8th catch our heart-strings, Christ's mother in the 14th is composed and we admire her restrained pain whilst in the 13th Station Brangwyn himself experiences the weight and enormity of what has occurred. In direct contrast to the bustling crowd is the pale, spiritual, enigmatic figure of Christ, who, as Chesterton points out, is thereby isolated, 'it does really make the central gure distinguished, in the exact sense of distinct'.

Libby Horner

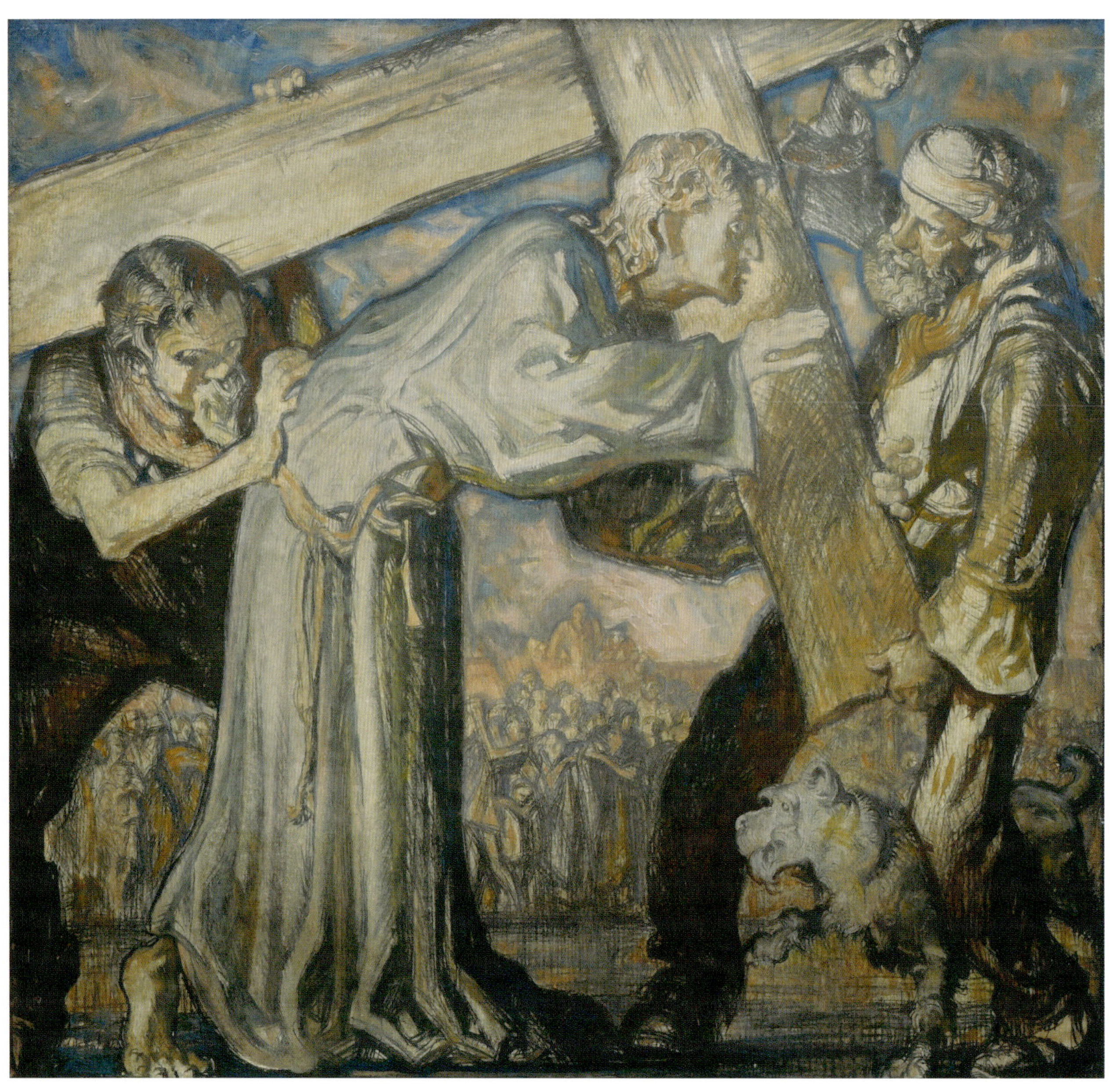

Frank Brangwyn (1867-1956), The 2nd Station: *Jesus Carries His Cross*, oil over lithograph, laid on board, 33 × 35 in. (85 × 90.5 cm).

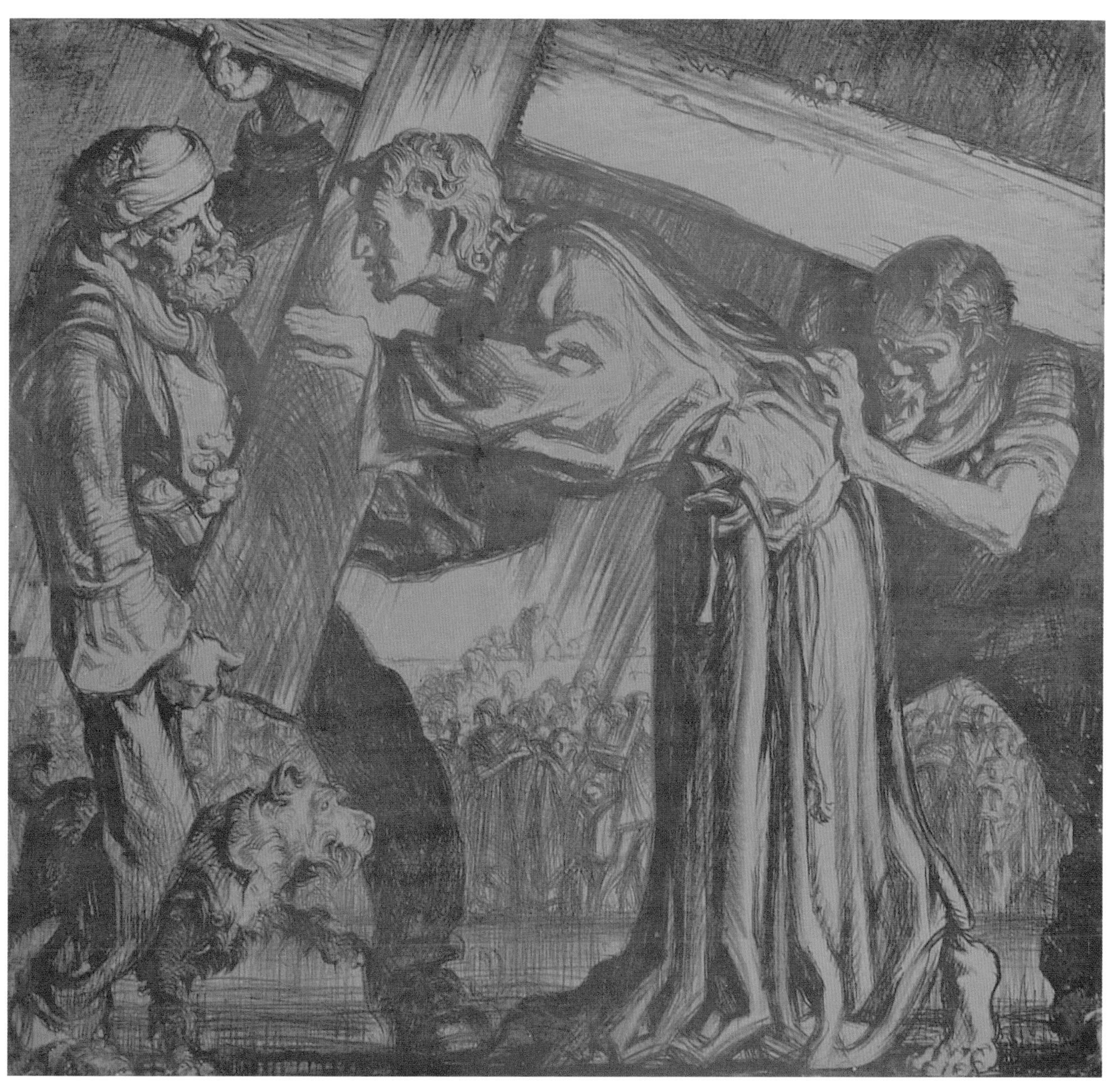

78 – **Frank Brangwyn** (1867-1956), *The 2nd Station: Jesus Carries His Cross*, 1934-35, signed with monogram, original zinc lithographic plate, 30 × 32 in. (76.2 × 81.3 cm)

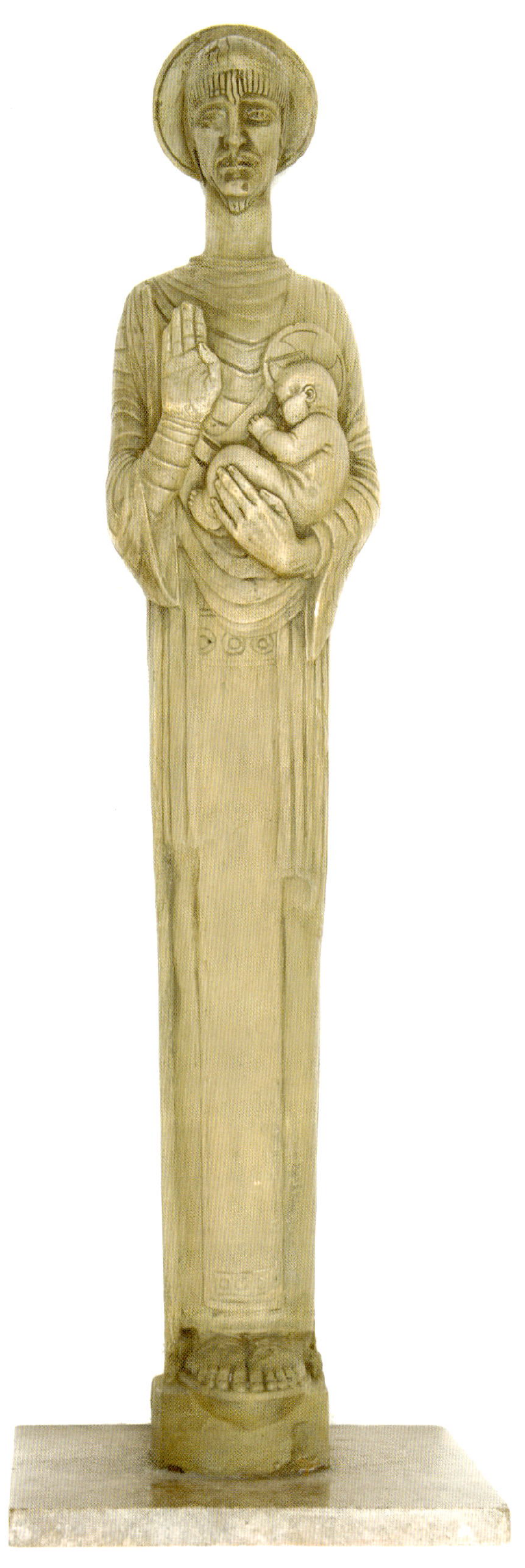

79 – James Woodford (1893–1976), *Infant Christ*, original patinated plaster, height: 12 in. (31 cm).
Provenance: Moore-Gwyn Fine Art.

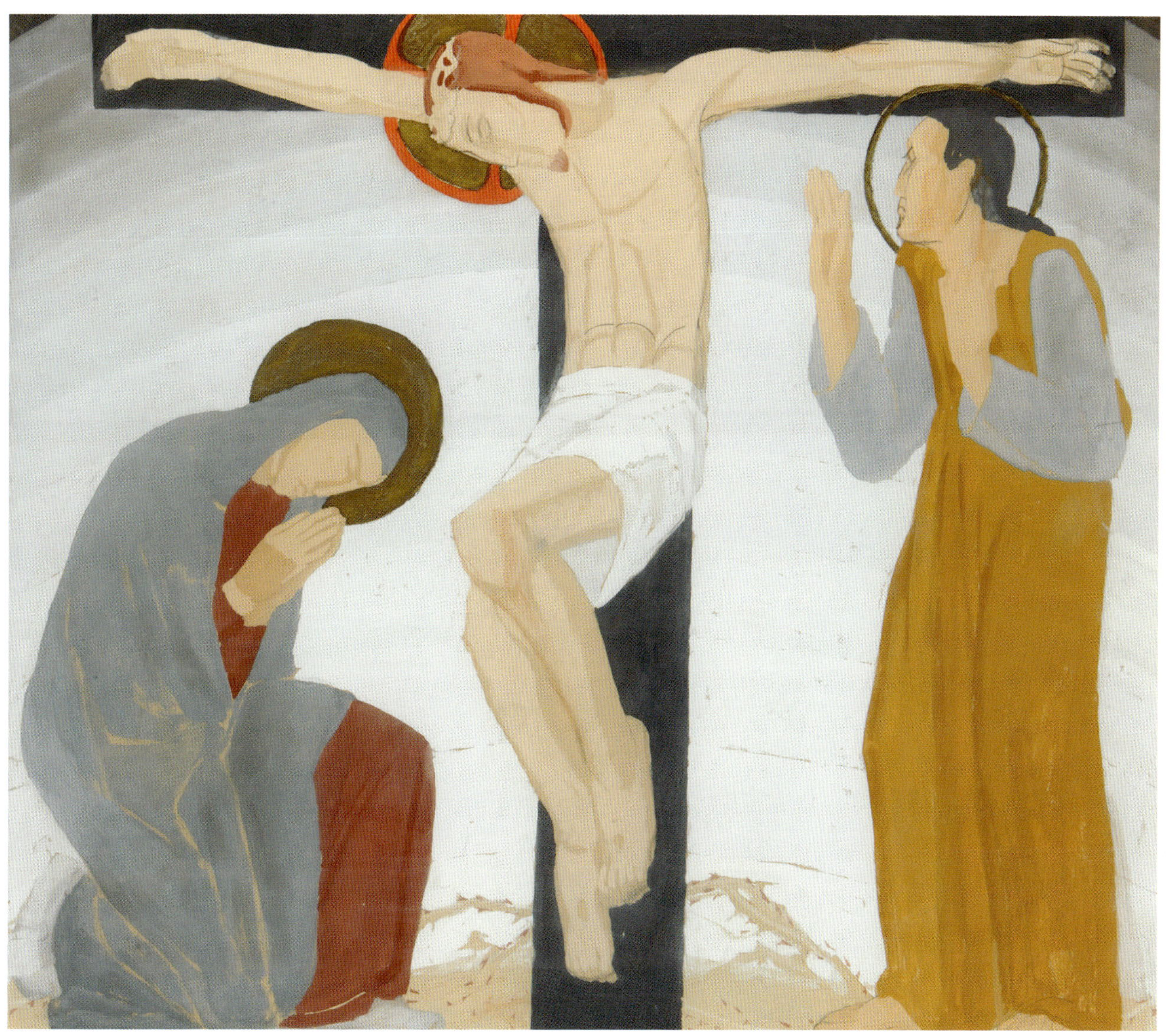

80 – Geoffrey Houghton Brown (1903-1993), *Crucifixion*, gouache on paper, 23 × 26 ¾ in. (58.4 × 68 cm).

Having trained in Paris, with Maurice Denis, in London, at the Slade School of Fine Art, and in Rome, in 1924 Geoffrey Houghton Brown became a Roman Catholic and, from then on, religion strongly influenced his artistic output. He became a member of the Guild of Catholic Artists and wrote several articles for its journal, *Art Notes*. In 1945, he helped established a Church Decorators' Society for the development of sacred art. Houghton Brown's style was inspired by Picasso, Byzantine art and contemporary Italian painting. He was a friend of the artist Roy de Maistre, Father Martin D'Arcy, and Oliver Messel.

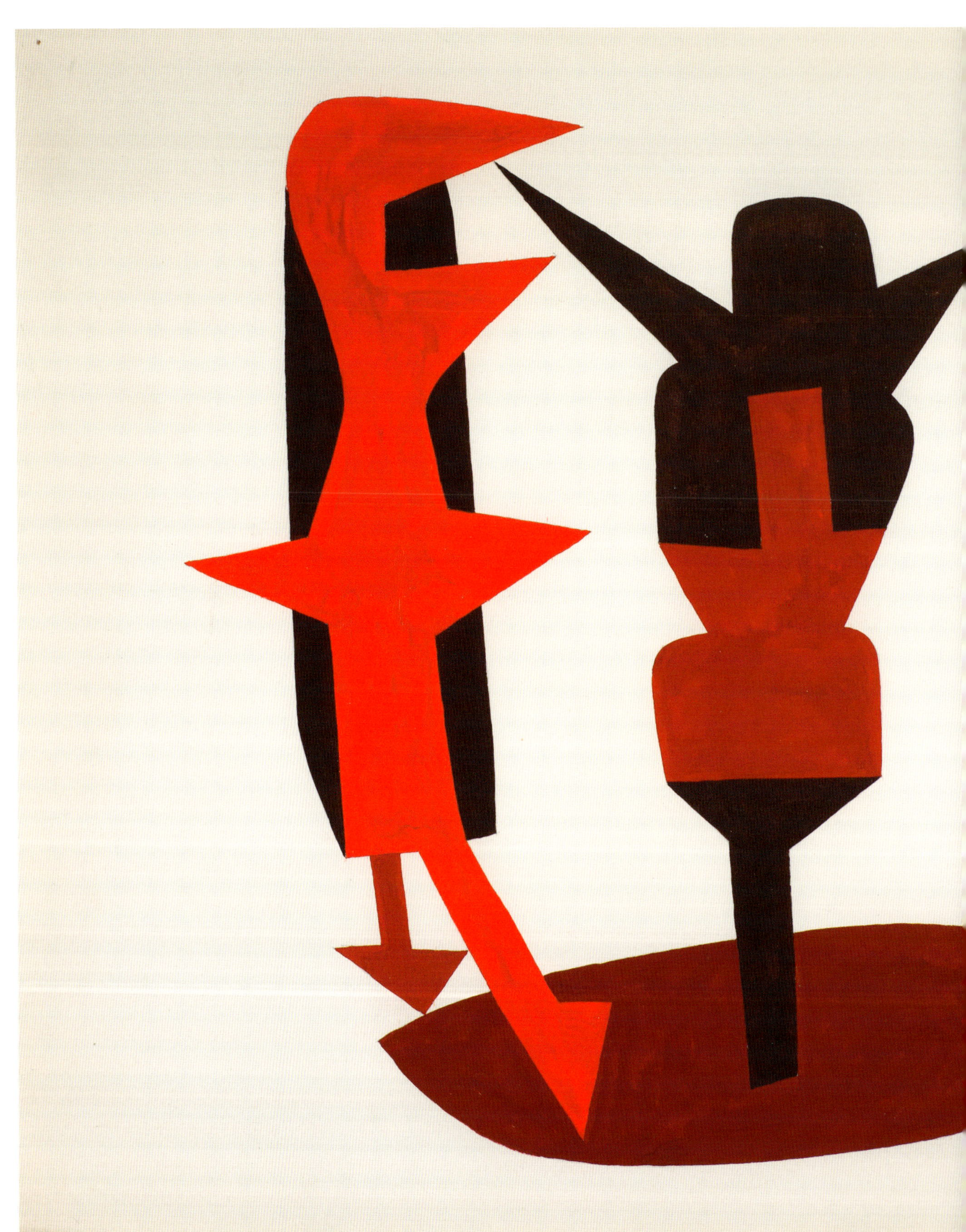

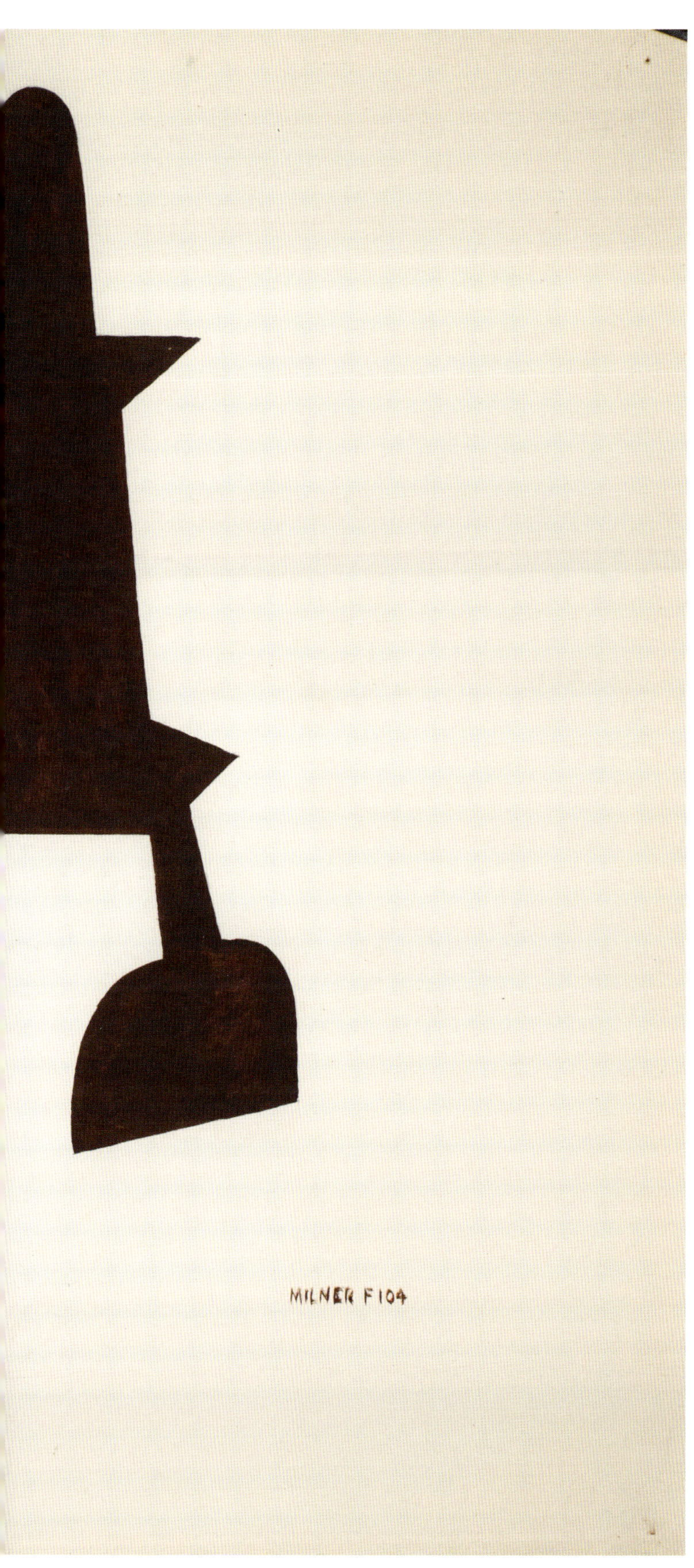

81 – Allan Milner (1910-1984), *F 104*, 1967,
gouache, 15 ¼ x 21 in. (38.4 x 53.3 cm).
Provenance: Private collection.

Milner exhibited in mixed exhibitions at the Mayor Gallery,
Redfern Gallery and Gimpel Fils and had solo shows at
E.I.T Mesens London Gallery (1949) and Woodstock
Gallery (1967). The numbers that appear alongside Milner's
signature are actually the titles of his pictures which were
classified by a series of figures, often prefixed by a letter.

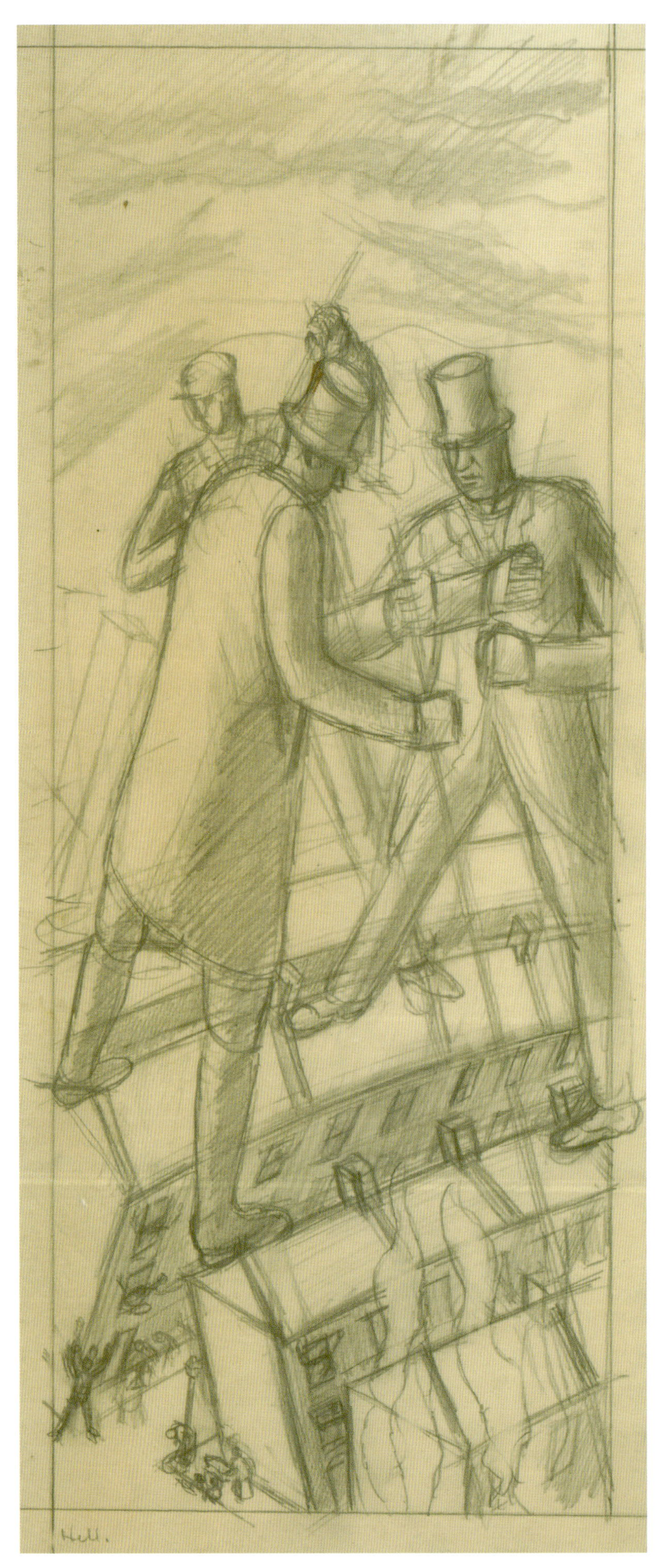
Hell.

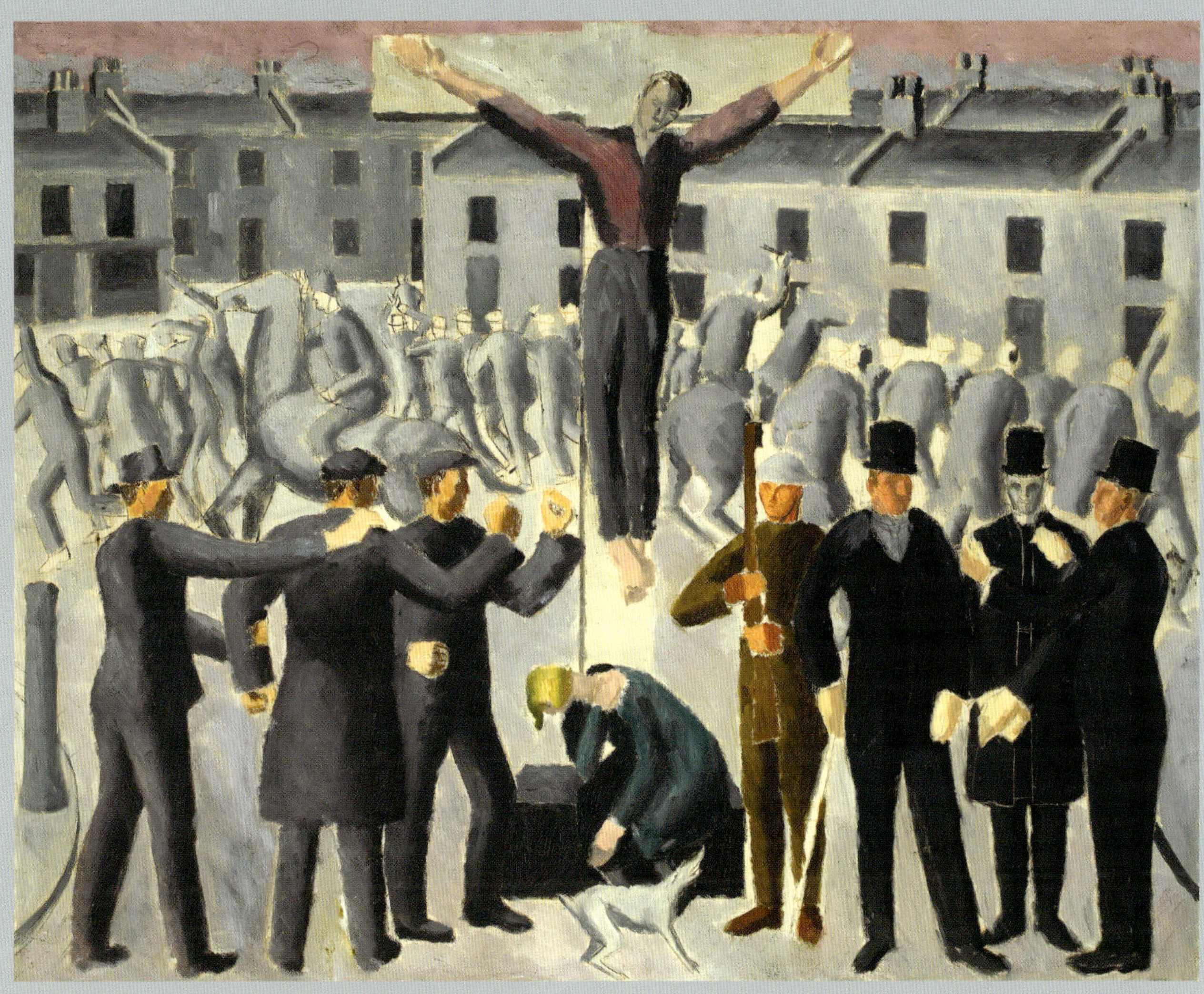

83 – Archibald Ziegler (1903-1971), *An Allegory of Social Strife*, late 1920s,
oil on panel over pencil and red crayon, 21 ¼ × 26 ½ in. (53.7 x 67.7 cm).
Provenance: Private collection.

This scene can be read as a polemical Allegory of the sacrifice of the working man as a victim of the ruling classes. It depicts the artist himself on the Cross. He is flanked on the left by pugnacious worker's leaders (a reference to Socialism?) and on the right men in formal attire representing the Establishment (a reference to Capitalism?). Brow-beaten workers, under attack, fill the background. A soldier stands guard to the Establishment figures, amongst which is a macabre, frock-coated figure whose pose and dog-collar alludes possibly to the Church. A study for this right hand group is inscribed by the artist with the title 'Hell'. Dating to the second half of the late 1920s – a period of mass unemployment and social unrest lasting until well into the 1930s – it recalls images of the 1926 General Strike, which Ziegler would have himself lived through as a young art student. Ziegler's striking composition is likely to have influenced the later well known self portrait as Christ (*Jesus The Jew*, 1942) by Emanuel Levy.

82 – Archibald Ziegler (1903-1971), *Hell*, inscribed with title, pencil on tracing paper, 14 ½ × 6 ¼ in. (36.8 x 15.5 cm).

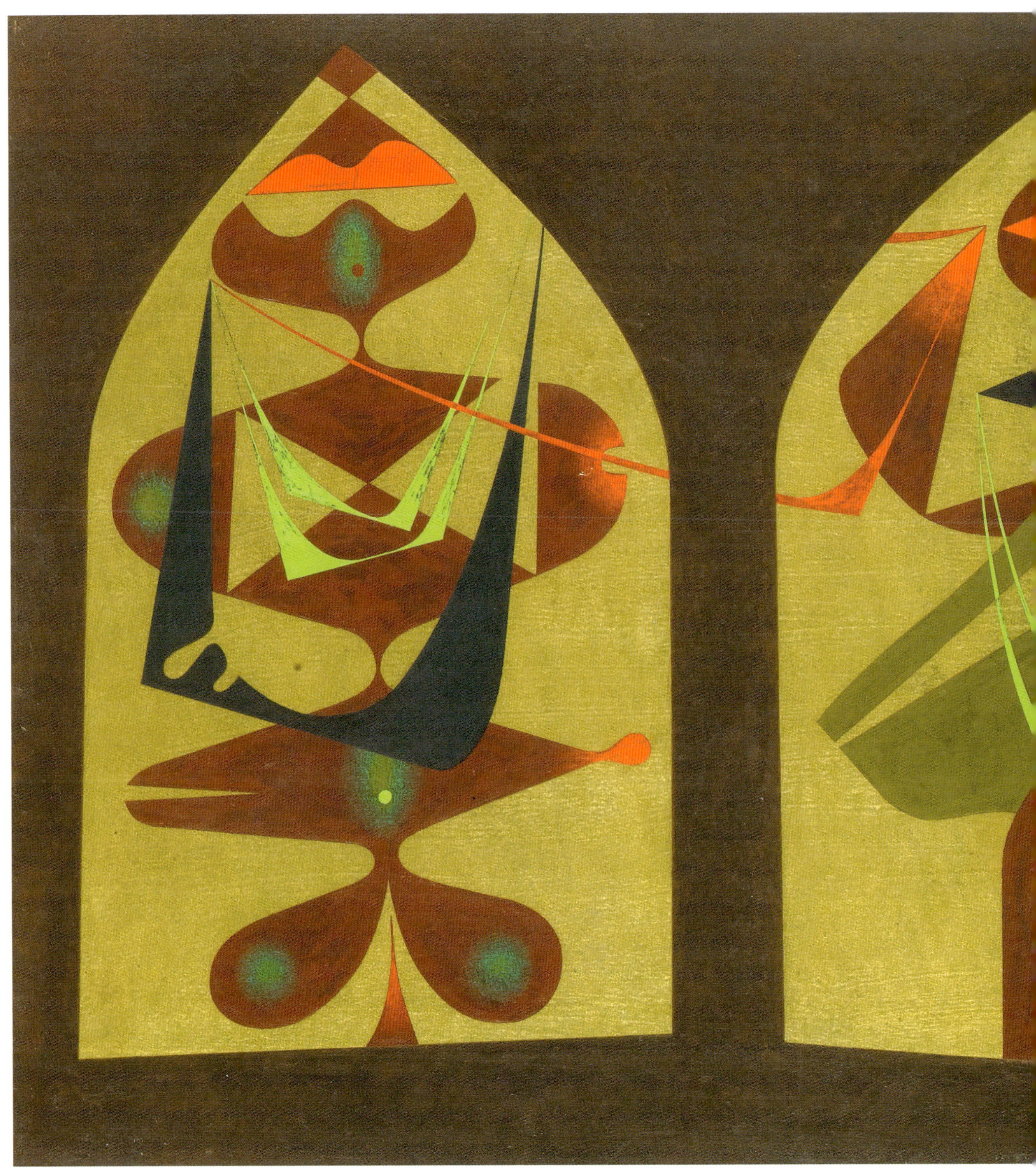

84 – Victor Reinganum (1907-1995), *Cavalry*, 1968, signed and dated 'Reinganum,'68', oil on board, 12 x 23 ½ in. (30.5 x 59.7 cm)

Reinganum attended the Academie Julian in Paris and was one of Leger's six private students in his studio in Montmartre.In 1926, with Nicolas Bentley, Reinganum formed the Pandemonium Group, a loosely knit group of "bright young things" that held regular exhibitions at the Beaux Arts Gallery, where they began their tentative experiments with abstraction.

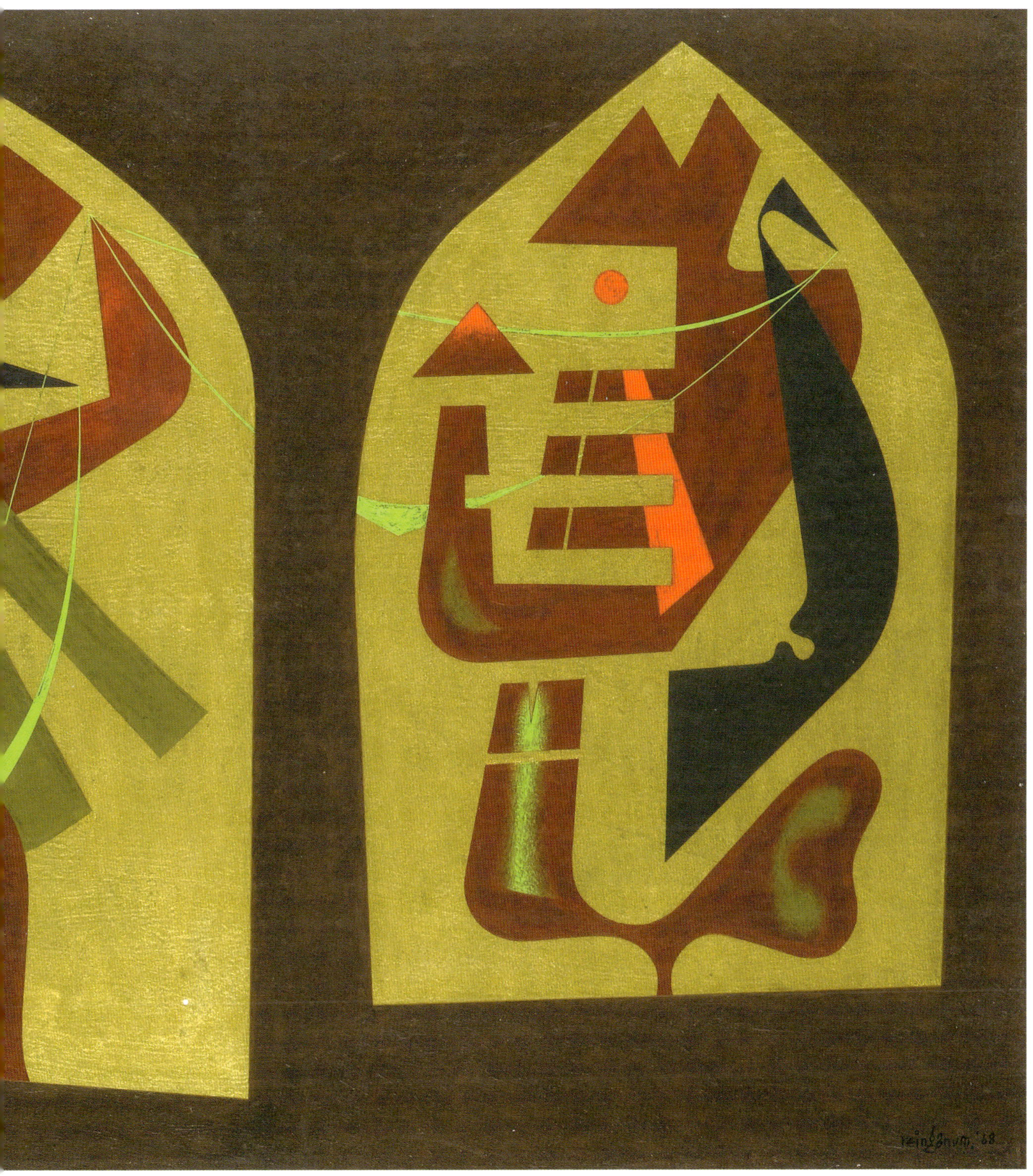

Reinganum disliked categories, both of medium and style, and did his best to avoid them. His paintings were exhibited under the banner "abstraction" but, gradually, the world at large dubbed him a Surrealist and he was swept up in the wave of British Surrealism exhibitions in the 1970s. His paintings have been shown in 20 exhibitions with "Surrealism" in their title, together with other members associated with the movement that included: Edward Burra, Eileen Agar, Merlyn Evans, Conroy Maddox, Tristram Hillier, John Piper and Roland Penrose.

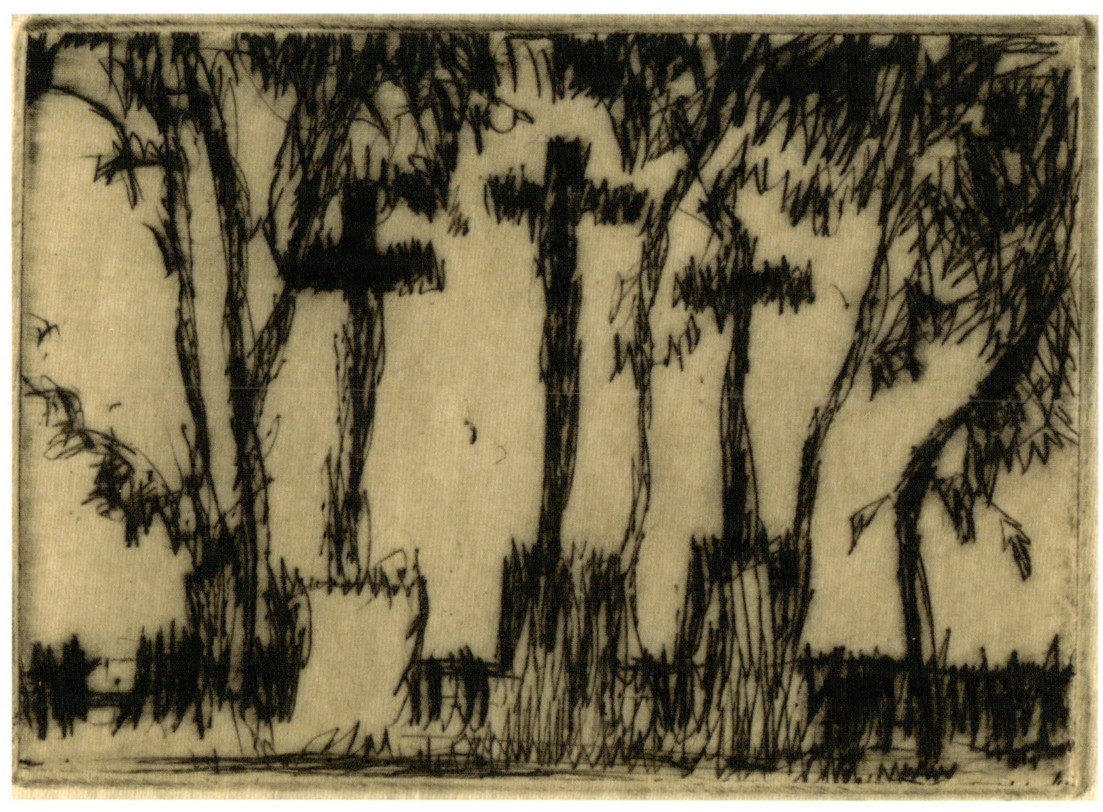

85 – Frank Brangwyn (1867-1956), *L'Ombre de la Croix – Three Crosses*, 1931,
dry point print, 2 × 3 in. (5 × 7.5 cm).

'Life here is nothing without God.
The time comes when one has to leave it all, then one says to oneself: what can I say I have done to please Him?'

In his own self-effacing way Brangwyn did much to please Him. Quite apart from the Stations of the Cross, he also produced in oil a set for Father Thomas Ryan's leper mission in Pretoria (1920-22), another for Arras Cathedral (1920-24) in memory of those who fell during The Great War, and a series in woodcut (1934-35). He designed the magnificent murals for St Aidan's church, Leeds and painted *Last Supper* murals for the Marist College, Middlesbrough (1937-45) and St Joseph's, Stokesley (1946). He produced over 70 illustrations for a projected *Life of St Francis*, 33 etchings for the *Book of Job*, covers for four of Hugh Redwood's evangelising books and 73 etchings for *L'Ombre de la Croix* (1931), a book about the life of Jews in contemporary Europe.

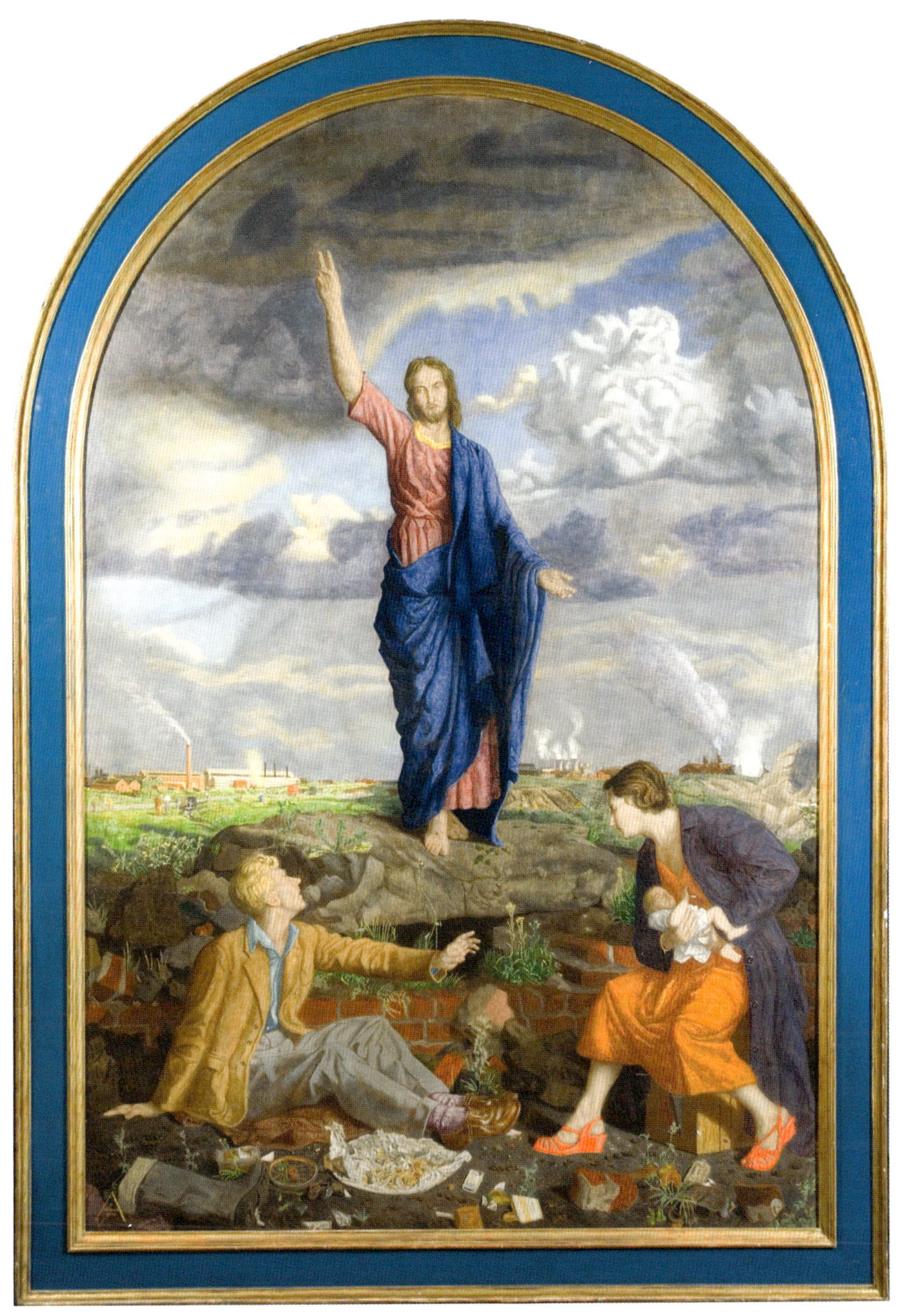

86 – George Warner Allen (1916-1988), *The Rubbish Dump, A Black Country Altarpiece*,
oil on canvas, 74 ½ × 48 in. (182.9 × 122 cm).
Provenance: Canon Abell Wood; by descent to James Wood; Nicholas Bagshawe.
Collection: Wolverhampton Art Gallery, acquired from Liss Llewellyn.

This work depicts an industrial landscape showing the factories and chimneys of the Black
Country. In the foreground a young family sit surrounded by the detritus of modern day
living, an indication of the grim reality of industrialisation and the hardship that surrounds
them. The figure of Christ is depicted rising above the rubbish dump, inspiring the people
to raise themselves out of poverty and offering a symbol of hope. It was painted for Canon
David Wood, who had married Allen's cousin and was working at the Black Country Industrial
Mission in Wolverhampton, based at St. George's Vicarage.

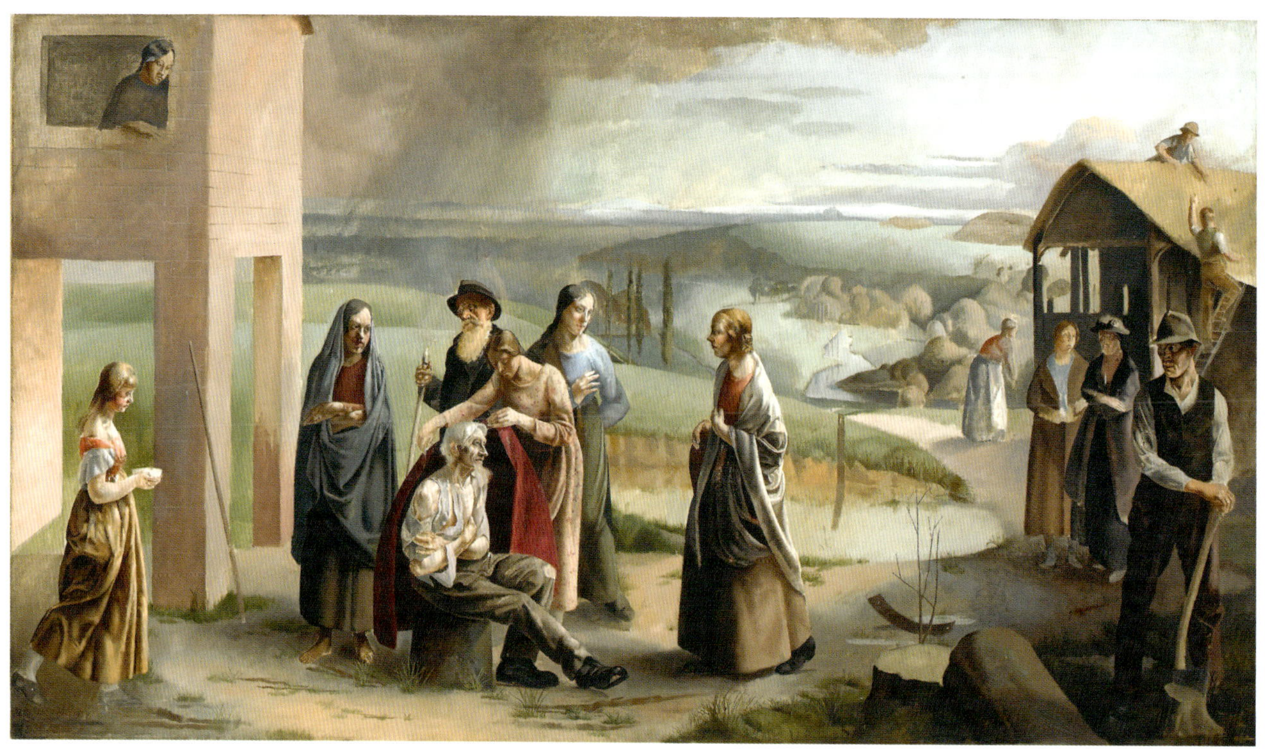

87 – Thomas Monnington (1902-1976), *Winter*, 1921-22,
oil on canvas, 48 × 85 in. (122 × 216 cm).
Provenance: The British School at Rome, Lowther Gardens, London; Sotheby's, London 14th October 1987, lot 118, purchased by Abbot and Holder; Alan and Susanna Powers.
Exhibited: Exhibition of works submitted in the final competitions for the Rome Scholarship of 1922, Royal Academy, February 1923; International Exhibition of Modern and Decorative Industrial Art, Paris, April-October 1925, British Section, Grand Palais (309).
Literature: *Illustrated London News*, 10 March 1923, vol.162, p.366, (Reproduced).

Winter was Monnington's winning submission for the 1922 British School at Rome Scholarship in Decorative Painting. The landscape is based on studies looking towards Clerebury Rings near Salisbury, undertaken during visits in 1921 to the artist's cousin Dr. R. C. Monnington. In a review in *The Observer*, (22 February 1923), P. C. Konody praised Monnington's painting for being steeped in the best traditions of the Italian Renaissance. His colour is dull, but there is a marked sense of style in his design.

A link with the Italian Renaissance can be demonstrated more specifically in relation to the work of Piero della Francesca: the young peasant leaning with both hands on a spade is a possible echo from the *Discovery and Proving of the True Cross* (San Francesco, Arezzo). The man sitting on a rock in the middle of the composition appears to be based on the figure of St.. Joseph (in reverse) in Piero della Francesca's *Adoration*.

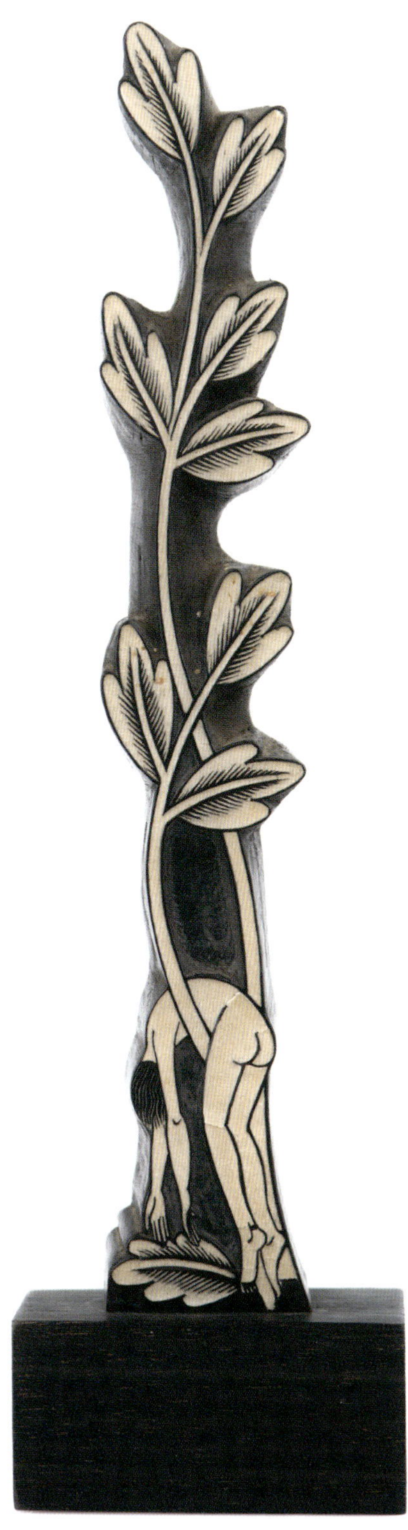

88 – Eric Gill (1882-1940), *Naked Man Dead*, c.1929,
incised with Gill's initials and numbered '284', block blind stamped 'T. Lawrence',
original woodblock carving with gesso, 7 x 1 ½ in. (17.8 x 3 cm).

This design was used as a border design for the Golden Cockerel Press edition of *The Canterbury Tales*
by Geoffrey Chaucer (Waltham St. Lawrence, 1929-31).

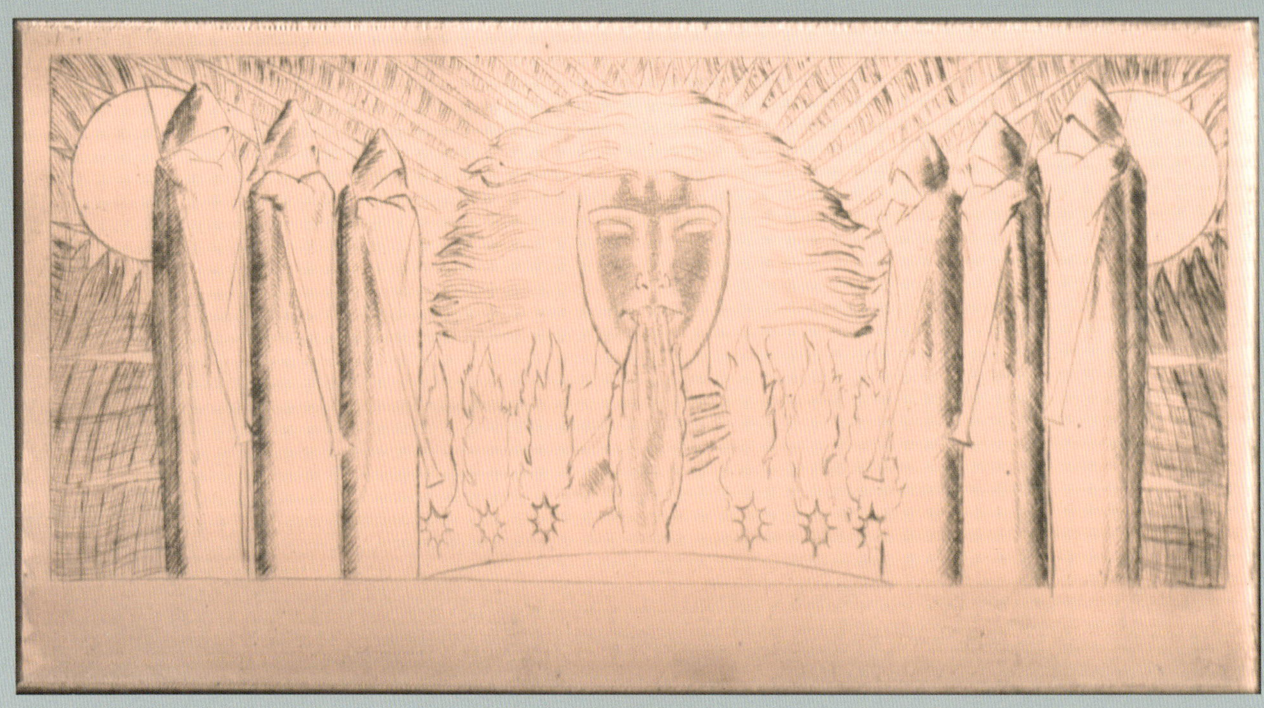

89 – Frederick Carter (1883-1967), *Silence in Heaven*, 1925,
Original copper plate, 4 x 7 ½ in. (10 x 19 cm).
Literature; *Frederick Carter A.R.E., A Study of his Etchings* by Richard Grenville Clark, The Apocalypse Press, 1998, page 68.

This plate is thought to have never been editioned in Carter's lifetime.

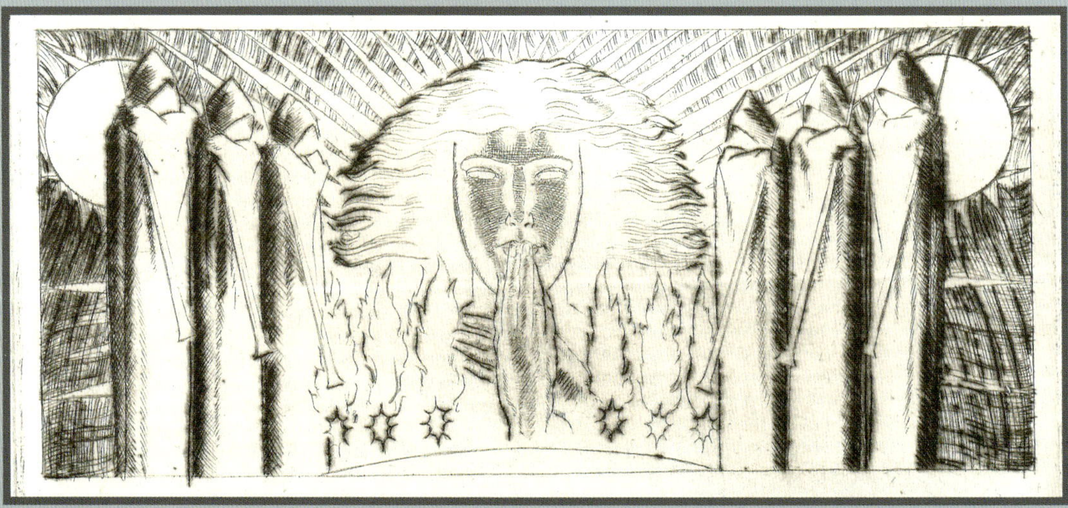

89 a – Posthumous print pulled from plate.

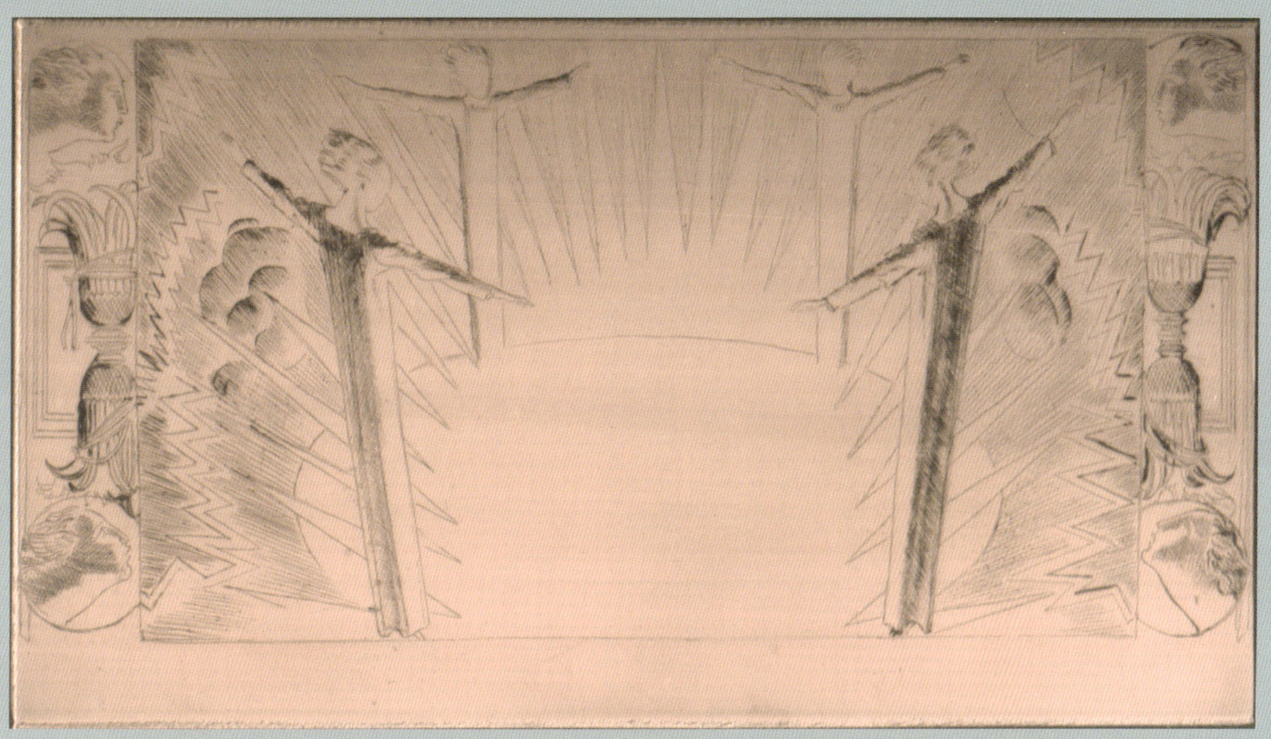

90 – **Frederick Carter** (1883-1967), *The Four Winds of the Apocalypse*, 1925,
Original copper plate, 4 ¼ × 7 ¾ in. (11 × 20 cm).
Literature; *Frederick Carter A.R.E., A Study of his Etchings* by Richard Grenville Clark, The Apocalypse Press, 1998, page 66.

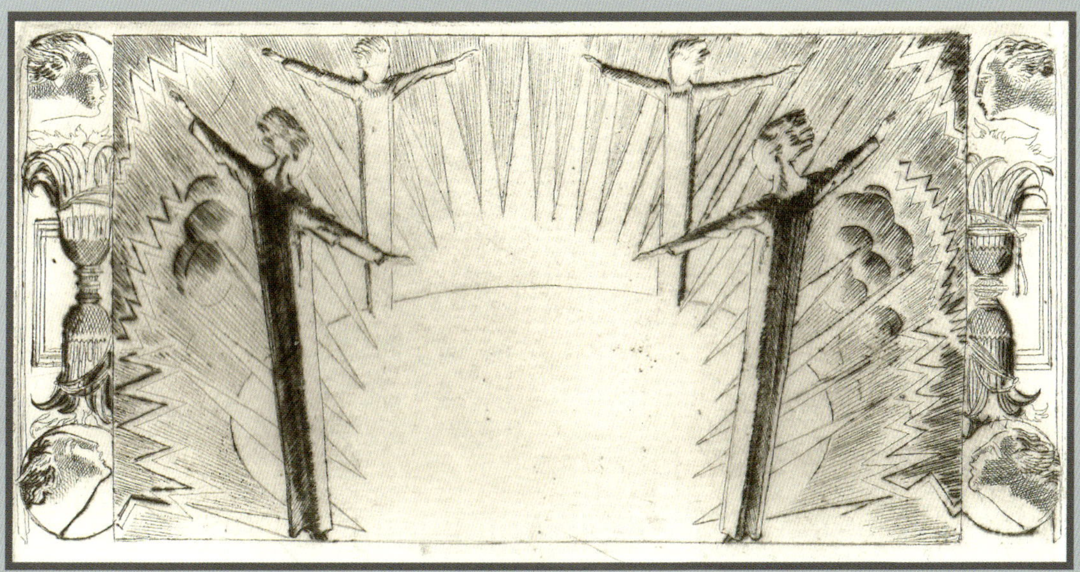

90 a – Posthumous print pulled from plate.

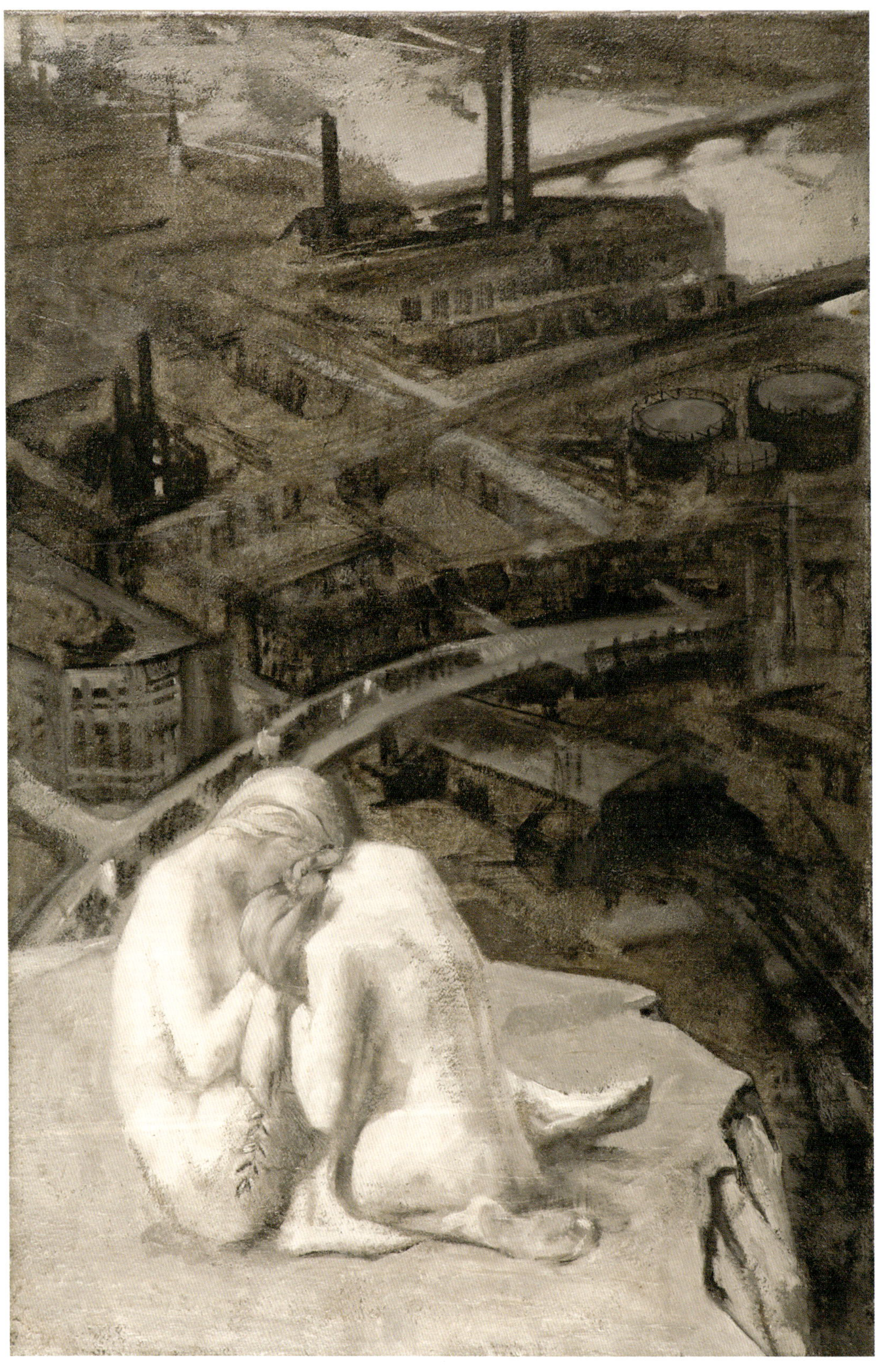

91 – **Dorothea Frances MacLagan** (1895-1982) *An allegory: Truth and Beauty comforting each other,* c.1920, oil on canvas, 18 × 11 ¾ in. (45 × 29.8 cm).

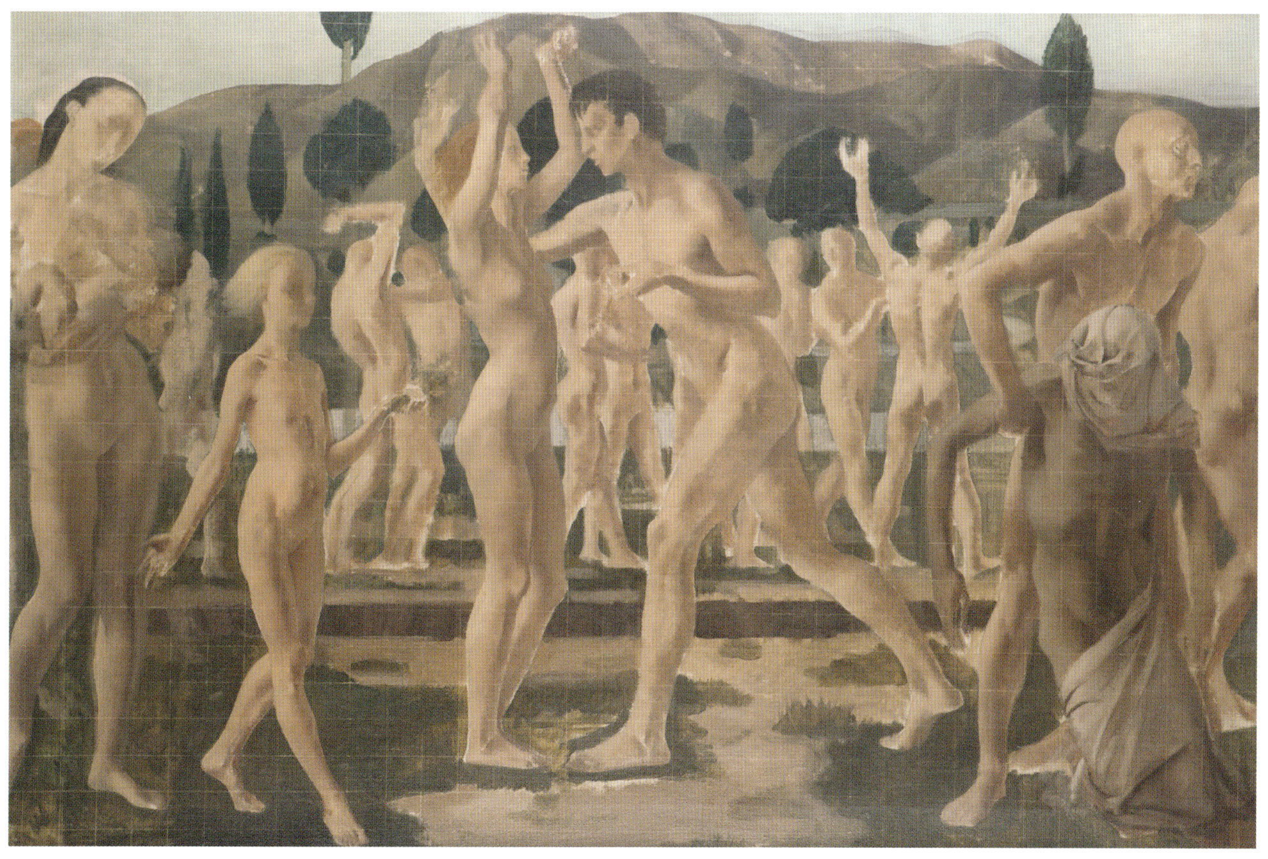

92 – Alfred Kingsley Lawrence (1893-1975), *An Allegory of Human Life*, 1923,
oil on canvas, 24 x 36 in. (61 x 91.5 cm).
Provenance: The British School of Rome; Jonathan Clark; Private collection.

A. K. Lawrence was the Rome Scholar in Decorative Painting for 1923. *An Allegory of Human Life* was one of the submissions with which Lawrence won the Scholarship. The finalists for the 1923 Scholarship in Decorative Painting were Constance Grant, who submitted *The Flight into Egypt*, Doris Stacey, *The Parable of the Lost Piece of Silver*, Hugh Stutfield, *Sophonisba's Cup* and Alfred Kingsley Lawrence *An Allegory of Human Life*.

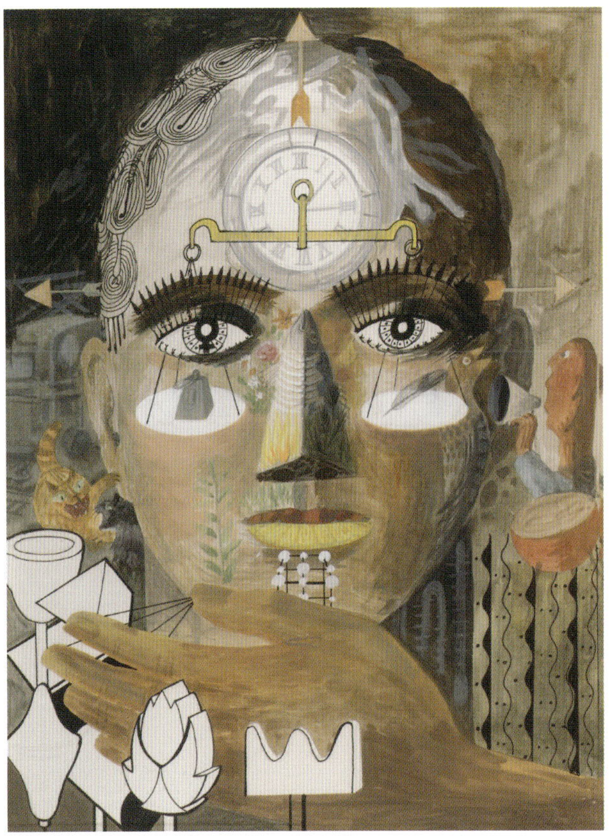 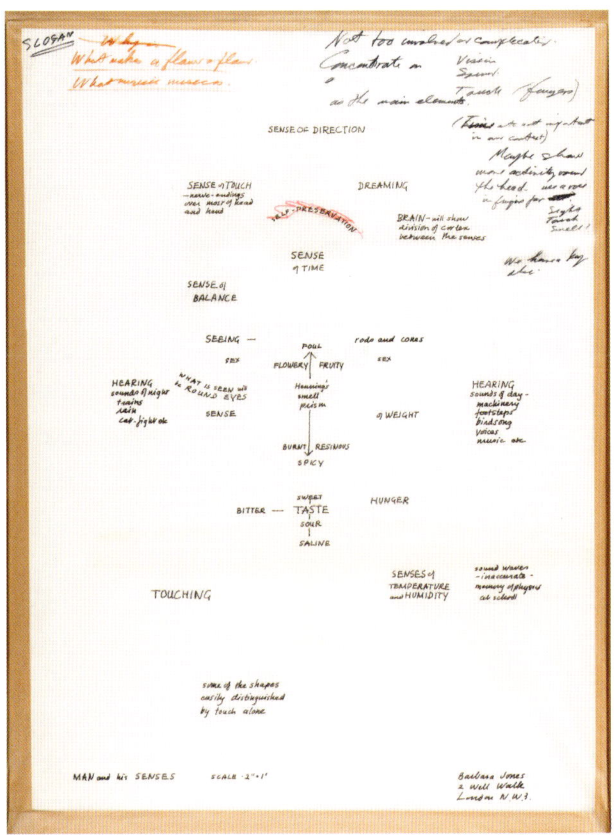

93 – Barbara Jones (1912-1978), *Study for Man and his Senses* (recto and verso), 1966-71, collage on paper, 17 ¾ x 11 ¾ in. (45 x 30 cm). Private collection.

94 – Barbara Jones (1912-1978),
Mural based on the theme 'Man at Work – a century of technical and social progress' for the International Labour Exhibition,
Central Office of Information, Turin, Italy, 1961,
two panels, oil on board, 168 ¾ x 120 ¼ in (428.6 x 305.4 cm)
Provenance: with the artist until 1978; thereafter in her studio with her assistant Tony Raymond.
Exhibited: Expo 61, the International Labour Exhibition, Central Office of Information, Turin, Italy, 1961.
Literature: Ruth Artmonsky, *Barbara Jones*, Artmonsky Arts, 2008, pp.89-95;
British Murals and Decorative Painting 1920-1960, Sansom & Co, 2013, pp.334-335.

Created to celebrate the centenary of the Italian State (1961), *Man at Work* was the mural that Jones remained most proud of during her lifetime. She went to considerable lengths to buy it back and return it to her studio after its appearance at Expo 61 in Turin.

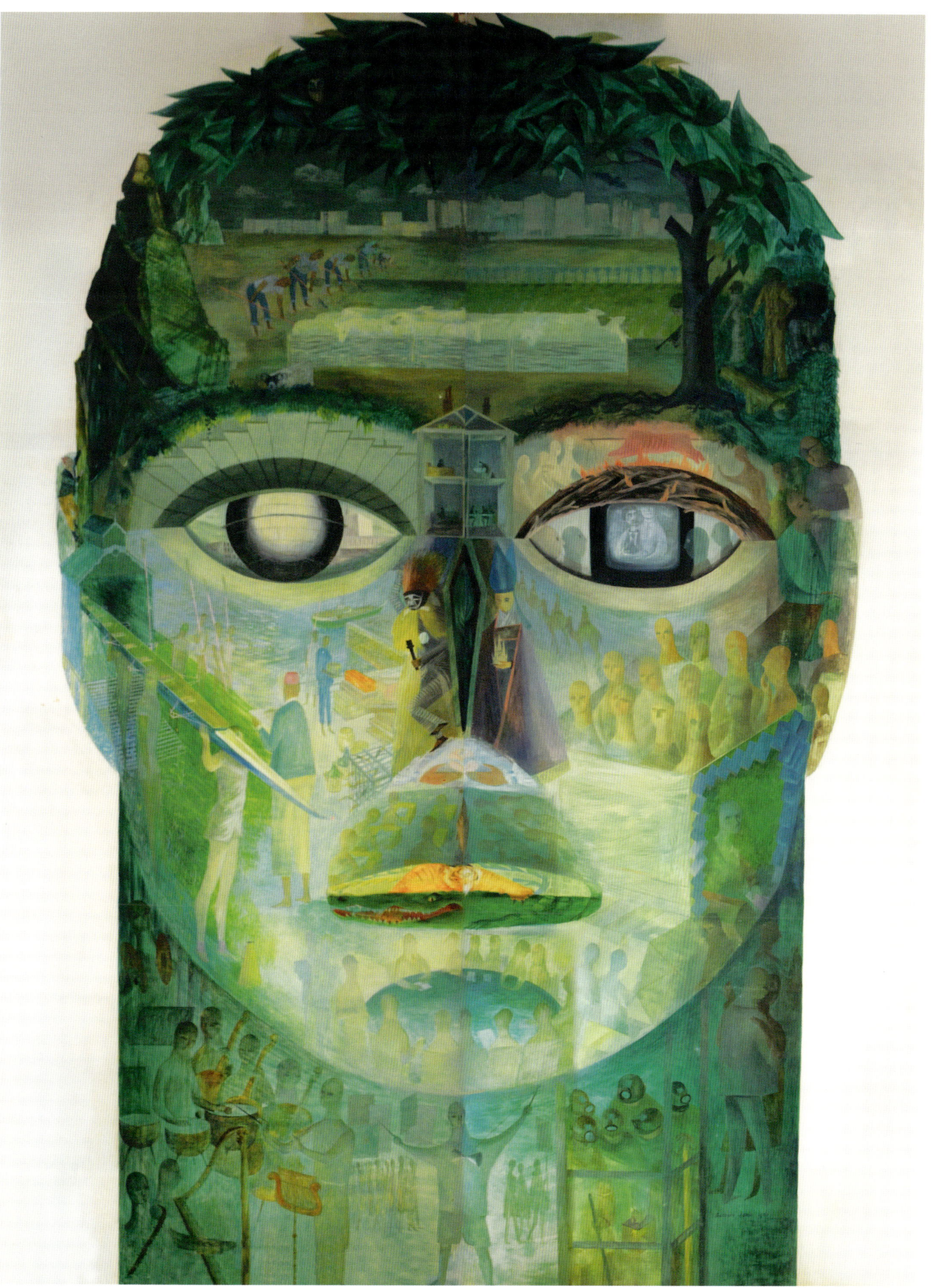

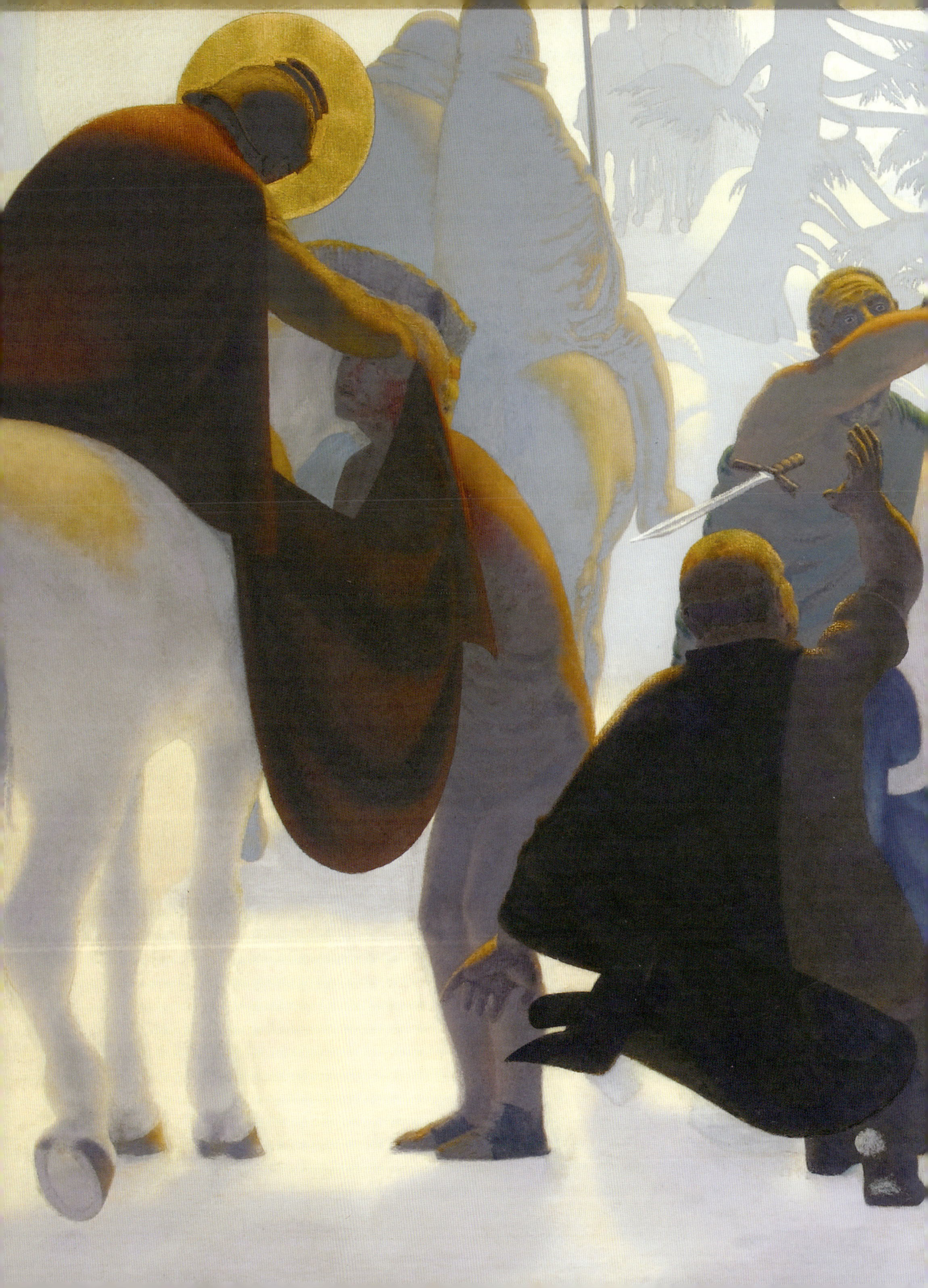

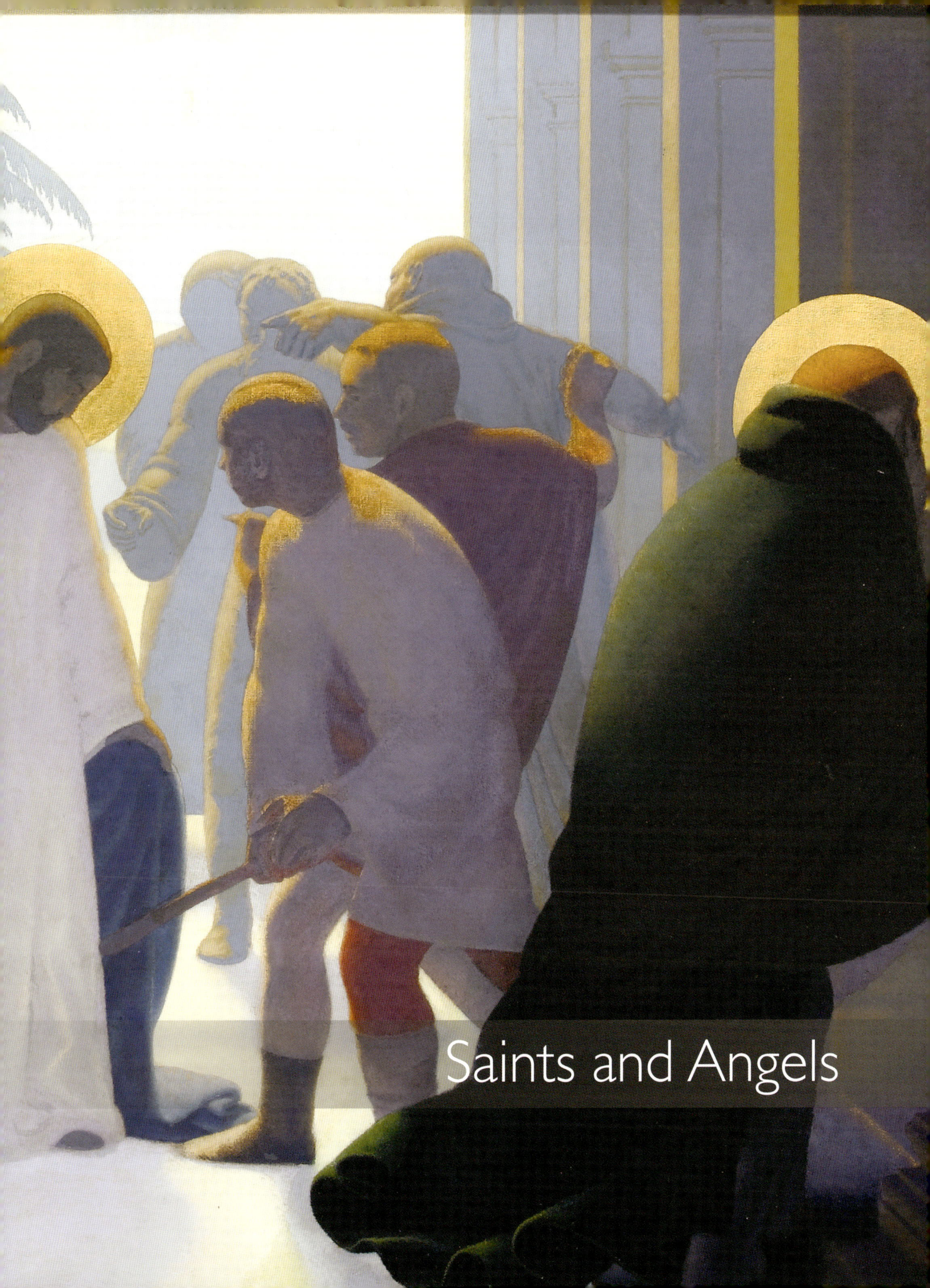
Saints and Angels

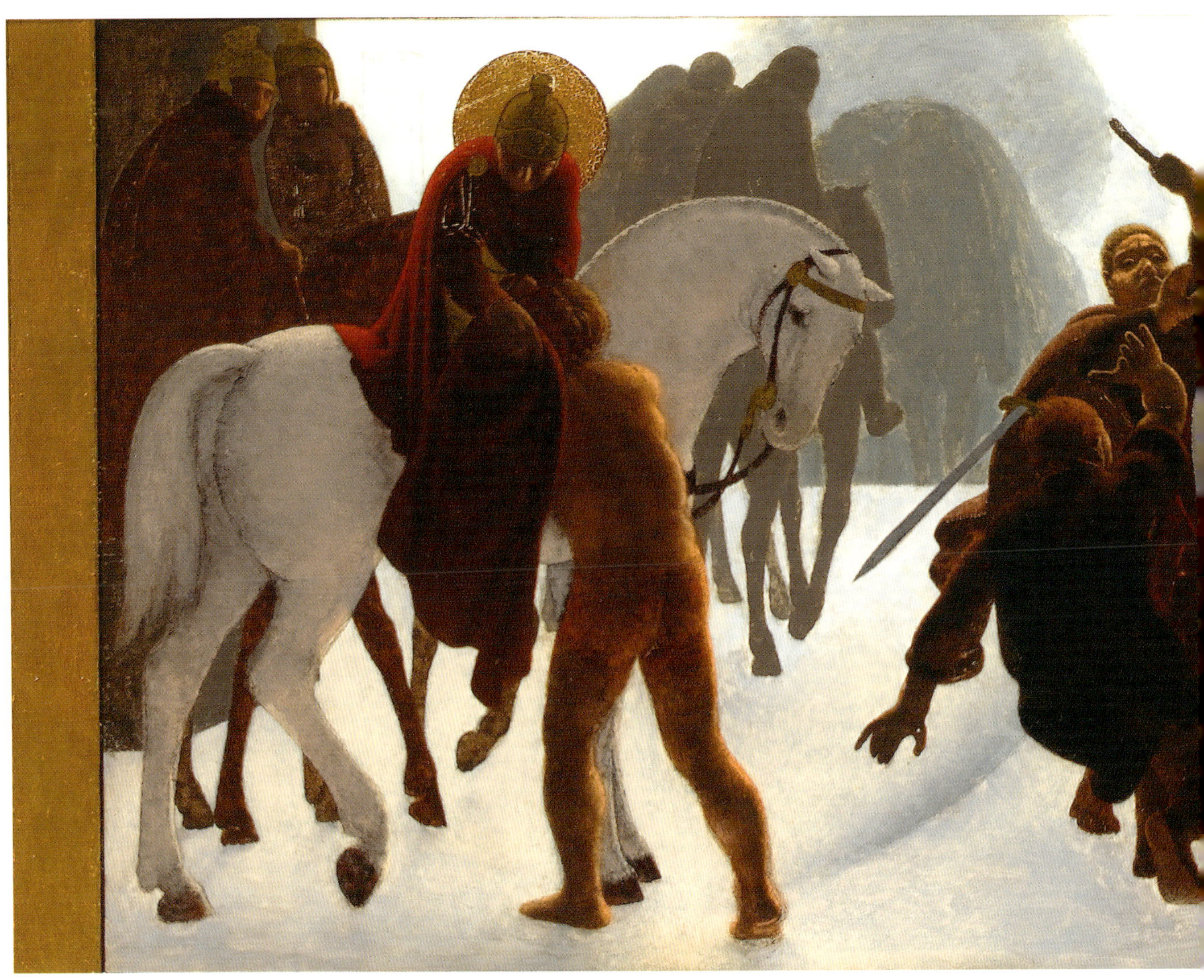

95 – Glyn Jones (1906-1984), Study for St Martin's Altarpiece, Canterbury Cathedral, c.1927, tempera on board, 14 × 37 in. (35.5 × 94 cm).

'In everything to do with this picture I have been conscious of grasping with something bigger than myself' (Glyn Jones, 8 April 1950, letter to Mr Rushbury).

In 1927, at the start of his three-year scholarship at the British School at Rome, Glyn Jones received a prestigious commission to paint three scenes representing the life of St Martin, to form a reredos in the Milner Memorial Chapel, Canterbury Cathedral. The panel of expert advisers who awarded the commission were Sir Herbert Baker, the architect of the Memorial Chapel, and Professor Tonks, under whom Jones had studied at the Slade, with Sir Arthur Steel-Maitland from the Ministry of Labour acting as General Secretary. Baker suggested that, before starting the painting, Jones should 'go to Assisi to see the St Martin's series of paintings there' (letter of 24 March 1927), and later wrote to say that Tonks and he were certain that Jones would 'produce a beautiful picture rich in imagery, design and colour' (17 November 1927). The commission meant a great deal to Jones. The painting became his opus magnum; he worked on little else during his entire sojourn in Italy, and even relinquished his third year of the scholarship in order to be able to concentrate on it without distraction.

On 30 July 1928 Jones received the devastating news that his painting was to be rejected: 'I am sorry to say that it was the opinion of the Committee, and also that of the Cathedral authorities, that the picture is … quite different from what they had expected and hoped from the sketch which you showed to us at an early stage….'' In view of the work which Jones had already expended, a fee of £125 was suggested, half the original value of the commission, and indeed half the value of the third year of the Rome scholarship that Jones had given up to finish the painting. Meanwhile the commission was handed over to Winifred Knights, whose painting of St Martin now hangs in the chapel. Jones never recovered from the disappointment of losing this commission; as late as 1950 he was still trying to persuade Canterbury Cathedral to accept his painting, and indeed appears to have still been trying to resolve the panel on the left-hand side, into which St Agnes was eventually placed.

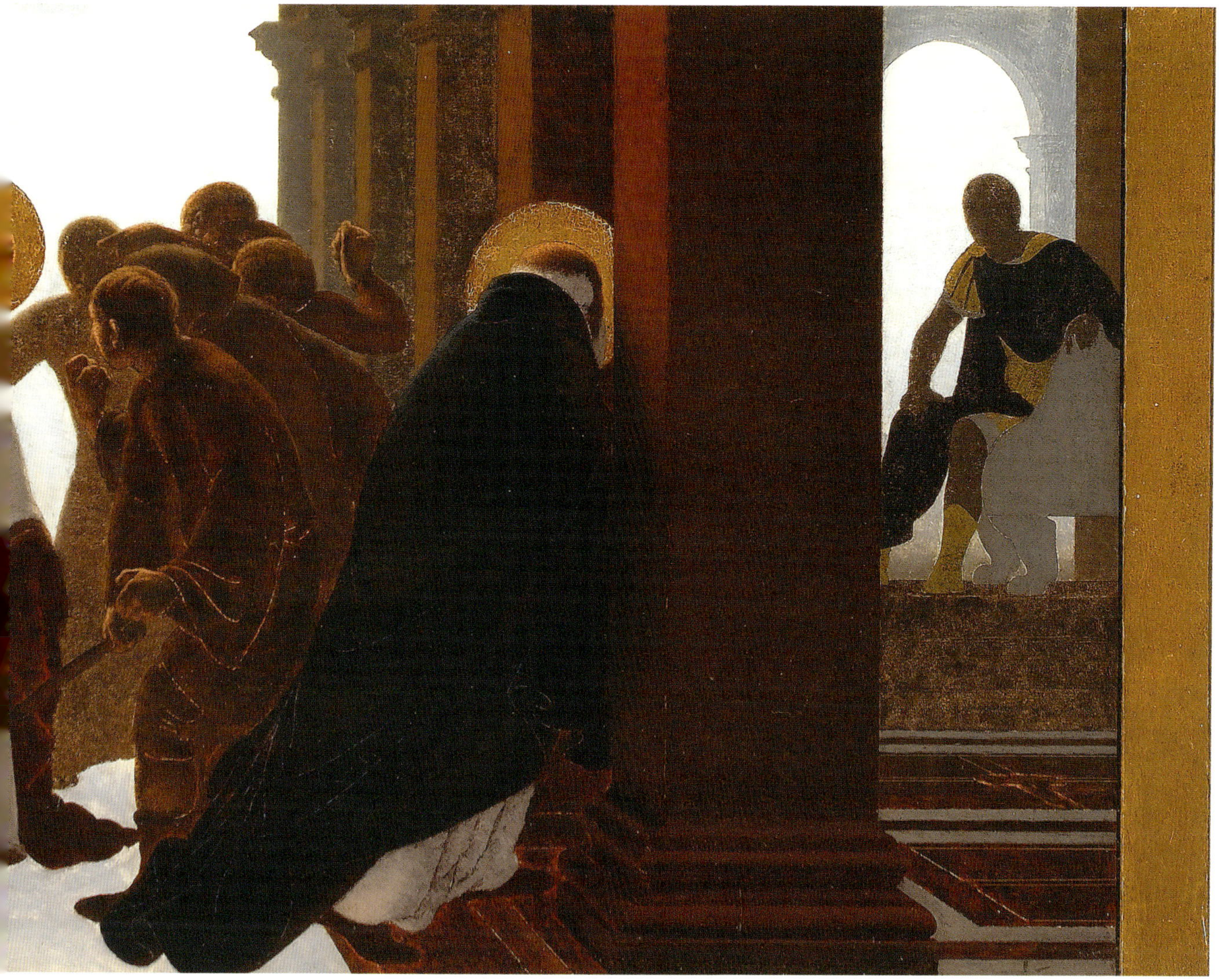

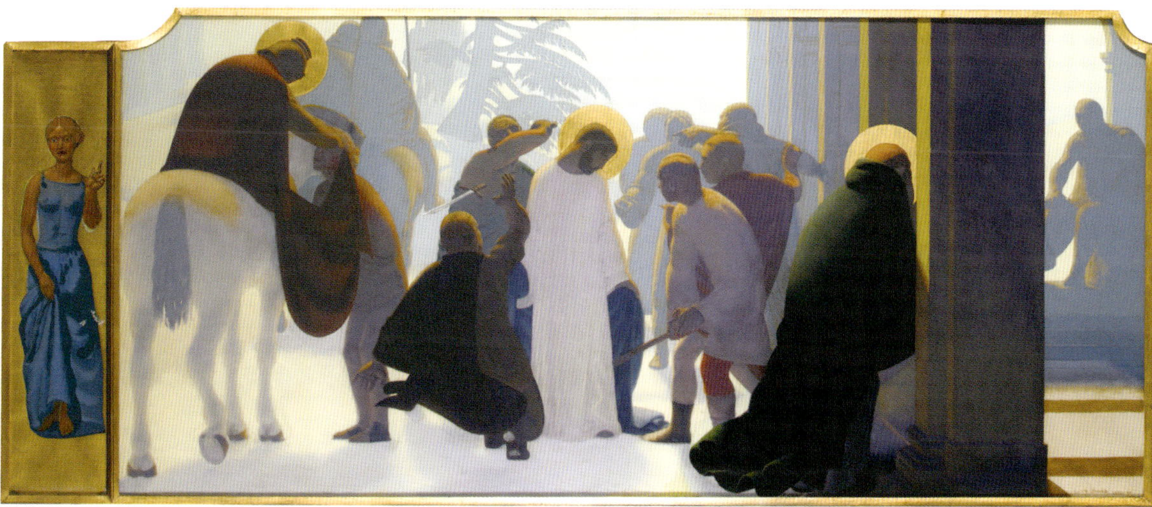

96 – Glyn Jones (1906-1984), St Martin's Altarpiece, Canterbury Cathedral, 1926-1950, signed and dated,
oil on canvas, 29 x 63 in. and 26 ¾ x 6 ½ in. (74.5 x 161.5 cm and 68 x 16.3 cm). Frame designed by Herbert Baker.

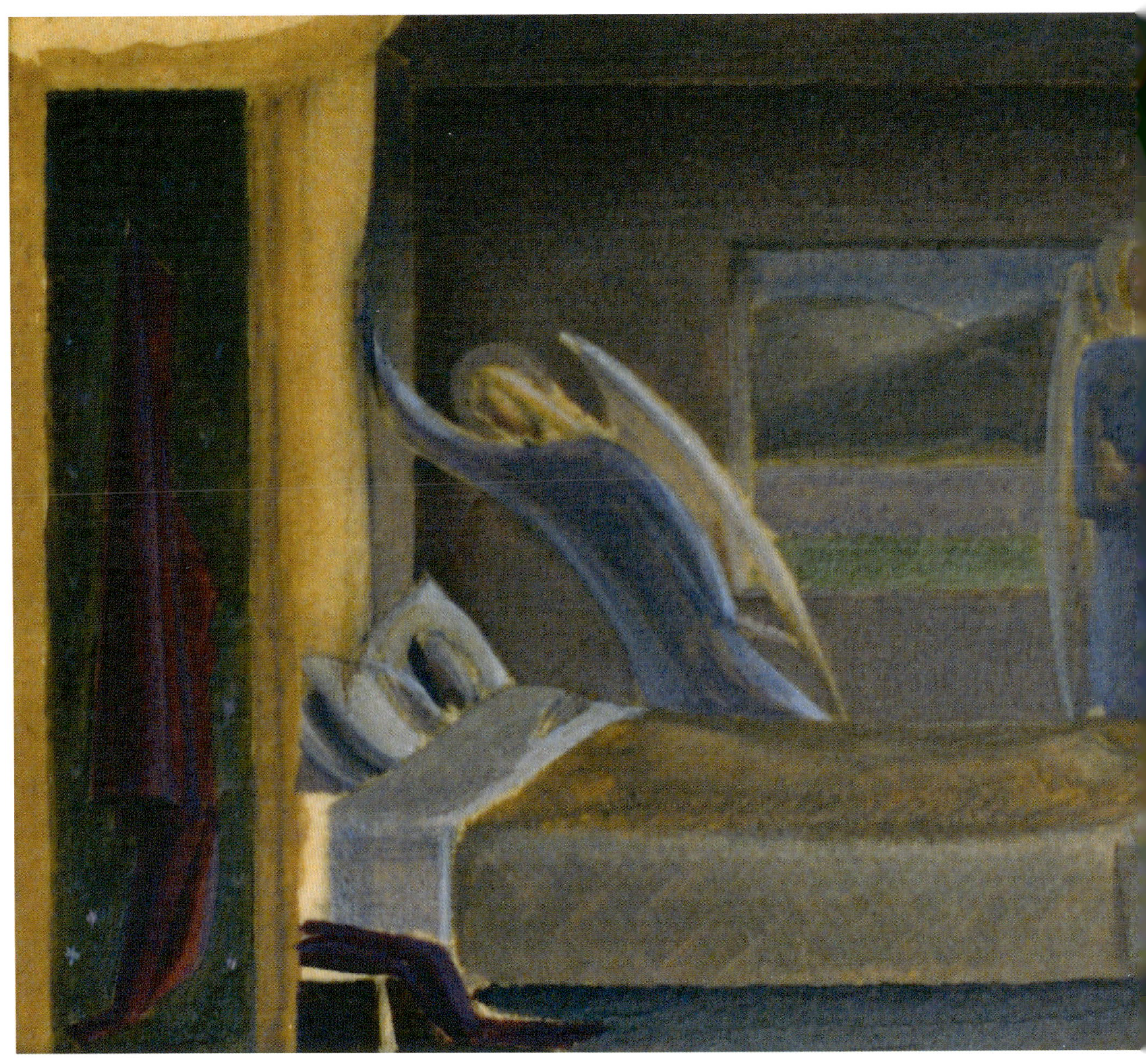

97 – **Winifred Knights** (1899-1947), First compositional study for *Scenes from the Life of Saint Martin of Tours*, 1928, thinned oil on tracing paper, 7 ¼ × 16 in.. (18.5 × 41 cm).

Literature: Sacha Llewellyn *Winifred Knights 1899-1947* (London: Lund Humphries in association with Dulwich Picture Gallery, 2016);

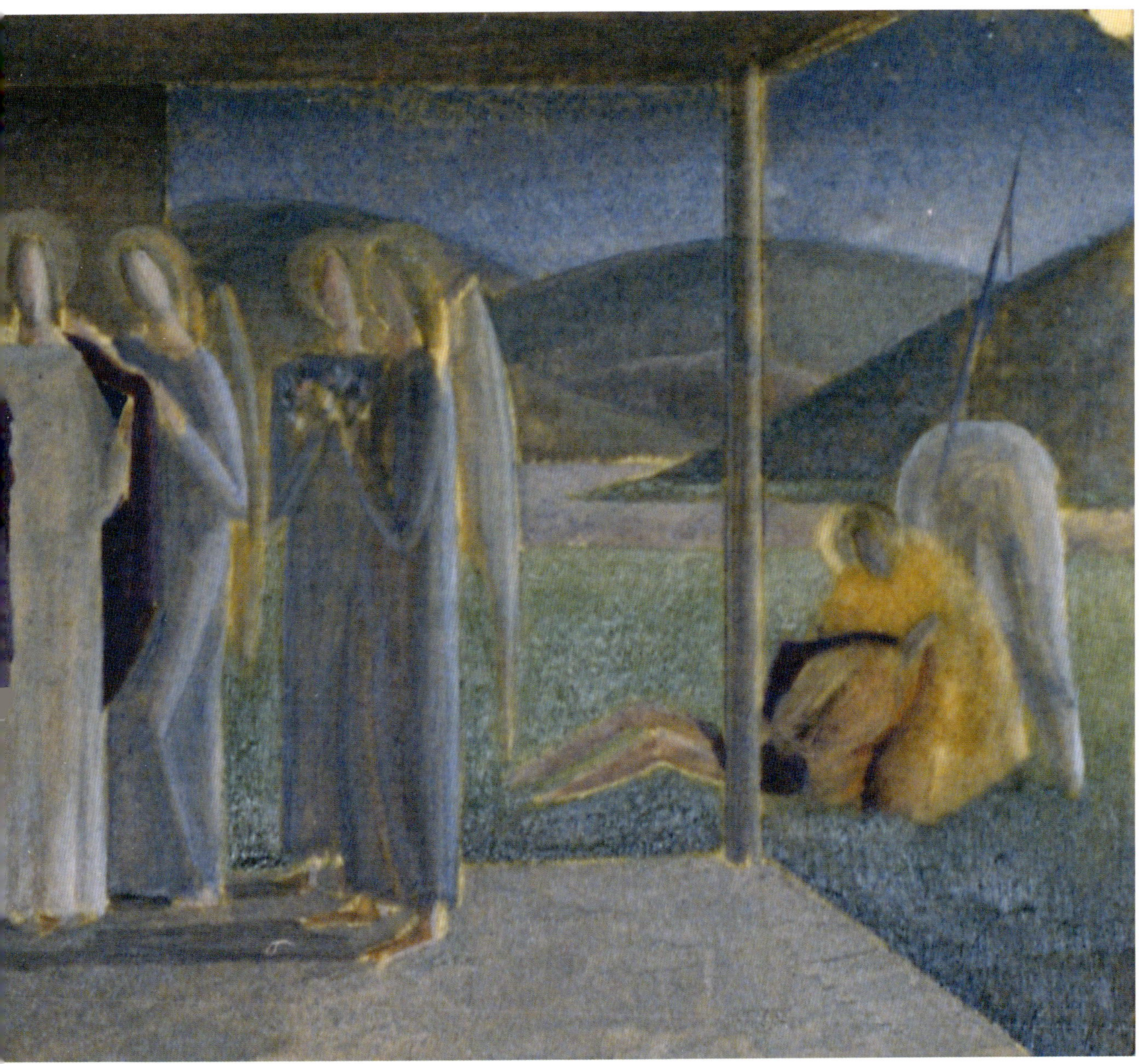

Scenes from the Life of Saint Martin of Tours was commissioned for the Milner Memorial Chapel by the Dean Dr. George Bell, later Bishop of Chichester, in conjunction with the architect Sir Herbert Baker. The Chapter Act Books from Canterbury Cathedral record that the painting was finished by December 1933, referring to it having been commissioned six years earlier. Numerous compositional studies that have survived for the painting demonstrate that Knights considered several interpretations of the subject and also bear witness to the difficulties that she had in working to the precise specifications of the architect Herbert Baker. The final composition incorporates three events from the life of St. Martin.

Simone Martini produced a cycle of frescoes on the theme of St. Martin of Tours in the Chapel of San Martino, Assisi, and it is to these images that Knights turned for inspiration. Like Simone Martini Knights situates the various Miracles within an Italian rather than French landscape. Bishop Bell described the work as 'one of the most lovely, delicate and deeply felt modern religious paintings that I know'.

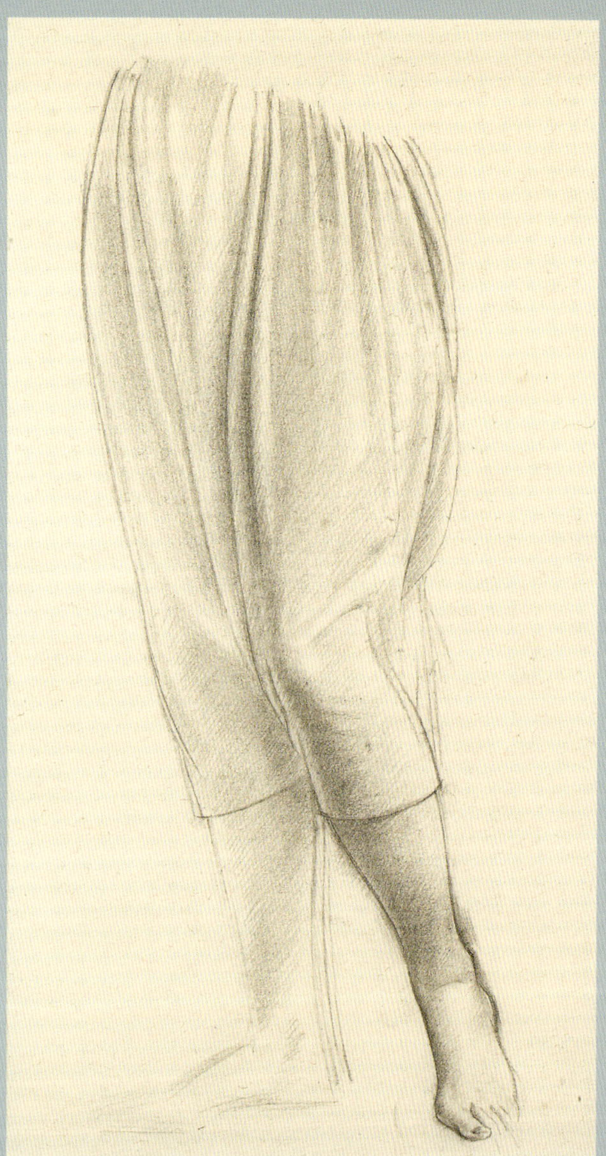 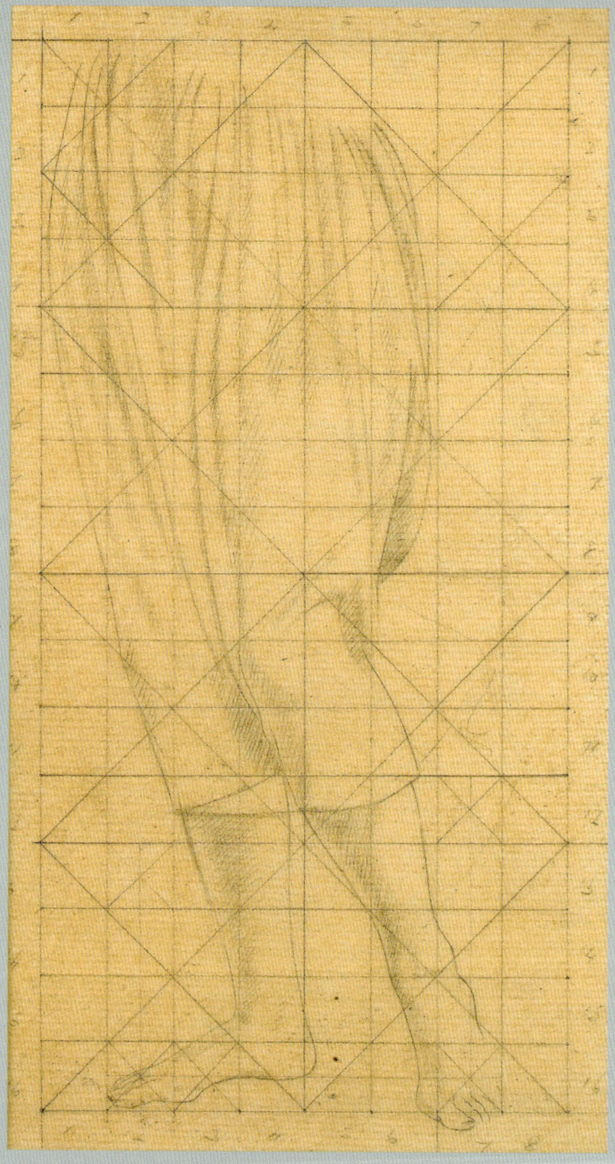

98 –**Winifred Knights** (1899-1947), 2 figure studies, *Scenes from the Life of Saint Martin of Tours*, c.1928, pencil, on paper and tracing paper, 8 × 4 ¼ in. (20.3 × 10.8 cm) each.

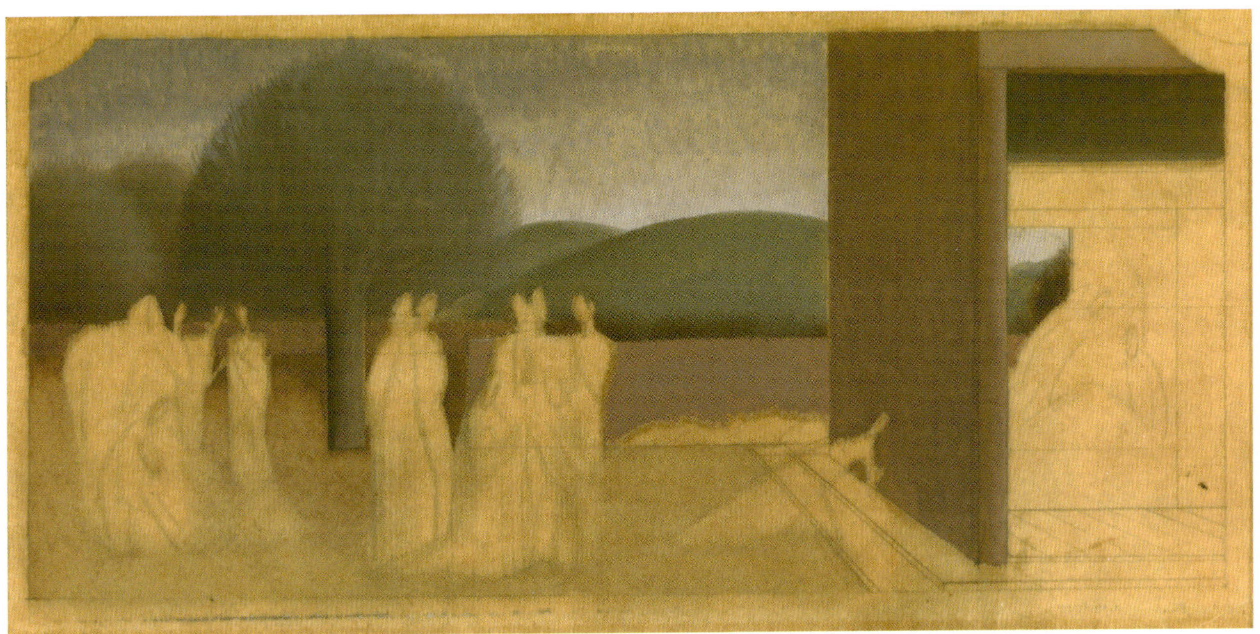

99 – **Winifred Knights** (1899-1947), Study for *Scenes from the Life of Saint Martin of Tours*, c.1929,
oil, pencil and wash on tracing paper, 5 ½ × 11 ¼ in. (14 × 28.6 cm).
Provenance: the artist's estate; private collection since 1995.
Literature: G.K.A. Bell, 'The Church and the Artist', *The Studio*, September 1942, vol. 124, no. 594, p. 81.

Knights was commissioned to paint the Milner Memorial altarpiece for Canterbury Cathedral in 1928; she finished it some five years later in 1933. It was to be the last major work completed by Knights.

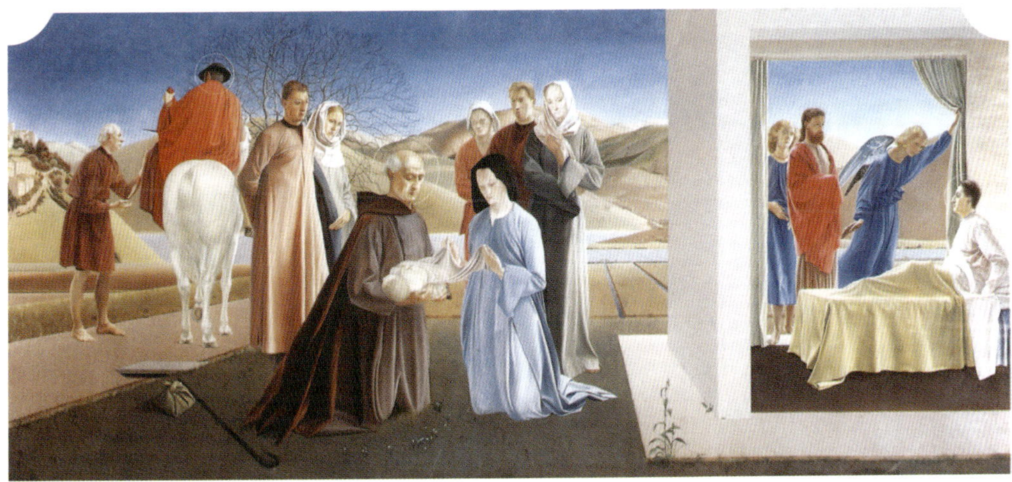

100 – **Winifred Knights** (1899-1947), *Scenes from the Life of St Martin of Tours*, 1928-1933,
oil on canvas, 30 ¼ × 74 ½ in. (76.5 × 189.5 cm),
Milner Memorial Chapel, Canterbury Cathedral.

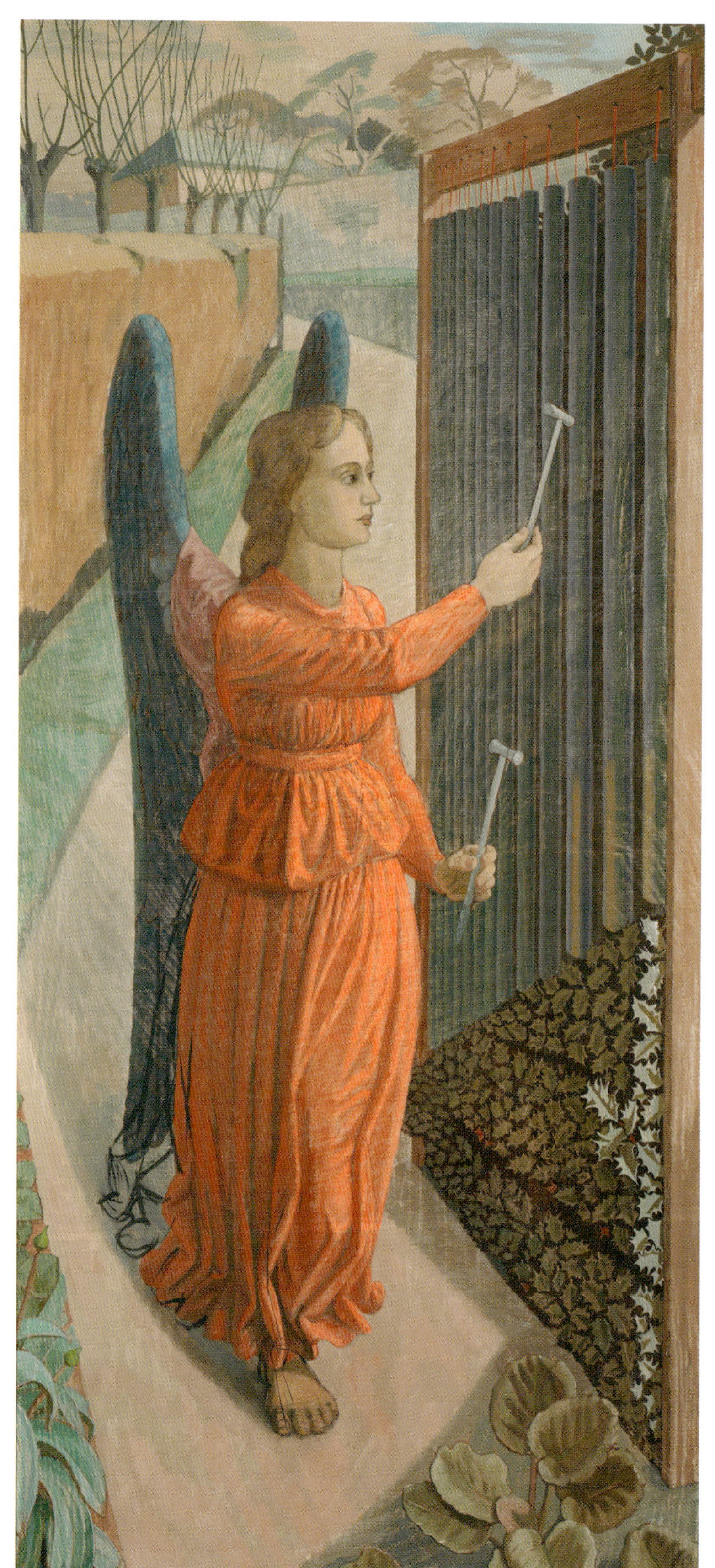

101 –
Charles Mahoney (1903-1968),
Angel playing tubular bells,
oil on canvas,
57 ½ x 25 ¼ in. (146.5 x 64.5 cm).

This is a full size study for the Angel to the left of the Altar at Campion Hall Chapel. Whilst the two compositions are almost identical, Mahoney only got as far as putting in the underdrawing in the Chapel design itself. In the finished painting, here, the wild folliage, which dominates the Chapel composition, is trimmed back to reveal a suburban setting, the walls and rooftops, less visible in the Chapel version, underpinning the composition.

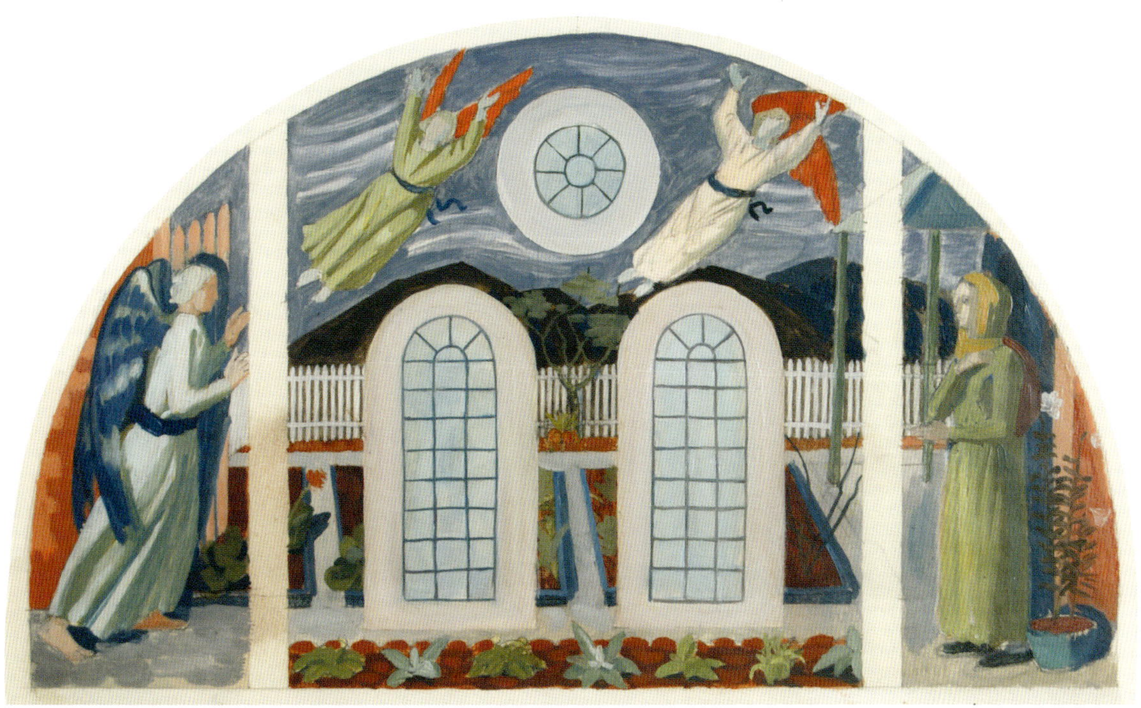

102 – **Charles Mahoney** (1903-1968), Design for the altar wall, *Annunciation in an Allotment*, c.1942, oil over pencil on paper, 11 ½ × 19 in. (29 × 48.2 cm). Provenance: The Artist's Estate. Literature: Sansom & Co, 2013, pp.85-86 and pp.232-243.

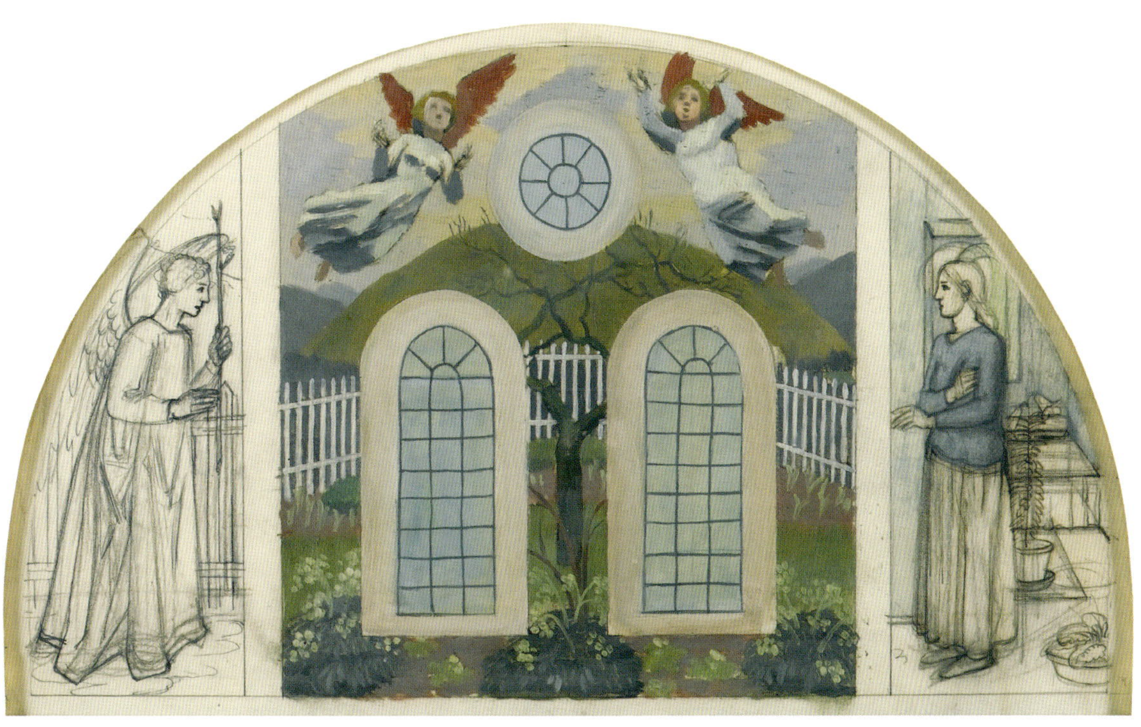

103 – **Charles Mahoney** (1903-1968), Design for the altar wall, *Annunciation in an Allotment*, partially coloured, c.1942, oil over pencil on paper, 11 ½ × 19 in. (29 × 48.2 cm). Provenance: The Artist's Estate. Literature: Sansom & Co, 2013, pp.85-86 and pp.232-243.

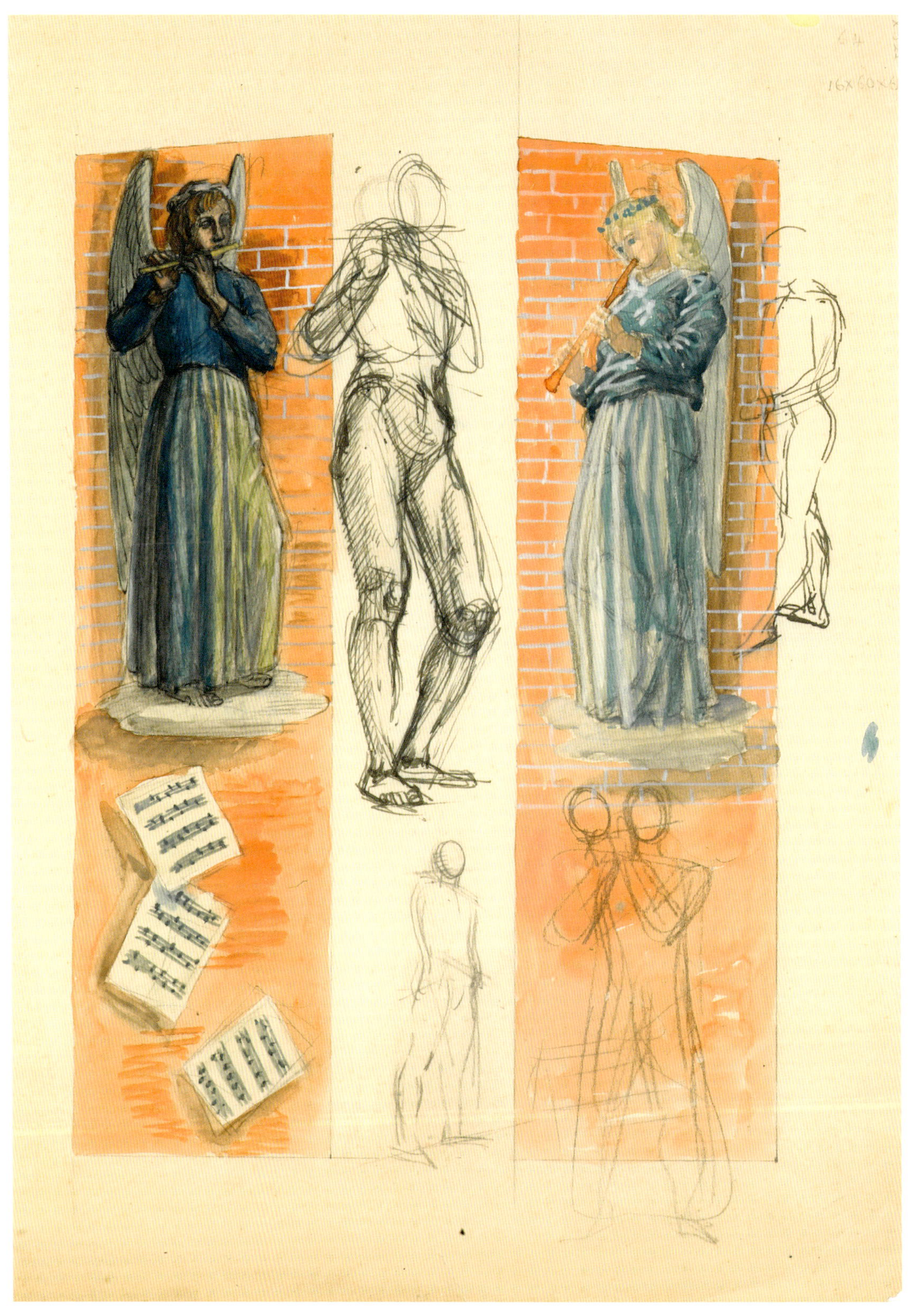

104 – **Charles Mahoney** (1903-1968), Study of angels for the altar wall of Campion Hall, mid 1940s, gouache on paper, 20 x 14 in. (50.7 x 35.5 cm).
Provenance: The Artist's Estate
Literature: *British Murals & Decorative Painting 1920-1960*, Sansom & Co, 2013, pp85-86 and pp232-243.

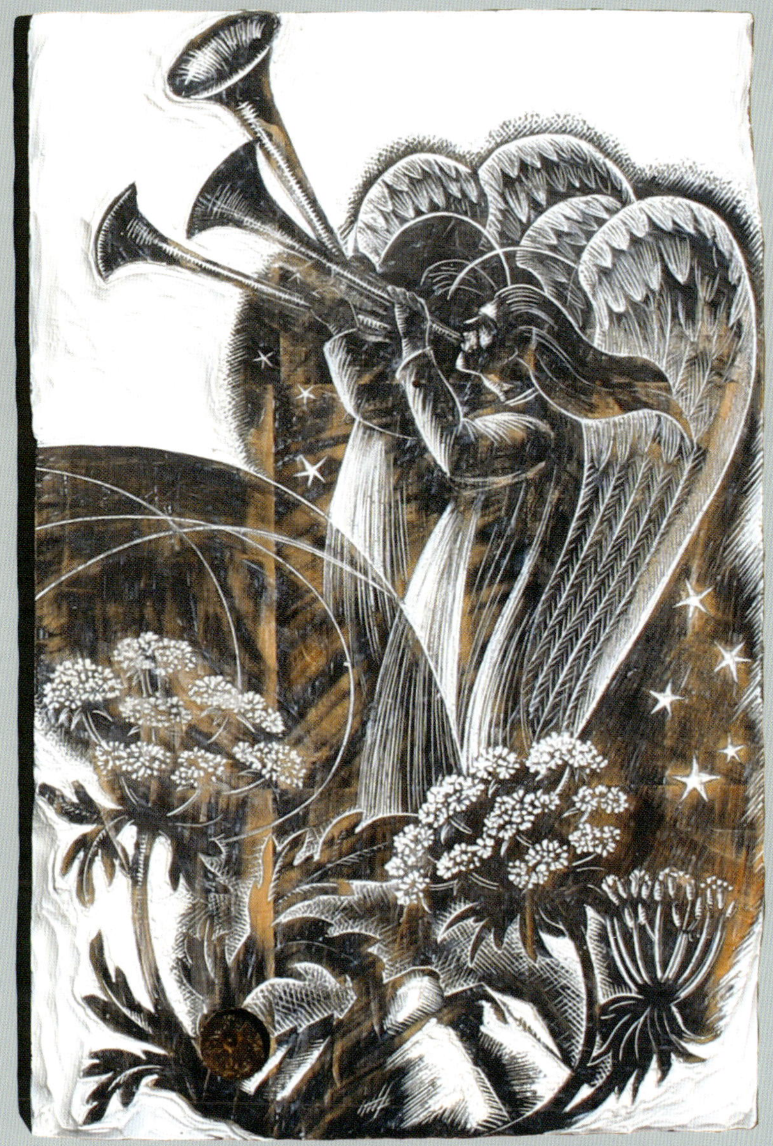

105 – **Clare Leighton** (1898-1989),
Angels and Trumpets, 'The Vision Splendid, BPL 762, 1965,
original woodblock cancelled, 6 × 4 in. (15.3 × 10.2 cm).
Provenance: The Artist's Estate

The Vision Splendid was originally printed in an edition of 50 as part of
Helen Plotz, *The Earth Is The Lord's* (New York: Thomas Y. Corwell). 1965.

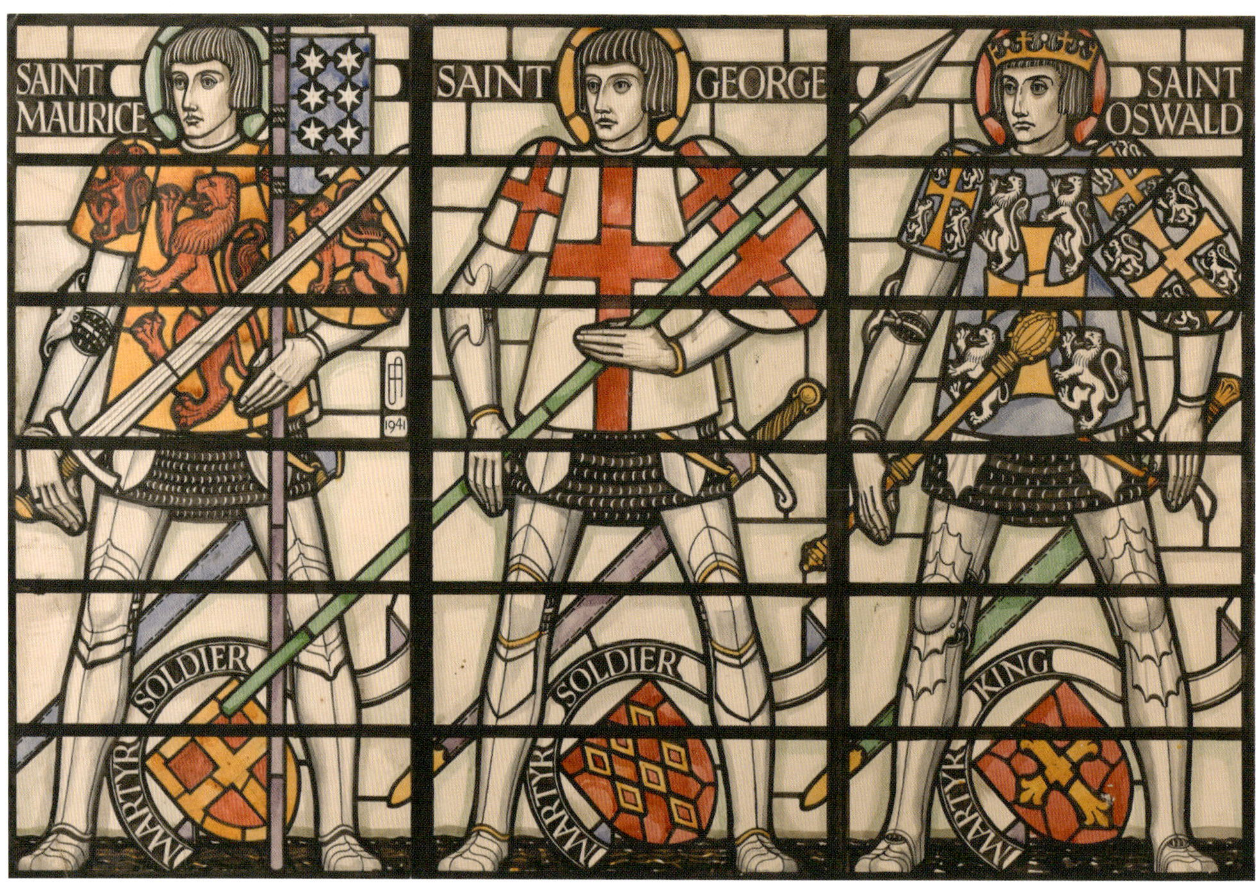

106 – Francis Spear (1902-1979),
Martyr Soldier, 1941, signed with monogram and dated, inscribed *Saint Maurice, Saint Oswald, Martyr Soldier, Martyr King*,
black ink and gouache on paper; 26 ½ x 17 ½ in. (67 x 44.5 cm).
Provenance: Simon Spear, the artist's son.
Exhibited: *WW2 – War Pictures by British Artists*, Morley College London, 28 October-23 November 2016, cat 132.
Literature: *WW2 – War Pictures by British Artists*, Edited by Sacha Llewellyn & Paul Liss, July 2016, cat 132, page 175.

107 – Francis Spear (1902-1979),
St. George and the Dragon, 1941, signed with monogram and dated, inscribed *S. George*,
black ink and gouache on paper; 42 x 18 ½ in. (104 x 47 cm). Provenance: Simon Spear, the artist's son.
Exhibited: *WW2 – War Pictures by British Artists*, Morley College London, 28 October-23 November 2016, cat 133.
Literature: *WW2 – War Pictures by British Artists*, Edited by Sacha Llewellyn & Paul Liss, July 2016, cat 133, page 176.

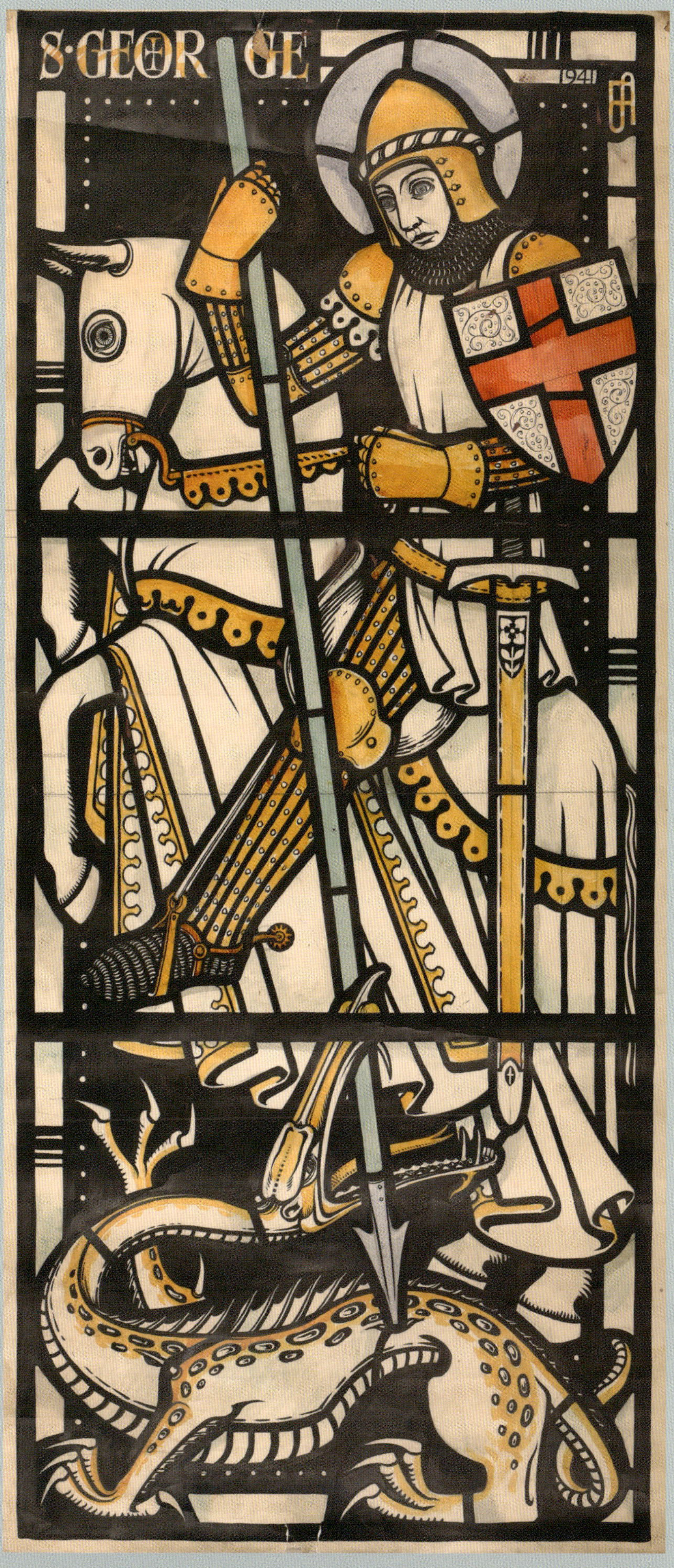

S·GEORGE
1941

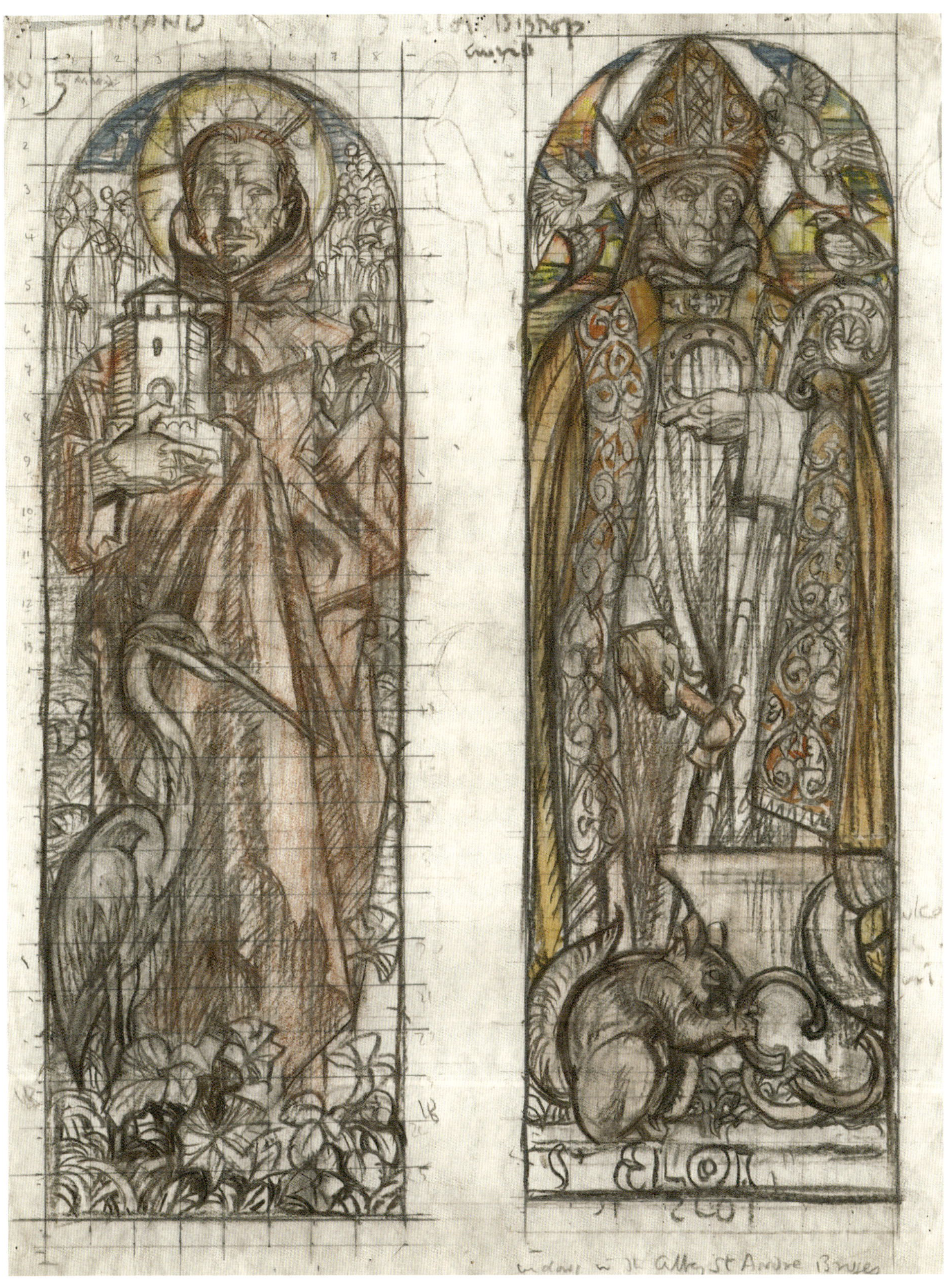

108 – Frank Brangwyn (1867-1956), Studies for St Amand and St Eloi – windows in the Abbey St André, Bruges, coloured chalk and pastel on paper, squared in pencil, 20 ½ × 15 ¾ in. (52.5 × 40 cm).

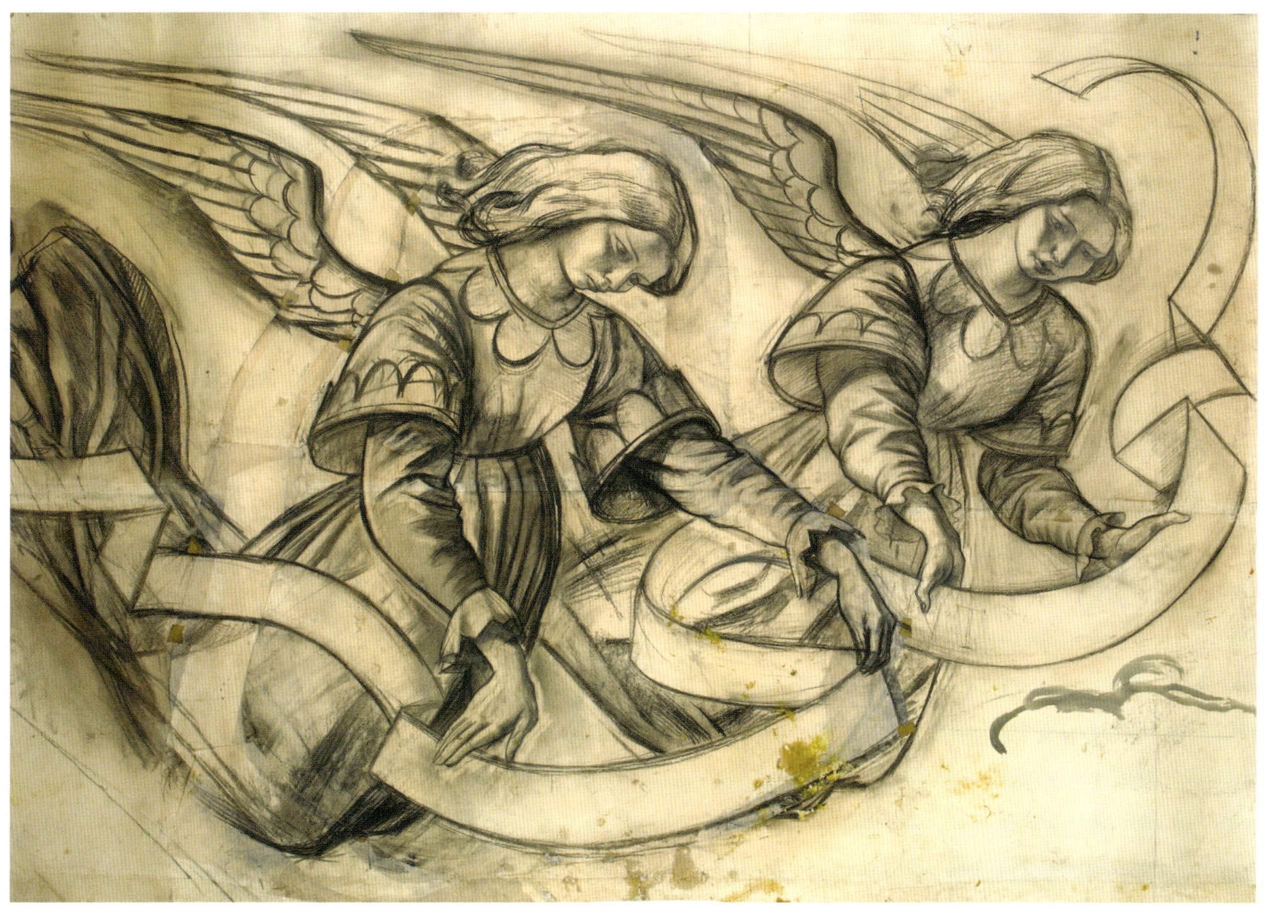

109 – Alan Sorrell (1904-1974), Study for Angels for St Peter's Church, Bexhill-on-Sea, 1951,
pencil and ink on paper, 51 x 75 in. (129.5 x 190 cm).
Provenance: The Artist's Family.

'At Old Bexhill, the parish was restoring the church and wished to recapture some of the quality of medieval wall paintings, a subject on which E.W. Tristram, former tutor in mural painting at the RCA, was the national authority. He recommended Sorrell, a choice approved by the Bishop of Chichester, George Bell, one of the few major patrons of new art in churches at the time. To either side of an opening in the north aisle arcade, where the two spandrels barely met in the middle, Sorrell designed a composition that balances the patrons of the church, Saints Peter and Paul on the left, with the local Saints Wilfrith and Richard in episcopal robes on the right. A flight of angels holding a text provides a link between the two halves across the sky at the top. There are many pitfalls in work of this kind, and Sorrell managed to avoid them with a work that is based on sound drawing and design, fitting into the medieval context but not self-consciously archaic.' (Alan Powers, 'Murals and Public Paintings', *Alan Sorrell, The Life and Works of An English Neo-Romantic Artist*, Sansom, 2013, p 127).

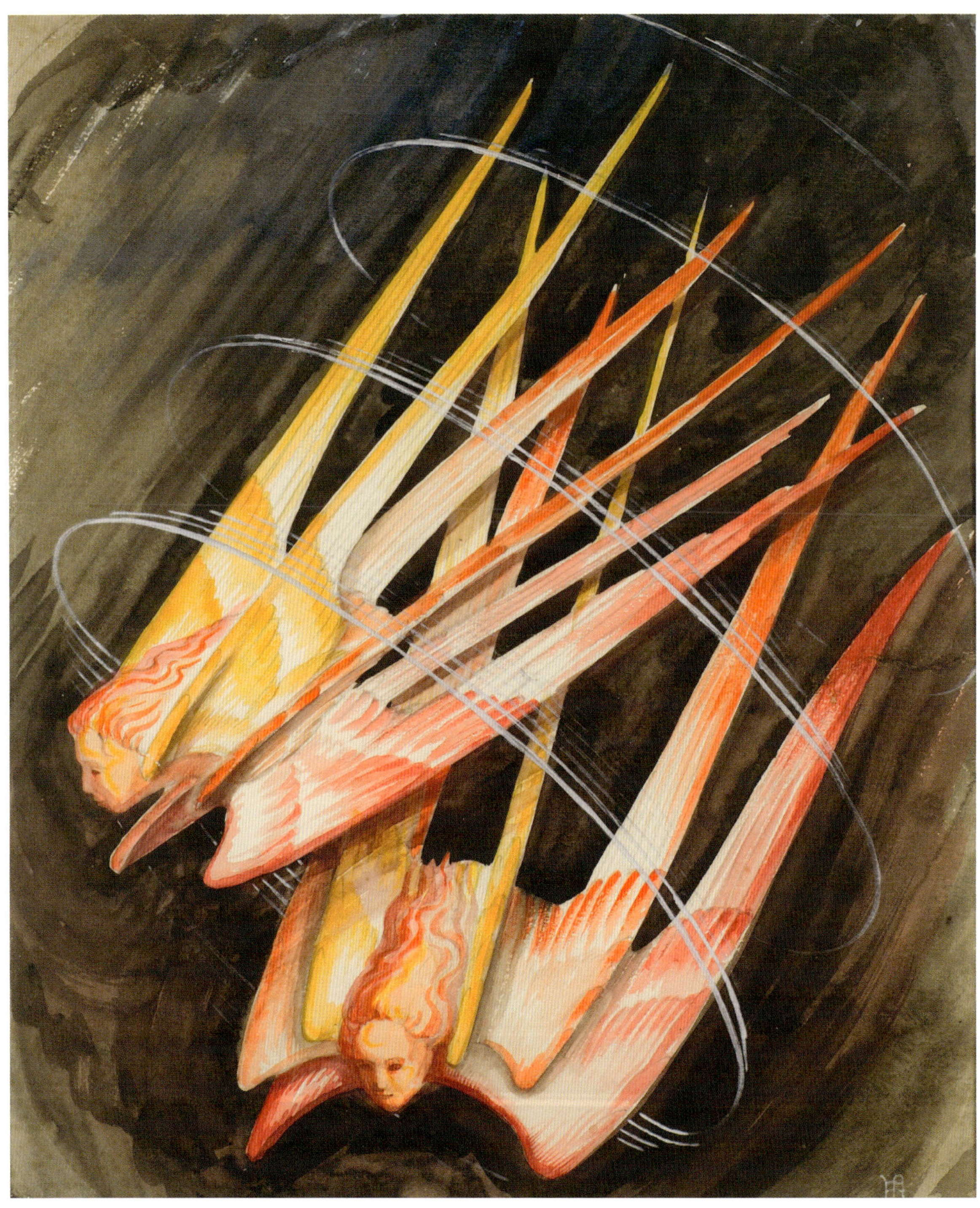

110 – **Francis Spear** (1902-1979), *Seraphine*, design for stained glass window, 1932,
signed with monogram, inscribed with title to reverse,
pencil, watercolour and gouache on paper, 15 x 21 in. (53.8 x 53.5 cm).
Provenance: Simon Spear, the artist's son.

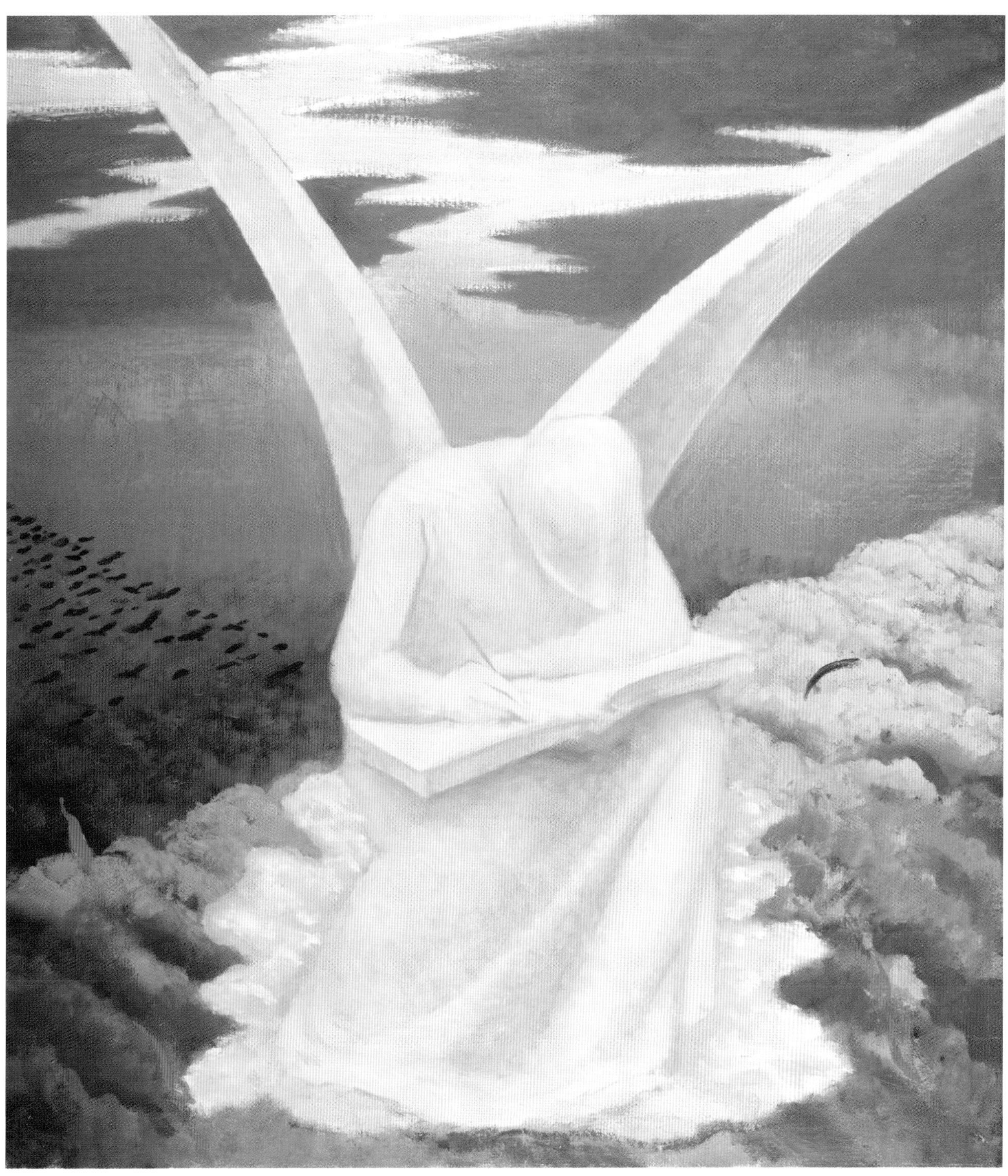

111 – **Dorothea Frances MacLagan** (1895-1982), *The Angel of Revelation*, c.1925,
oil on canvas, 18 × 11 ¾ in. (45 × 29.8 cm).

This striking image is likely to show the Archangel Gabriel – known as the angel of revelation or announcement. He plays a significant role in Christianity, Islam, Judaism, and many other faiths, acting as a messenger for God. In the Bible, Gabriel can be found in the books of Luke and Daniel.

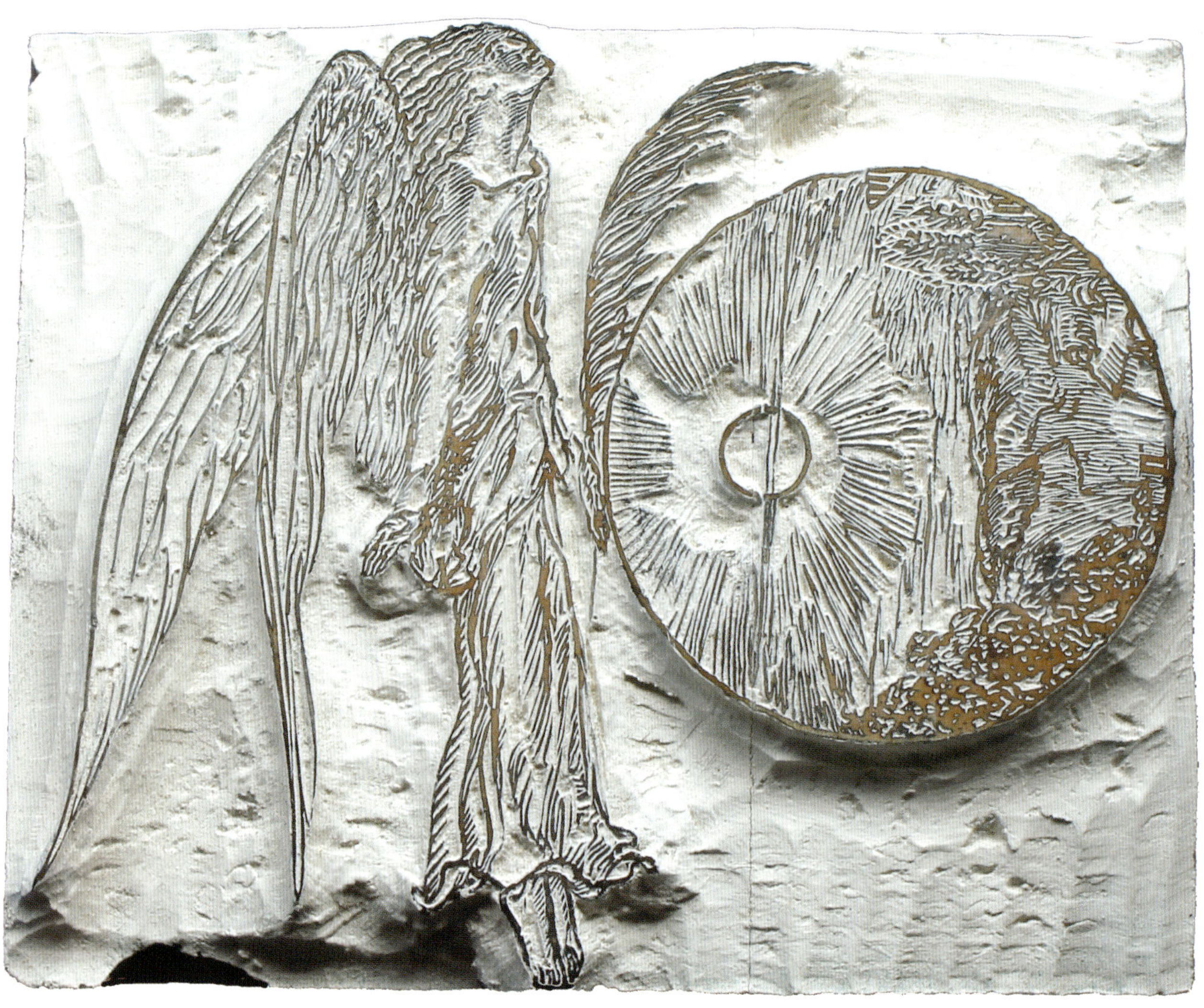

112 – **Frederick Carter** (1883-1967), *The Angel Messenger*,
original woodblock, 2 ½ × 3 ½ in. (6.8 × 8.8 cm).

During the 1920s, Carter became a mystic and worked on illustrations for D.H. Lawrence's *Apocalypse* (1929).

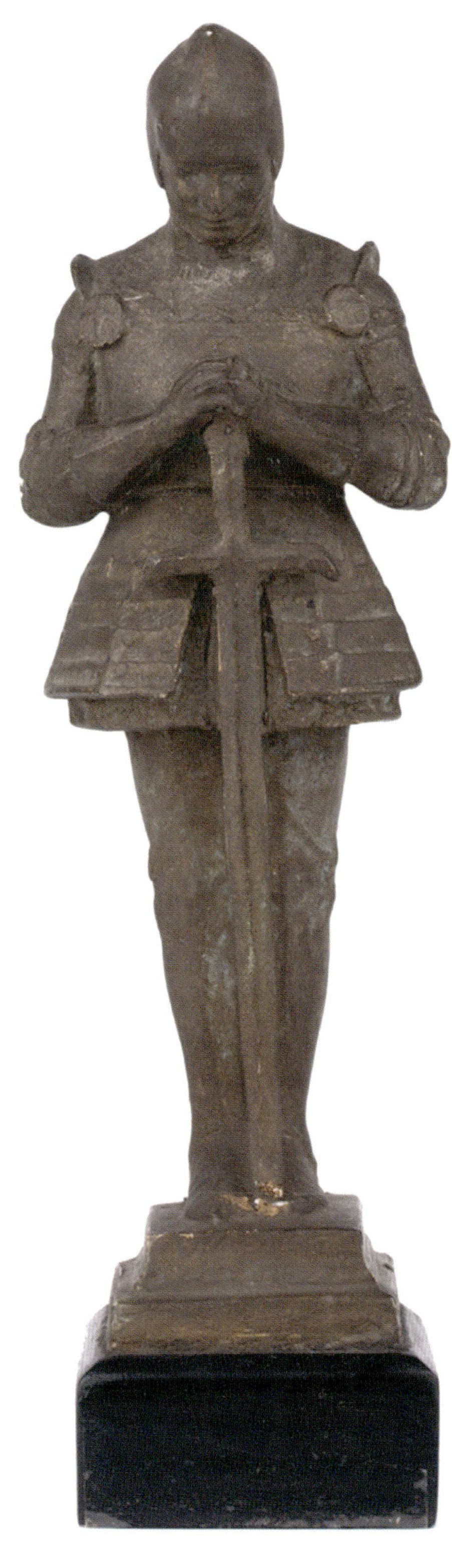

113 – **Margaret Wrightson** (1877-1976), *St George* – the original maquette for Cramlington War Memorial, Northumberland, c.1921, the original plaster maquette, height: 8 in. (20.5 cm).

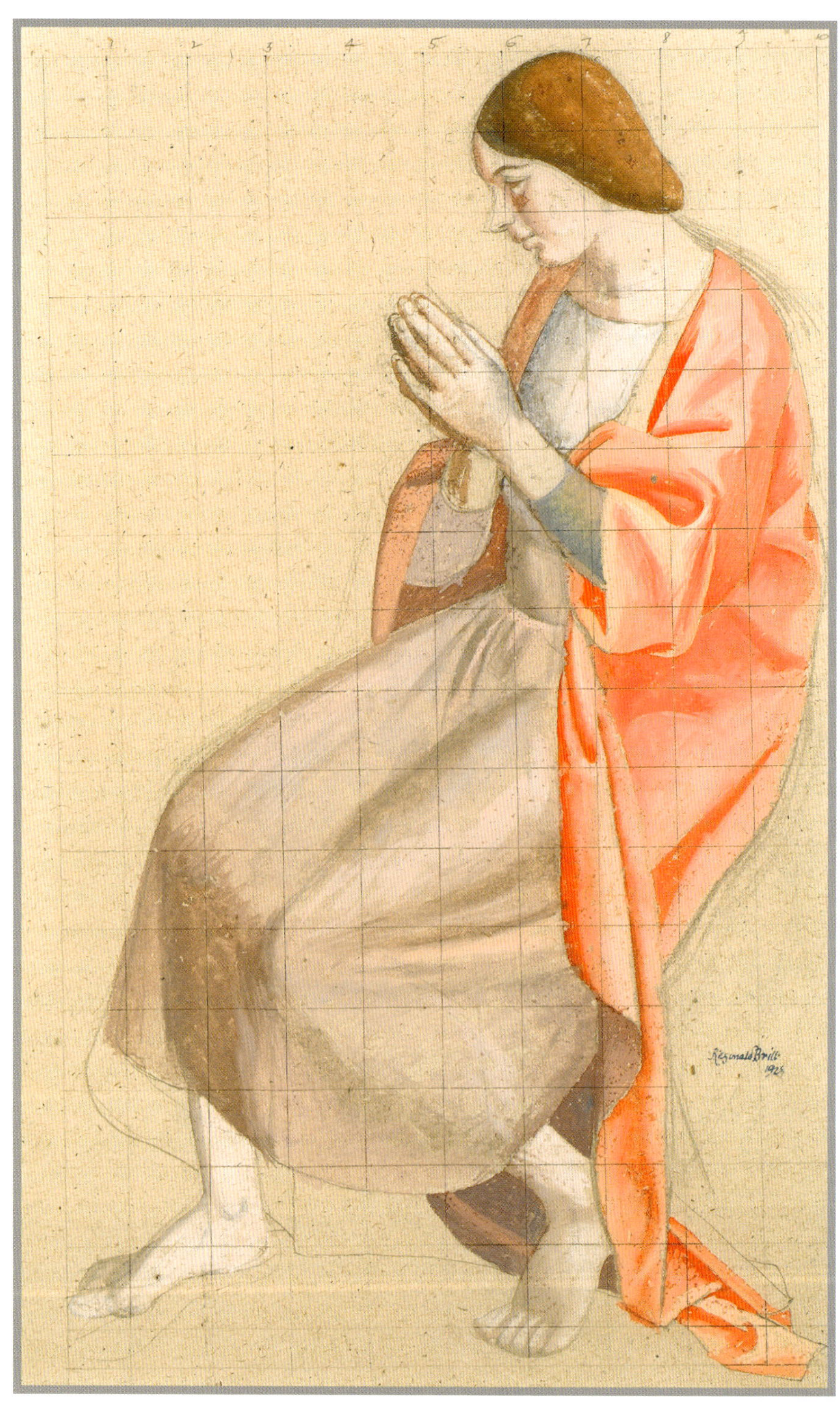

114 – Reginald Brill (1902-1974), Study of Praying Angel for *Adam and Eve*, 1927,
signed and dated in pen& ink, titled on four lables to the reverse,
gouache on brown textured paper, squared in pencil, 18 x 13 in. (46.5 x 33 cm).
Provenance: Richards/Webb.
Exhibited: Kingston University, (Permanent loan 13th July 1998).

Adam and Eve was the painting with which Brill won the 1927 Rome Scholarship in Painting.

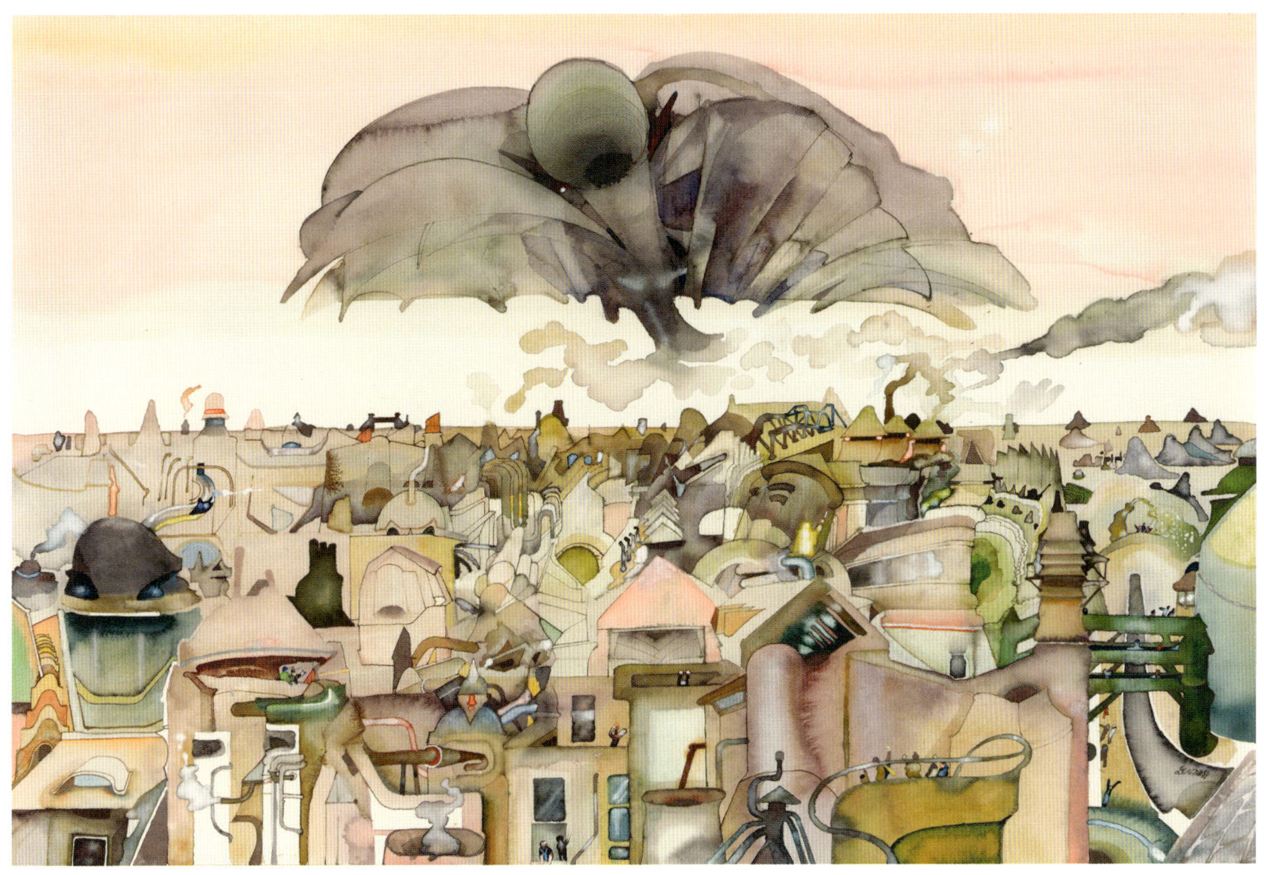

115 – **David Evans** (1929–1988), *The Angel of Mons*, 1978, signed, watercolour on paper, 26 ¼ × 39 ¼ in. (67 × 100 cm).

Provenance: The artist's studio.
Literature: *David Evans (1929-1988)*, edited by Sacha Llewellyn & Paul Liss, published by Liss Llewellyn Fine Art, 2017. Cat 134, pp172-173.

Evans subjects range from the sacred to the profane and the mundane to the exotic; though frequently with the edges blurred: *Noli Me Tangere*; The *Wages of Sin and Co* (1979); *Scenes from Provincial Life* (1979); *South Sea Bubble* (1978); *The Angel of Mons* (1978). The Old Testament and Pagan world provided a ready stream of themes in which Evans' imagination could flow freely, responding with science-fiction style reinterpretations of age old subjects: *Tower of Babel* (1981-82); *David and Goliath*; *Dies Irae* (1978), *Venus Observed* (1979); *Sirens*; *The Witch of Endor*; *Opus Surgieum*; *Saxons* (1978); *Landscape with Angels*.

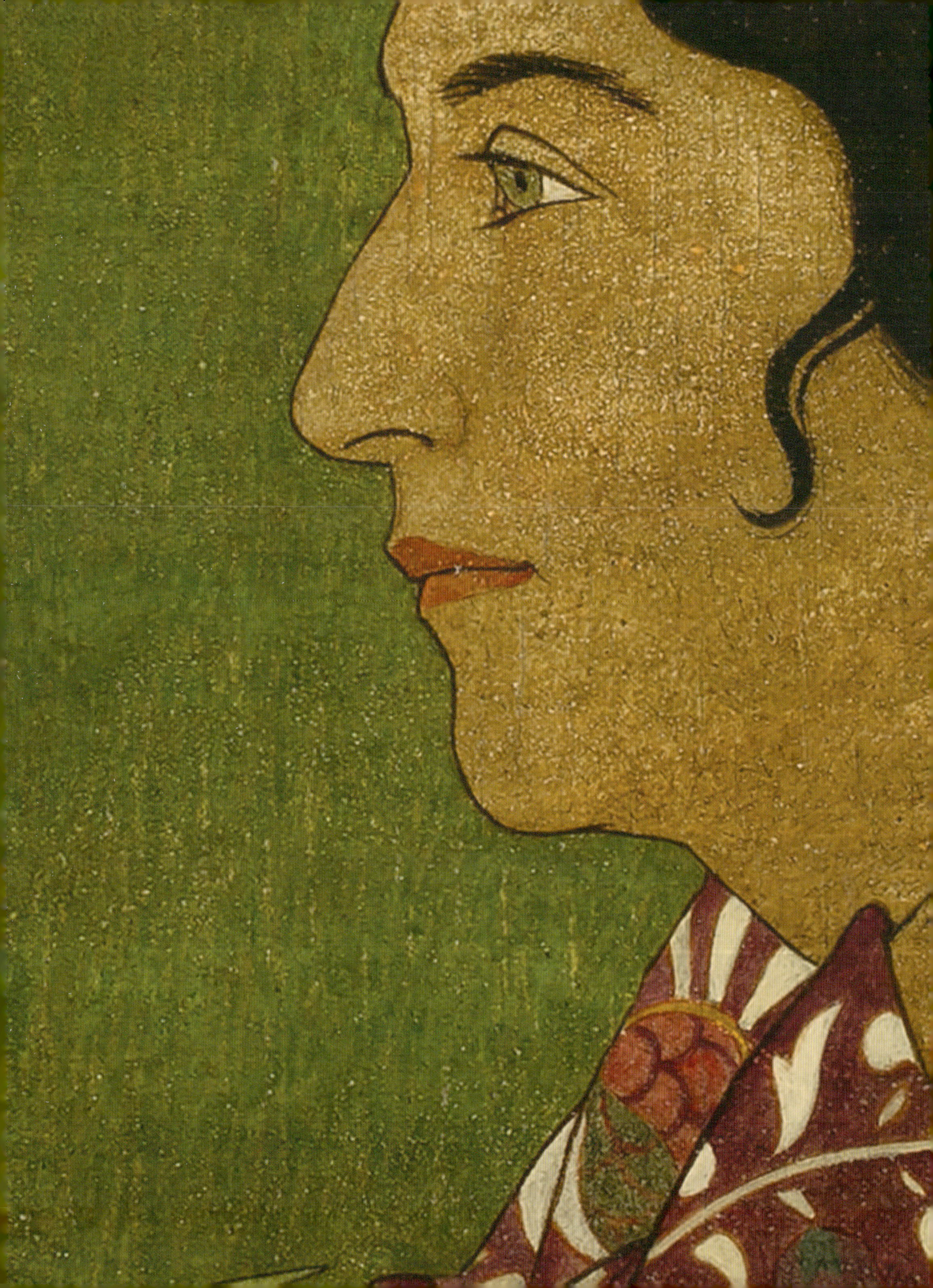

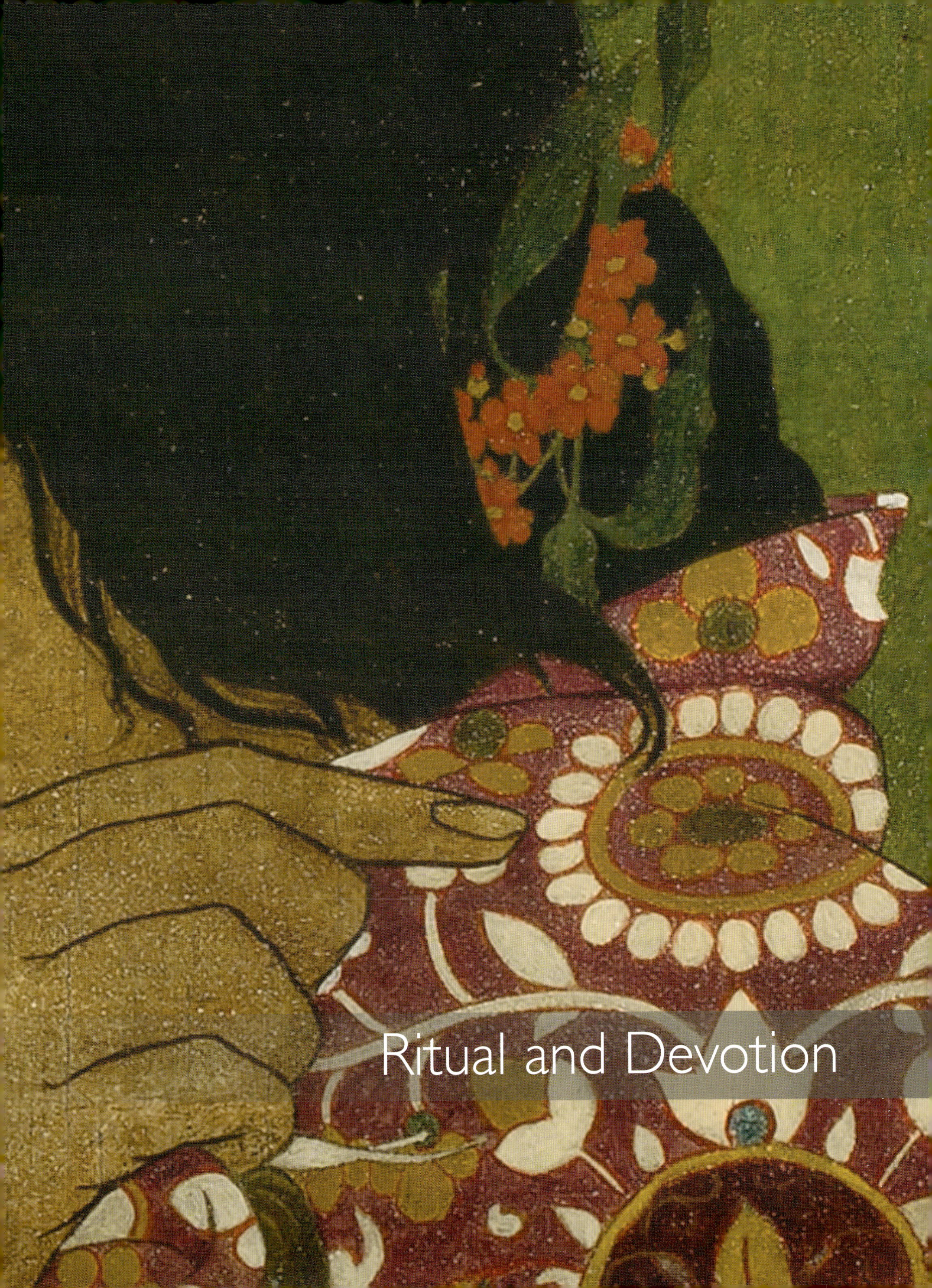
Ritual and Devotion

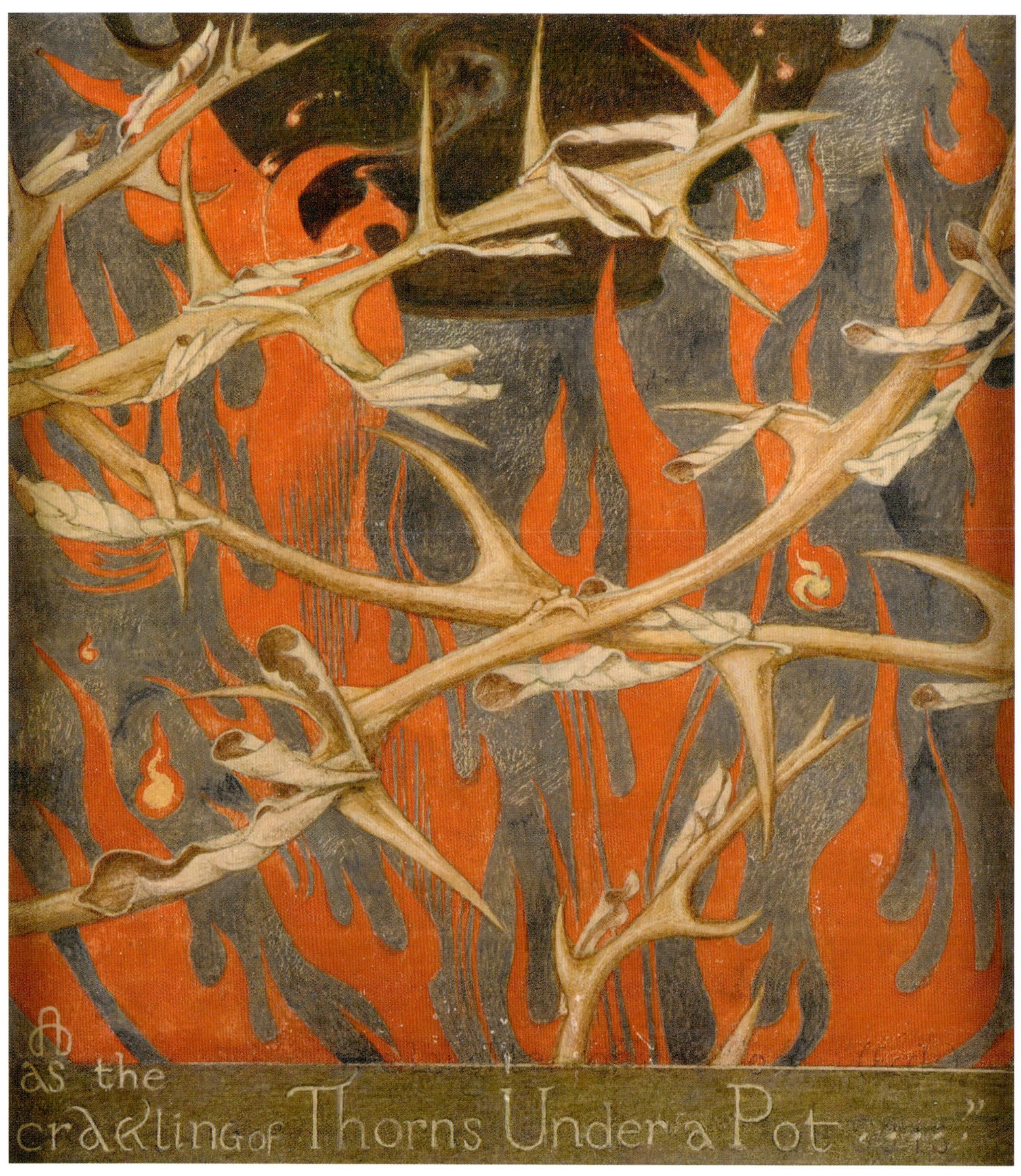

116 – **Maxwell Armfield** (1881-1972), *As the crackling of thorns under a pot...*, 1920s,
signed with monogram and inscribed with title; also inscribed in pencil 'The laughter of fools',
tempera on panel, 10 × 9 ½ in. (25.5 × 24 cm).
Provenance: The Fine Art Society 1987; Private collection New York.

According to a note written by Armfield in 1971 (note book no. VIII, p695) the title comes from Ecclesiastes 7.6: 'For as the crackling of thorn bushes under a pot, So is the laughter of the fool; And this too is futility'. Armfield might also have had in mind Psalm 58:9: 'Before your pots can feel the fire of thorns He will sweep them away with a whirlwind, the green and the burning alike'.

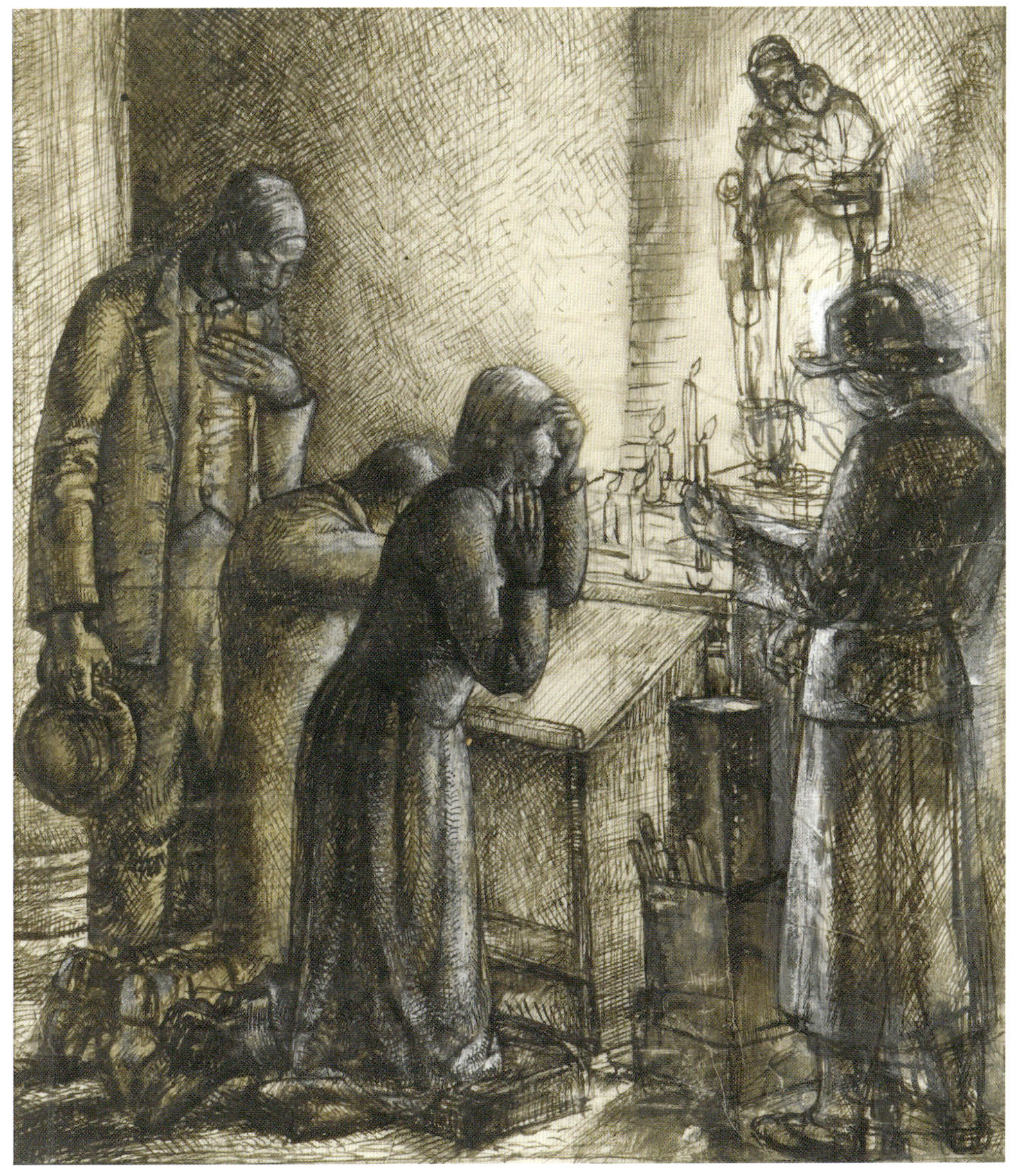

117 – **Evelyn Gibbs** (1905-1991), *The Chapel*, 1928, pen & ink with white highlights, 5 ¾ x 5 ¼ in. (14.8 x 13.2 cm).

Evelyn Gibbs trained as a graphic artist and more particularly as a printmaker in etching and engraving. Born in Liverpool in 1905, the granddaughter of an Edinburgh engraver, she enrolled at Liverpool School of Art in 1922, winning a scholarship to the Royal College of Art in 1926 and from there a further scholarship to the British School at Rome in 1929, allowing her to continue and expand her practice.

Her tutor at the RCA was the excellent Malcom Osborne who encouraged his students to observe people and landscapes in everyday life. *The Chapel* was based on studies made in Westminster Cathedral.

'It is interesting to compare this with another print made the same year, *The Graveside* – an engraving where four figures attend a burial site. In *The Chapel*, prayers are being offered and candles lit in memory of the departed. The women are so similar in these two works as to suggest the story of a bereavement, but the treatment is very different. Daylight and space are rendered cleanly behind the grieving figures in *The Graveside*, whereas the sombre enclosed space in *The Chapel* depends upon shadows and the candlelit area around the statue of the Virgin and Child. Here, Gibbs uses emphatic hatching and cross hatching to intensify the religious and emotional atmosphere, and it is all there in the original drawing, ready to transfer, in reverse, to the copper plate.'

Pauline Lucas, author of *Evelyn Gibbs: Artist and Traveller* (2001).

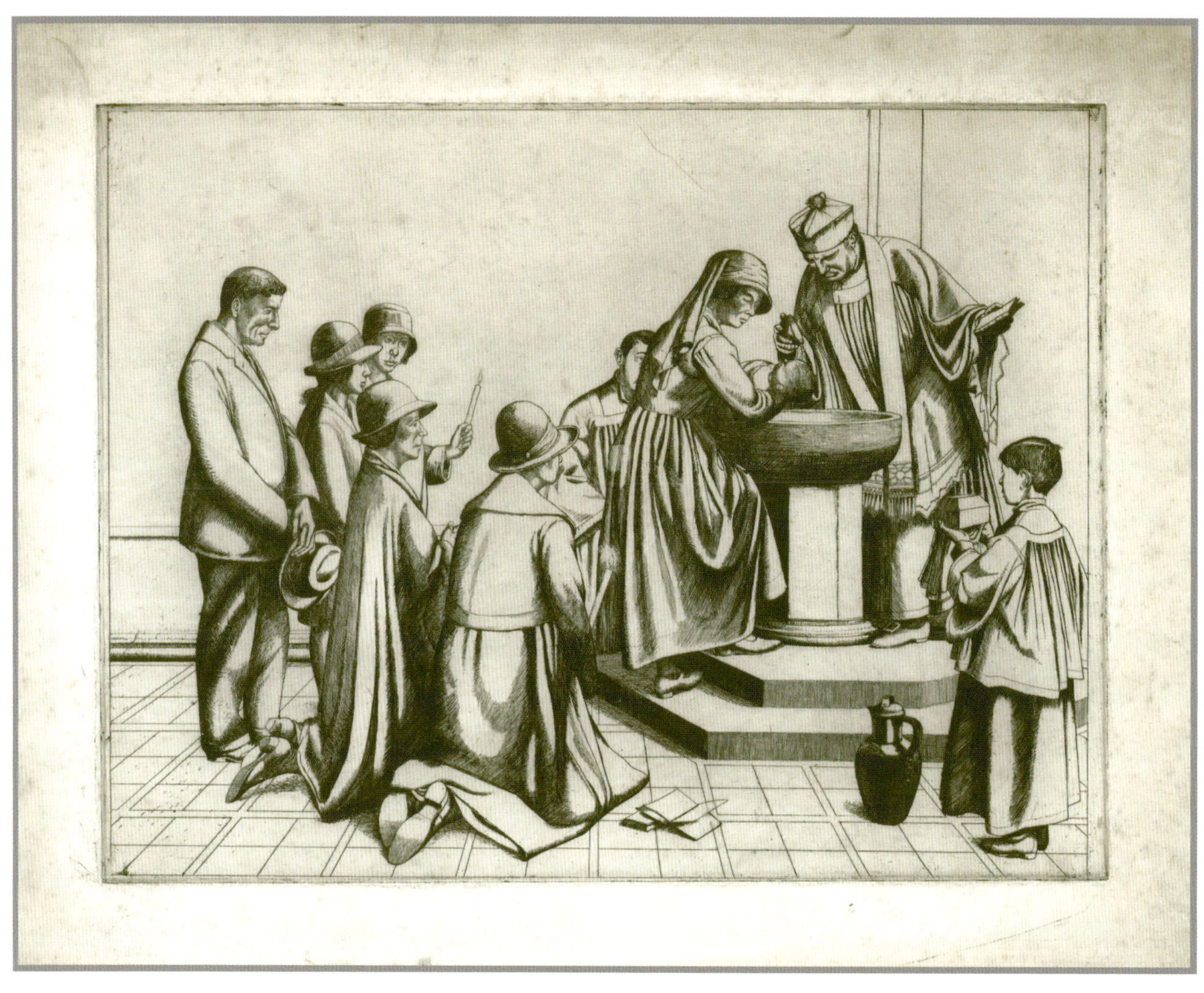

118 – **Frederick Austin** (1902-1990), *A Baptism*, 1926, etching, 8 x 11 in. (22 x 28 cm).

As one of the largest and most elaborate of Frederick Austin's etchings, this relatively sparse composition, arranged in the manner of a traditional frieze, reflects aspects of the early Renaissance art which so interested Frederick Austin, and which drew him to Rome the following year.

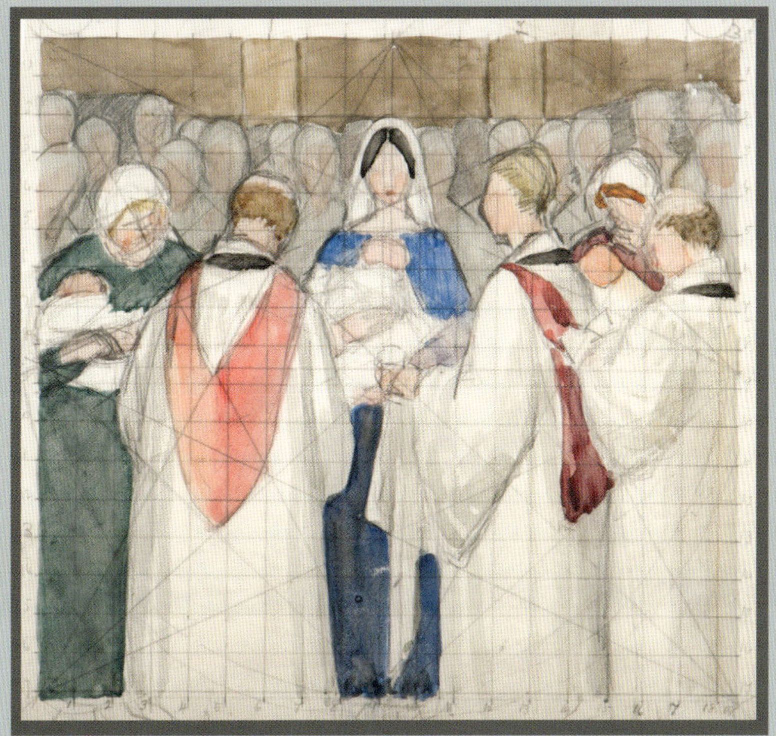

119 – **Phyllis Dodd** (1899-1995), Study for *Baptising little Pearce 2*, c.1925,
squared and inscribed with measurements,
pencil and watercolour on paper, 6 ¼ × 6 ½ in. (15.8 × 16.8 cm).
Provenance: The artist's daughters.

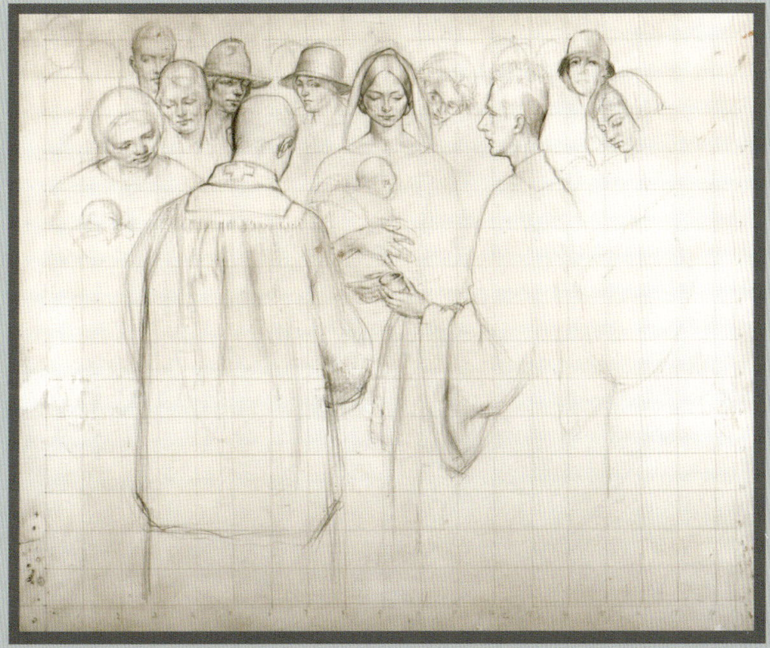

120 – **Phyllis Dodd** (1899-1995), Study for *Baptism of Little Pearce*, c.1923,
squared, pencil on paper, 12 ½ × 15 ¼ in. (31.8 × 38.6 cm).

Pencil notes in the margins of this drawing identify the models for the crowd as
including the artist herself, Enid Marx, Muriel Minter and Gerald Cooper.

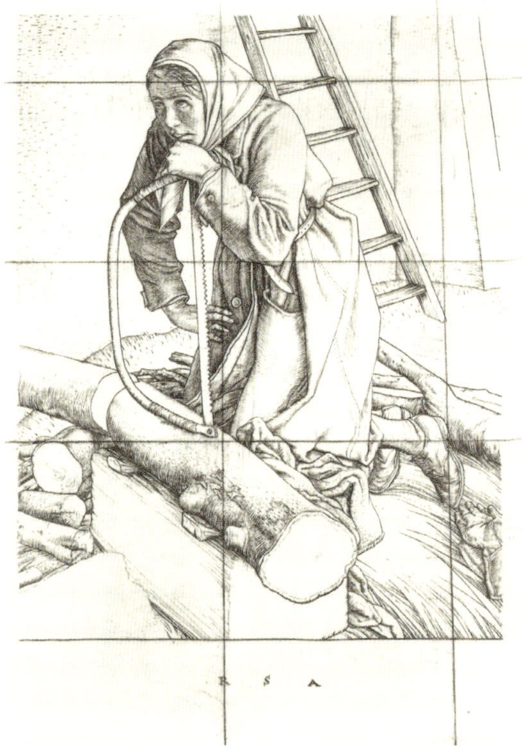

121 a – Print pulled from plate posthumously.

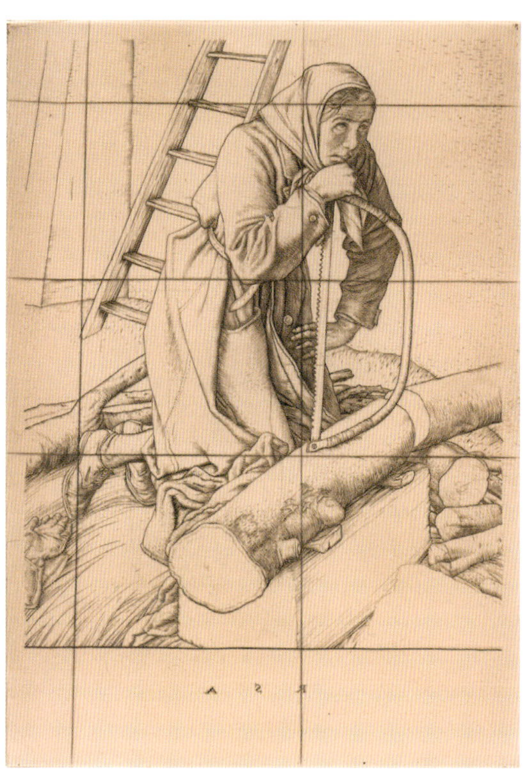

121 – **Robert Austin** (1895-1973), *Widow of a Hero*, 1944, original copper plate (cancelled), line engraving, signed in the plate, 9 ¼ × 7 in. (23.5 × 17.5 cm).

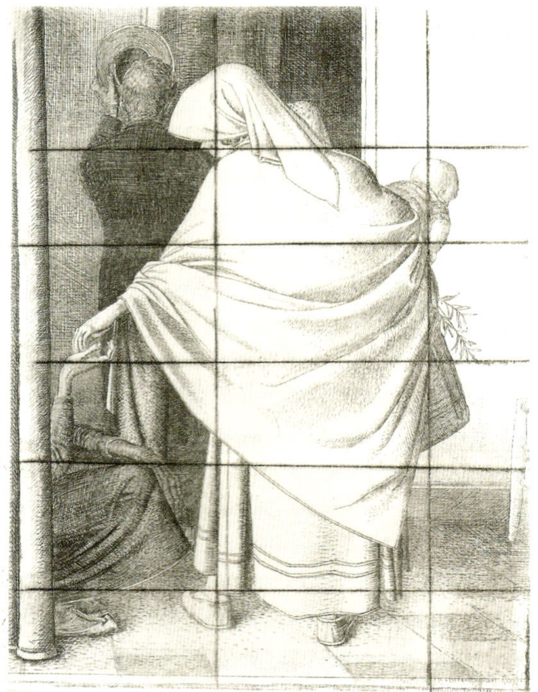

122 a – Print pulled from plate posthumously.

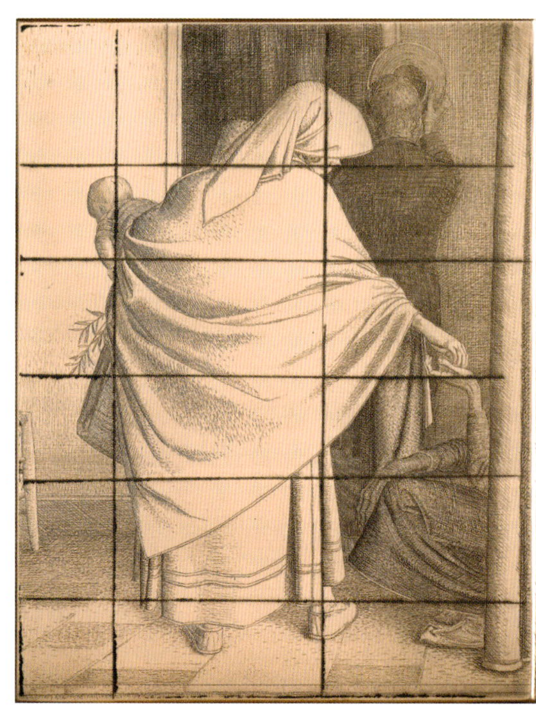

122 – **Robert Austin** (1895-1973), *Palm Sunday*, 1925, original copper plate (cancelled), etching, 5 ¾ × 4 ¾ in. (15 × 12 cm).

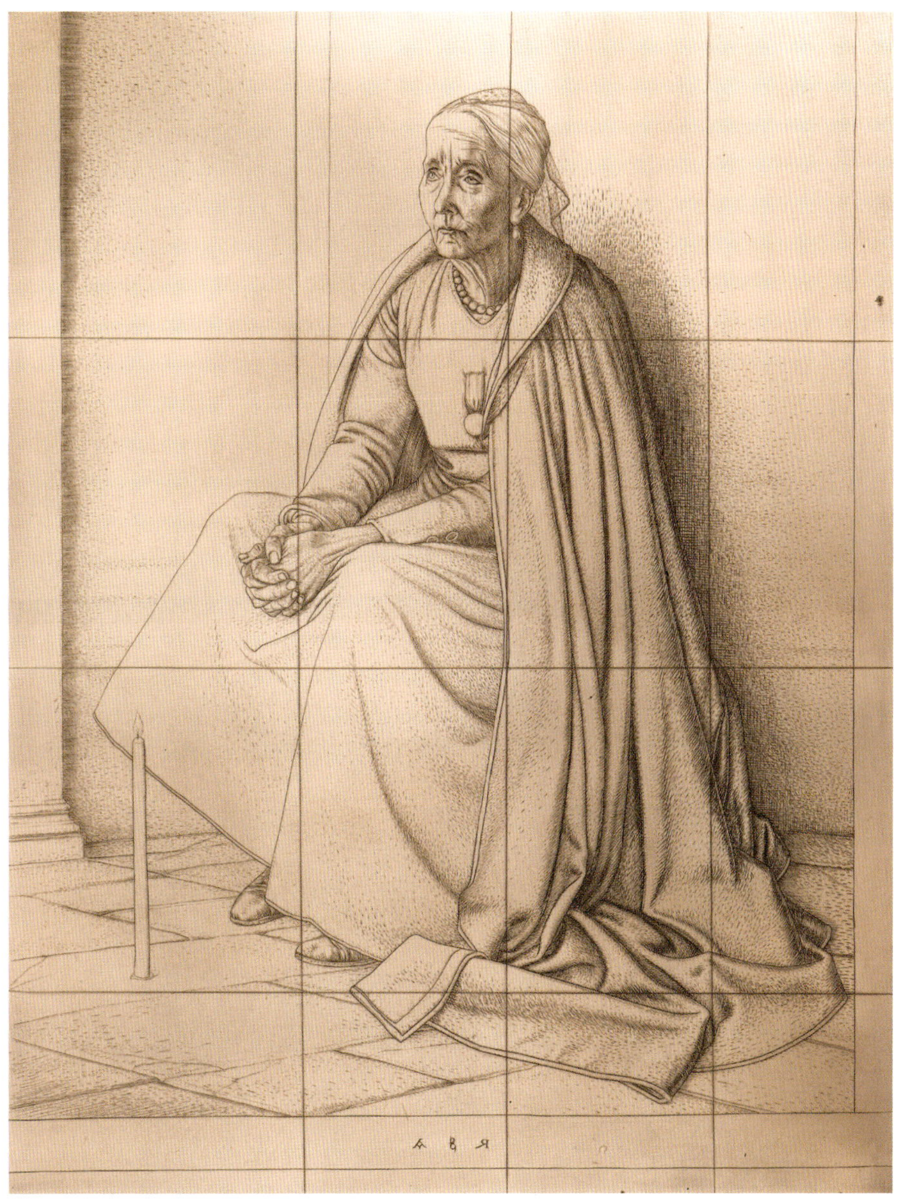

123 – **Robert Austin** (1895-1973), *The Mother*, line engraving, signed in the plate,
original copper plate (cancelled), 11 ½ × 8 ½ in. (29.5 × 22 cm).

 As Rome Scholar in Engraving, Austin produced some of the most enduring images of Italian peasants, sharing with D.H. Lawrence an admiration for a culture 'so primitive, so pagan, so strangely heathen, and half-savage' (D. H. Lawrence, *Sea and Sardinia*, 1921).

Campbell Dodgson, Keeper of Prints and Drawings at the British Museum, who compiled the standard reference work on Austin, compared him to Albrecht Dürer, noting that Austin had 'more than a touch of that master in him' (Dodgson, Robert Austin, exh. cat., Twenty-One Gallery, London, 1930).

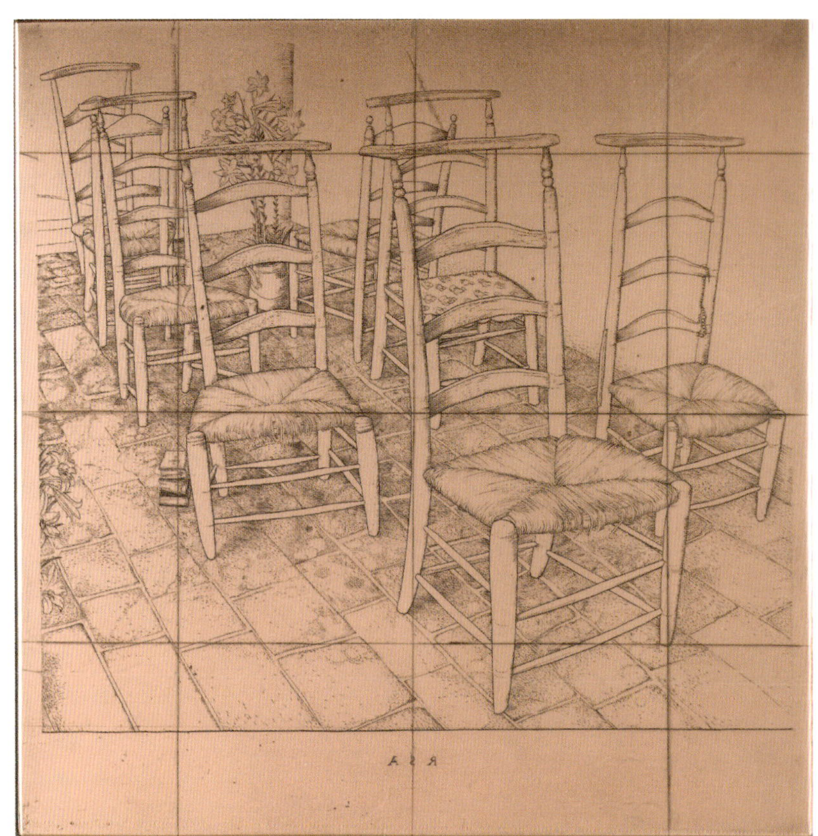

124 – **Robert Austin** (1895-1973),
Empty Church – Concarneau, 1949,
original copper plate (cancelled),
line engraving, signed in the plate,
6 ¼ × 6 ½ in. (16.2 × 16.9 cm).

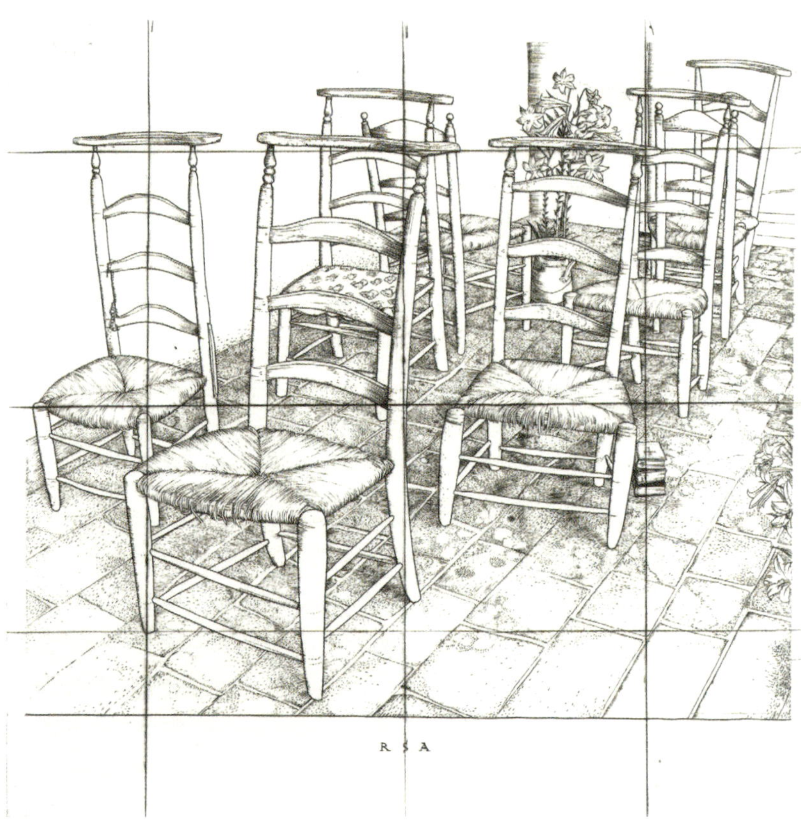

124 a – Print pulled from plate posthumously.

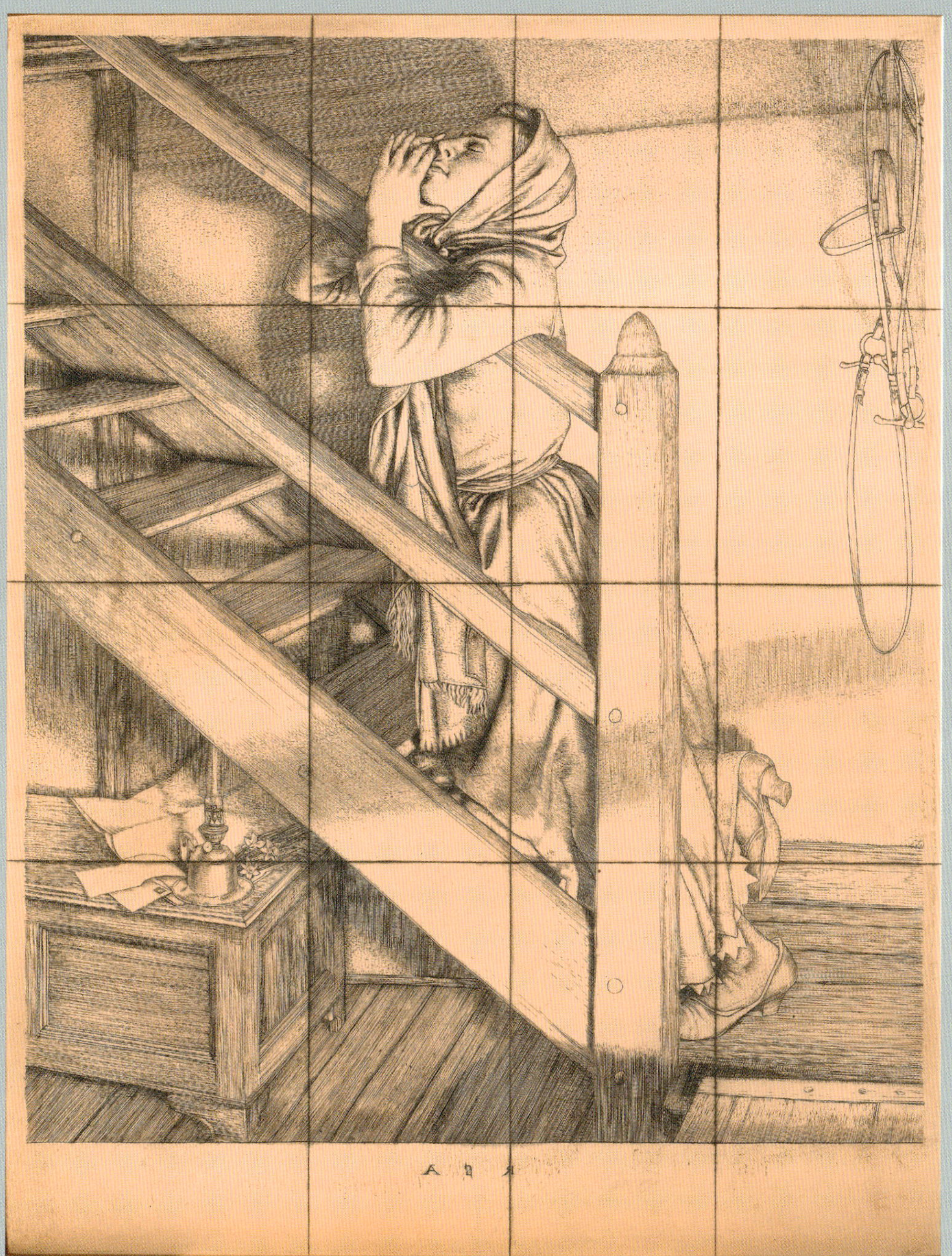

125 – Robert Austin (1895-1973), *Evening*, 1939, line engraving, signed in the plate,
original copper plate (cancelled), 8 ¾ x 6 ¾ in. (22.5 x 17.2 cm).
Provenance: Provenance: the artist's family.
Literature: Campbell Dodgson, Robert Austin, exh. cat., Twenty-One Gallery, London, 1930; Gordon Cooke,
Drawings and Prints by Robert Austin, exh. cat., The Fine Art Society, London, 2001

Evening, a composition created during the early years of the war, is one of Austin's most accomplished engravings.
The model praying was Eleanor Hudson, (Austin's student and mistress) a watercolourist, etcher and designer
best known for her depictions of women at work during the Second World. One of Austin's signature prints
Evening might be seen as a pendant to the same sized image Girl on a Stairs which Austin produced in the early
years of WW2. Both compositions, which evolve around solitary figures in at the bottom and top of a stair
case, enveloped by shadows and silence, convey a sense of mystery. The setting of *Evening* was The Chapel at
Burham Overy Staithe, (Norfolk) where Austin had his studio when not working in London.

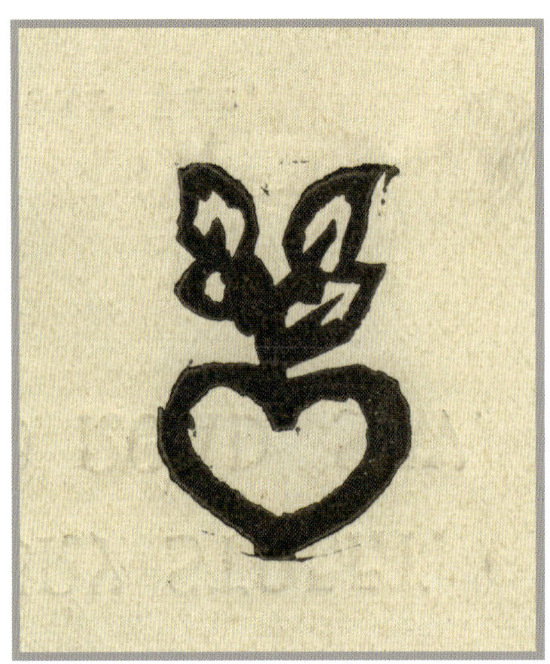

126 – **Frank Brangwyn** (1867-1956),
Flaming Heart (V-3587), c.1919, signed in pencil,
Wood cut, 1 ¼ × 1 in. (3.1 × 2.5 cm).

127 – **Maxwell Armfield** (1881-1972), *Pacific Portrait*, c.1915-1922, signed and dated, inscribed 'op 80' in rectangular cartouche,
tempera on plywood panel, 23 ¾ × 19 ¾ in. (44.5 × 38 cm).
Provenance: The Fortunoff collection [HF12]; Privaye collection.
Exhibited : Royal Society of Portrait Painters, 1929 (74); The Fine Art Society 1971; The National Galleries of Scotland, True to Life, 2017, (3)
Literature; Patrick Elliot & Sacha Llewellyn; *True to Life, British Realist Painting in the 1920s & 1930s*, July 2017, , Cat. 3, page 58.

Pacific Portrait was exhibited at the Royal Society of Portrait Painters annual exhibition in 1929. However, the title suggests that it was done in America. Armfield and his wife Constance sailed for New York in Spring 1915, probably in part to avoid his being called up to fight in the First World War (he was a Quaker turned Christian Scientist and would have stood as a conscientious objector). They stayed in New York. An exhibition of his work led to the commission from a railway company for a painting of the Grand Canyon, and they duly set off for Colorado. They then travelled on to California, where they set up a drama course in Berkeley. They subsequently lived in New York and returned to England in 1922. This portrait was presumably painted in California. It is clearly inspired by Italian Quattrocento portraiture, by the likes of Antonio del Pollaiuolo, Domenico Ghirlandaio and Alesso Baldovinetti:

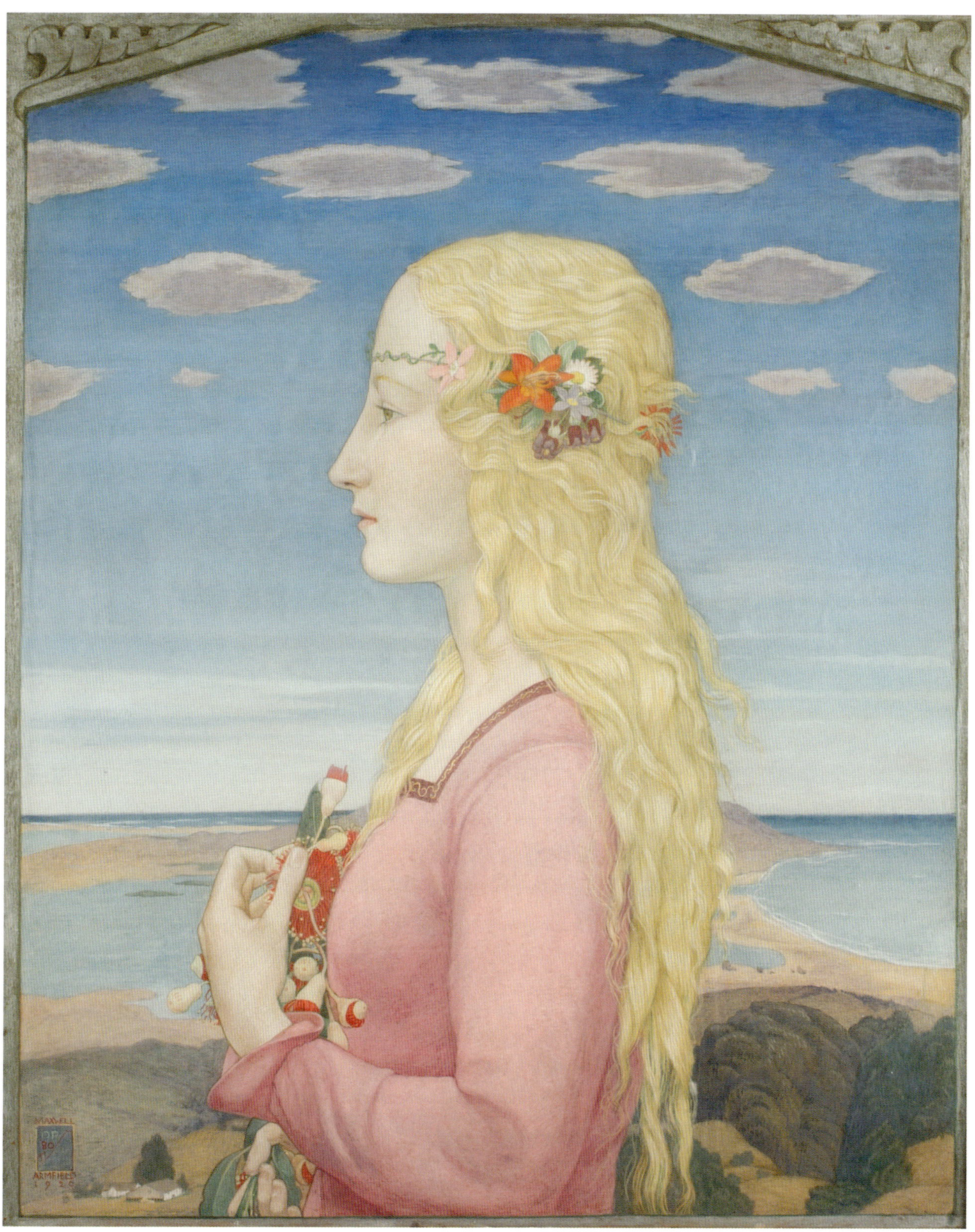

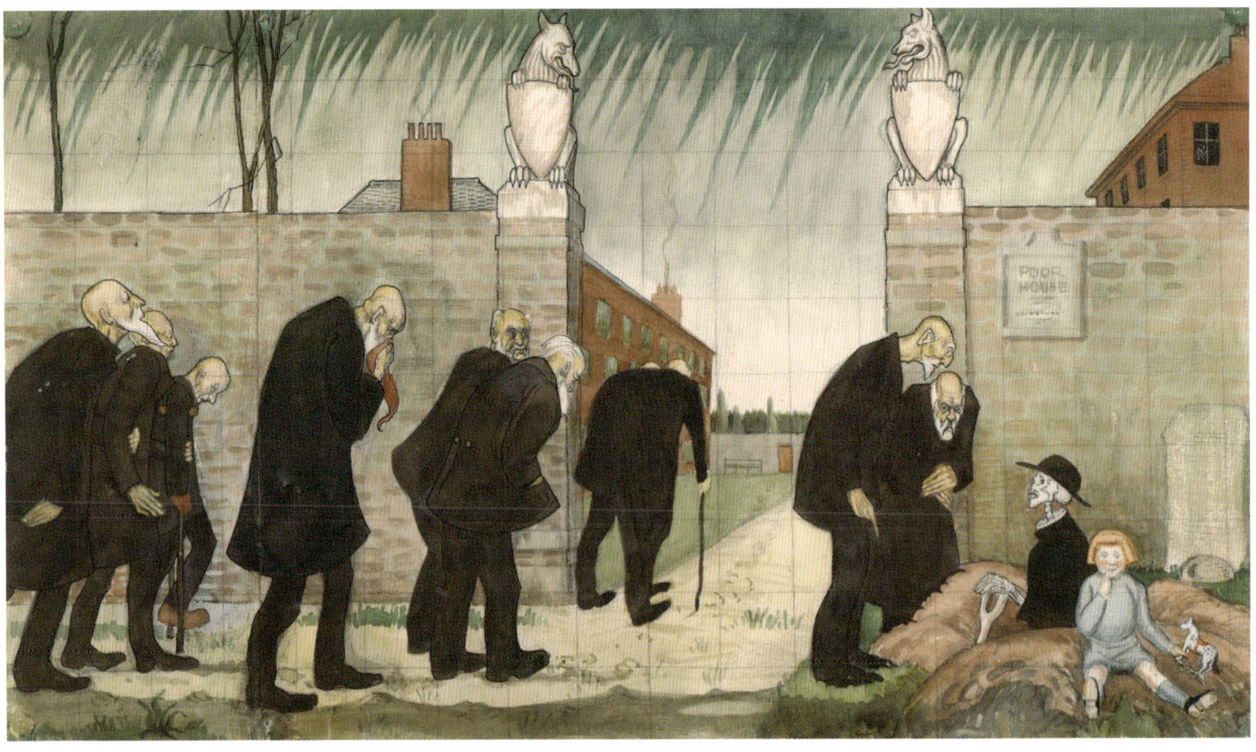

128 – Douglas Percy Bliss (1900-1984),
The Poorhouse – RCA Composition, 1923, signed, titled and dated in pencil,
pen & ink and gouache on paper, 10 × 17 ½ in. (25.4 × 44.4 cm).
Provenance: Prudence and Rosalind Bliss

"In *The Poor House*, 1923, derelict old men shufffle through the gates of the institution whle to the right a skeleton gravedigger prepares a hole watched by a young boy. A later engraving of the same scene shows a gravestone with the name Douglas Percy Bliss carved upon it."

Malcome York,
Gargoyles and Tattie-Bogles, The Lives and Work of Douglas Percy Bliss & Phyllis Dodd, The Fleece Press, 2017, p 34.

129 – Eric Ravilious (1903-1942),
Clerical Outfitter, 1938, from *Highstreet* by J. M. Richards,
original lithograph, full sheet, 9 × 6 in. (23 × 15.2 cm).

First published in 1938, this classic book introduces the British high street, pairing the timeless illustrations of Eric Ravilious with an engaging text by architectural historian J. M. Richards. Shops include the family butcher, the cheesemonger, the knife grinder, and the oyster bar. Only 2,000 copies of the original book were printed before the lithographic plates were destroyed in the London Blitz during World War II. As a result, it has become one of the most collectible of all artist's books from this period.

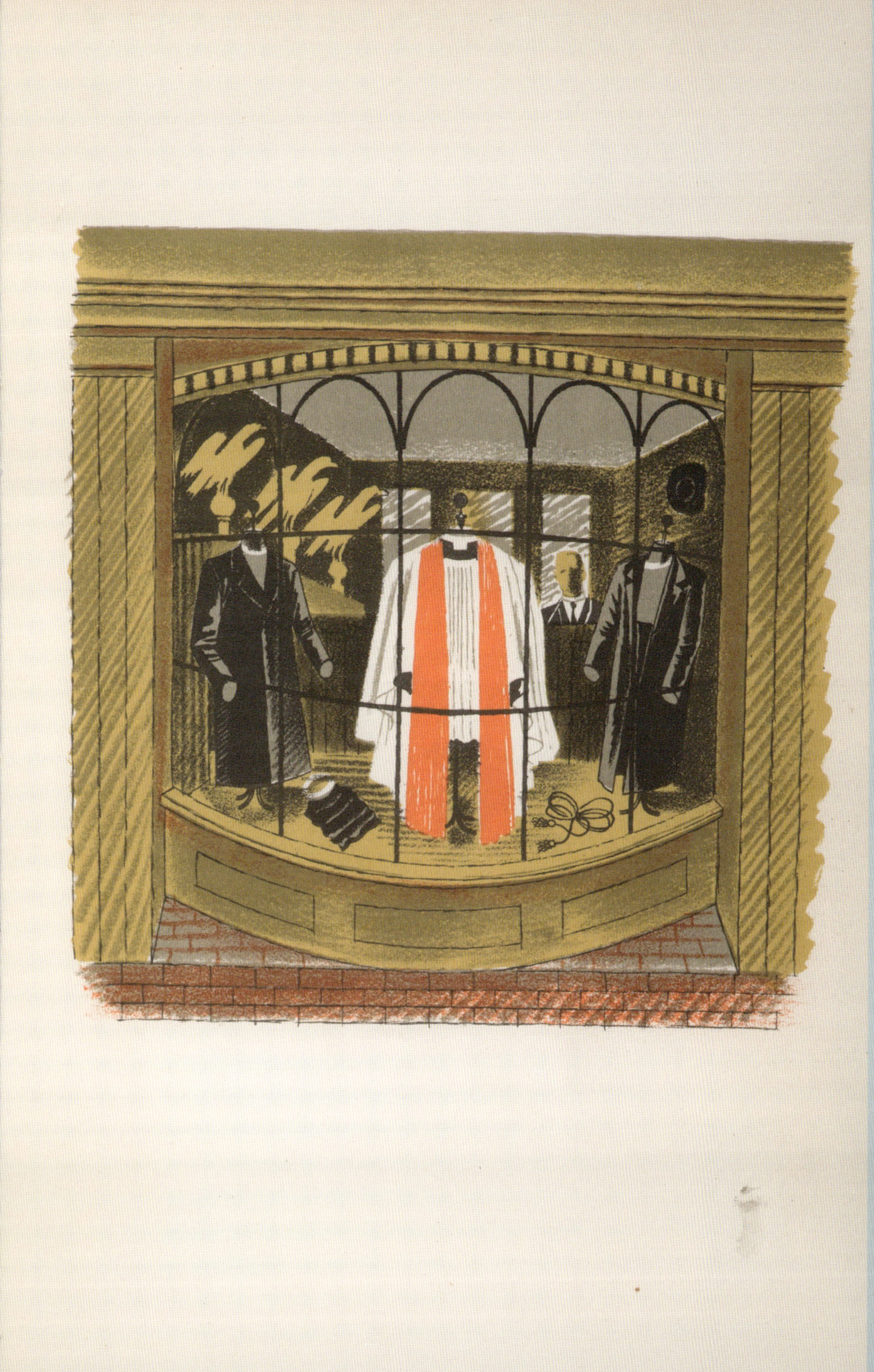

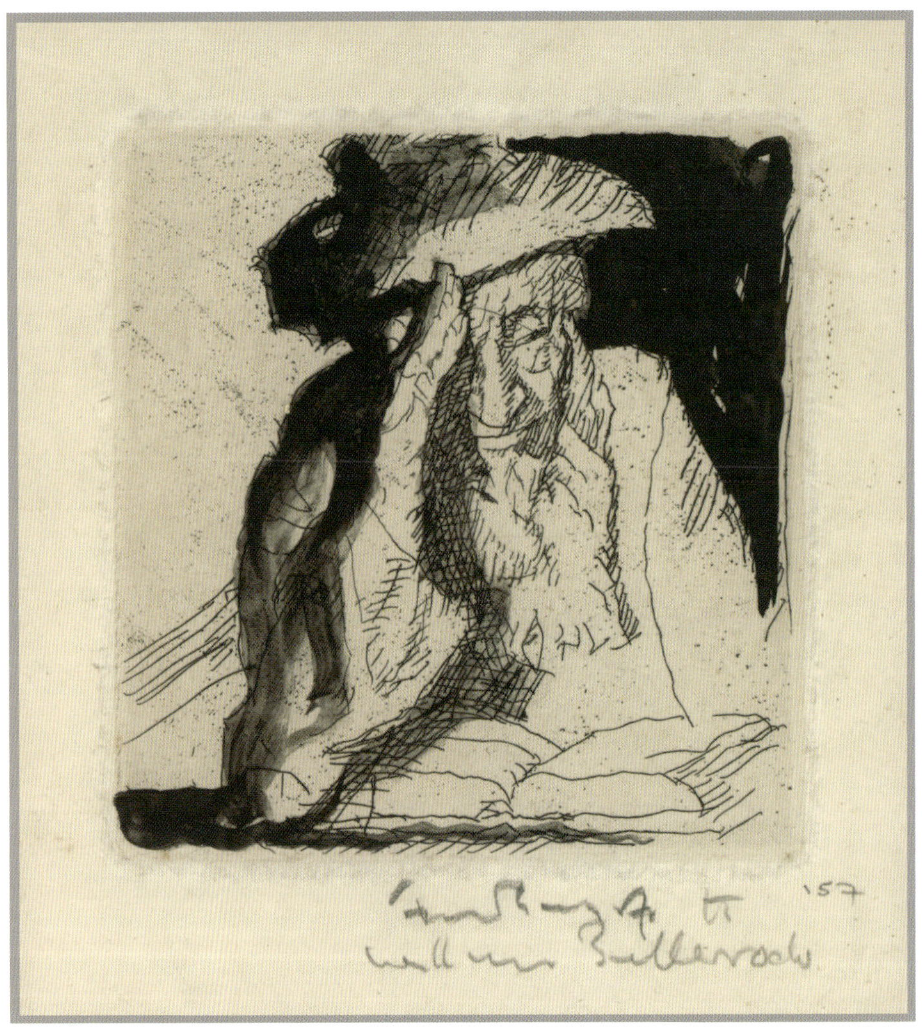

130 – Frank Brangwyn (1867-1956), *L'Ombre de la Croix – Book 1*,
signed and dedicated to William Belleroche,
black ink over etching (unique), 3 ¾ x 3 ¾ in. (9.5 x 9.5 cm).
Provenance: William de Belleroche.
Literature: Jerome & Jean Tharaud, *L'Ombre de la Croix*, Paris 1931, p15, Book 1.

The text for *L'Ombre de la Croix*, written by the brothers Jerome and Jean Tharaud, was published by Editions Lapina, Paris, 1931, in two volumes, and was illustrated with 73 Brangwyn etchings. The book describes the lives of Jews in contemporary Europe and many of Brangwyn's illustrations appear to depict the town of Belz in Poland, which was a centre of pilgrimage. Brangwyn is not known to have visited Poland and current research suggests that a large proportion of the etchings were based on photographs.

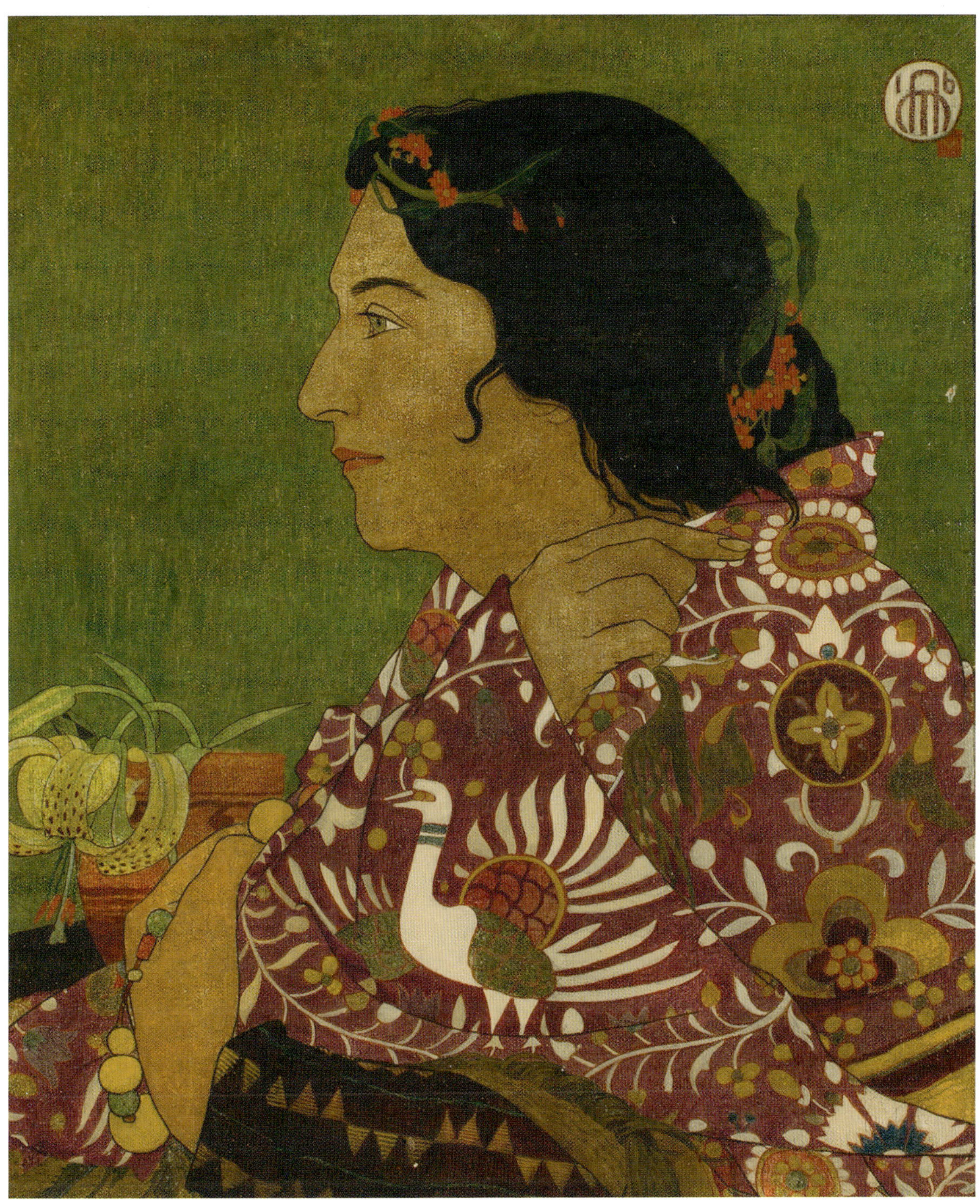

131 – **Maxwell Armfield** (1881-1972), *Profile portrait of a Navaho Indian*, signed with monogram,
Oil on board, 17 ½ x 15 in. (44.5 x 38 cm).
Provenance: The Fortunoff collection [HF 24].

During his time in California Maxwell Armfield was particularly struck by the ingenuity of the patterning of the native woven blankets, and made a series of oil studies – mostly in profile – of local figures wearing them. Two of these are reproduced in his book 'An Artist in America' (Methuen, 1925) in which he wrote: 'The Navaho, who originally stole the Hopi flocks, have made good use of their theft, and now weave as well, if not better than their masters, the blankets which are such blazing comments on the wild natural phenomena amongst which they live.'

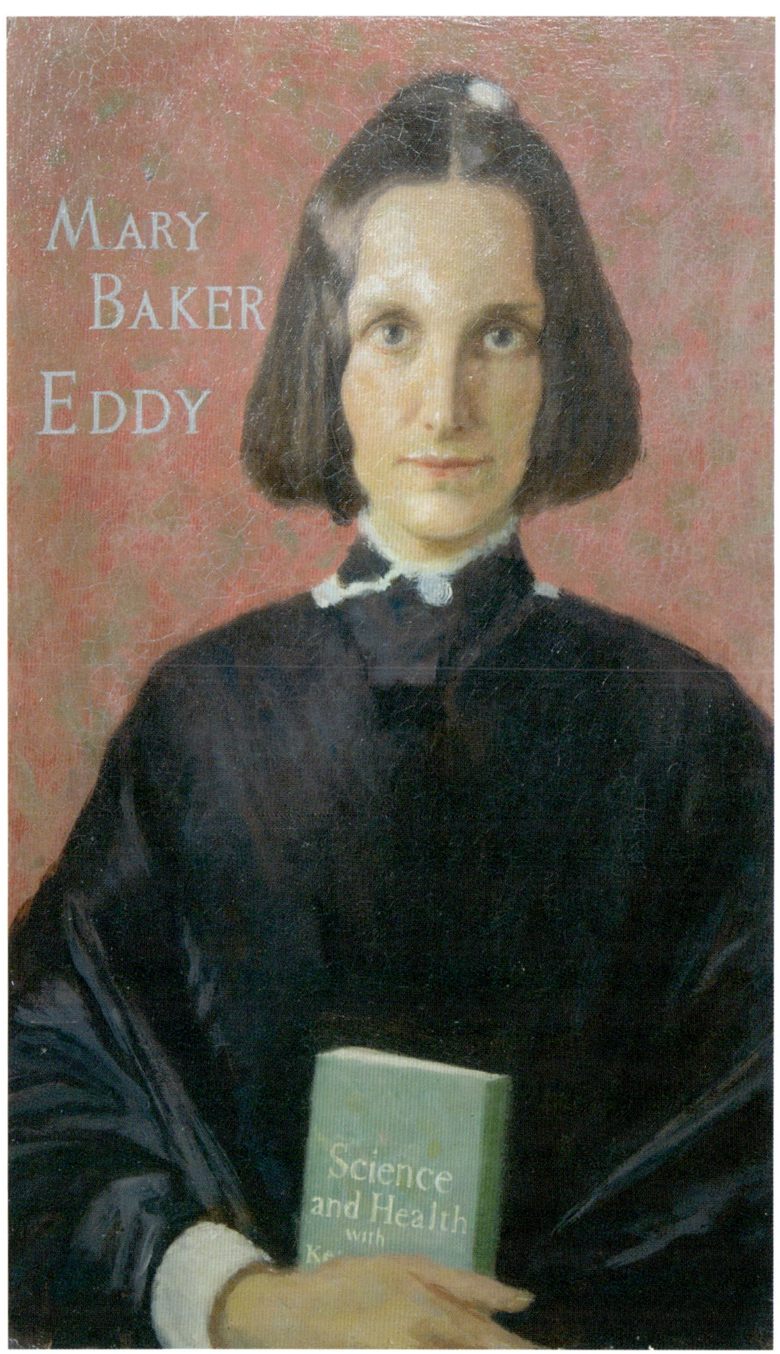

132 – **Hubert Arthur Finney** (1905-1991), *Portrait of Mary Baker Eddy*, c.1930, oil on board, 24 x 14 ½ in. (61 x 36.8 cm)
Provenance: the artist's son.
Collection: Wolfsoniana, Miami; acquired from Liss Llewellyn.

Mary Baker Eddy (1821-1910) was the founder of Christian Science, a new religious movement in the United States in the latter half of the 19th century. Eddy wrote the movement's textbook *Science and Health with Key to the Scriptures* (first published 1875) and founded the Church of Christ, Scientist in 1879. She also founded the Christian Science Publishing Society (1898), which continues to publish a number of periodicals, including *The Christian Science Monitor* (founded in 1908).

According to Finney's son H.A. Finney had a strong admiration for Mary Baker Eddy almost a fascination and some of this is exhibited in the portrait itself. His interest in Mary Baker Eddy existed quite some before his conversion to Christian Science, towards the end of his life. Many of Finney's RCA contemporaries, such as Evelyn Dunbar, were committed Christian Scientists.

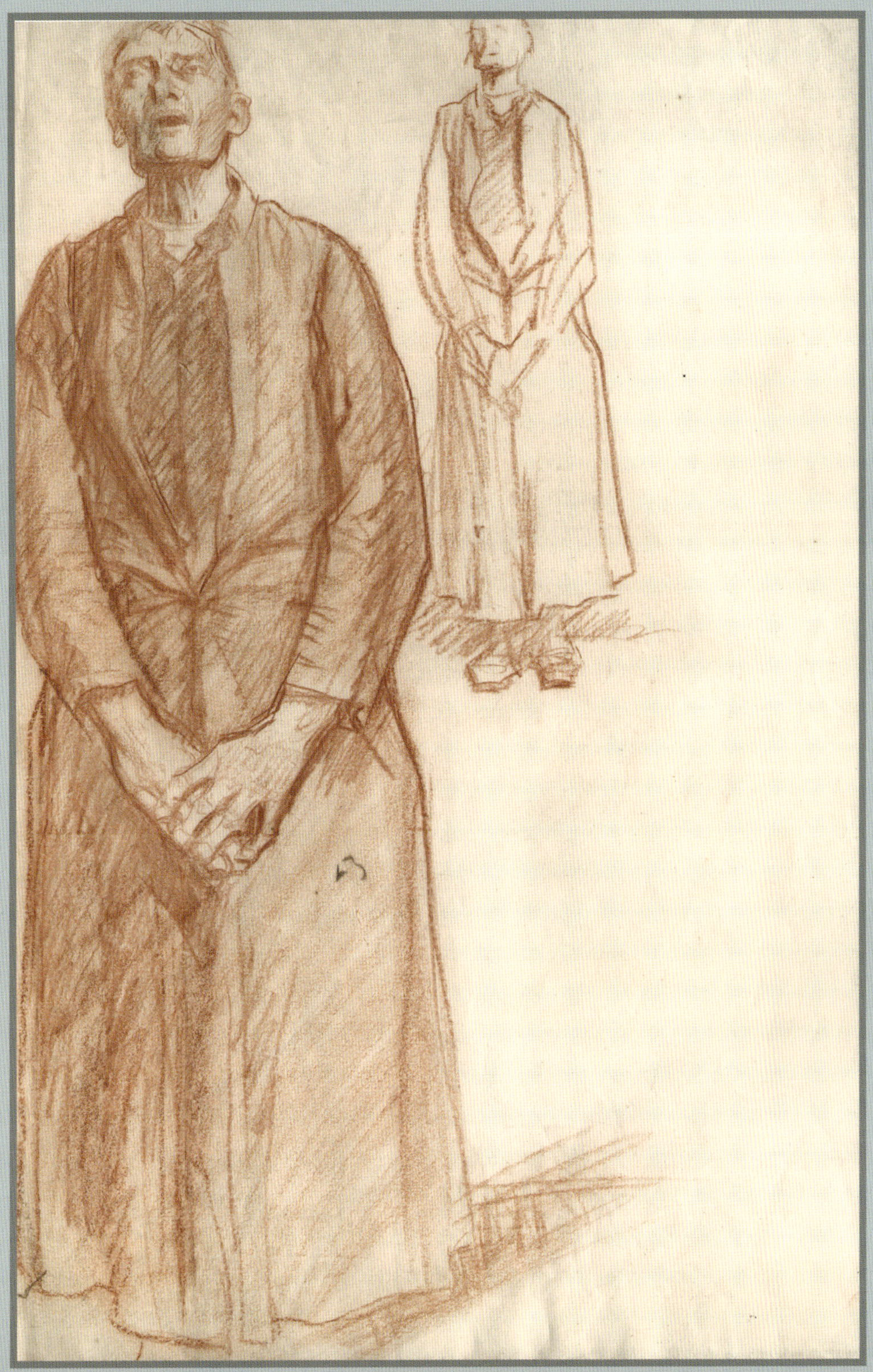

133 – Frank Brangwyn (1867-1956), *Man Singing*, (study for Christ's Hospital, panel 7),
signed with initials, red chalk on paper, 17 ½ x 11 in. (44.2 x 28 cm).
Provenance: Father Jerome Esser.
Literature: *Frank Brangwyn, Drawings from the Collection of Father Jerome Esser,*
          Liss Fine Art 2015, cat. 34, page 36.

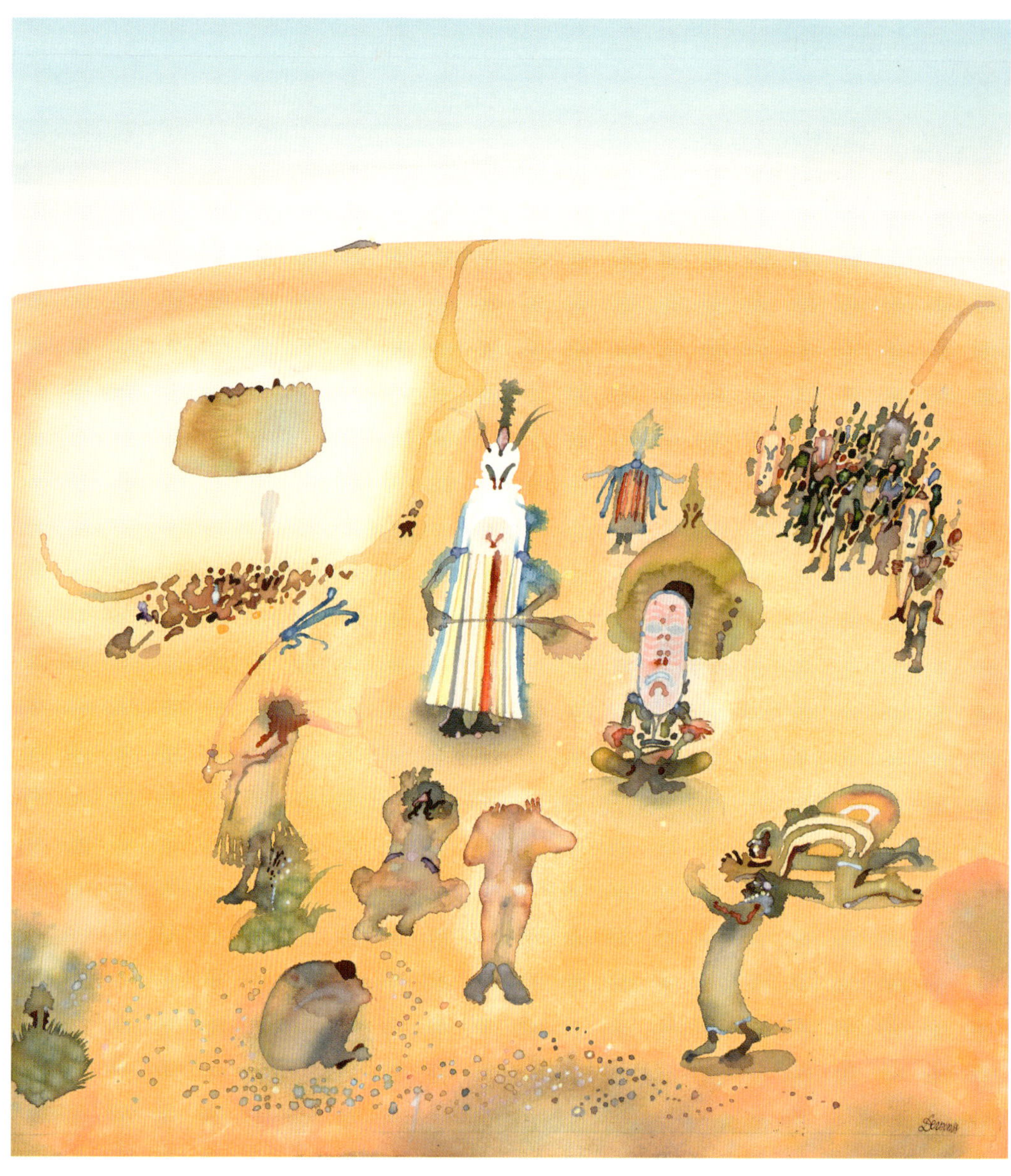

134 – **David Evans** (1929-1988), *Ritual,* signed,
watercolour on paper, 29 ¼ × 26 in. (74 × 66 cm). Provenance: The Artist's Studio

In a letter to The Redfern Gallery dated 1 January 1981 Evans said that in choosing the titles he aimed for something that would be 'beguiling'. His titles are typically characterised by innuendo and humour : *Horrendous Rex; Murphy Rules; The Land of Nod.* Many titles remain enigmatic. In his imagination Evans travelled far afield: *Rhine Journey; Tipperary; Scapa Flow* (1977); and further still: *Asia Major, Indian Landscape; Slavonic Dances; Arabian Days* (1980).

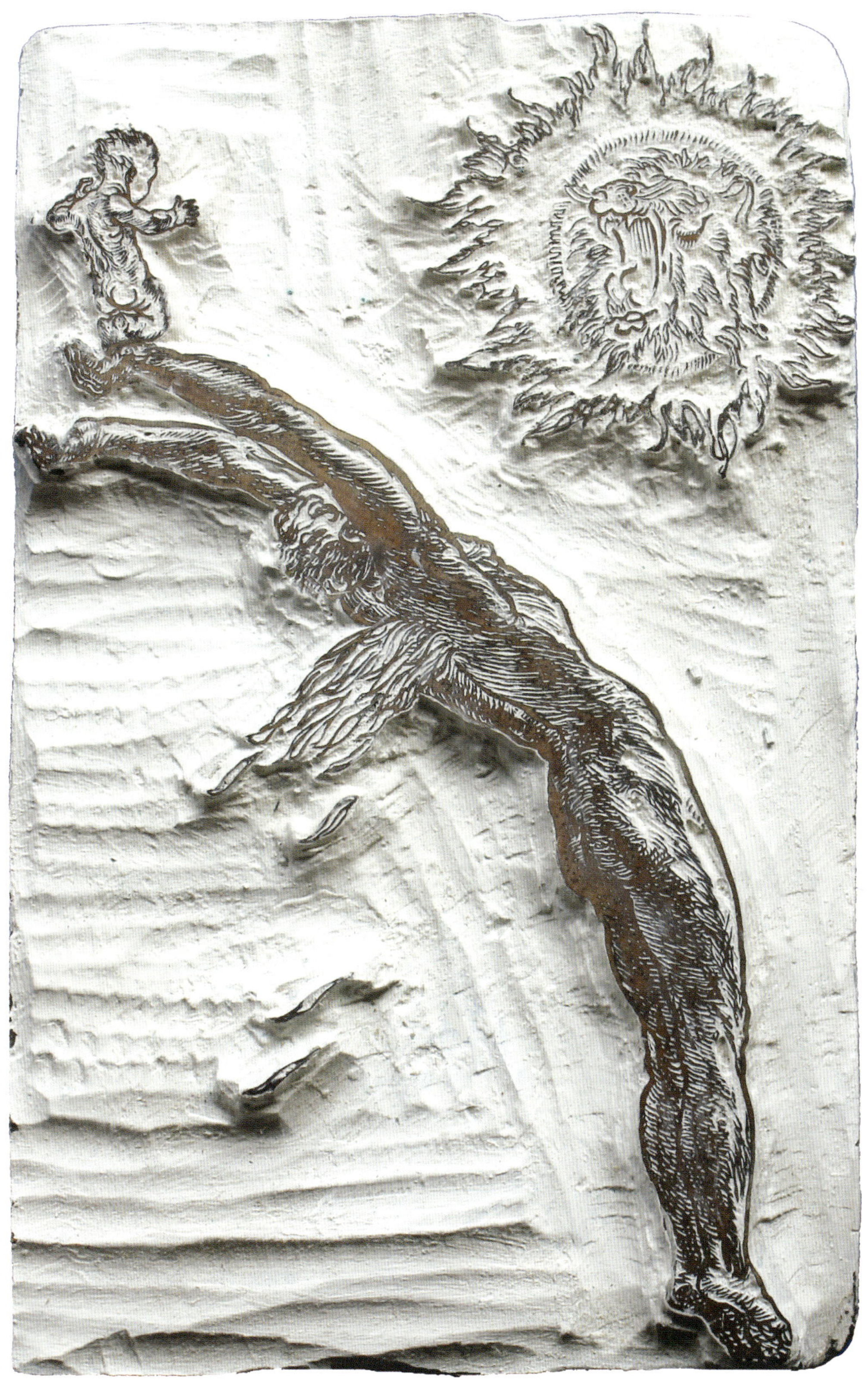

135 – **Frederick Carter** (1883-1967), *Babe of Fire,*
original woodblock, 4 ¼ × 2 ½ in. (10.9 × 6.8 cm).

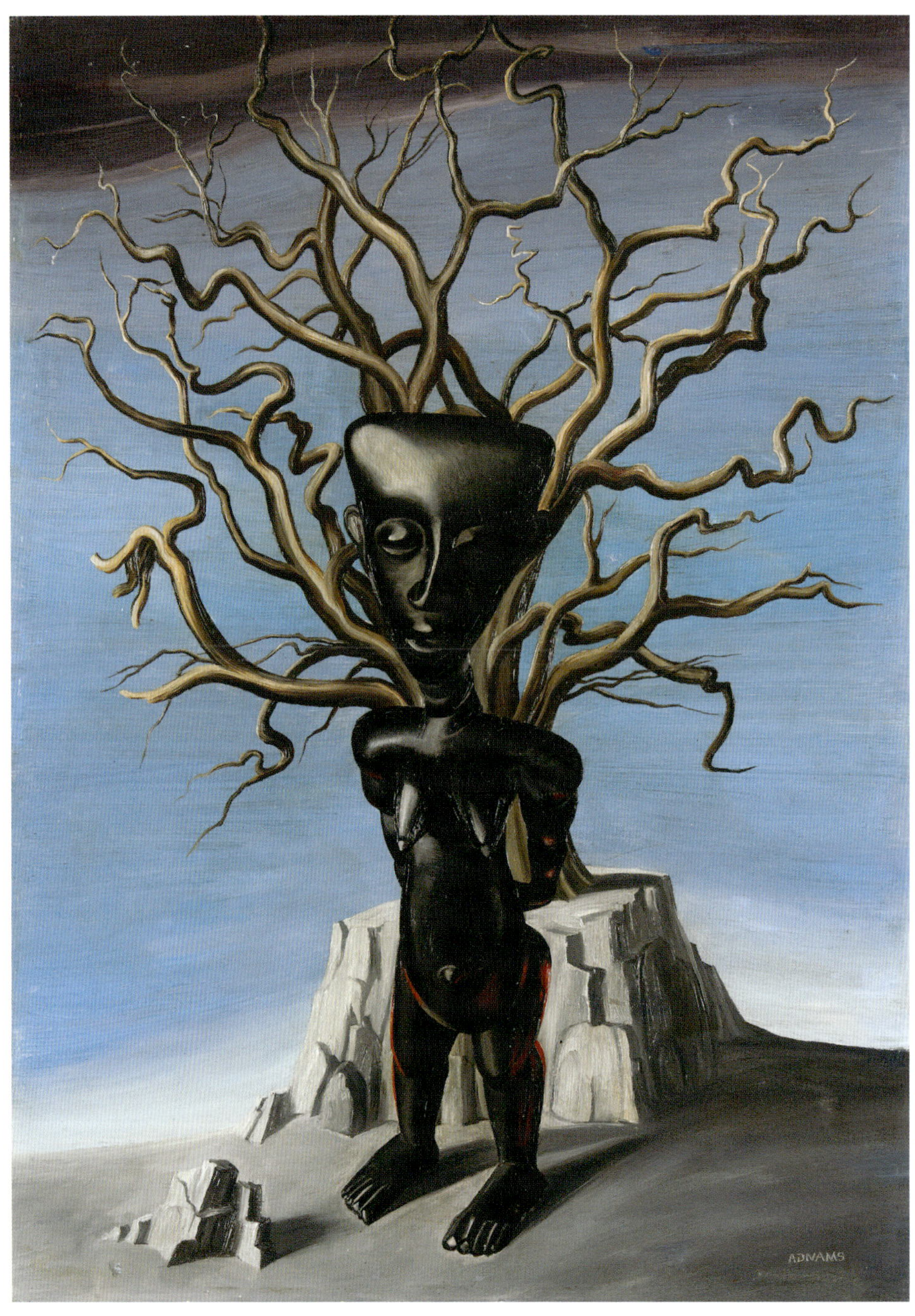

136 – Marion Elizabeth Adnams (1898–1995), *Medusa Grown Old*, 1947,
oil on panel, 21 ½ x 15 ½ in. (55 x 39.5 cm).
Provenance: Private Collection.

In 1947, Marion Adnams borrowed a small African sculpture from the city's museum for closer study.
'One day I made a drawing of her, and, when it was finished, dropped it down on the floor by my chair.
By chance, it landed on a drawing I had done the day before – a drawing of an ancient English oak
tree, with gnarled, twisting branches. They framed the head of the African figure, and there she was
Medusa, with snakes for hair.' In Christian symbolism, Medusa represents death, and thus becomes an
embodiment of the Devil.

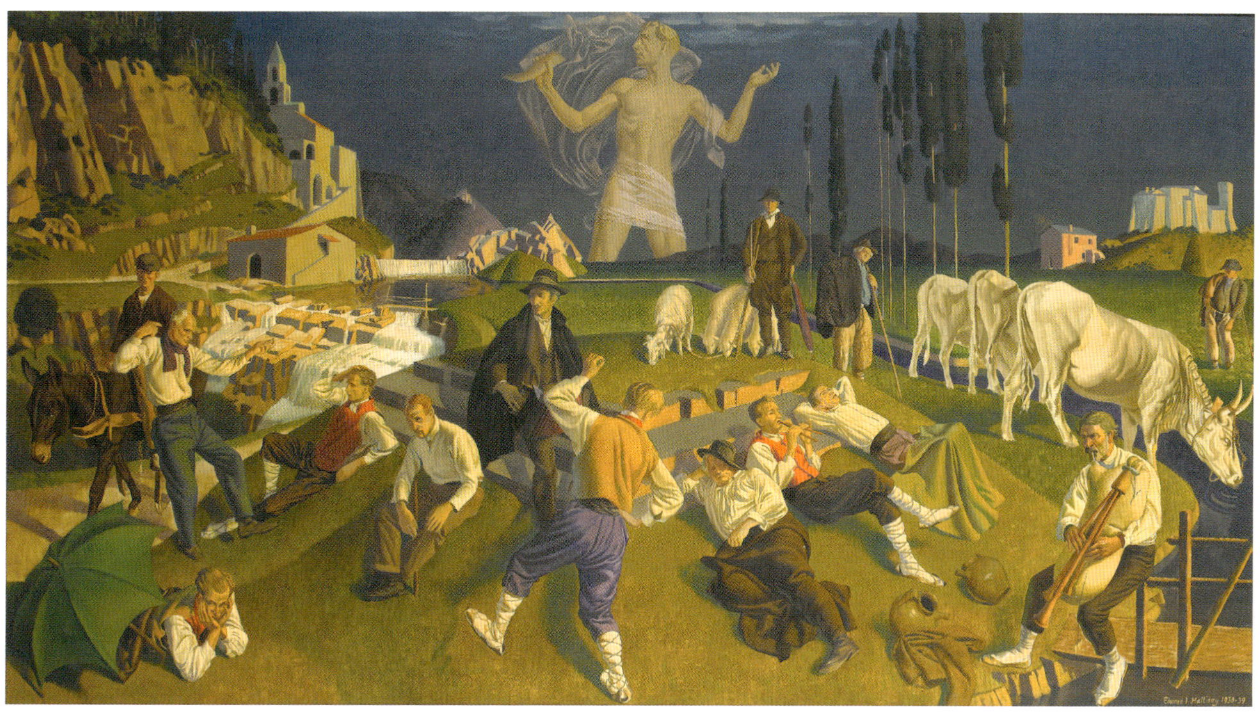

137 – Edward Irvine Halliday (1902-1984), *Hypnos*, 1928, signed lower left,
oil on canvas, 30 × 54 in. (74.7 × 134.7 cm).
Provenance: Commission by Sir Benjamin Johnson for his house Abbot's Lea, Woolton, 1927. Completed in 1928; given to Halliday as a gift
in 1937 upon the death of Johnson. Private Collection.
Exhibited: Royal Academy, 1939, under the title *Evening in the Campangna*, (with new date added 1930-9 but no changes to the composition).
    The Thirties. The Arts in Italy Beyond Fascism, Palazzo Strozzi, Jan 2013.
Literature: *Edward Halliday, Art for Life, 1925-1939*, Anne Compton, pp 18-21, reproduced p. 20 and on front cover.
    British Murals & Decorative Painting 1920-1960, Sansom & Co, 2013, pp.190-203;
    True to Life, British Realist Painting in the 1920s & 1930s, Patrick Elliot & Sacha Llewellyn, July 2017, Cat. 45 page 91.

Hypnos was commissioned in 1927 by Sir Benjamin Johnson, for his house Abbot's Lea, Liverpool, and completed in 1928 during the last
year of Halliday's Rome Scholarship. Johnson was an insomniac, hence the choice of Hypnos, god of sleep, and the painting hung in the
corridor outside Johnson's bedroom. The iconography was devised by Dorothy Hatswell, a classicist and assistant librarian at The British
School at Rome, whom Halliday married in 1928. The painting includes portraits of Halliday's friend and fellow Rome Scholar in Painting
Robert Lyon as well as Bobby Longdon, a friend and classics scholar at The British School at Rome.

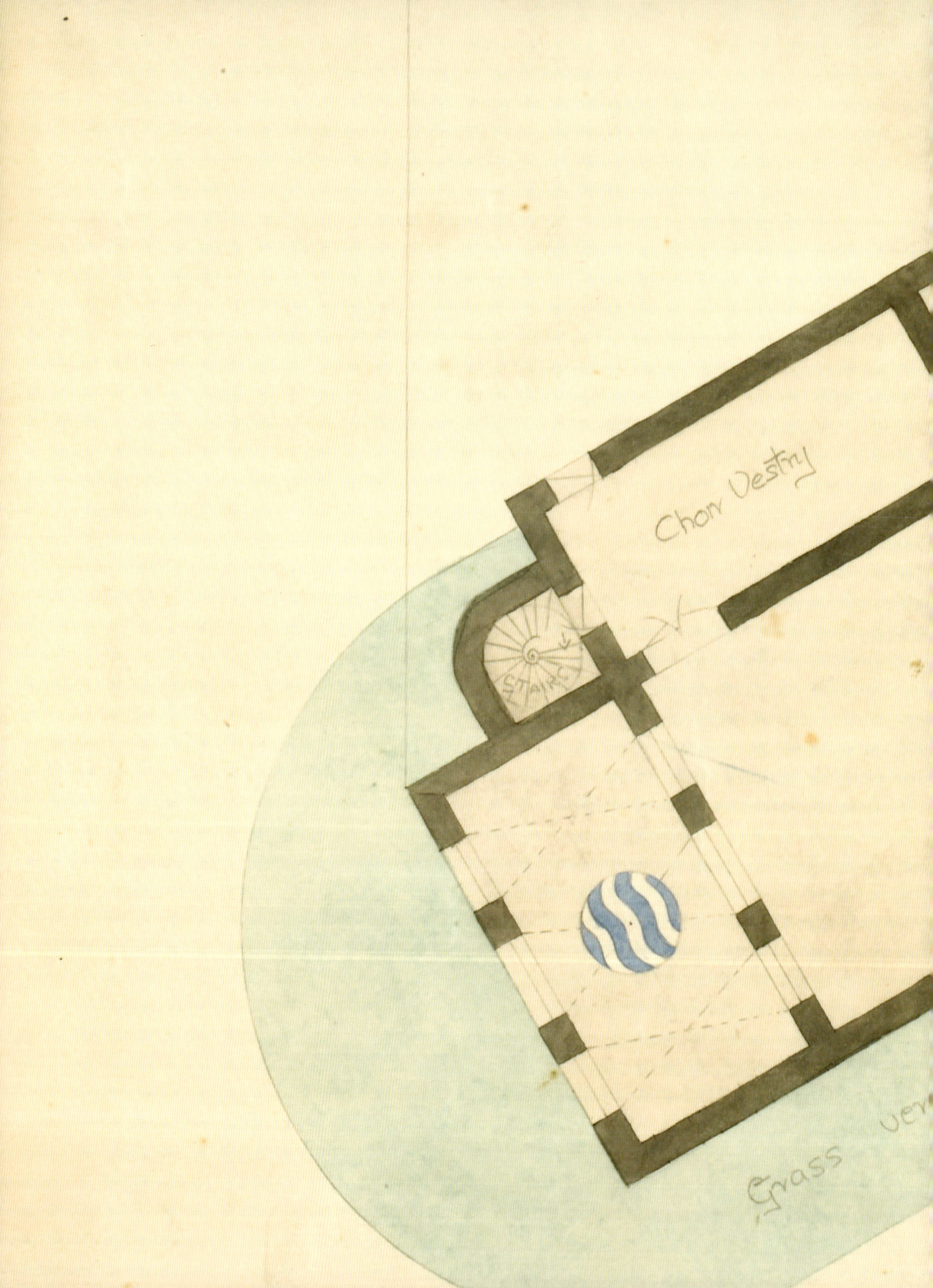

Choir Vestry
STAIRS
Grass ve

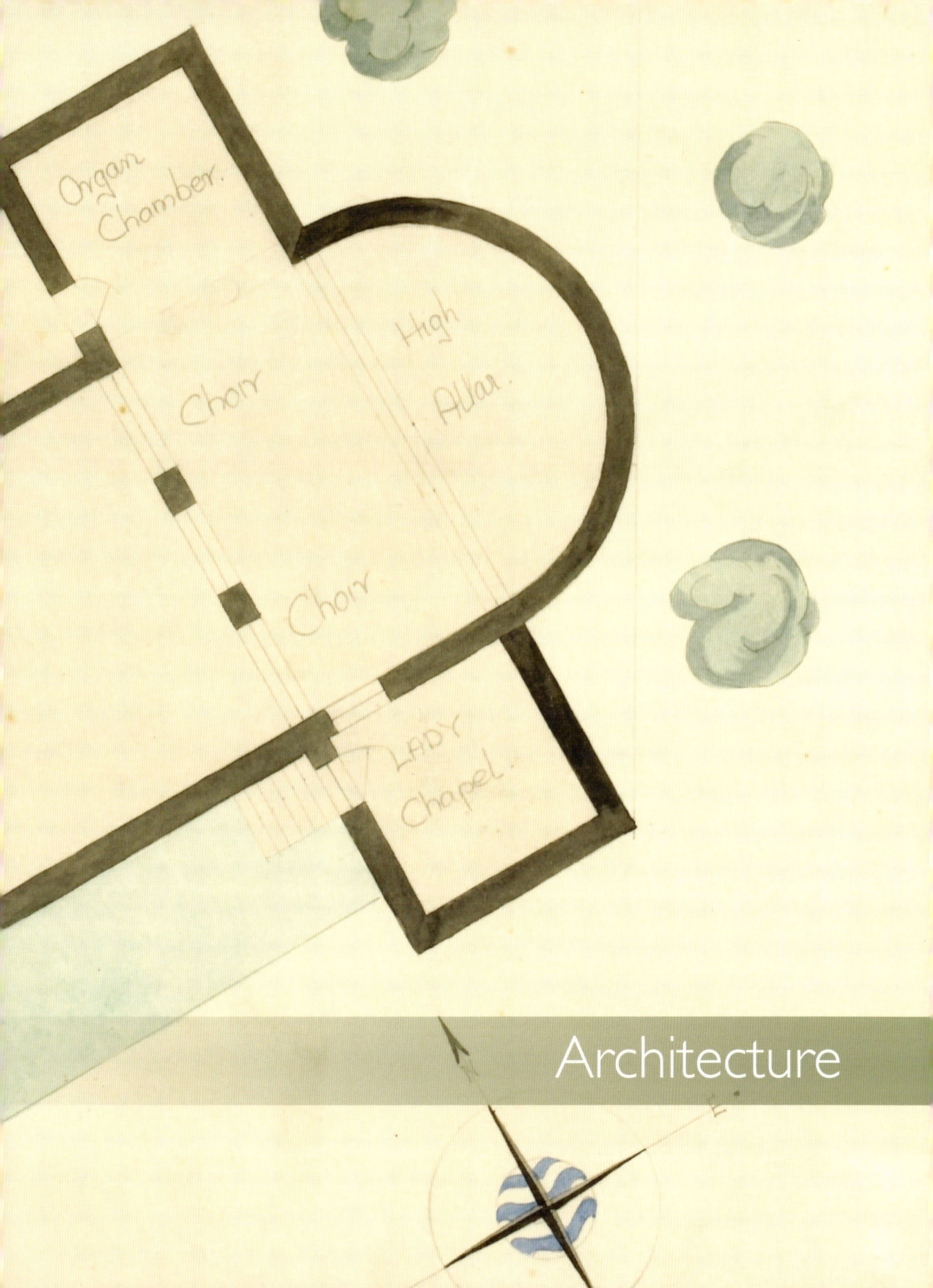

Architecture

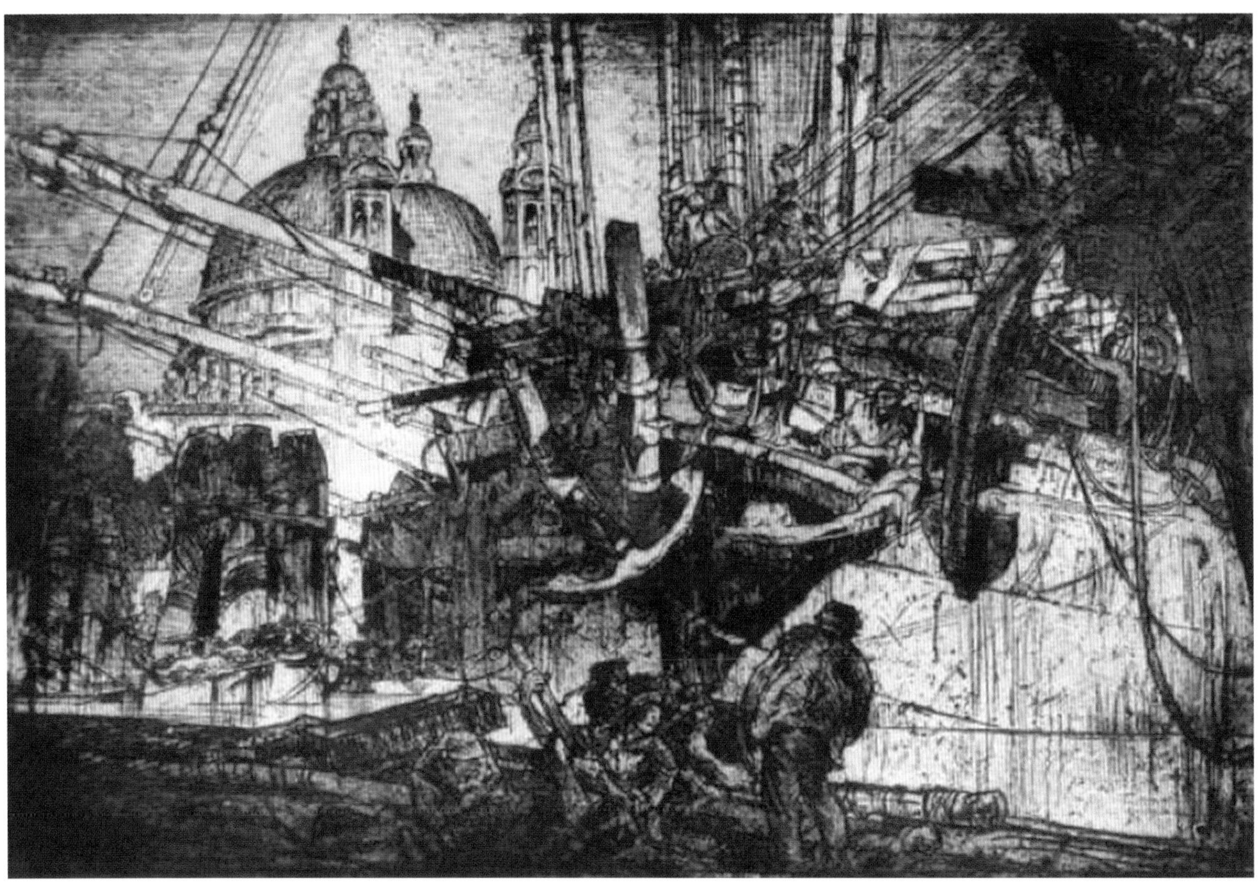

138 – **Frank Brangwyn** (1867-1956), *Santa Maria della Salute*, 1906,
etching, printed posthumously from the origianl plate, 30 × 35 in (76.2 × 89 cm).
Provenance: Sparrow, Prints and Drawings by Frank Brangwyn, 161.
Literature: Sparrow, Walter Shaw. Frank Brangwyn and His Work. Boston: Dana Estes, 1911.

Santa Maria della salute is arguably the most celebrated of all of Brangwyn's prints. It was awarded the gold medal at the 1907 Venice International Exhibition and the Grand Prize at the 1906 Milan International Exhibition.

A few etchings have very important names, though the subjects that these names ask us to see, are almost hidden by boats or barges. This joke has been noted by many writers. Frank Newbolt says, for instance: "'The Porte St. Croix at Bruges,' that massive structure of town defence, is dwarfed by enormous barges"; and Henri Marcel is struck by the "Santa Maria della Salute", seen behind the masts and rigging of tall ships fastened to groups of piles. On our right a medley of picturesque anchors and cranes makes a complicated framing for Santa Maria, whose leaden domes stand out rather clearly against the sky. I like this genre. Not only does it blend architectural motifs with sailoring and commercial activities; it suits Brangwyn, and discovers him as much as he discovers its charm and variety.

Brangwyn is thought to have visited Venice for the first time in 1896. He designed the British Room for the Venice Biennale in 1905 and 1907 and always felt a strong association with the city and its celebrated tradition of painting. In 1922 he illustrated Edward Hutton's book The Pageant of Venice.

139 – **David Evans** (1929-1988), *Cathedral*,
pencil and gouache on paper, 19 ¾ × 13 in. (50 × 33 cm).
Provenance: The artist's studio.
Literature: *David Evans (1929-1988)*, edited by Sacha Llewellyn & Paul Liss, published by Liss Llewellyn Fine Art, 2017. Cat 31, page 57.

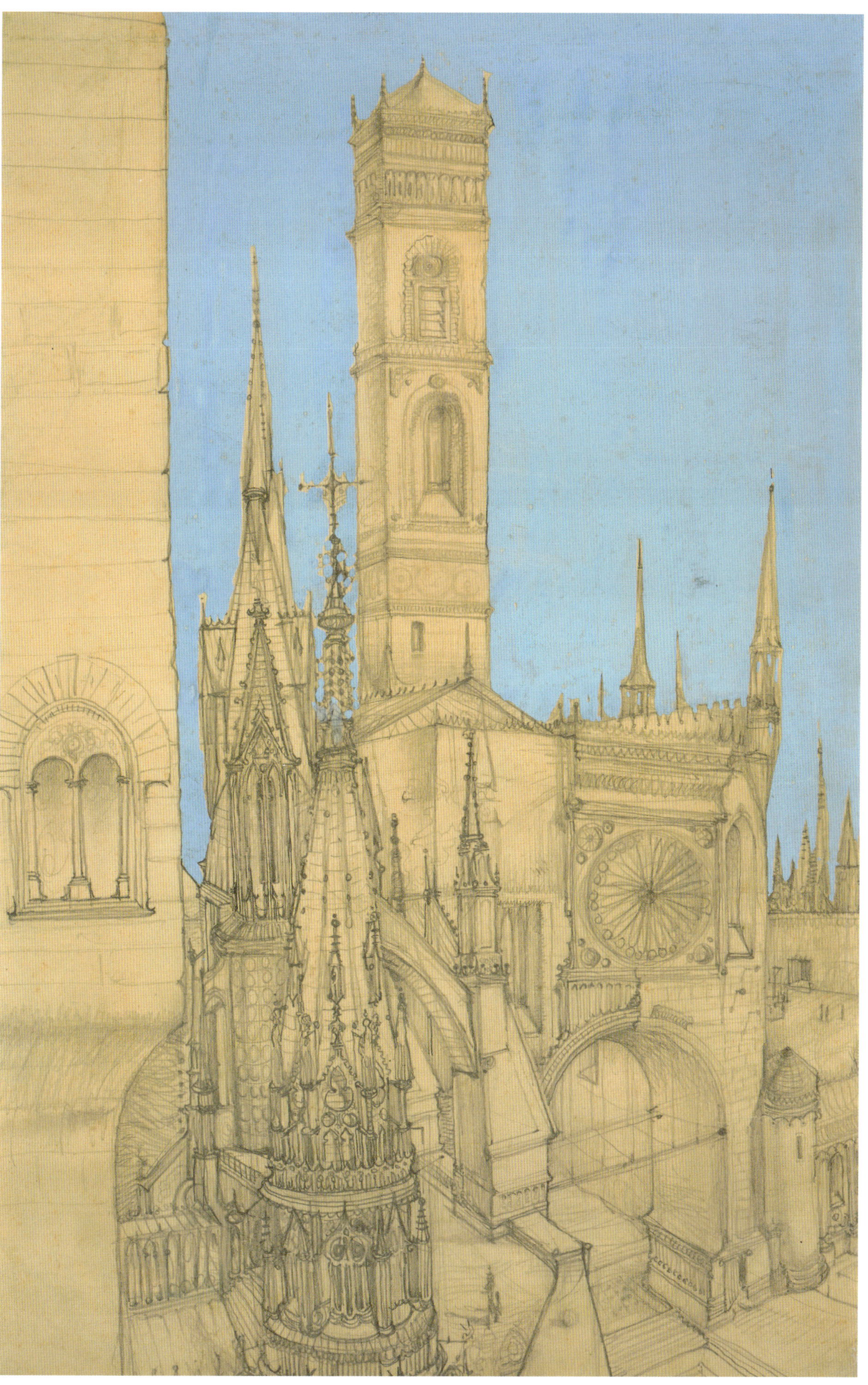

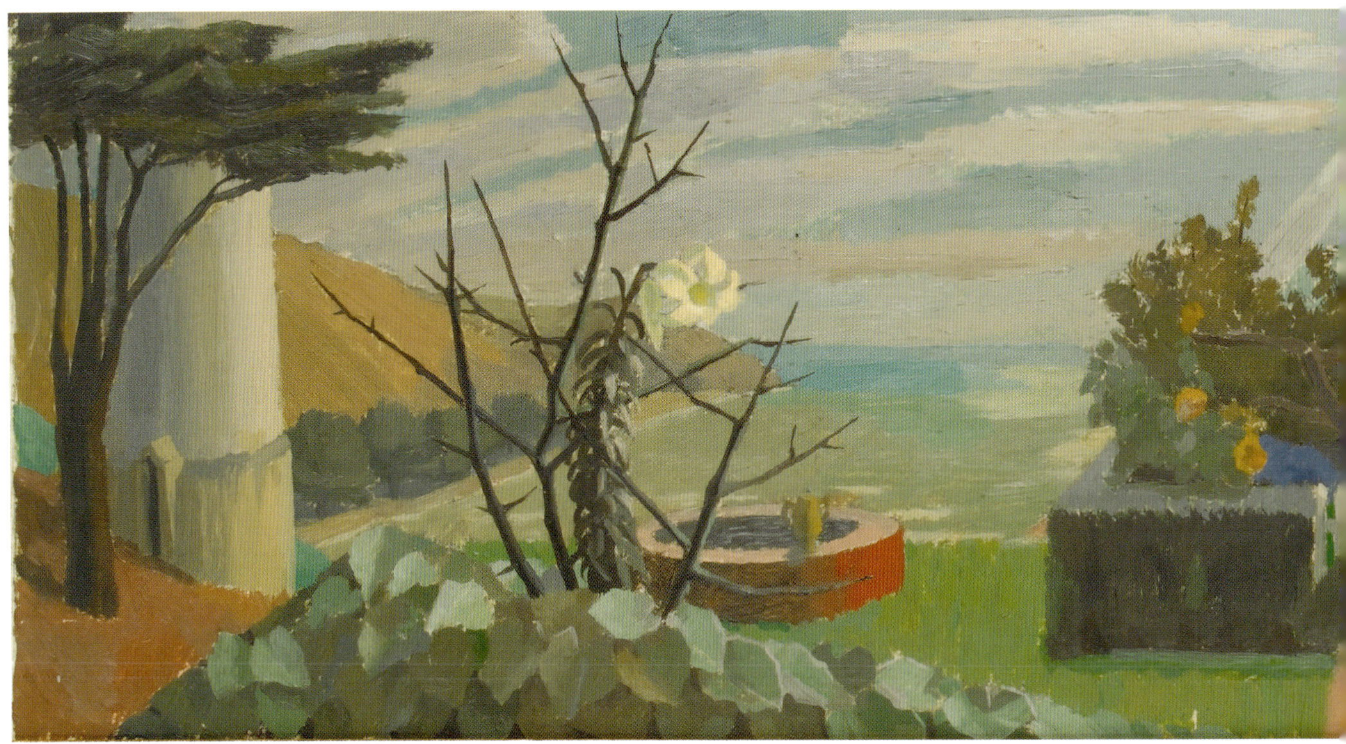

140 – Charles Mahoney (1903-1968), *Symbols of Mary*, mid 1940s, oil on paper, 7 ½ × 30 in. (19 × 76.2 cm).

Mahoney was commissioned to produce a mural scheme for the Lady Chapel at Campion Hall in 1941. This is a study for the final composition of the wall panel above the altar. It is amongst the most evocative of Mahoney's designs and is full of the compositional devices that characterise his best work.

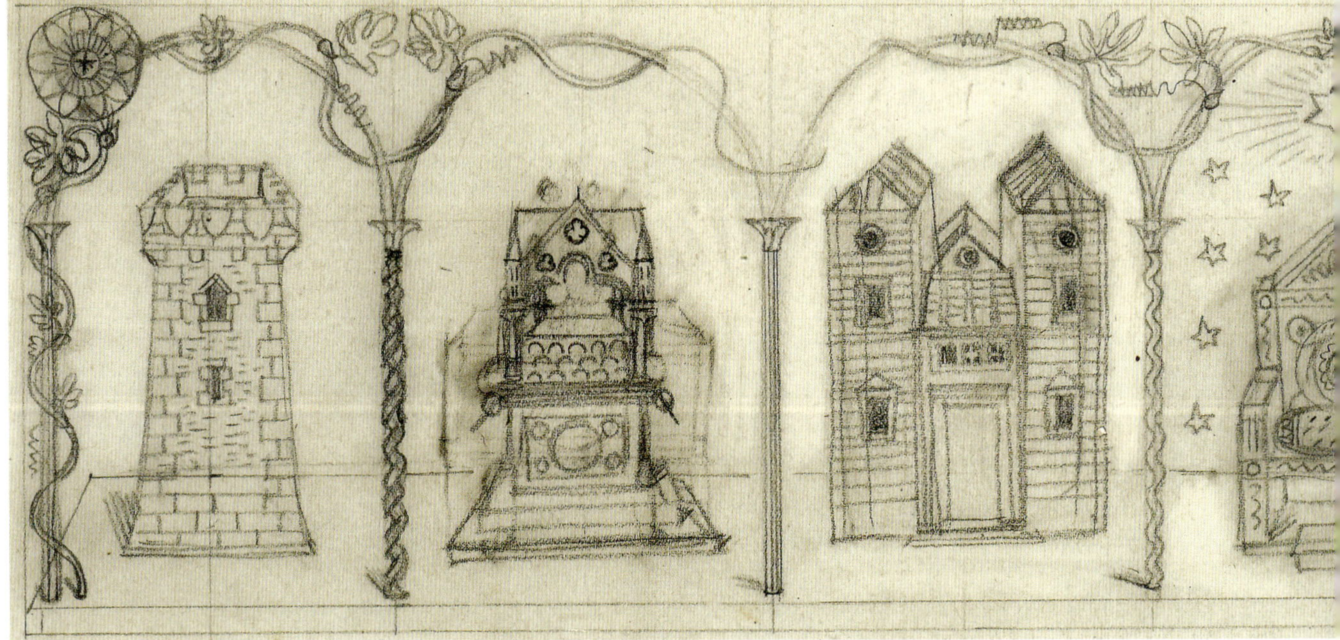

141 – Charles Mahoney (1903-1968), *The Emblems of the Virgin*, design for Campion Hall altarpiece, c.1941, pencil on paper, 5 ¼ × 22 in. (13.5 × 56 cm).
Provenance: the Artist's Estate.

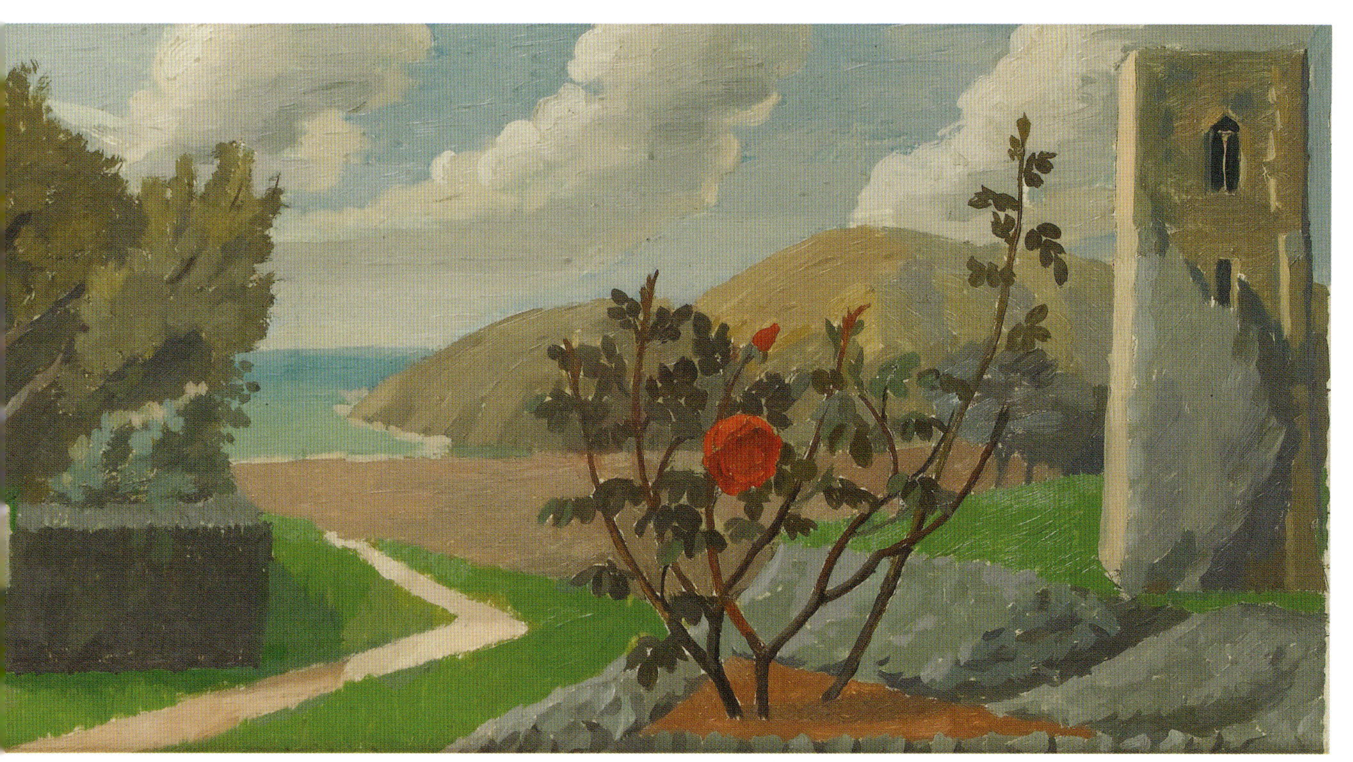

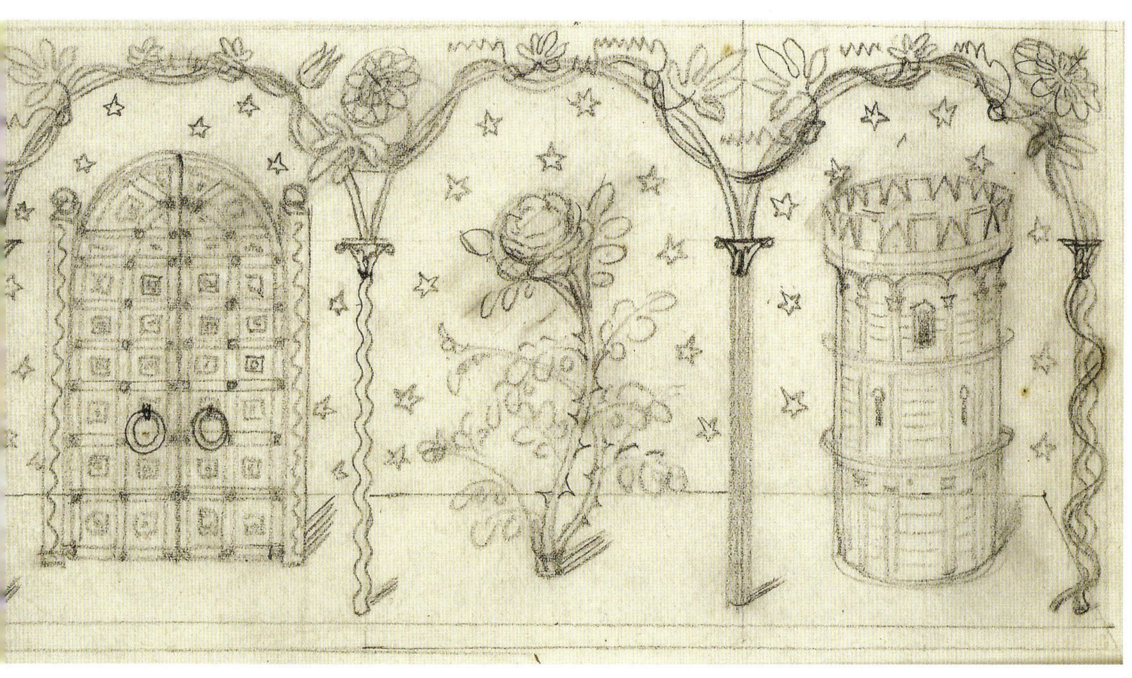

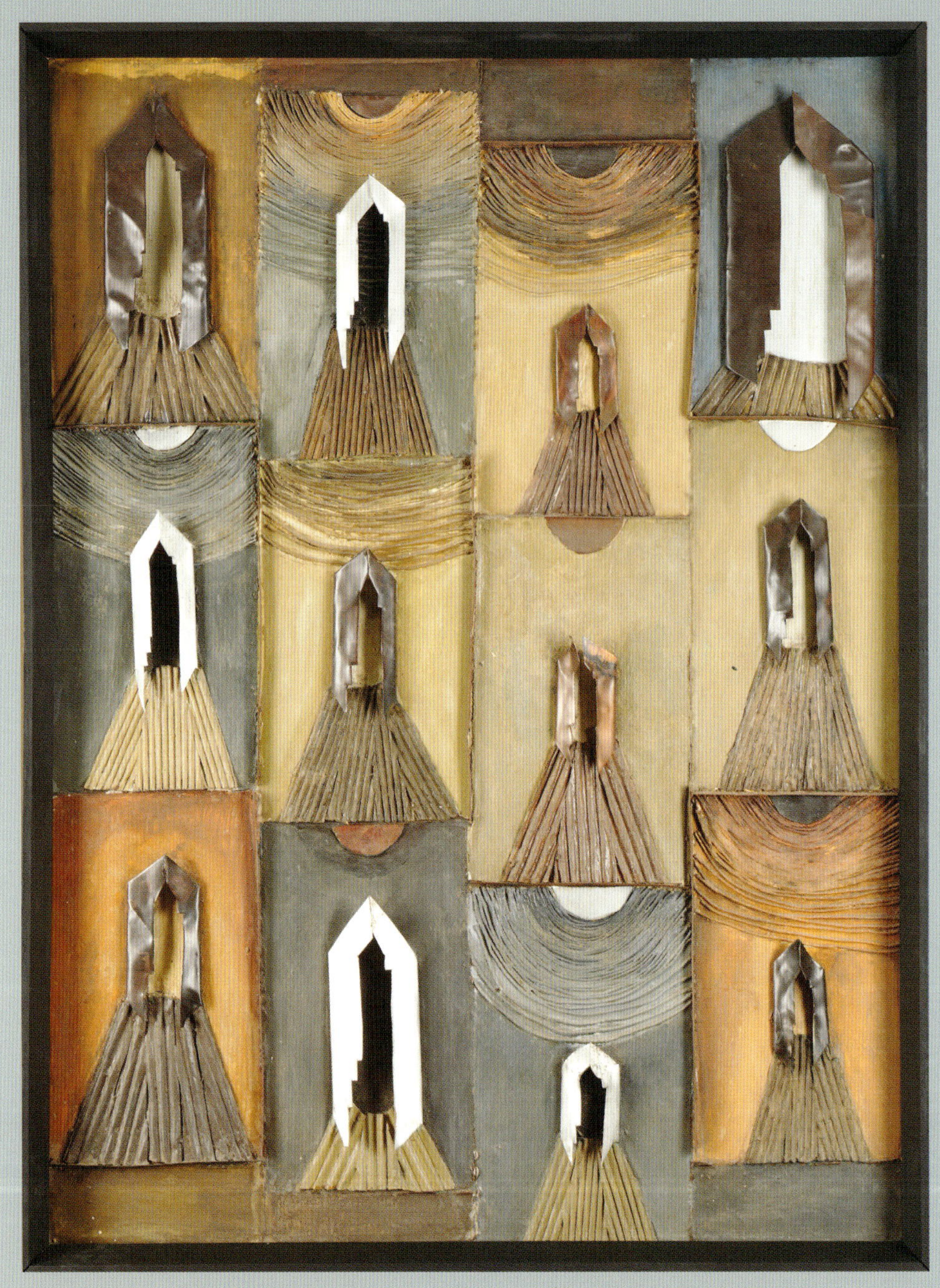

142 – **Rachel Reckitt** (1908-1995), *Towers and Helmets*, mixed media, sheet metal, 36 × 27 ½ in. (91.5 x 70 cm).

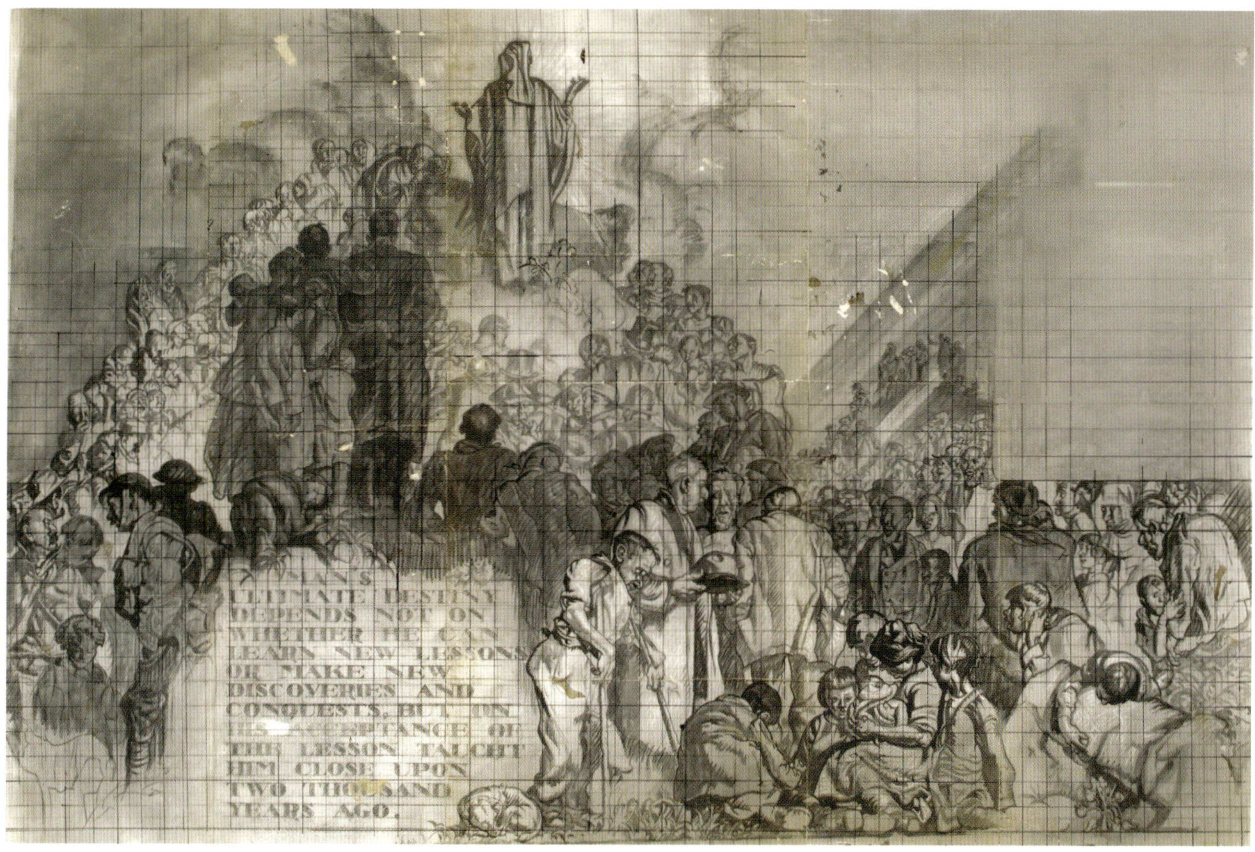

143 – Frank Brangwyn (1867-1956),
Working photomontage for *Man's Ultimate Destiny*, (mural scheme for the Rockefeller Center, New York),
squared, with pen & ink and highlights in white oil paint, 33 ½ x 51 ¼ in. (85 x 130 cm).

Brangwyn's celebrated murals for the Rockefeller Center decorate the main atrium around the entrance to the lifts.

This working photomontage, which was probably developed by Alfred Sinden, was worked upon by Brangwyn with multiple grids for enlarging the image on to the final canvas. The cartoon from which the photograph is taken is one of four in the collection of the William Morris Gallery, London Borough of Waltham Forest. This photograph shows the final composition in which the figure of Christ has effectively turned his back upon Rockefeller.

Picasso and Matisse were originally asked to paint murals for the newly built Rockefeller Centre, but after they declined Brangwyn, the Spanish artist José Maria Sert and the Mexican Diego Rivera were subsequently appointed. Critics complained that American artists should have been chosen for such a prestigious commission.

Further controversy followed in May 1933 when Rivera was prevented from finishing his mural after it was discovered that he had included a portrait of Lenin, and sympathizers of the artist clashed with police outside the building. The authorities also objected to the bright colours of the panel (Sert and Brangwyn had both agreed to paint monochrome works) and the mural was taken down and replaced by a new mural by Sert.

In September 1933, Brangwyn himself faced controversy. Officials from the Rockefeller Center objected to the figure of Christ being included in the fourth panel, representing the Sermon on the Mount. Raymond M. Hood, one of the architects of the Center, explained that, 'some people here felt that it would not be fitting to put the figure of Christ in a business building. They thought that might be too strong a representation of an individual religion'. It was suggested that Brangwyn represent Jesus by a light shining from heaven. However the artist merely reversed his figure, so that Christ facing the populace became the back of a nameless cloaked man.

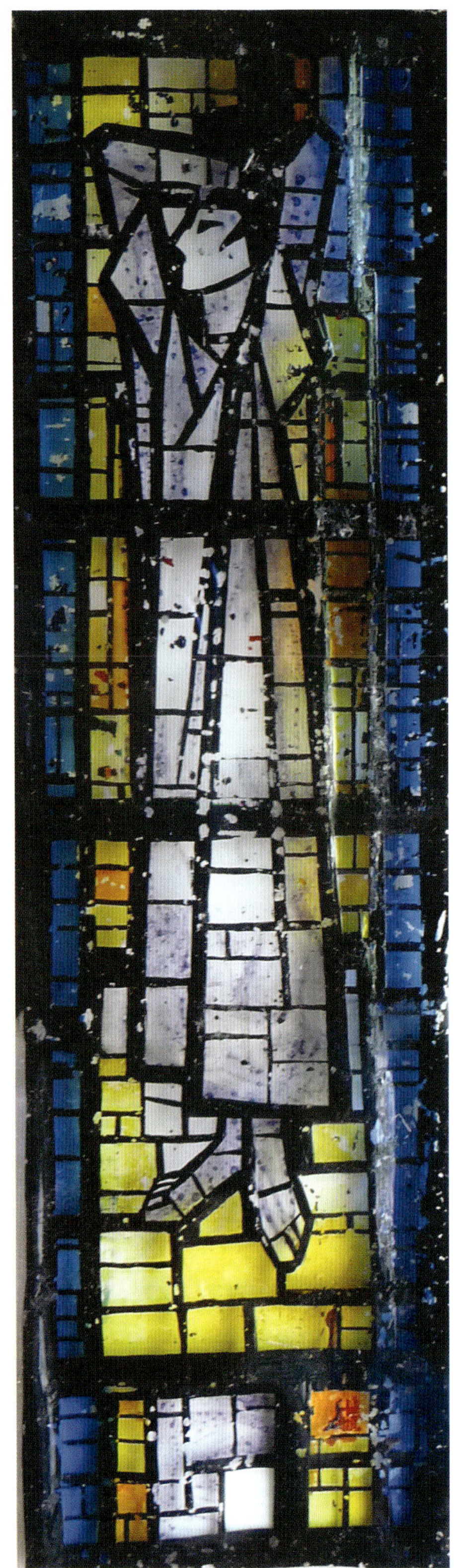
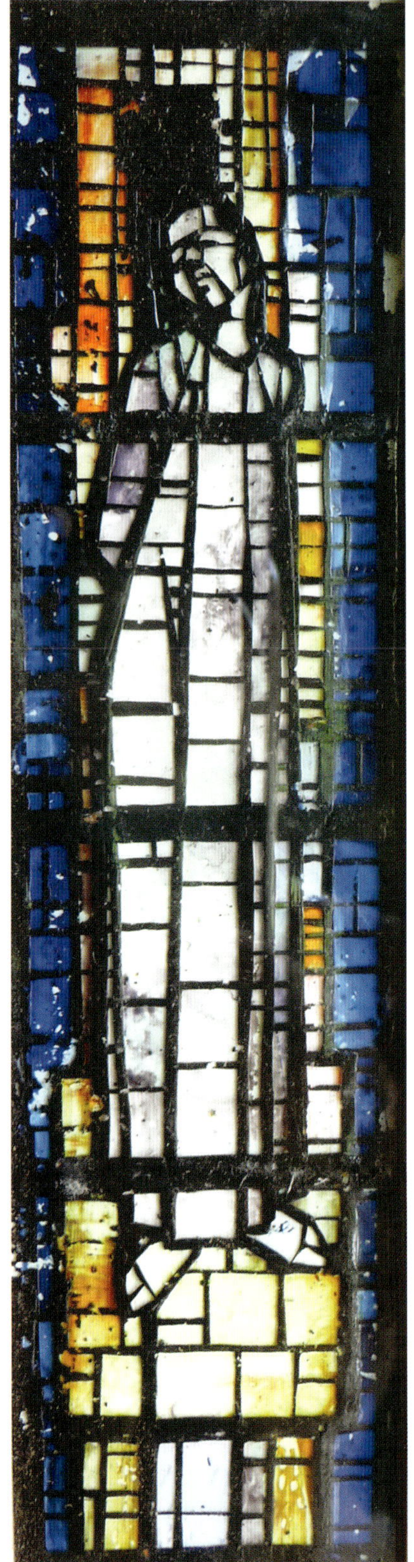

144 – Gerald Anthony Coles, (1929-2004),
a Design for stained glass window, coloured ink on melanex, 7 ¼ × 2 in. (18 × 5 cm).
b Design for stained glass window, coloured ink on melanex, 6 ¼ × 1 ½ in. (15.8 × 4.5 cm).

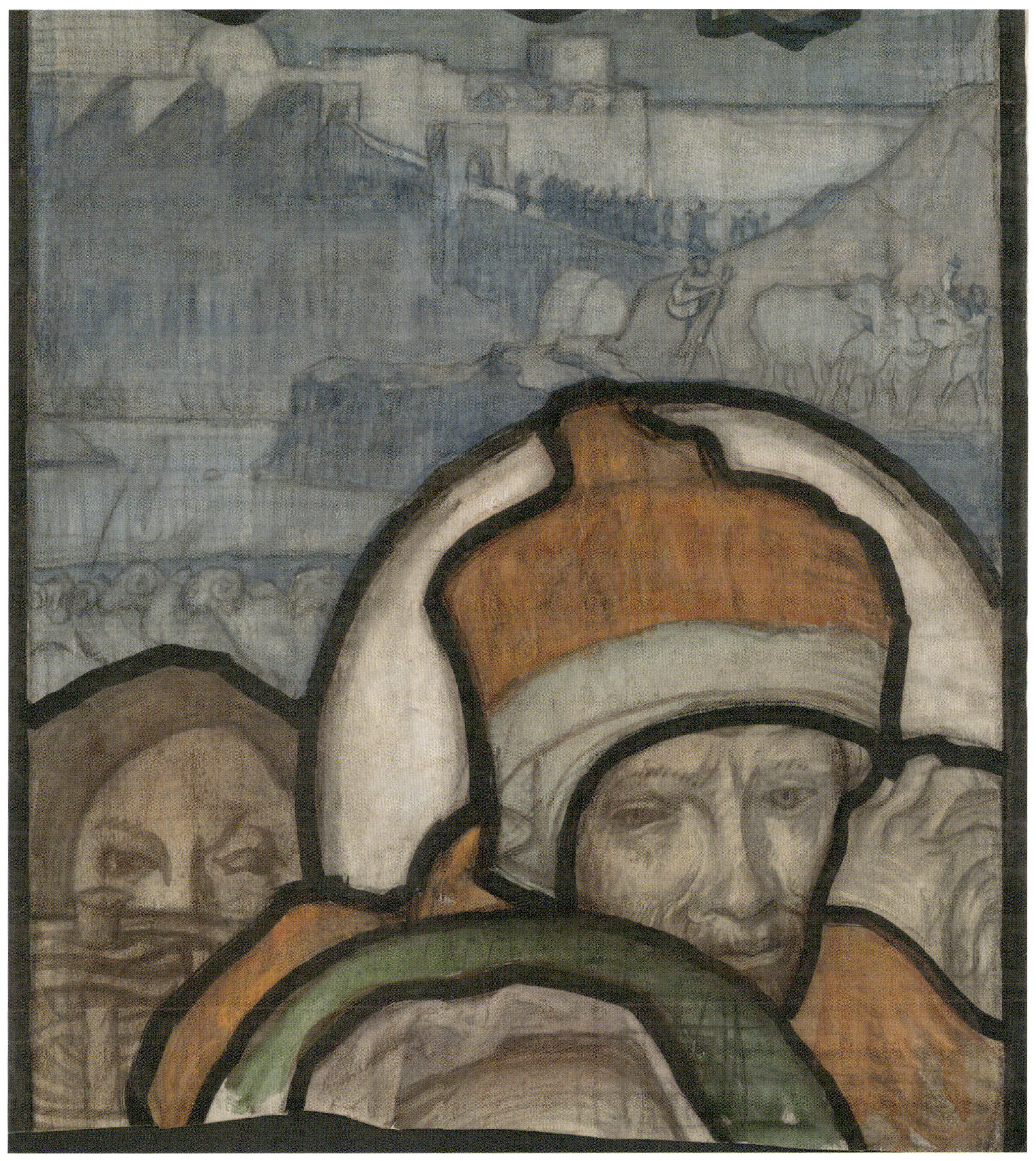

145 – **Frank Brangwyn**, (1867-1956), Study for central panel of Nativity window, St Mary the Virgin, Bucklebury, Berkshire, gouache on paper; 19 ½ x 18 in. (50 x 46 cm).
Provenance: Father Jerome Esser.
Literature: *Frank Brangwyn, Drawings from the Collection of Father Jerome Esser,*
        Liss Fine Art 2015, cat. 37, pages 39-41.

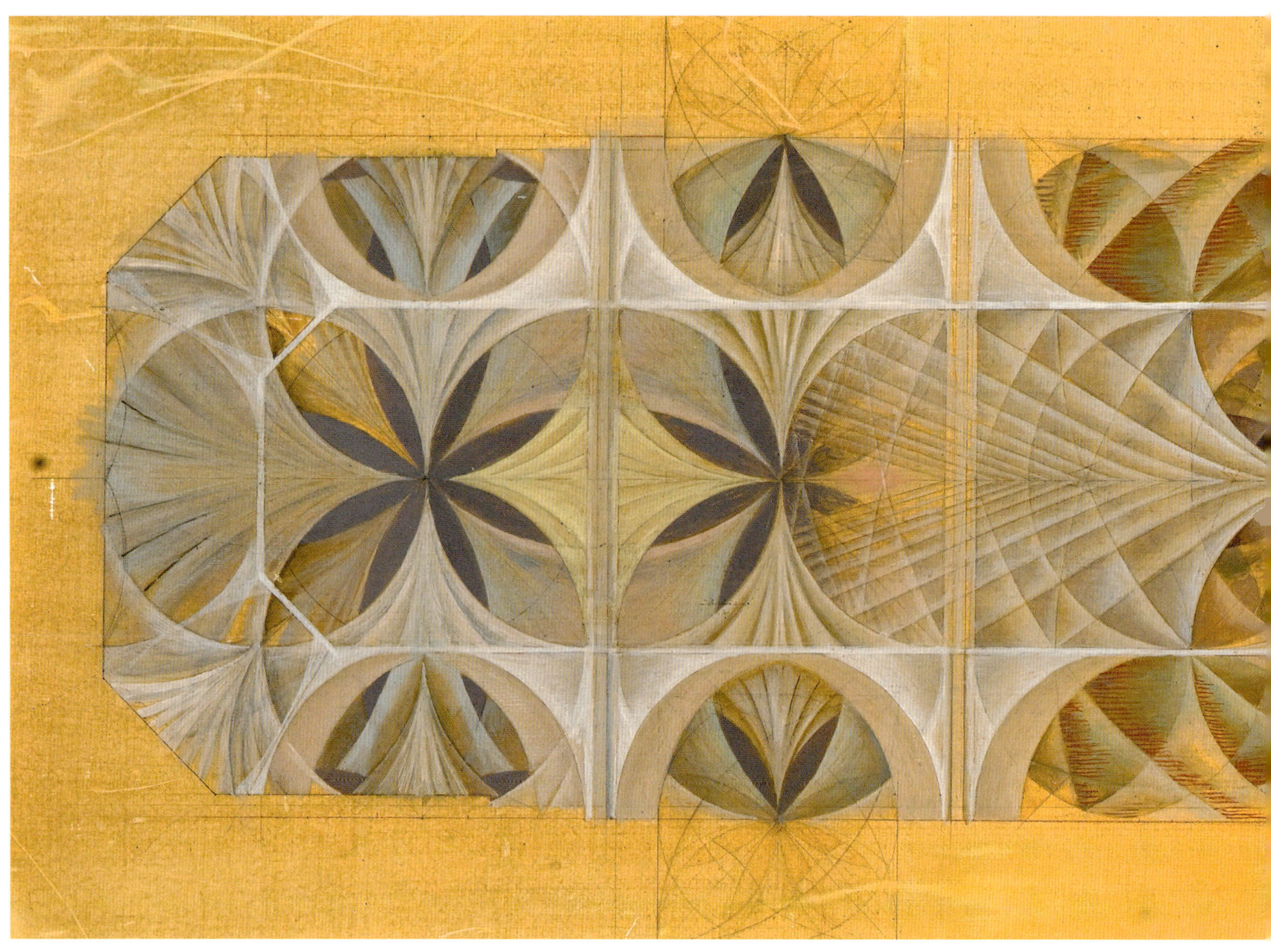

146 – Thomas Monnington (1903-2068),
Design for the ceiling of the Mary Harris Memorial Chapel of Holy Trinity, University of Exeter, 1956,
oil on board, 19 ½ × 48 ½ in. (49 × 123 cm).
Provenance: Evelyn Monnington.
Exhibited: The Fine Art Society, 1997, no. 134.
Literature: *British Murals & Decorative Painting 1920-60*, Samson & Co, 2013, pp.310-325.

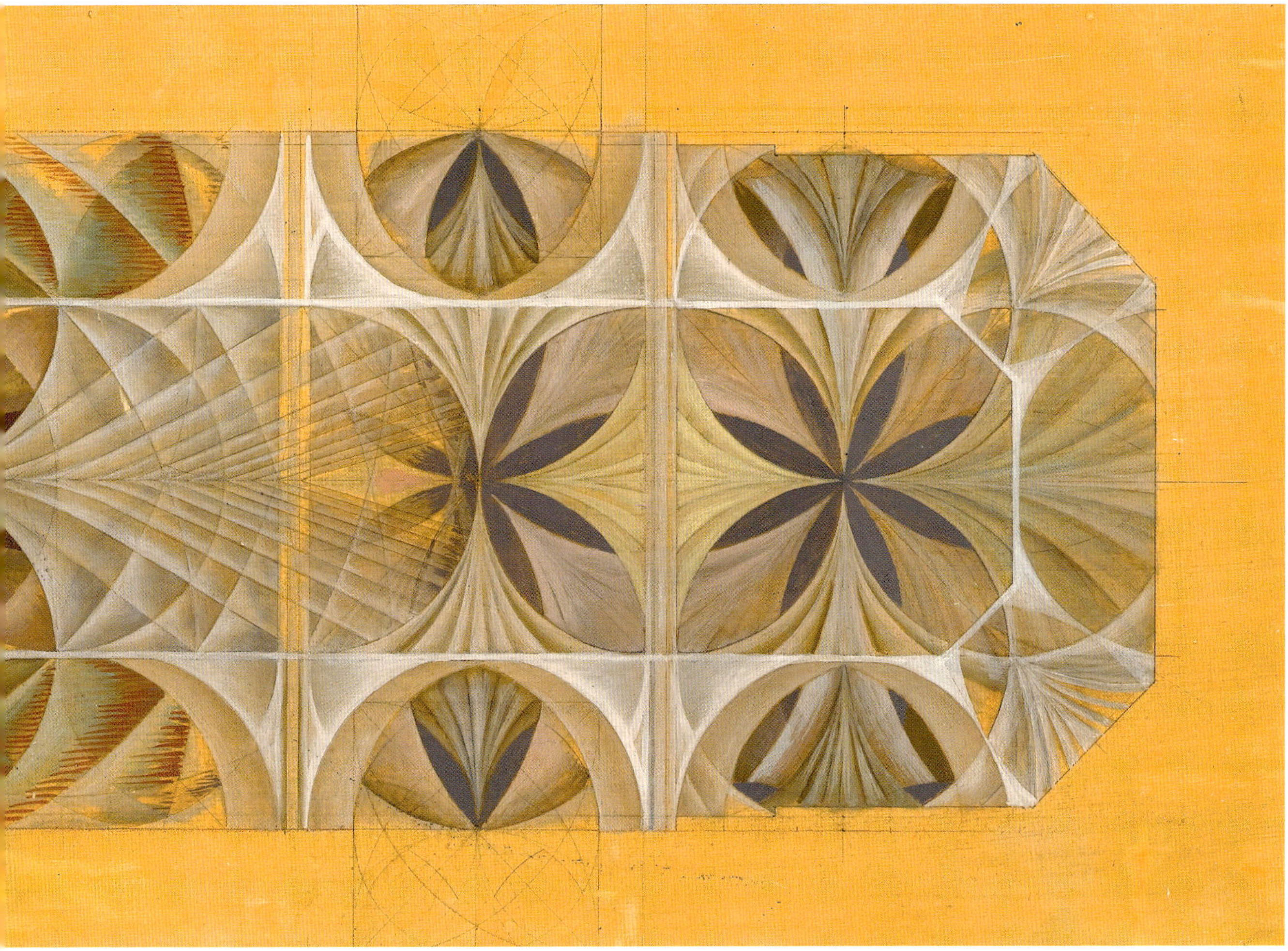

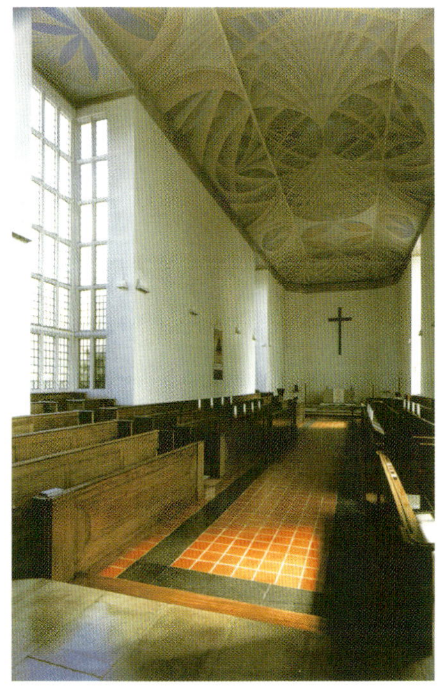

147 – The Mary Harris Memorial Chapel of Holy Trinity was designed by Vincent Harris R.A. (architect of the Bristol Council House) in memory of his mother.

Harris commissioned Monnington to paint the 112 x 28 ft ceiling in 1956. Monnington's assistants Scott Medd and W.B. (Peter) Lowe took 11 months to execute the designs. Lowe recalls: 'Tom maintained that it was difficult to draw angels in the twentieth-century, and was comforted by the enduring qualities of geometry and light.

The design, based on simple geometry, was visualised as over-lapping webs of transparent light extending into and partly veiling the mysteries of space'. 'The ceilings at Bristol and Exeter have matured well – unlike the earlier St Stephens Hall – and can safely be hailed as twentiethcentury masterpieces, and the studies for them, prepared with the precision and patience of a master, appear today both strong and vital.' (Peyton Skipwith, *Thomas Monnington*, published by Paul Liss in association with The Fine Art Society, 1997, p.9.)

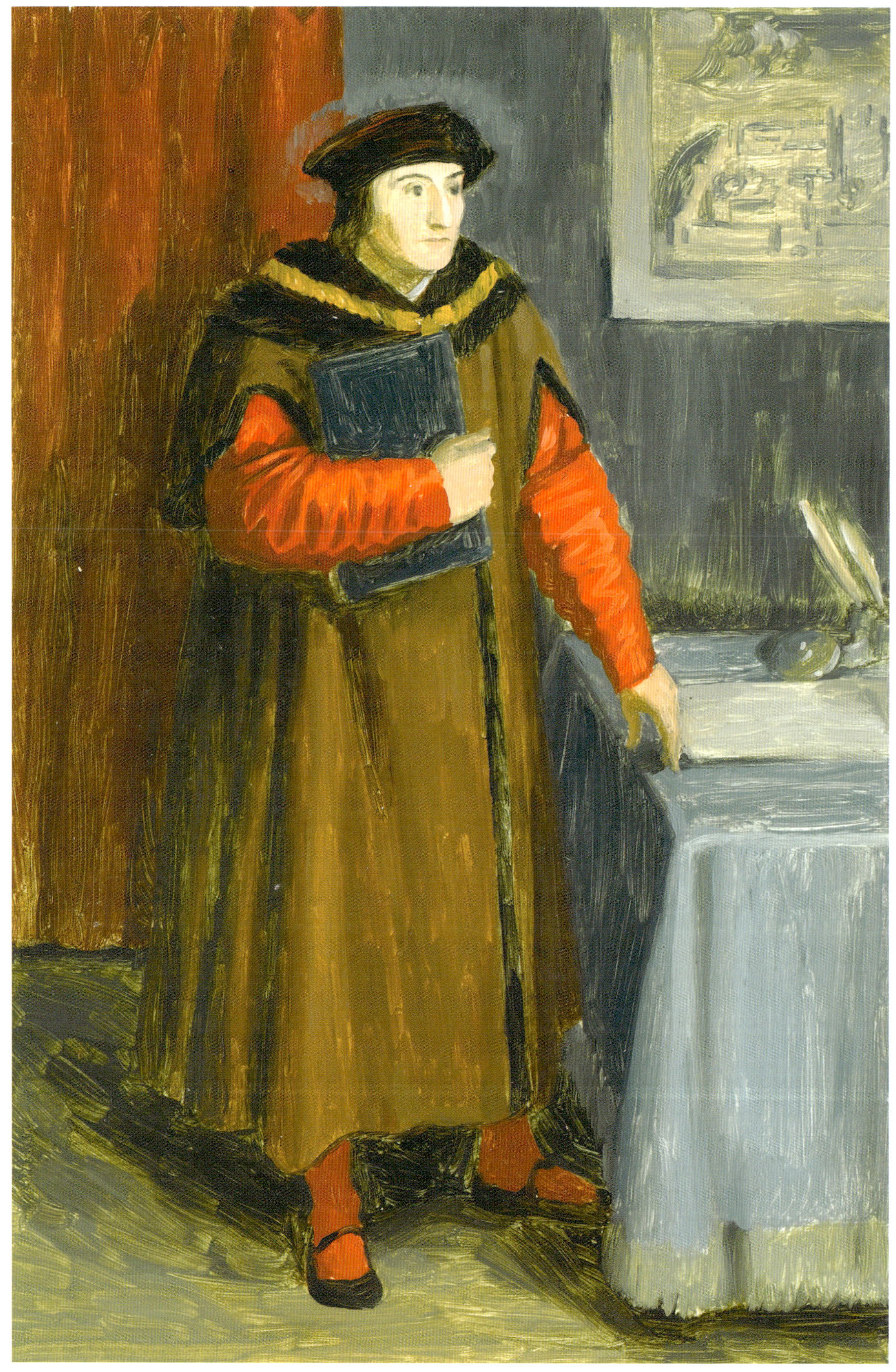

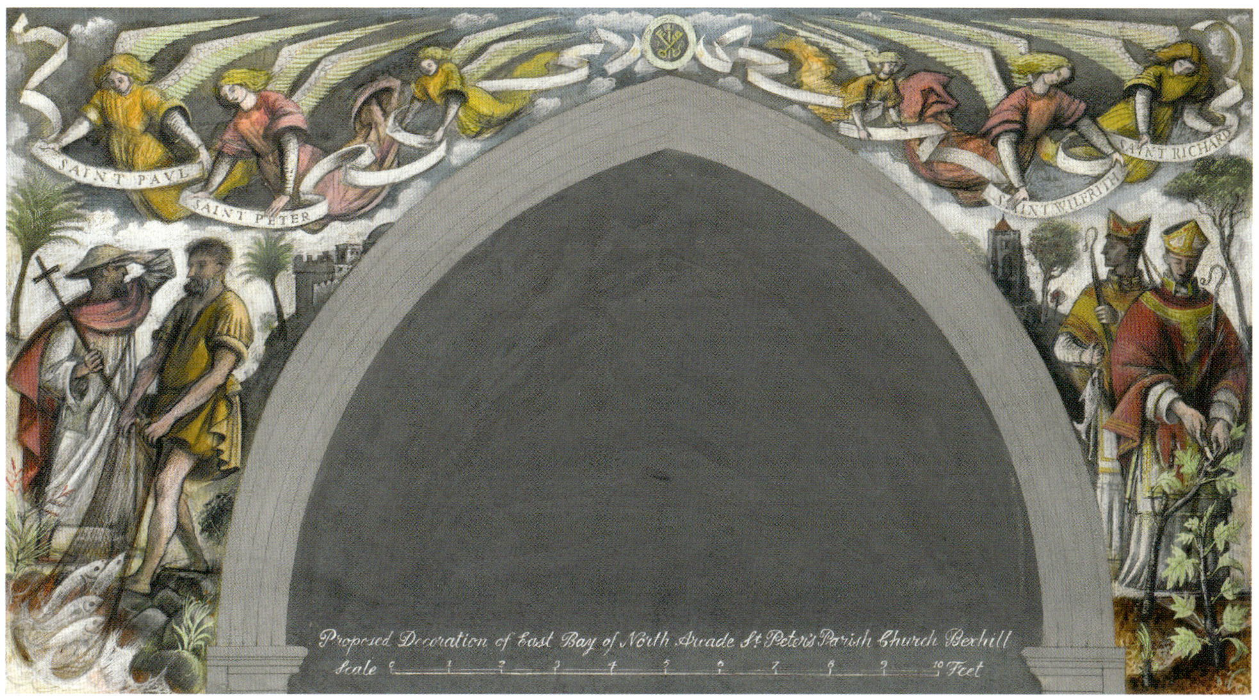

149 – Alan Sorrell (1904-1974),
Study for North arch of St Peter's Church, Bexhill-on-Sea, 1951,
pencil, ink and gouache on paper, 11 ½ x 21 in. (29 x 53.5 cm).
Provenance: The artist's son, Richard Sorrell
Literature: Sacha Llewellyn & Richard Sorrell (ed), *Alan Sorrell; the Life and Works of an English Neo-Romantic Artist*, (Bristol: Sansom & Co.)
2013, p 127-128.

This is a presentation sketch for the mural that was carried out at Bexhill.

148 – Charles Mahoney (1903-1968),
First design for the Thomas More Altar, Cheyne Row, London, mid 1930s,
oil on paper; 12 x 8 in. (30.5 x 20.2 cm). Provenance: The Artist's Estate

This is a study for a mural undertaken for the Holy Redeemer Church, Chelsea.
Mahoney's altarpiece for the Roman Catholic Church of Our Most Holy Redeemer and St Thomas More was unveiled on April 1, 1938.
In the background the Tower of London with a scaffold being erected can be seen on one side with More's house in Chelsea on the other.
Thomas More's name was added to the dedication of the Roman Catholic Church following his canonisation in 1935, (the quadricentenary
of his martyrdom). The church is located close to the house where he lived in Chelsea from 1524 until he was taken to the Tower and
subsequently executed on July 6, 1535.

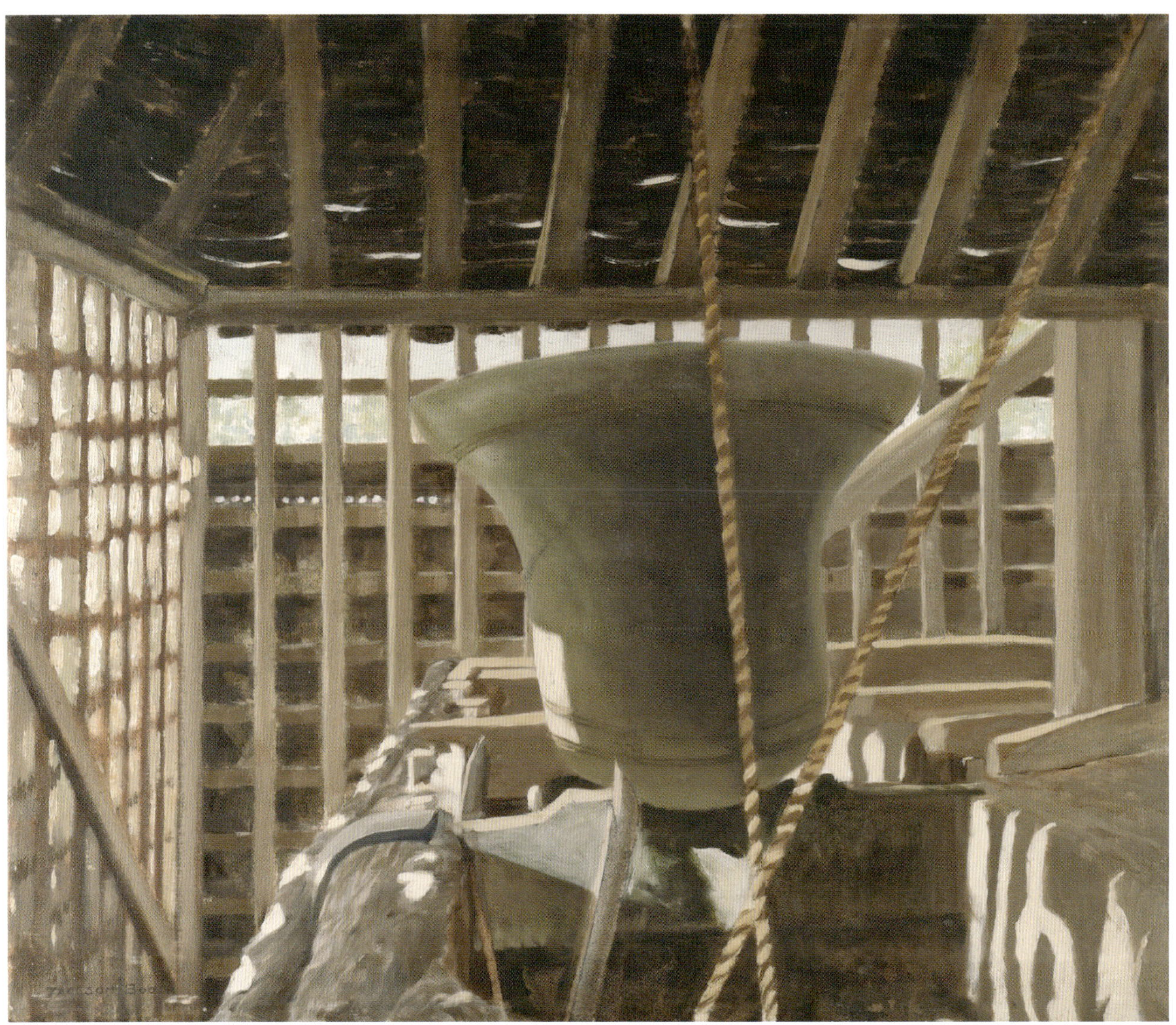

150 – Jackson Booth,
The Bell Cage of St Mary's Church, East Bergholt, Suffolk, c.1950, signed and indistincly inscribed on the stretcher,
oil on canvas, 20 × 24 in. (50.8 × 61 cm).
Provenance: Julie Collino.

The Church of St Mary the Virgin was built in the 15th and 16th centuries, but is well known for the absence of a tower or spire to house the bells. Work began on a tower in 1525, but Cardinal Wolsey's fall from grace in 1530 brought construction to a halt and the following year a wooden bell cage was erected in the churchyard. This temporary structure still exists although not in its original position. It was moved from the south to the north side of the church in the 17th century because the occupant of Old Hall objected to the noise of the bells. The bells are exceptional in that they are hung upside down and not rung from below by ropes attached to wheels, as is usual in change ringing, but the headstock is manipulated by hand by ringers standing beside the bells.

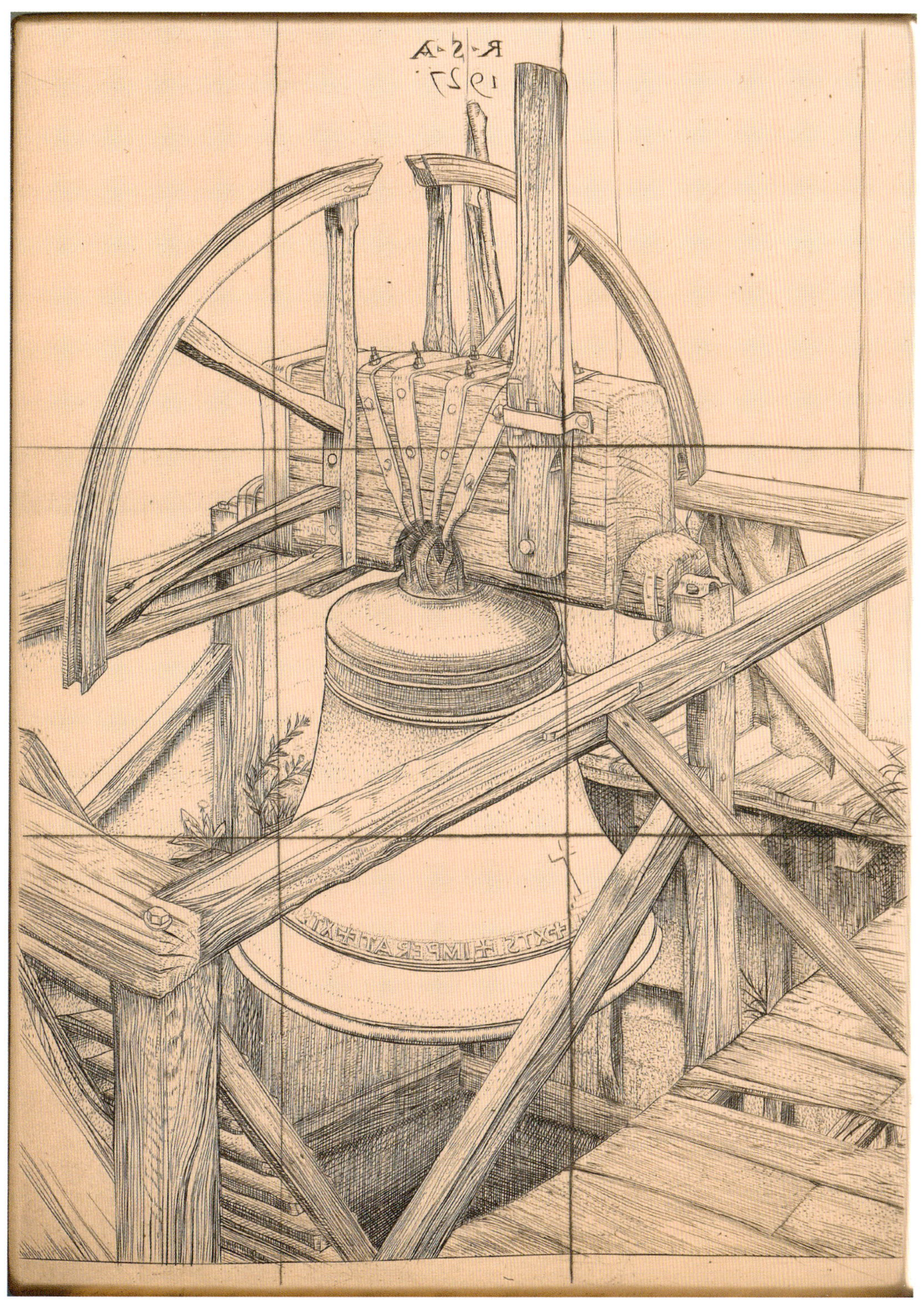

151 – **Robert Austin** (1895-1973), *The Bell, N° 2*, 1927, line engraving, signed and dated in the plate, original copper plate (cancelled), 6 × 4 ½ in. (15 × 11.5 cm).
Provenance: the artist's family.

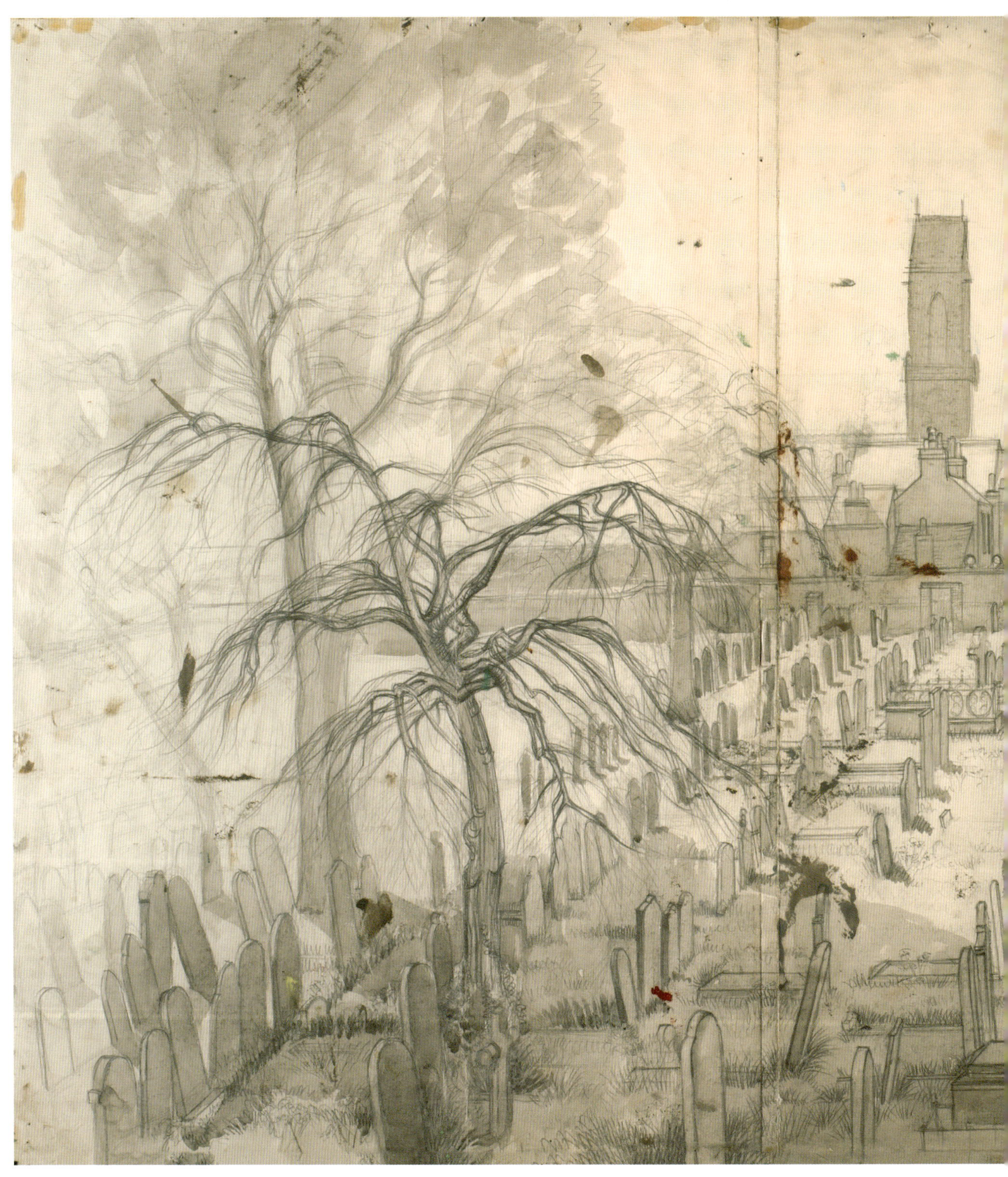

152 – **Marion Elizabeth Adnams** (1898–1995), Study for *Spring in the Cemetery, Uttoxeter Road, Derby*, 1956,
pencil and wash on paper, 21 ¾ × 42 ½ in. (55.7 × 108 cm).
Provenance: The Artist's Estate.

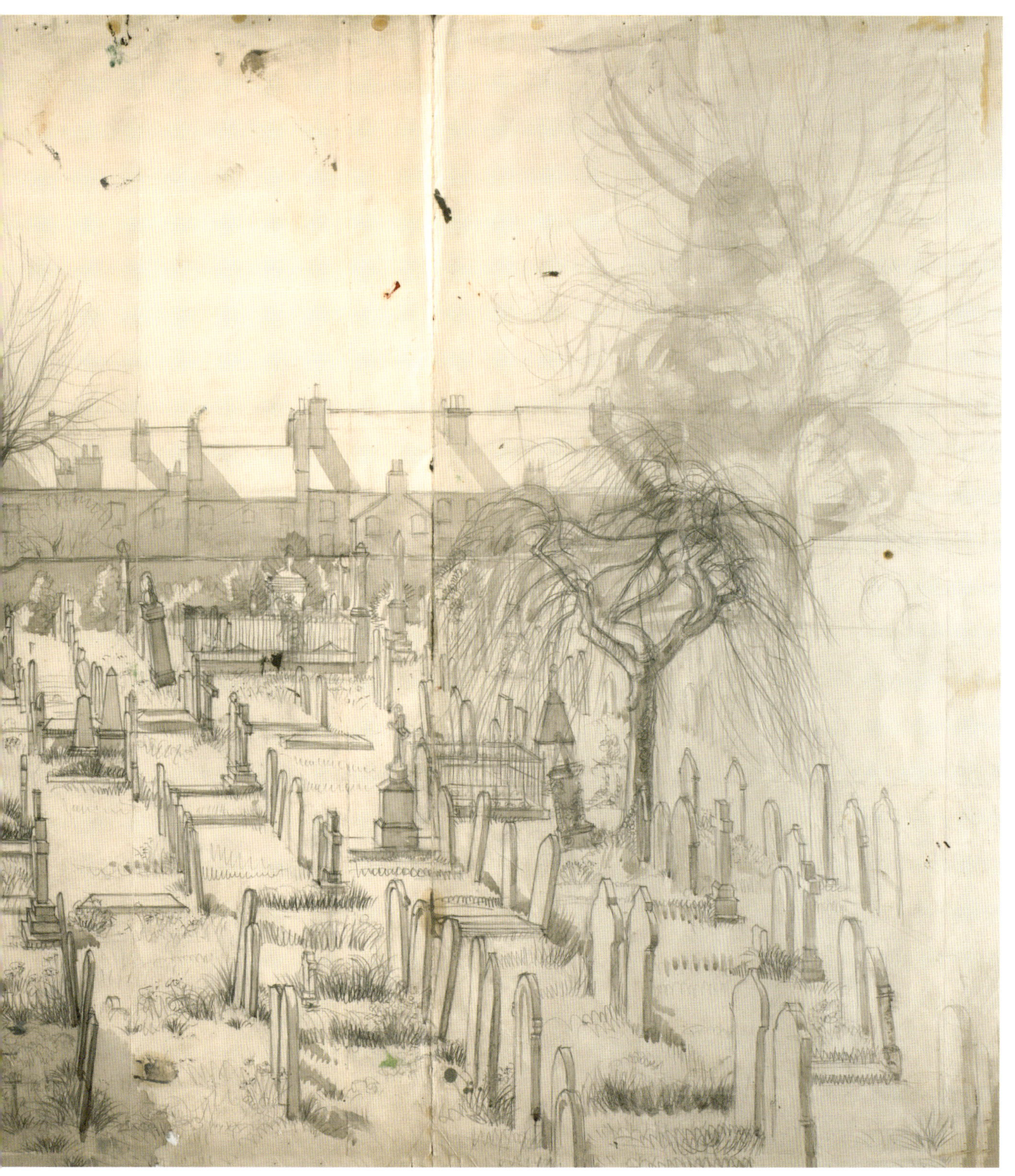

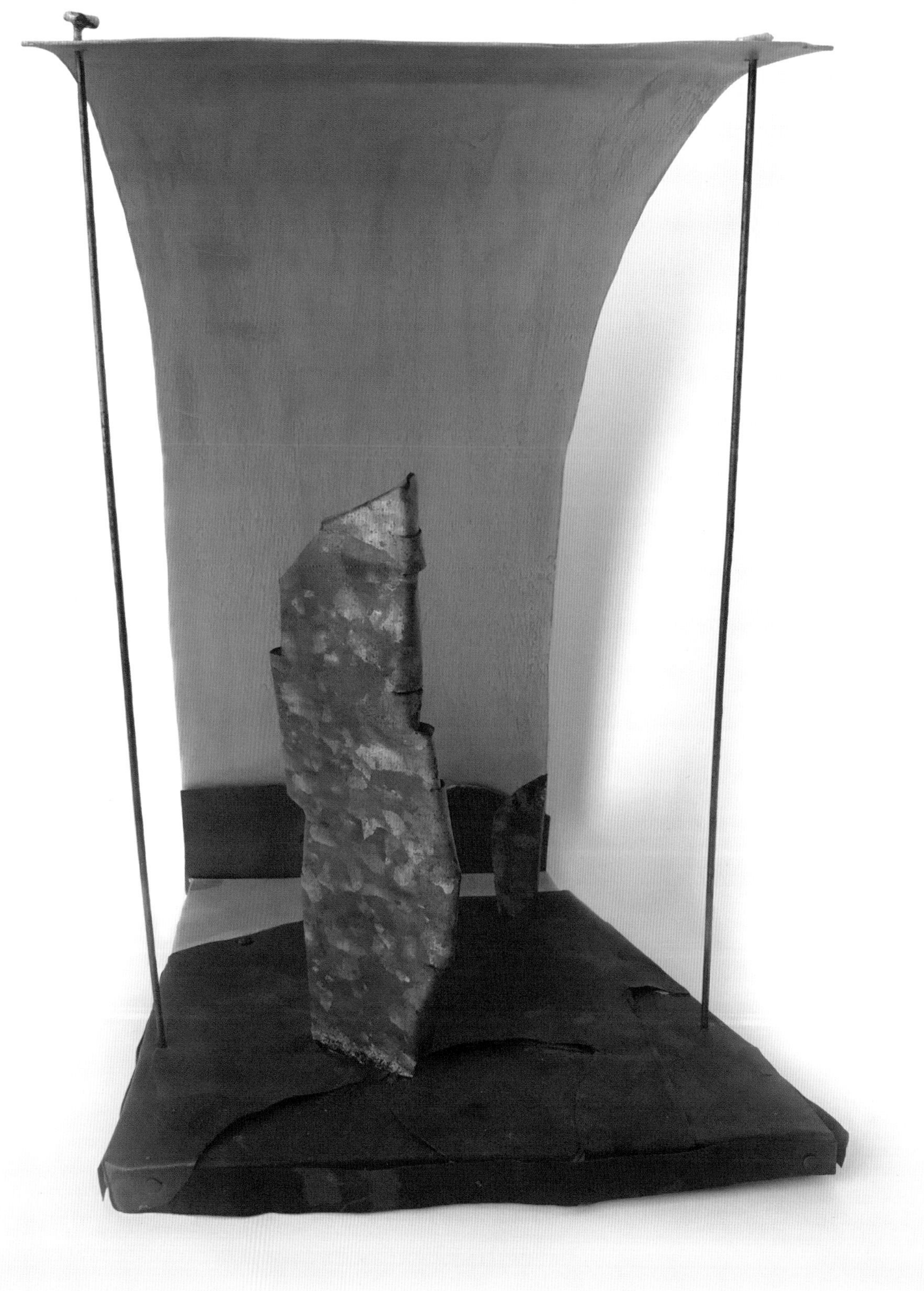

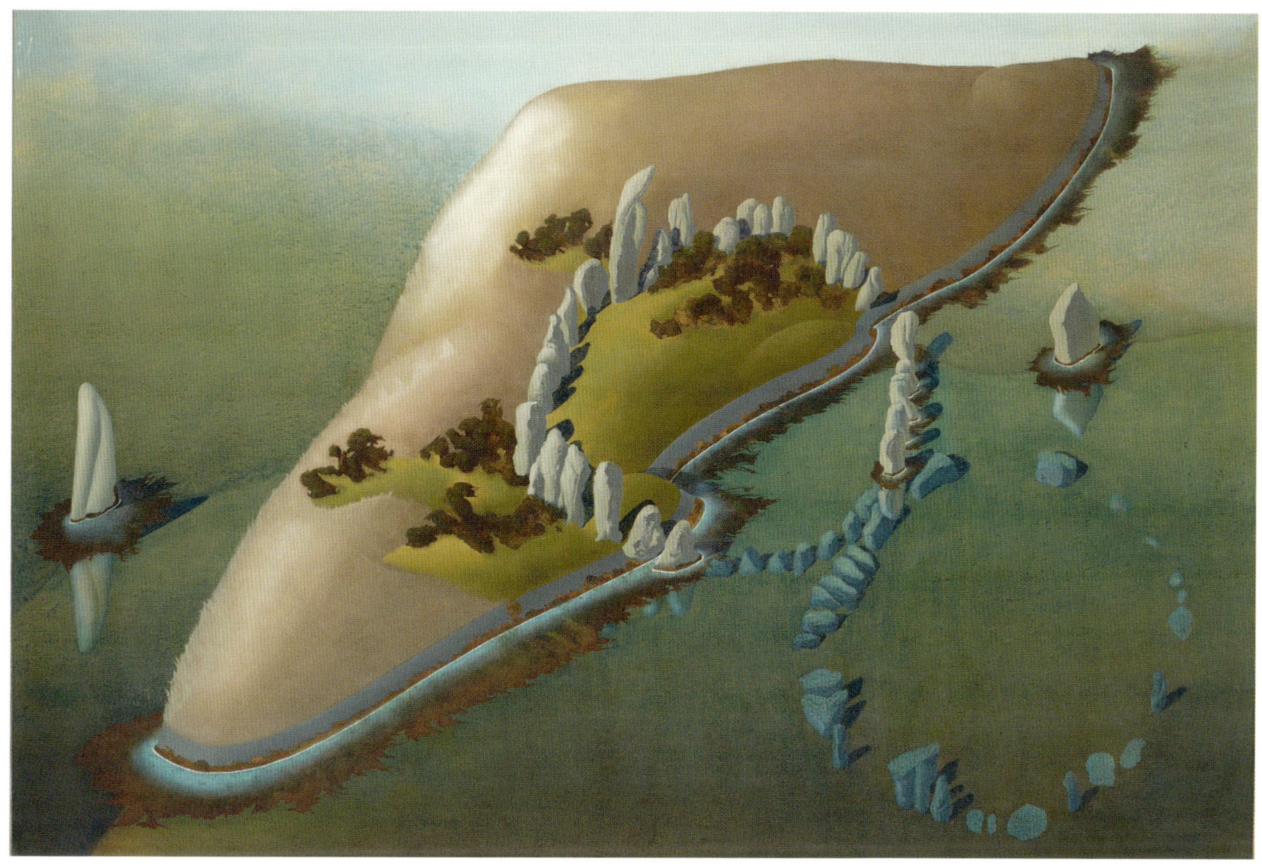

154 – **Ithell Colquhoun** (1906–1988), *La Cathédrale Engloutie*, c.1950, signed and inscribed,
oil on canvas, 51 ¼ × 76 ½ in. (130.1 × 194.8 cm).
Provenance: The Israel Museum, Jerusalem, Arturo Schwartz collection.
Exhibited London, Royal Academy, 1952, no. 755. Israel Museum, 2000-2001, no. 133.

This painting was inspired by the stone circles on the small Island of Er-Lannic, Brittany. According to Colquhoun 'perhaps the daily immersion of this temple, dedicated to the powers of both sea and earth was intended by its builders.' The title is a reference to the Prelude for piano by Claude Debussy. Colqhuoun revisited the same subject in her later painting *Rocky Island* (1969).

153 – **Rachel Reckitt** (1908-1995), *Monolith*,
metal and wood, 18 × 12 in. (45.7 × 30.5 cm).

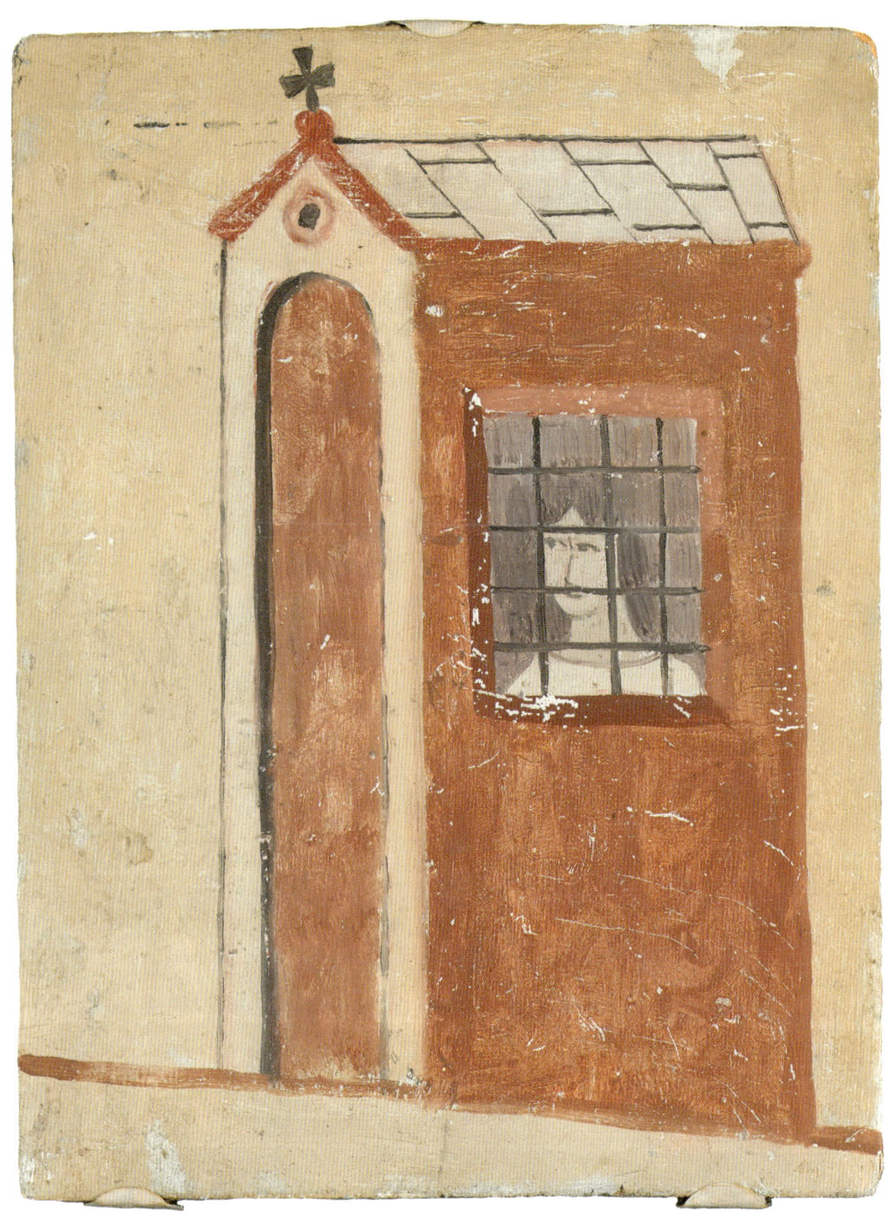

155 – **Kenneth Rowntree** (1915-1997), *Chapel*,
oil on panel, 9 ½ x 7 ¼ in. (24 x 18.5 cm).

156 – **Marjorie Hayes** (1913-2005),
The Church of St Mary (south-west elevation and ground plan), 1941,
titled, inscribed with notes,
watercolour and pencil on paper, 21 x 14 in. (53.5 x 36 cm).

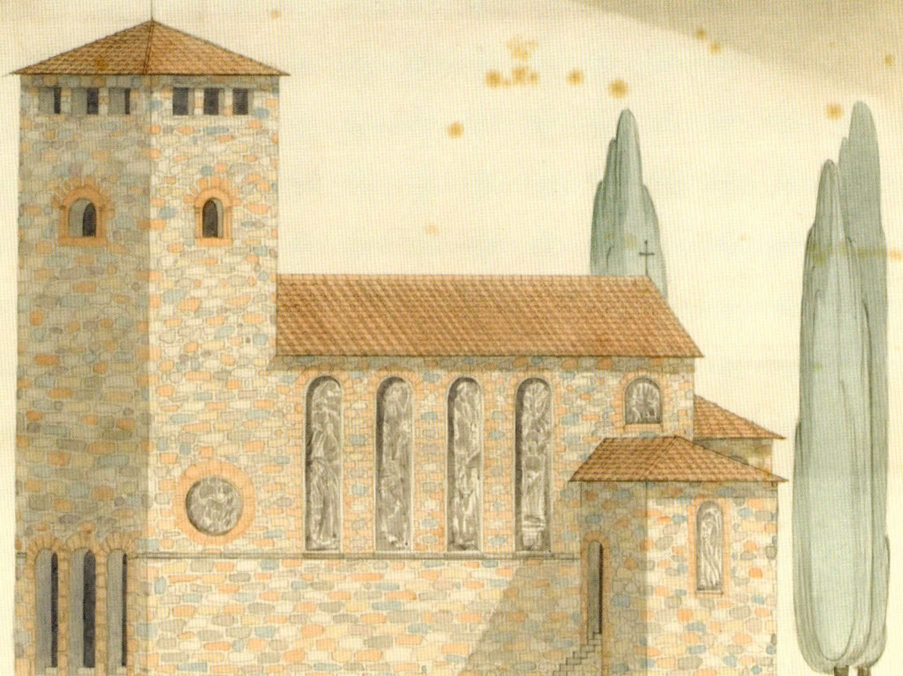

South-West Elevation.

GROUND PLAN

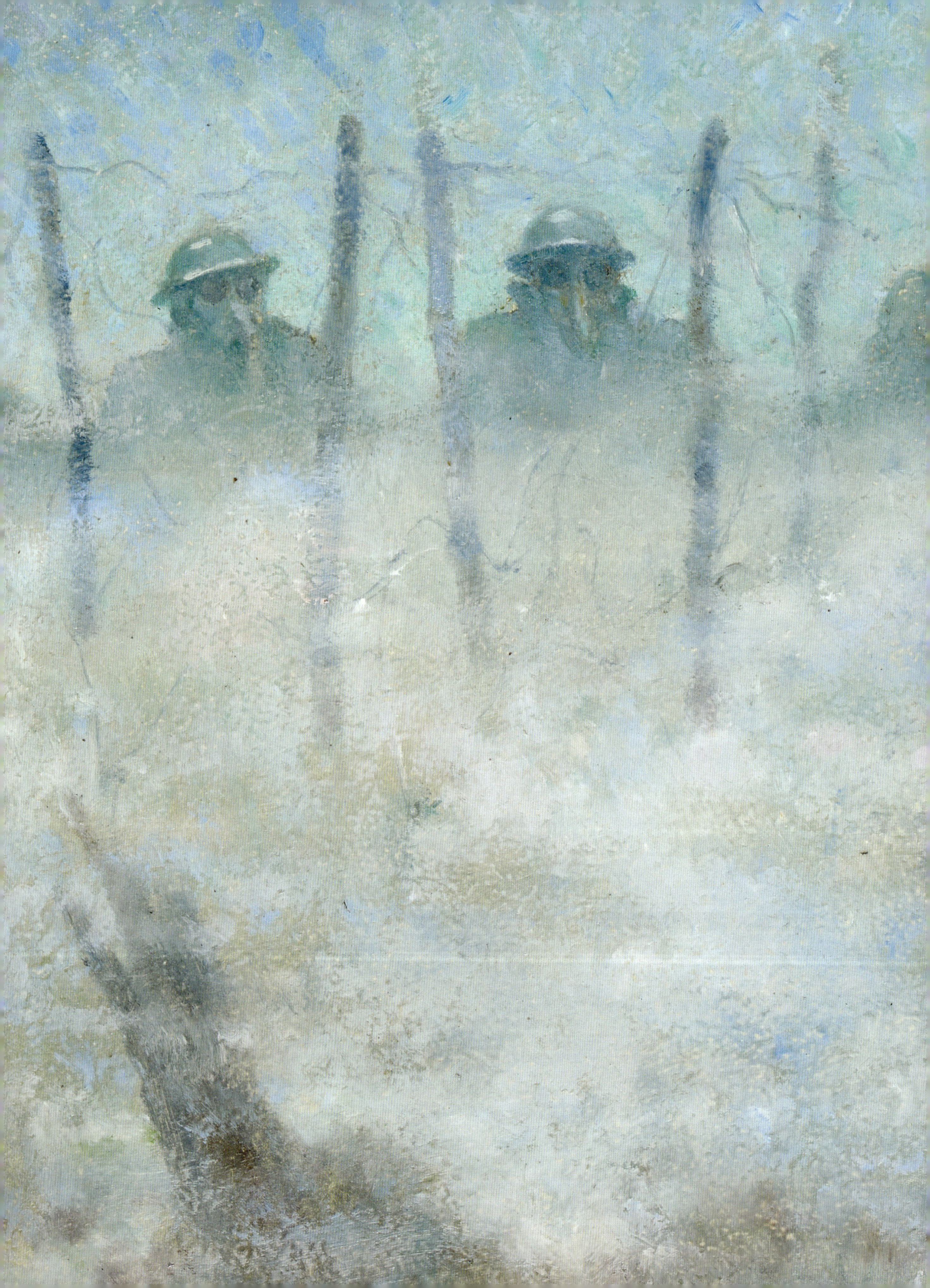

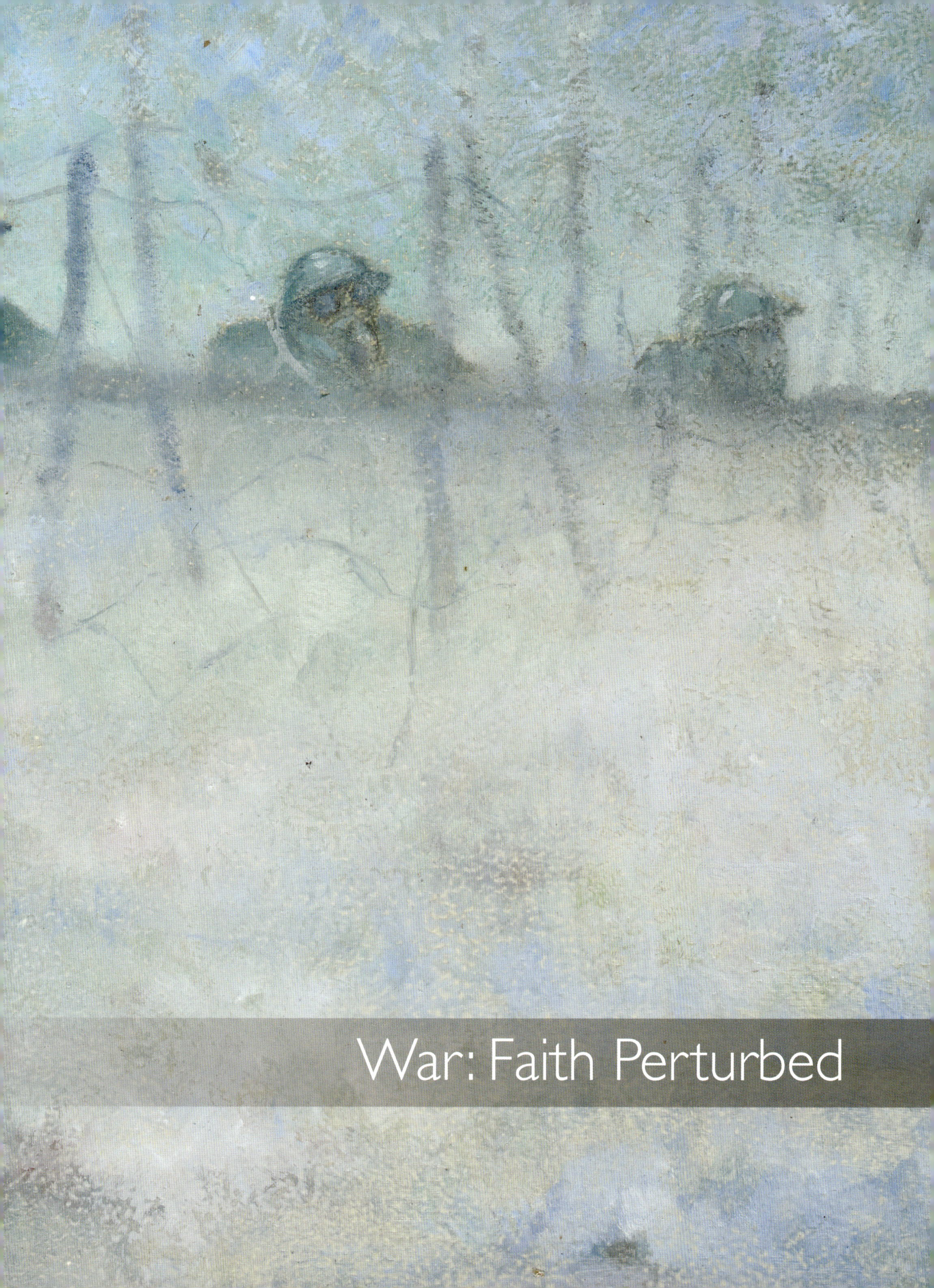
War: Faith Perturbed

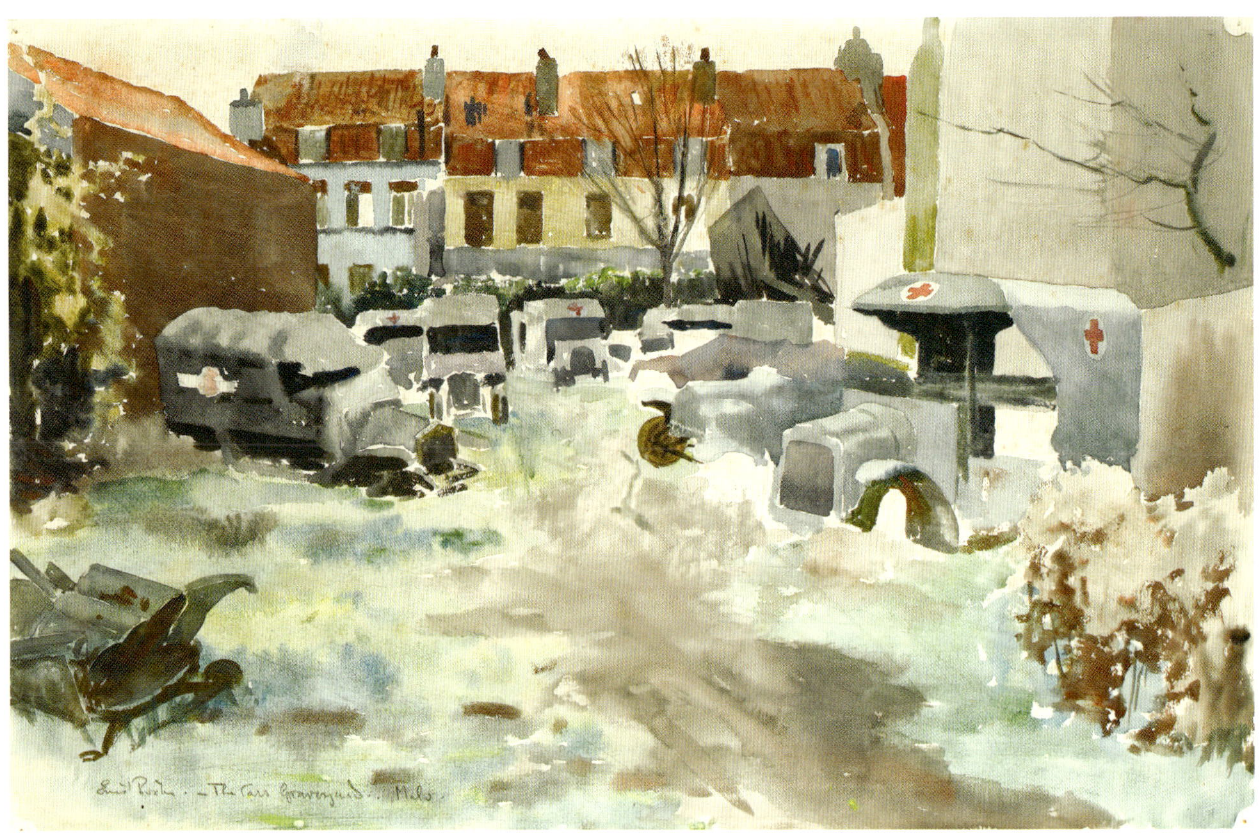

157 – Ernest Procter (1886-1935), *The Cars Graveyard, Malo*, c.1919, signed, inscribed with title, gouache on paper, 12 ¼ × 19 in. (31 × 48.2 cm).

Many conscientious objectors, such as Ernest Procter, served in the Medical Corps, rather than as soldiers. Between 1916-17 Procter was a member of and official artist for the Friends' Ambulance Unit (FAU) in Dunkirk, a voluntary organisation founded by individual members of the British Religious Society of Friends (Quakers), in line with their Peace Testimony. The FAU operated from 1914-19 and was chiefly staffed by registered conscientious objectors such as Procter. Altogether it sent more than a thousand men to France and Belgium, where they worked on ambulance convoys and ambulance trains with the French and British armies. Procter later served on the Western Front with two units of the Section Sanitaire Anglaise, at Nieuport Bains and at Verdun. He was appointed Official War Artist for the Ministry of Information from 1918-19.

158 – Ernest Procter (1886-1935), *Peronne 3.1.1919*, signed, dayed and inscribed with title, crayon and gouache on paper, 19 ½ × 12 ½ in. (49.5 × 31.8 cm).

Peronne, in Northern France, is close to where the Battle of the Somme took place. This watercolour shows the flamboyant Gothic west front of the Eglise Saint-Jean-Baptiste which by 1917, like most of the town, had been almost entirely destroyed..

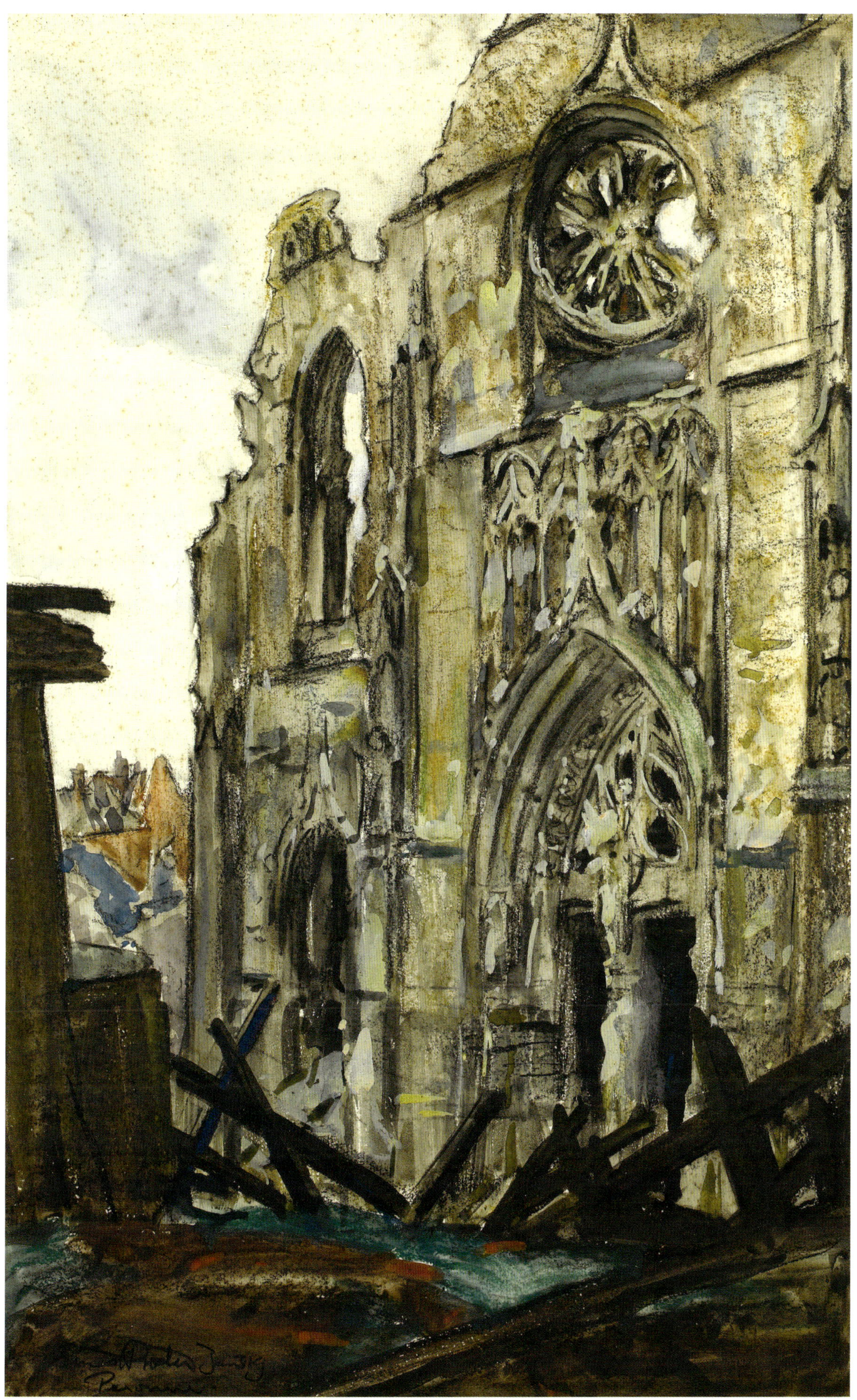

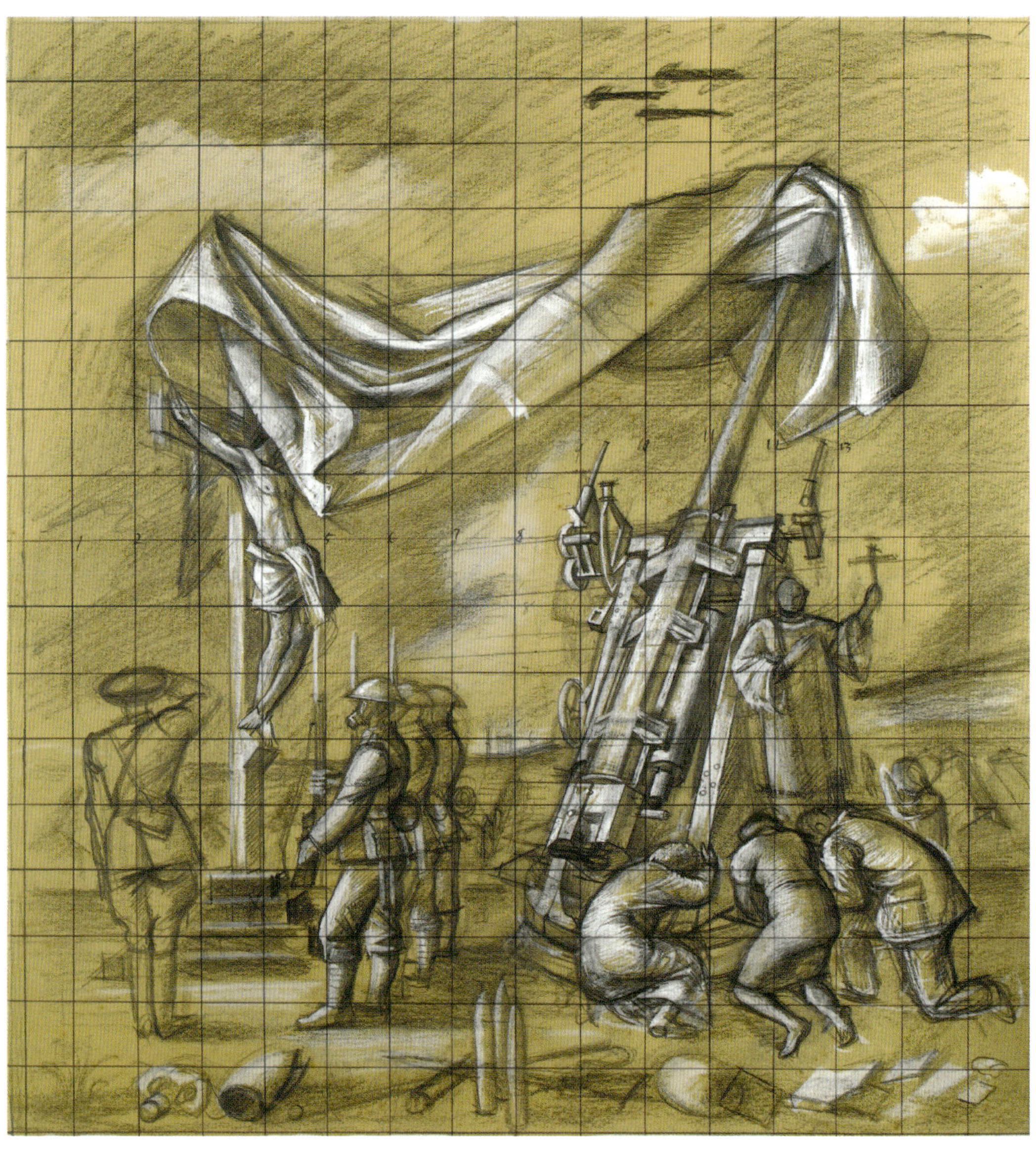

159 – Alan Sorrell (1904-1974), *A Confusion of Symbols*, 1939, signed, titled and dated *June 24, '39*,
pencil and gouache on paper, 17 ¾ × 15 in. (45.4 × 38.2 cm).
Exhibited: *WW2 – War Pictures by British Artists*, Morley College London, 28 October -23 November 2016, cat 129.
Literature: *WW2 – War Pictures by British Artists*, Edited by Sacha Llewellyn & Paul Liss, July 2016, cat 129, page 172.

During the Second World War Sorrell served in the RAF, where he was able to make first-hand visual records of the daily life in the Air Force. Although twenty six of these pictures were acquired by the War Artists' Advisory Committee and Sorrell had canvassed for Rothenstein's support to put his name before the WAAC, in both private and public he questioned the morality of War. Indeed he was not scared of challenging his superiors – when he enrolled in the RAF he refused to work on terrain models of cities he considers of "irreplaceable artistic importance", what he later referred to as his "one man mutiny". His image, *A Land Fit for Heros* openly challenged perceptions of the Hounour and Glory that surrounded WW1.

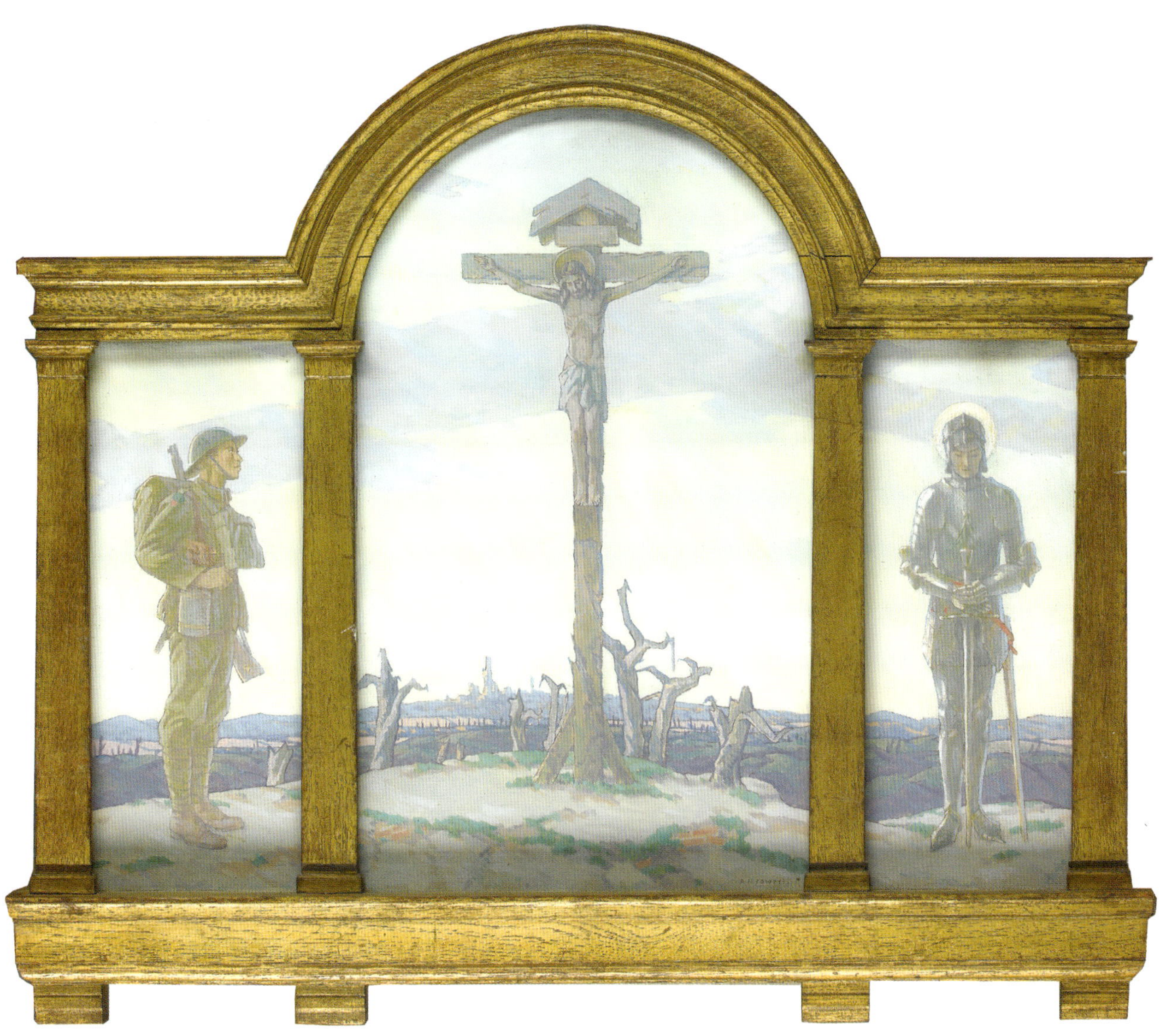

160 – **Percy Jowett** (1892-1955),
England (triptych), c.1918,
tempera on board, 25 ¼ × 30 in. (64 × 76 cm) overall.

"About this time the Principal [of The Royal College of Art] engaged a part-time teacher who possessed a distinguished personality and this was a significant event for the school. His name was P.H. Jowett and he had returned from the war and at times suffered from shell-shock. He visited the school two or three days a week and by the inspiration of his teaching gained our confidence and almost hero worship, transferring his own enthusiasm for drawing, and the beauty of classical construction of the human figure, to all who came under his instruction. I remember still with clarity, his beautiful selective demonstration drawings, which we eventually cut out and treasured."

Unpublished Autobiography of Hubert Arthur Finney, 1971, quoted by kind permission of Nicholas Finney

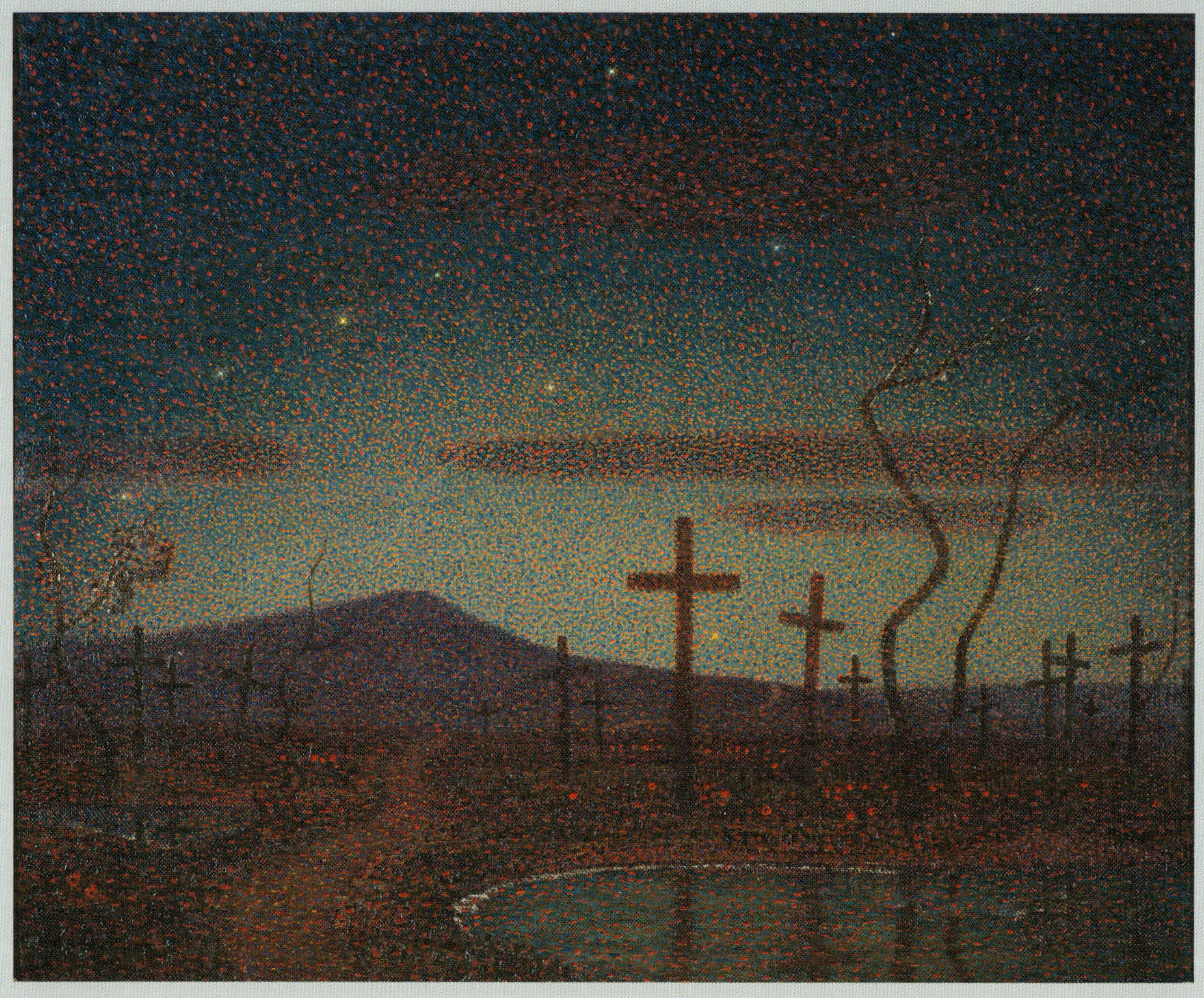

161 – Claude Francis Barry (1883-1970), *Monte Cassino*, c.1944,
oil on canvas, 25 x 31 in. (63.5 x 80 cm). Provenance: the artist's estate; cat.463. Private Collection.
Literature: Katie Campbell, *Moon Behind Clouds: An Introduction to the Life and Work of Sir Claude Francis Barry*, Jersey 1999, repr. p.74.

Barry spent most of the inter-war years etching and painting on the Continent. He had a particular fondness for Italy and it was only with reluctance that, at the start of the war, he abandoned his studio in Milan and moved back to England to return to St Ives.

Both a pacifist and an enthusiast for Italy, it is not surprising that he responded strongly to the Italian Campaign, producing a series of poignant paintings and etchings, especially around the subject of Monte Cassino. Though a victory for the Allies, the Battle of Monte Cassino, which took place between January and May 1944, resulted in appalling lossses: 54,000 Allied casualties and 20,000 Germans. It also resulted in terrible damage to the town of Monte Cassino and the total destruction of the historic monastery. Barry himself suffered a devastating loss during the closing weeks of the Italian campaign: an American bomb exploded in Milan, destroying his studio with all of his etching plates.

'The last fifty years are the most terrible of which history has any record and many of those, myself included, who have lived through them have often wished that they had never been born' (Claude Francis Barry, quoted in Katie Campbell, *Moon Behind Clouds*, Jersey 1999, p.74).

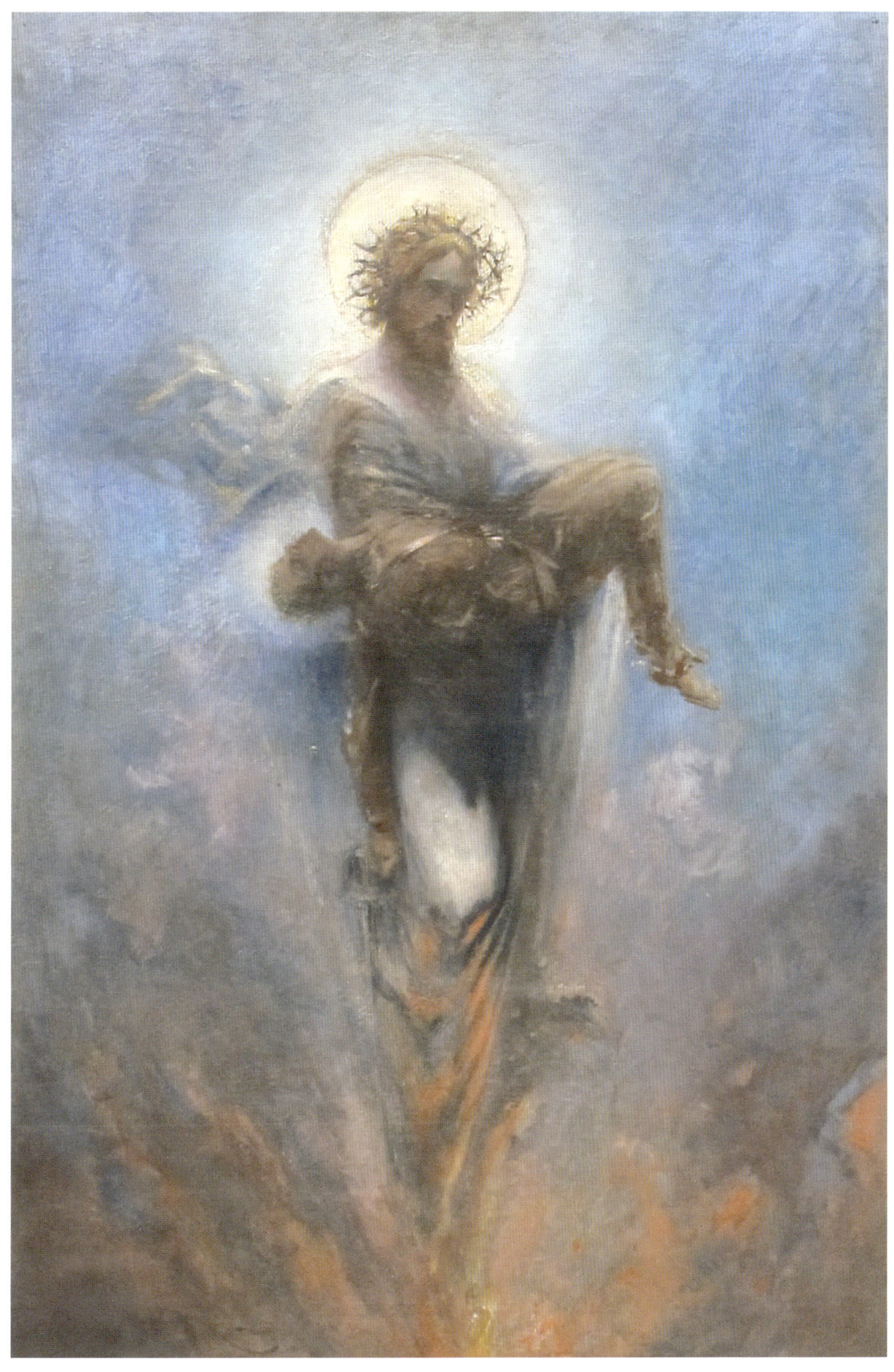

162 – **Hal Hurst** (1865-1938), *The Hero*, 1915, signed
oil on canvas, 45 x 30 in. (114 x 76 cm).

A photograph of Hurst working on *The Hero* appeared in *The New York Times Mid-Week Pictorial* on 22, April 1915.

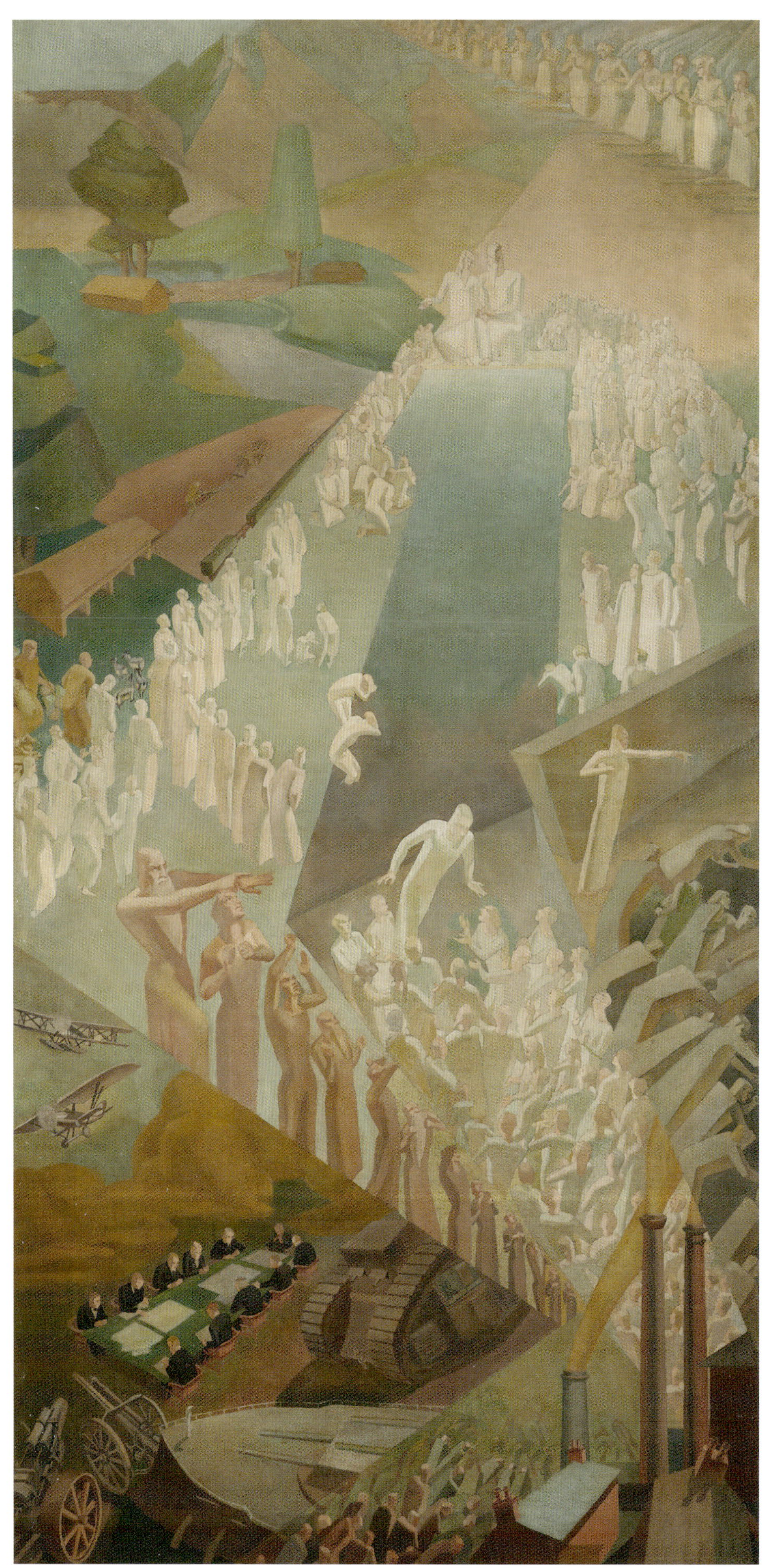

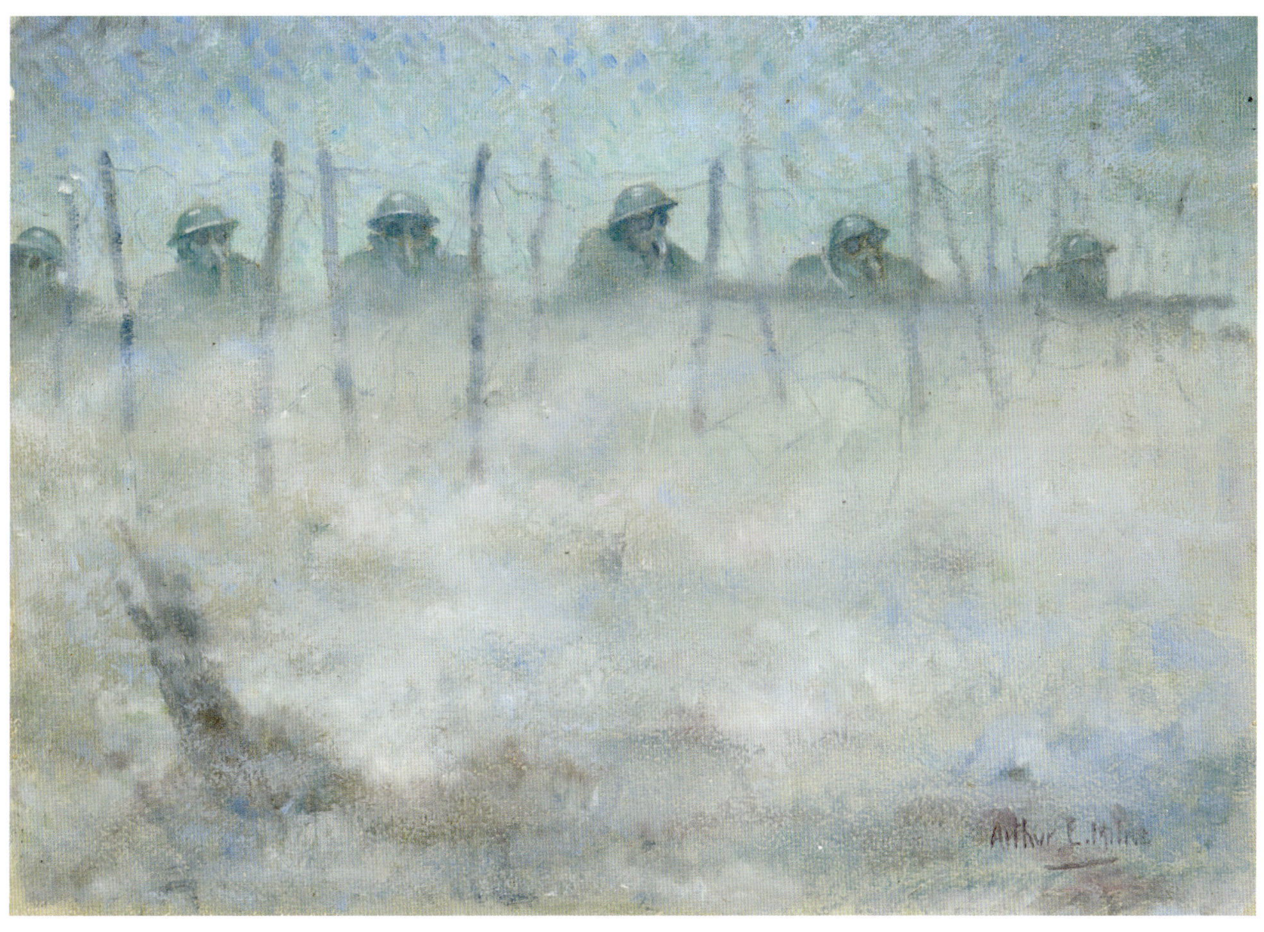

164 – Arthur Edwards Milne (1889–1981), *The Weird Barrier*, signed, inscription on verso, gouache on board, 9 ½ x 13 ¾ in. (24 x 35 cm).

163 – Slade School (?), *Allegory of War, The Last Judgement*, early 1920s, oil on canvas, 59 ½ x 29 ¾ in. (151 x 75.5 cm).
Provenance: Private collection, 1980s; Tadema Gallery until 2018.

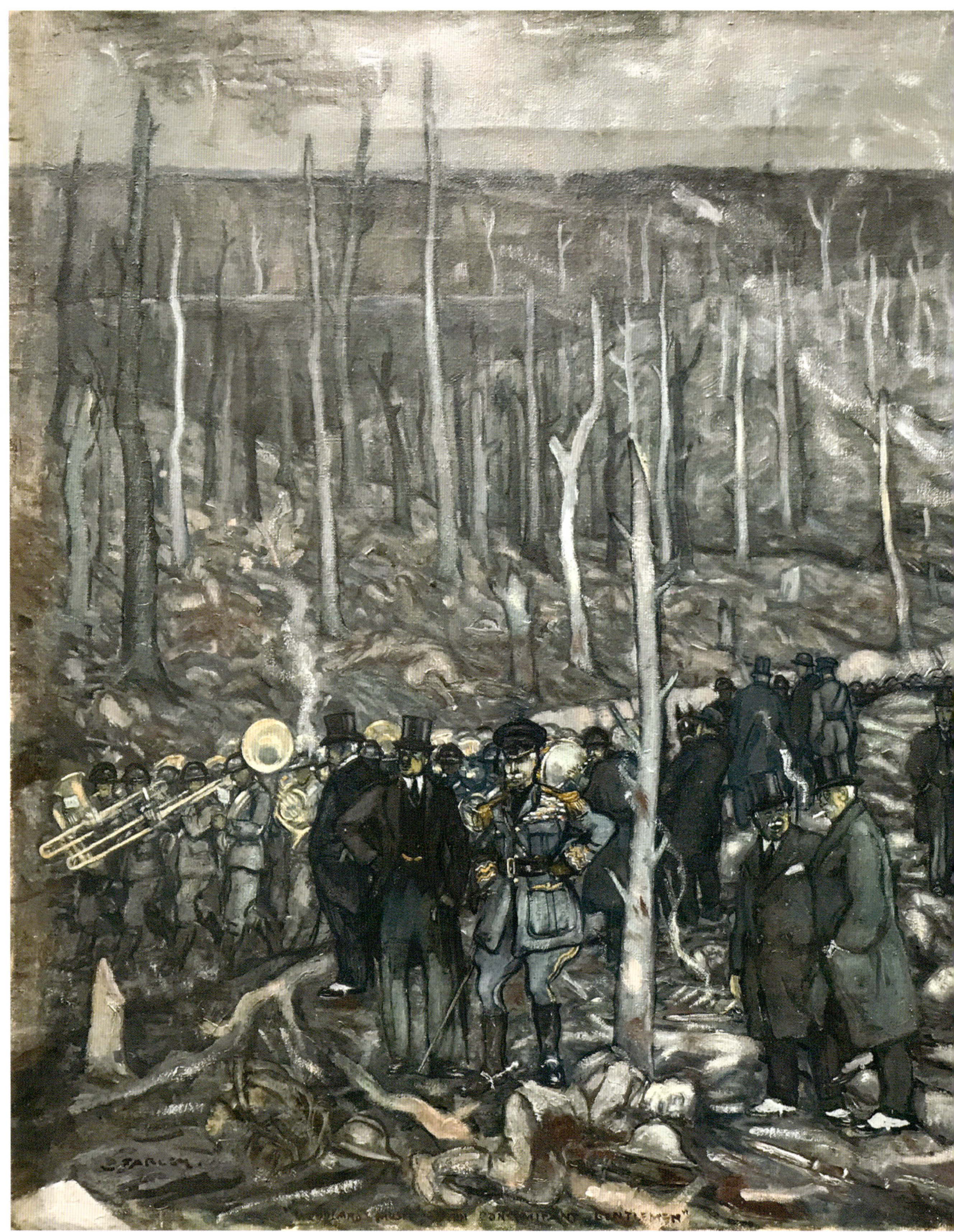

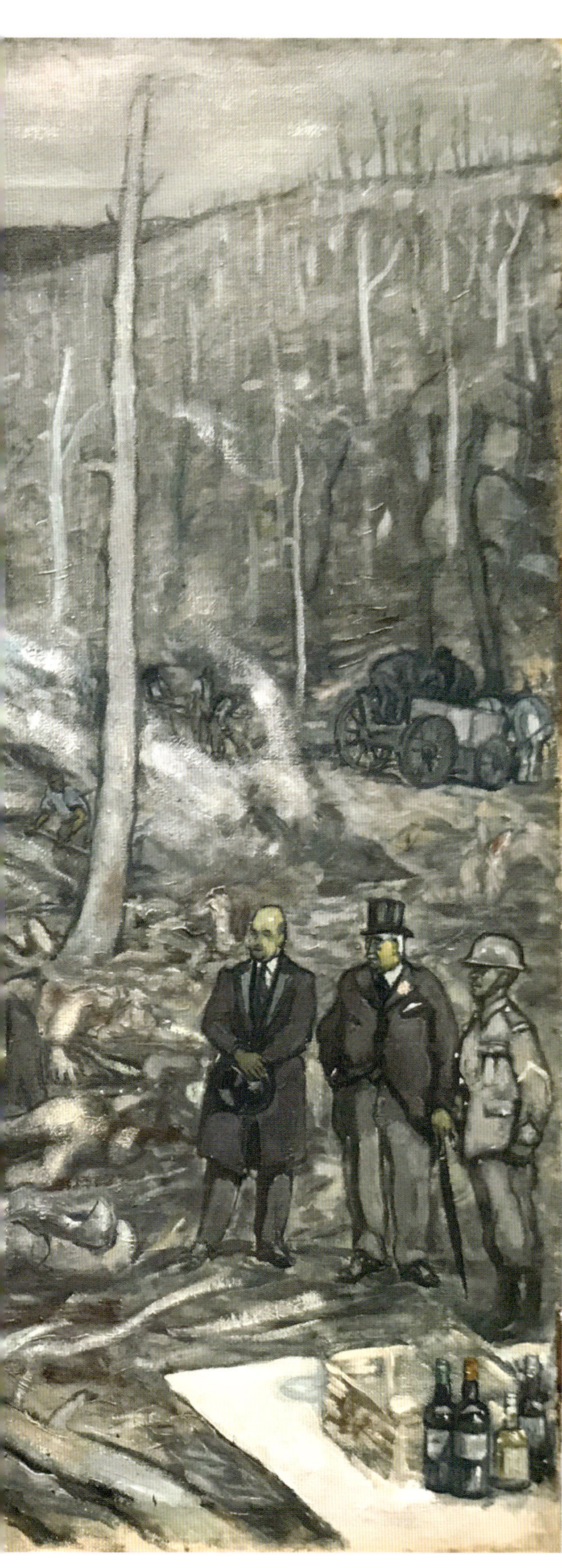

165 – **William Farley** (1891-1961),
Woodland Music with Concomitant Gentlemen,
signed, inscription on verso,
oil on canvas, 20 ½ × 26 ¼ in. (52 × 67 cm).

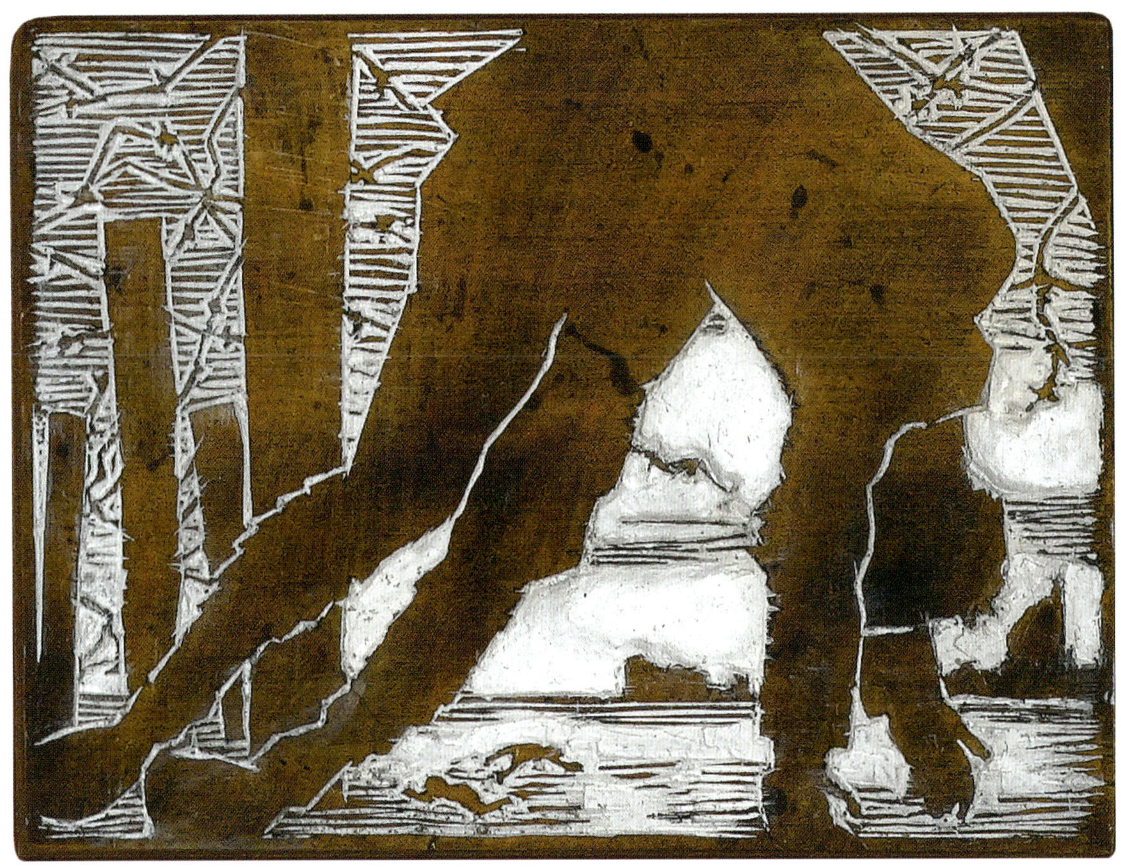

166 – **John Moody** (1906-1993), *War*, 1928,
the original woodblock, 3 x 4 in. (7.6 x 10.2 cm).

Margaret Ley, a talented miniaturist, and William Sewell, a talented artist and book illustrator, first met when students at Herkomer's Art School. In this poignant portrait of 1927, John Moody expresses the grief felt by Margaret on the tenth anniversary of her husband William's death – he died in 1917, aged 41, at the battle of Arras. Still in mourning, she holds in her hand a species of the Cardamine plant, known for its healing properties for heart ailments.

Born in 1906, Moody had been too young to participate in the war, but suffered its consequences. His poignant woodcut, *War*, produced in 1928, sums up his sense of the futility of war and and antagonism towards the 'old order' which had condemned so many to a needless death.

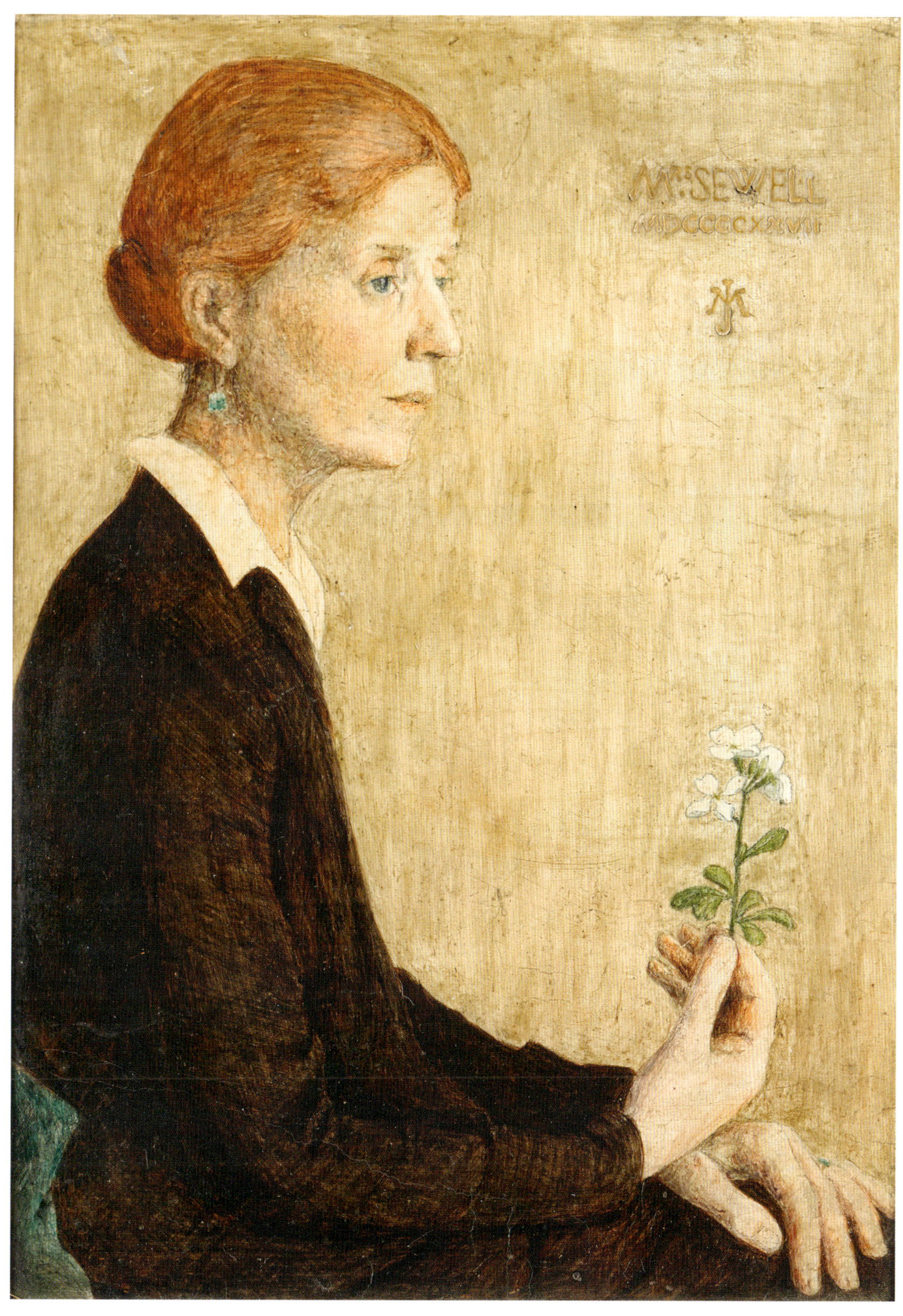

167 – **John Moody** (1906-1993), Margaret Sewell, 1927,
egg Tempera on board, 8 ¼ × 6 in. (20.9 × 15.2 cm).
Provenance: The Artist's Estate

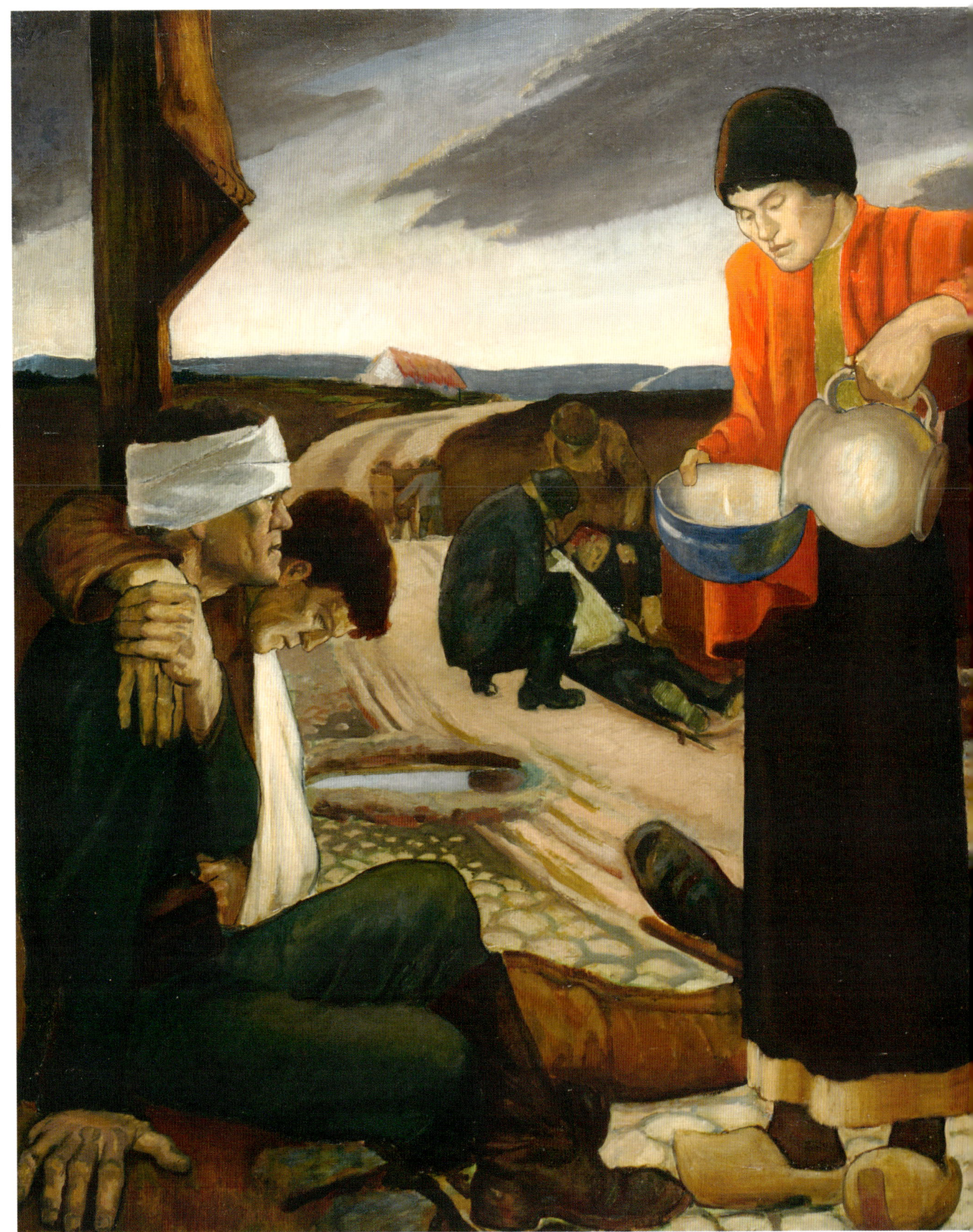

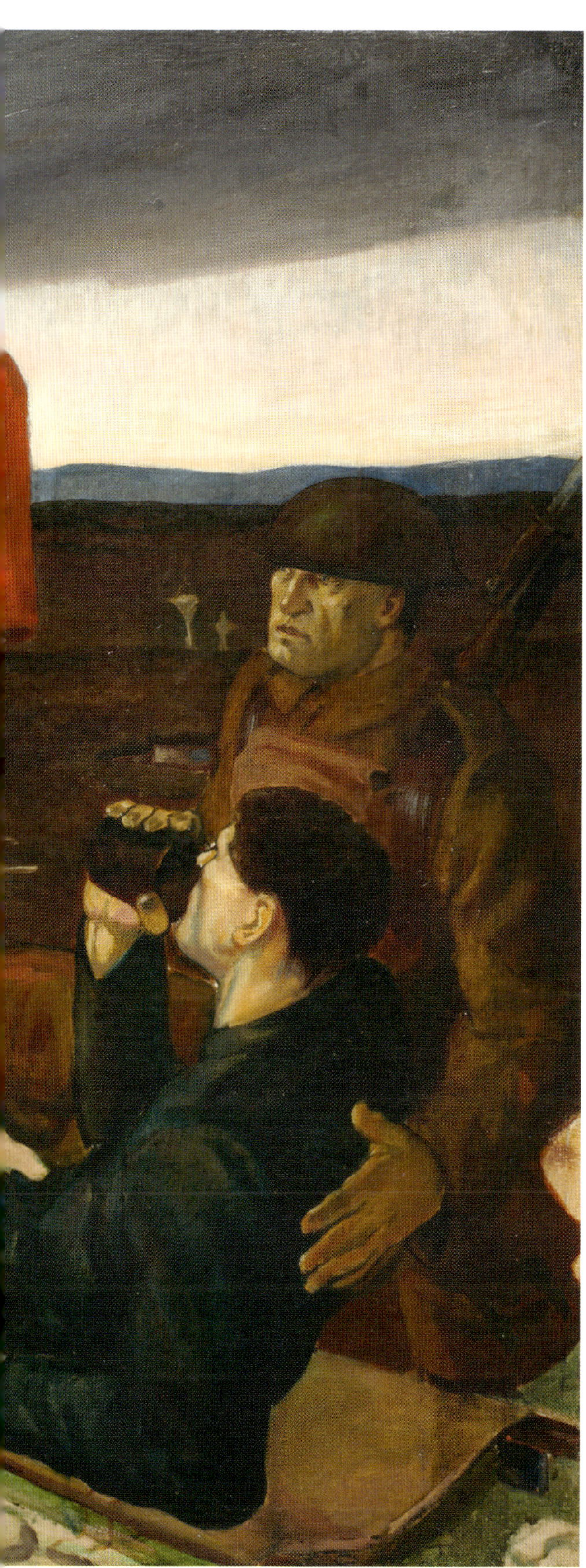

168 – **English School,** *The Good Samaritan*, c. 1920,
oil on canvas, 34 x 40 in. (86.5 x 101.5 cm).

A similar subject, where women attend to battle-weary soldiers, irrespective of their nationality, was portrayed by Charles Sargeant Jagger at the Anglo-Belgian War Memorial in Brussels. This end of WWI scene, by an as yet unidentified hand, may be set at the Belgian Front, the hills being typical of the Ardennes. Visible to the top left are the feet of a wayside figure of Christ.

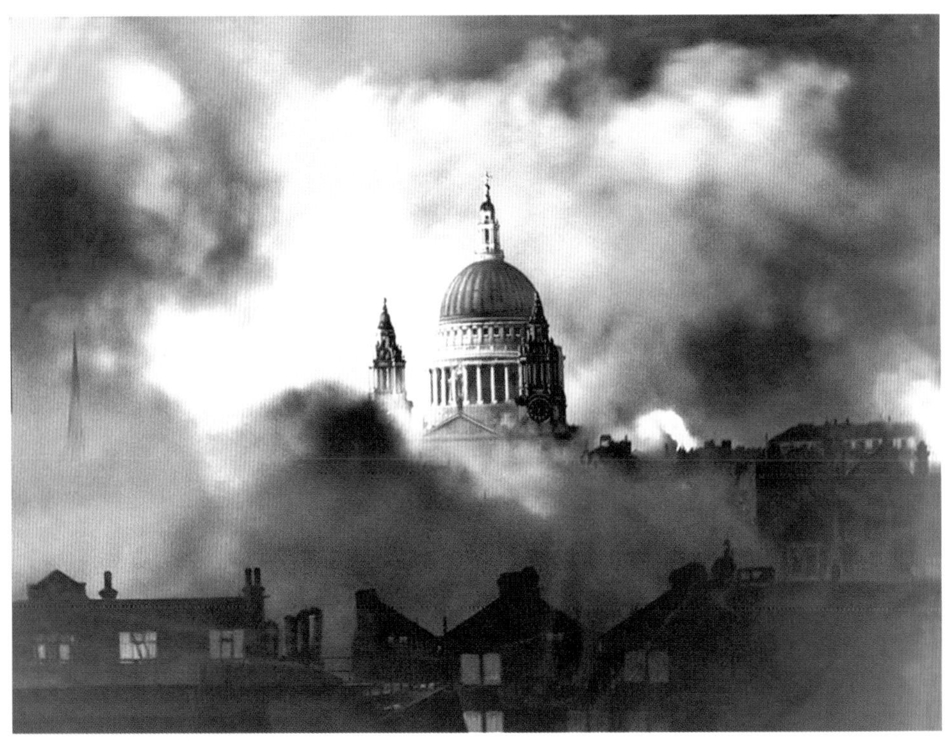

169 – Saint Paul's Cathedral during the Second World War.

170 – Frank Potter (1885-1958), *Self-Portrait as an Auxiliary Fireman*, c.1941,
oil on canvas, 62 ¼ × 40 ¼ in. (158 × 102 cm).
Provenance: Andrew Leslie, Leva Gallery, 1974; private collection.
Exhibited: *WW2 – War Pictures by British Artists,* Morley College London, 28 October -23 November 2016, cat 38.
Literature: Grant M.Waters, Dictionary of British Artists Working 1900–1950, Eastbourne Fine Art Publications, Eastbourne, 1976, vol. 2, illus. no. 70.
WW2 – War Pictures by British Artists, Edited by Sacha Llewellyn & Paul Liss, July 2016, cat 38, page 76.

This painting shows the artist as an Auxiliary Fireman, his plastron-fronted tunic buttoning on the right side and his fireman's hatchet in a holder attached to his belt. Potter, who had served in WW1, (enlisting in 1916 at the age of 29), would have been too old to fight in WW2, but served on the home front as an Auxillary Fireman assisting in the clean-up of bomb damage to the capital.

Potter was one of the founder members of the Decorative Art Group in the summer of 1916 with Ethelbert White, C.R.W. Nevinson, and Carlo Norway. As a print maker Potter produced views of London landmarks and his dry points bear comparison to those of C.R.W. Nevinson.

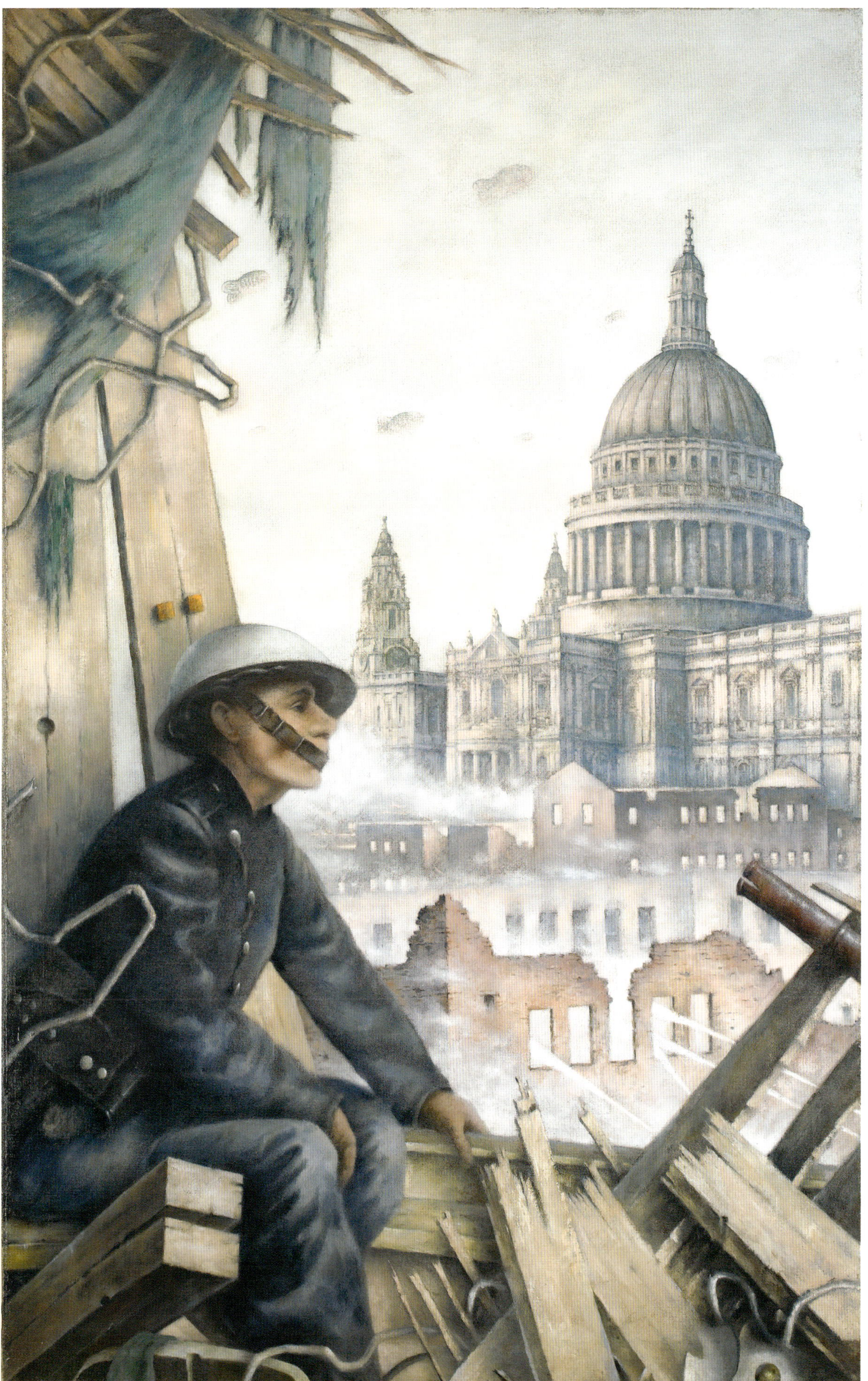

171 – Olive Mudie-Cooke (1890-1925),
Vlamertinge, c.1920, inscribed with title,
lithographic print, 11 × 8 in (27.9 × 20.4 cm).
Provenance: The Redfern Gallery

In 1919 Mudie-Cooke came to the attention
of the Women's Work Sub-Committee of the
newly formed Imperial War Museum which
acquired a number of her paintings for its
fledgling collection. This purchase included her
most famous picture, *In an Ambulance: a VAD
lighting a cigarette for a patient.*

In 1920 the British Red Cross commissioned
her to return to France to record the activities
of the Voluntary Aid Detachment units who
were still providing care and relief there. Her
paintings from this visit include examples of
war damage, the shattered landscapes of the
former battlefields and women tending graves
in a cemetery.

Some of these images were reproduced in a
limited edition of lithographs entitled: *With the
VAD's in France, Flanders and Italy.*

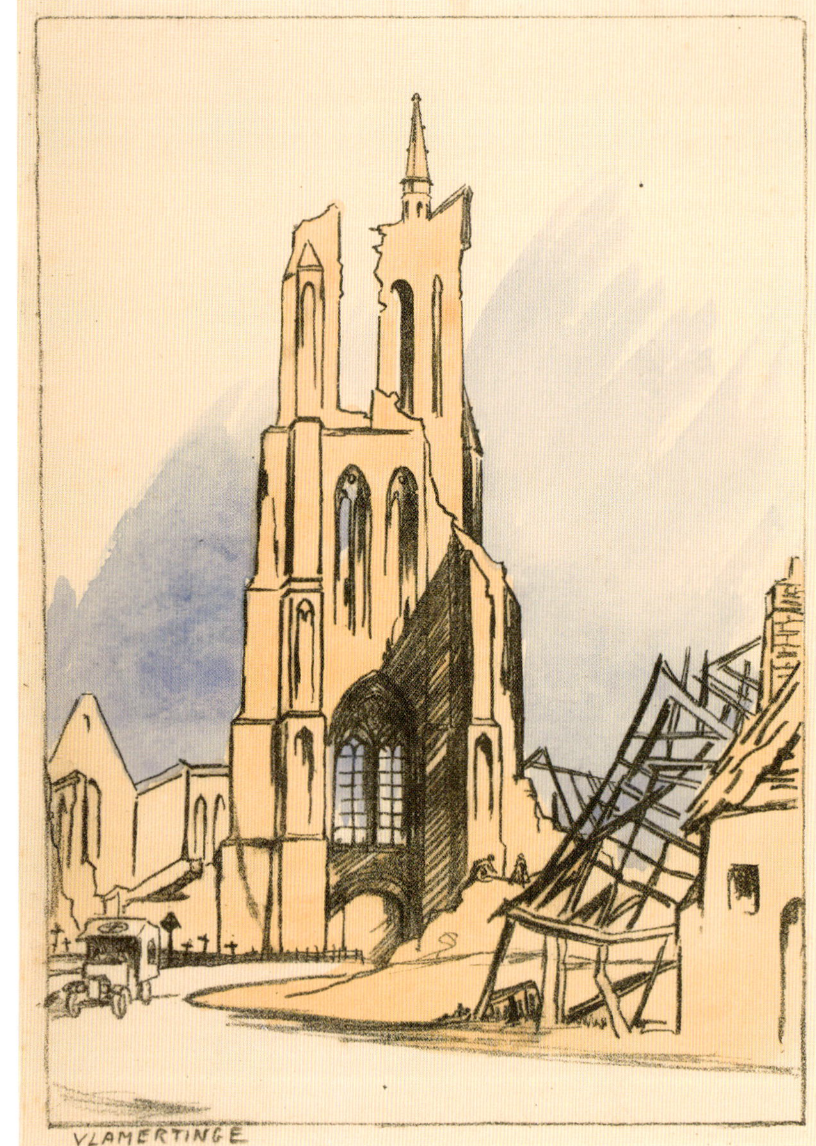

172 – Edward Irvine Halliday (1902-1984),
War and Peace, 1939, signed and dated, inscribed *Altar* and '1 inch to a foot',
ink and gouache on paper, 30 × 17 in. (76.2 × 43.2 cm).
Exhibited: *WW2 – War Pictures by British Artists*, Morley College London, 28 October -23 November 2016, cat 122.
Literature: *WW2 – War Pictures by British Artists*, Edited by Sacha Llewellyn & Paul Liss, July 2016, cat 122, page 163.

During the war Halliday worked as an air traffic controlled for the RAF and later was transferred to Intelligence and worked on intercepting German
radio signals. Altar offers a deeply personal and kaleidoscopic vision of war and peace. Conceived in 1939 for an unidentified (and presumably never
completed) altar the dominance of the disproportionately large central figure of Christ recalls that of Hypnos in *Evening on the Roman Campagna*,
which though painted in 1928, was exhibited at the Royal Academy in the same year that this composition was conceived.

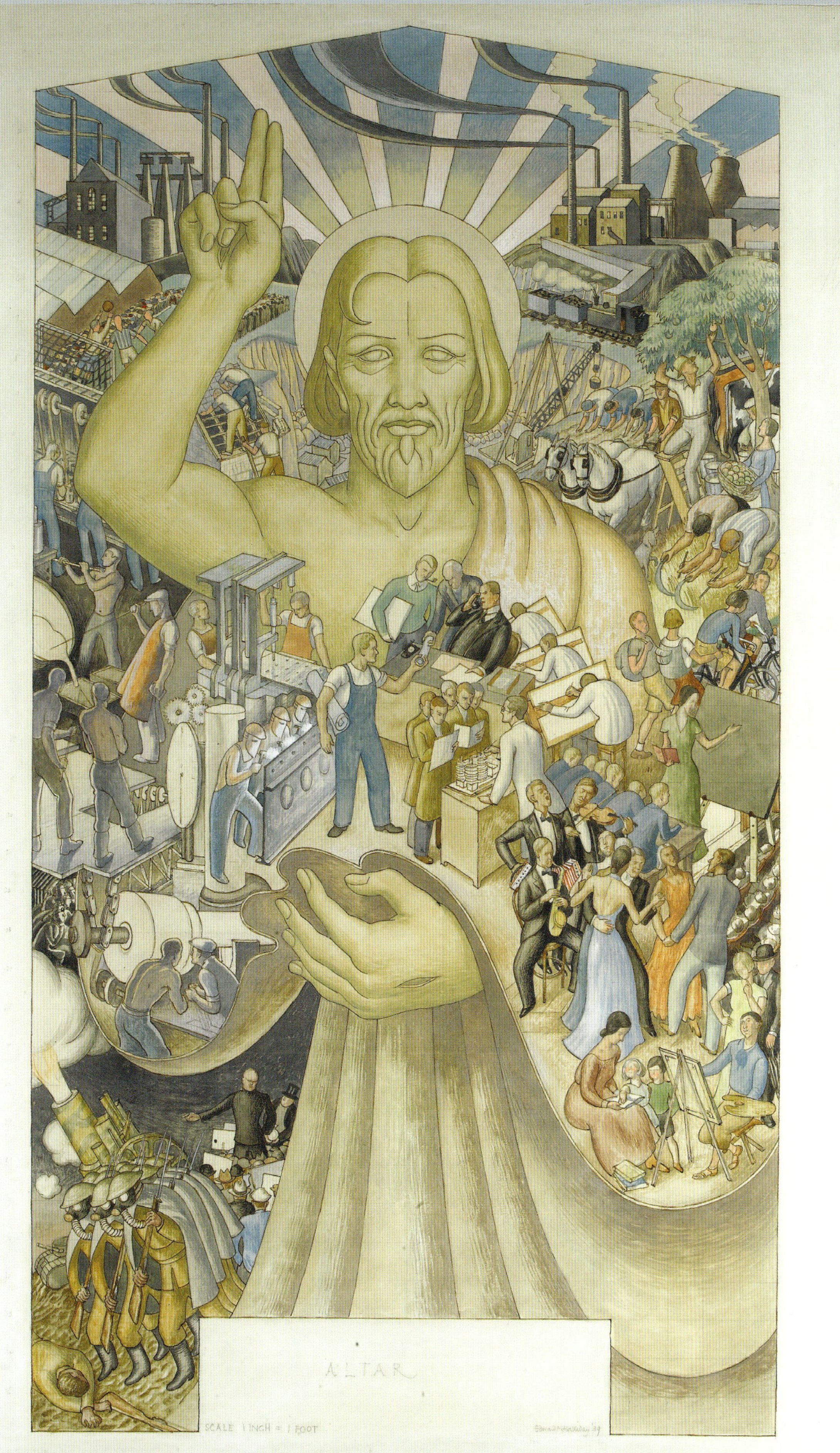

ALTAR
SCALE 1 INCH = 1 FOOT

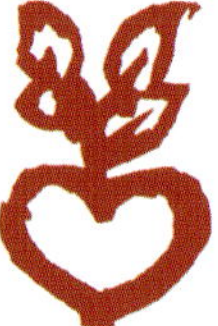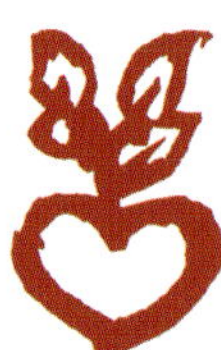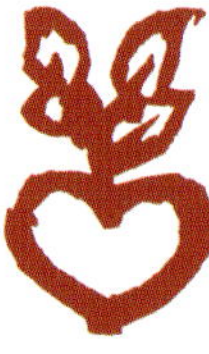

 ARTISTS INDEX

John Moody (1906-1993),
War, 1928, *210*
Margaret Sewell, 1927, *211*

Victor Hume Moody (1896-1990),
The Judgement of Solomon, c.1930, *60*

Olive Mudie-Cooke (1890-1925),
Vlamertinge, c.1920, *216*

John Napper (1916-2001),
The Night That Pontius Pilate Died, 1991, *24*

Anne Newland (1913-1997),
Study for *The Legend of Ceres*, c.1938-39, *86-87*

Frank Potter (1885-1958),
Self-Portrait as an Auxiliary Fireman, c.1941, *215*

Ernest Procter (1886-1935),
The Cars Graveyard, Malo, c.1919, *200*
Peronne 3.1.1919, *201*

Eric Ravilious (1903-1942),
The Famous Tragedy of the Rich Jew of Malta, 1933, *62-63*
Clerical Outfitter, 1938, *167*

Rachel Reckitt (1908-1995),
How high the Heavens are, late 1960s, *7*
Towers and Helmets, *182*
Monolith, *194*

Victor Reinganum (1907-1995),
Cavalry, 1968, *120-121*

Frederick Cayley Robinson (1862-1927),
Orphan girls entering the refectory of a hospital, 1916-20, *15*
Pastoral, c.1930, *85*

Kenneth Rowntree (1915-1997),
Chapel, *196*

Alan Sorrell (1904-1974),
Study for Angels for St Peter's Church, Bexhill-on-Sea, 1951, *147*
Study for North arch of St Peter's Church, *189*
A Confusion of Symbols, 1939, *202*

Francis Spear (1902-1979),
Christ Derided, Nov 1942, 1942, *107*
Martyr Soldier, 1941, *144*
St. George and the Dragon, 1941, *145*
Seraphine, design for stained glass window, 1932, *148*

Gilbert Spencer (1892-1979),
The Ten Commandments, c.1938, *56-59*

Stanley Spencer (1891-1959),
Sandham Memorial Chapel, Burghclere, Hampshire, 1928-29, *16*
Study for *Christ Carrying the Cross*, 1920, *109*

John Tunnard (1900-1971),
A point on the horizon line, *30*
Orange Flame, *31*

Annie Fearon Walke (1877 -1965),
Christ the Worker, 1923, *18*

James Woodford (1893–1976),
Nereid – fountain group, c.1947, *4*
Infant Christ, *114*

Peter Wright (1919-2003),
Madonna and Child, *83*

Margaret Wrightson (1877-1976),
St George, *151*

Archibald Ziegler (1903-1971),
Hell, *118*
An Allegory of Social Strife, late 1920s, *119*

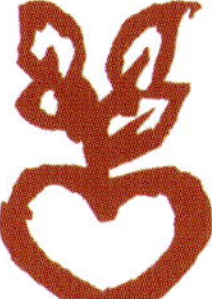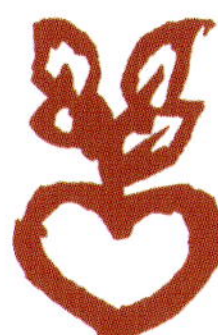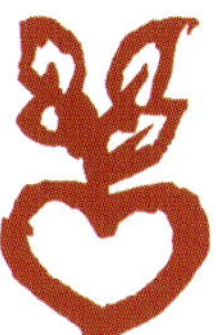

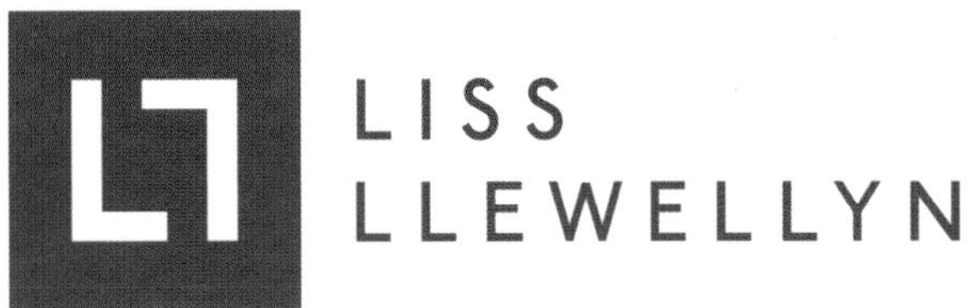

Founded in 1991 by Sacha Llewellyn and Paul Liss, LISS LLEWELLYN are exhibition organisers, publishers and Fine Art dealers specialising in the unsung heroines and heroes of British art from 1880 to 1980. During the last twenty-five years LISS LLEWELLYN have worked in association with museums and cultural institutions in the United Kingdom and abroad to develop a series of in-depth exhibitions to encourage the reappraisal of some of the lesser-known figures of twentieth century British art.

EXHIBITIONS

LISS LLEWELLYN exhibitions have been staged at Sir John Soane's Museum (London) / Pallant House Gallery (Chichester) / Cecil Higgins Gallery (Bedford) / Harris Museum (Preston) / Alfred East Gallery (Kettering) / Young Gallery (Salisbury) / Royal Albert Memorial Museum (Exeter) / Royal Museum and Art Gallery (Canterbury) / Fry Art Gallery (Saffron Walden) / Beecroft Art Gallery (Southend) / The Church of England / The British School at Rome.

PUBLICATIONS

LISS LLEWELLYN have published over twenty books on British Art and Artists. Our last four publications have all been longlisted for the Berger Art History Prize. *Alan Sorrell – The Life & Works of an English Neo-Romantic Artist* was chosen as one of the best art books of 2013 by Brian Sewell. *Evelyn Dunbar – The Lost Works* was chosen as one of the best books of 2015 by *The Guardian*.

FINE ART DEALING

Our website offers over 1500 works of art for sale. Email campaigns are sent out every three weeks and over 500 items of new stock are introduced every year. 95% of our works are sourced privately. We aim to deal with museum quality works.
Our choice not to run a gallery or participate in art fairs leaves us free to follow our interests without succumbing to the pressures of an exclusively retail environment.

MUSEUMS

LISS LLEWELLYN sells to museums throughout the UK, in Europe, America, Canada, Australia, and New Zealand. Our clients include:

Tate / The Victoria & Albert Museum / The permanent collection of the House of Commons / The Imperial War Museum / The Science Museum / The British Museum / The National Portrait Gallery / The Fitzwilliam / The Ashmolean / Leeds City Art Gallery / Jerwood Gallery / Southampton Art Gallery / Wolverhampton Art Gallery / Cheltenham Art Gallery / The Ferens City Art Gallery / Scottish National Gallery of Modern Art / Garden Museum (London) / The Hull University Art Collection (Hull) / Williamson Art Gallery and Museum (Birkenhead) / The Bowes Museum (Co. Durham) / Central St Martins Museum and Study Collection / Geffrye Museum (London) / The Whitworth Art Gallery (Manchester) / Metropolitan Museum of New York / Yale Center for British Art / National Gallery of Canada / Le Musée National du Moyen Âge (Paris) / Palazzo Strozzi (Florence) / Art Institute (Chicago) / Wolfsonian Museum (Miami Beach, Florida) / Musée Cluny (Paris) / The Frick Library (New York) / The Museum für Kunst und Gewerbe (Hambourg) / The Gates Foundation

We have gifted work to the following museums:

V&A, British Museum, UCL Art Museum, National Maritime Museum, Ben Uri, Tate Archive, Imperial War Museum, The Garden Museum. and The Wolfsonian, Miami. The collection that we created for Laporte in 2000 was the winner of the Corporate Collection of The Year Award.

LISS LLEWELLYN

Adam House,
7-10 Adam Street,
London WC2N 6AA

T: (+44) 7973613374   PAUL@LISSLLEWELLYN.COM   SACHA@LISSLLEWELLYN.COM

www.LISSLLEWELLYN.COM